VILLIERS
Everybody's Engine

Rob Carrick & Mick Walker

REDLINE BOOKS

Acknowledgements:

Inspiration for this book came originally from an idea by the late Brian Woolley, who willingly gave his advice, guidance and help on all two-stroke matters. During his career as a tuning wizard and latterly as a respected journalist with EMAP, he was an encouragement to us when we initially embarked on our early writing partnership.

Other two-stroke enthusiasts who deserve acknowledgement for their help and the material contained in this book are Dave Bradley and Tim Griffin of the Greeves Riders Association; Pete Thorne of Aspire Classics; journalist Richard Rosenthal; kart racing engineer Simon Bateman; vintage racer and engineer John Wood; Francis-Barnett works rider Tony Bryant; record-breaker James Moore; and long term off-road racer, sales representative and company executive with Norton Villiers Triumph, Mike Jackson.

The Sammy Miller Museum and the National Motorcycle Museum also deserve recognition for their help, as do the Norman and the DOT Owners Clubs who supplied additional information and illustrations.

Make SURE that the Motor Cycle You choose has a Villiers ENGINE

ISBN: 978 0 9555278 4 5

Designed and published by Redline Books

www.redlinebooks.co.uk

Printed in Italy by Printer Trento

REDLINE BOOKS

Contents

Appendices

REDLINE BOOKS

1 Bicycle Products

John Marston

The beginnings of the sprawling empire that went on to rule the world of small capacity two-stroke engines can be traced back to 1851, when John Marston commenced his apprenticeship with Edward Parry, a Japanner and Tinsmith of Paul Street, Wolverhampton in the English West Midlands. The young Marston spent the next eight years learning the trade of Japanning, the applying of the many coats of a special baked-on paint to achieve a deep and highly glazed surface finish, and this was to be his trademark when he started the Sunbeam group, a company who were always praised for the top quality finish of their products.

Having learned his trade, Marston set up his own business in Bilston, and during the next twelve years built up a reputation of producing work of the highest calibre. In 1871 Edward Parry died and John Marston bought the Paul Street business, continuing the Parry tradition of supplying fine quality work, against the competition posed by the many other companies in that area.

By now a very respected businessman, John Marston became active in local politics and was elected as a member of the Wolverhampton Town Council in 1882. In 1887 he became a Justice of the Peace and two years later became the Mayor of Wolverhampton, a position he held for a further two years. It was during his early days as a Justice of the Peace that John Marston's thoughts turned to that of a transportation device for the more well-heeled members of his community, for now the bicycle boom was under way.

The 'tailor made' bicycle

Having sampled a proprietary brand of bicycle, John Marston was not impressed, for having short legs he was unable to reach the pedals in comfort. As there was no choice in frame sizes it appeared that that would be the end of any bicycle riding for him, but for the intervention of the works foreman William Newell. Wanting to do his boss a favour, Newell built John Marston a 'tailor made' bicycle that was superior in design, build and finish to any other machine on the road. This one machine set a trend and the Sunbeam bicycle was born. Production commenced, with the first bicycle emerging from the Paul Street works in December 1887. This was the "Safety Bicycle" which was again built and developed by the works foreman, at a cost of £8.00. Having sold this first machine to the local Ironmonger, Marston embarked on a production run,offering both bicycles and tricycles for sale the following year.

Oil Bath Chaincase

Refinements were incorporated in the production bicycles, one of these being the Oil Bath Chain Case. Born of an idea and suggestion by John Marston's son Charles, who had joined the company in 1895 at the tender age of sixteen, the chain case fulfilled two important functions. Firstly the case carried the oil to lubricate the chain and secondly it kept the chain clean and away from road dirt. An added bonus to this arrangement was that the rider's trousers were kept clean and free from the grease traditionally used on the chains of early bicycles. John Marston used one of these machines on a regular basis to pursue his civic duties, commuting around Wolverhampton.

The bicycle by now had been named; being known as the Sunbeam Cob. And, as production was increasing by the year, John Marston decided to concentrate on this side of the business, disposing of his Japanning and Tinware interests. Towards the end of the 19th Century the Sunbeam workforce moved to larger premises and carried on with bicycle production.

The Sunbeam bicycle

The Sunbeam bicycle was a quality product, which only used the finest equipment available, much of which was purchased from outside manufacturing organisations.

Amongst these items were the pedals, but John Marston thought that they were not of a high enough quality for his machine, and despatched young Charles to the USA to find the necessary manufacturing machinery. The pedal making machinery was found and came from Messrs Pratt & Whitney (later famous for its aero engines) of Hartford, Connecticut, but on shipment to Wolverhampton it was found to be too big to fit into the Sunbeam workshops. Not to be thwarted, Marston acquired the adjoining building to house the machinery to produce the pedals for the Sunbeam bicycles. The premises comprised a row of three converted houses that totalled some 600 sq yds, enough to house the machinery and an eight strong workforce. The power required to drive the machinery (a shaft was extended through the wall) was taken from the next-door Sunbeam workshop and production of the superior pedals commenced. Charles was put in charge of the operation, which was named the Villiers Cycle Components Co, for the building stood at the corner of Villiers Street, named in honour of the respected MP for Wolverhampton – Charles Pelham Villiers.

The pedal-making operation

John Marston saw fit to establish the pedal making operation as an independent company, to produce the individual components for his Sunbeam bicycles, for being independent they could sell surplus production to the cycle industry as a whole. It was at this time that a Marston policy was formulated, only to sell to the trade and not the general public, as some other establishments were doing. This policy had a lasting effect and was still in operation at the company's end in 1966.

A few components manufactured by Villiers

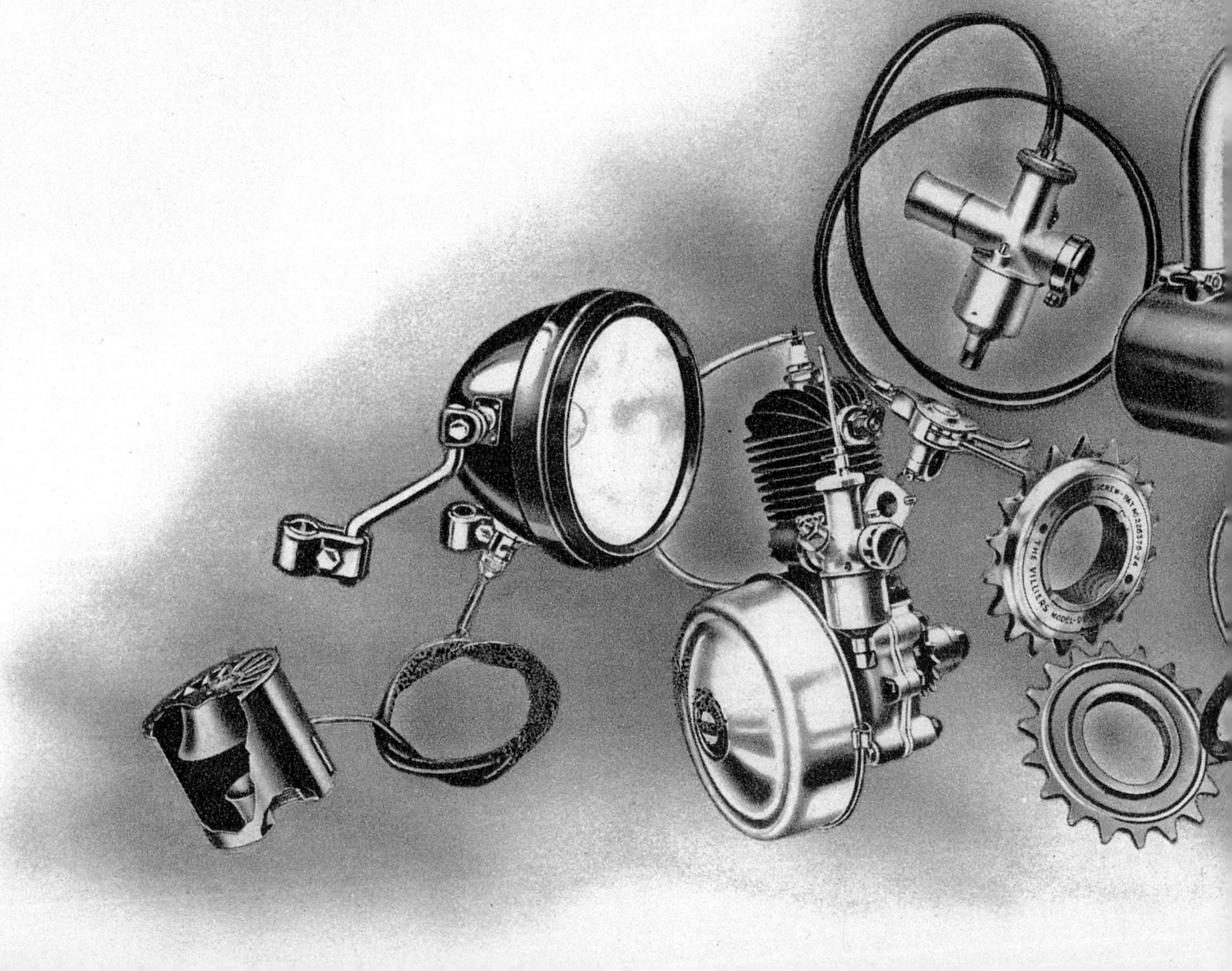

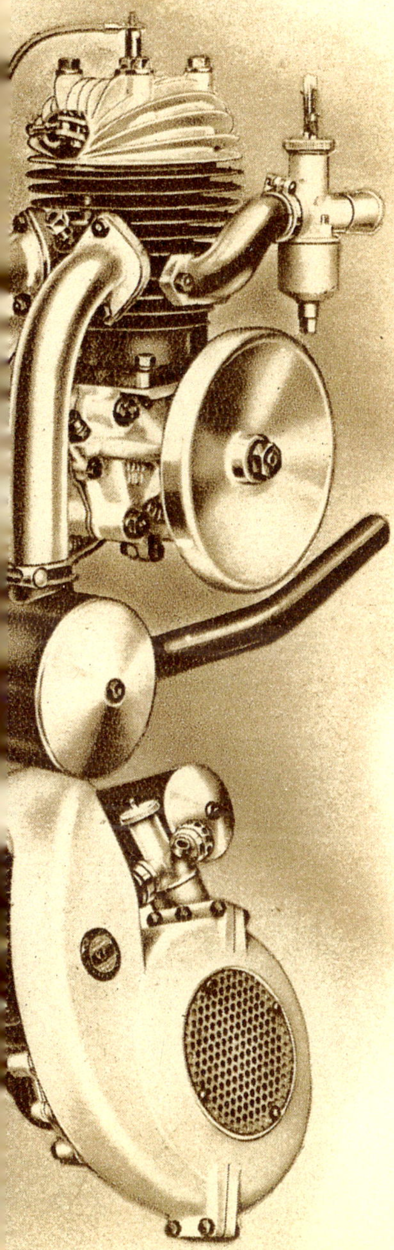

As pedal production hit its zenith, an outlet for the surplus stock had to be found and John Marston approached Frank H Farrer, who was then the manager of the Palmer Tyre Co in Coventry and had a strong connection with the cycle trade, with a view to merchandising the product. Frank accepted the challenge and was soon supplying most of the quality bicycle manufacturers in the area. Trade in pedals was so good that in 1902 Frank sold his Coventry business interests and joined the Villiers Company on a full time basis. At this time the production portfolio was increased to include the manufacturing of a free-wheel device for the bicycle. The free wheel was becoming a popular accessory and Villiers investigated the models available, coming up with a design that was both lighter and simpler than the opposition but still robust enough to be reliable.

The new company

The new company made many developments within the cycle industry but it was the free wheel that set them on the road to financial independence and soon the pedal manufacturing side was dropped altogether. Villiers ultimately became the world's biggest producer of freewheels, the output of the Wolverhampton factory after the Second World War exceeding 80,000 units per week (that is over four million a year), which were shipped out in wooden crates, 200 at a time. By the mid 1950s freewheels were packed in non-returnable fibreboard containers, 100 to each container, for easier onward transportation to the end users.

The Sunbeam factory was at this time operating at maximum production capacity, and to concentrate on this aspect of his business interests, John Marston decided to sell the Villiers Cycle Component Co to his son Charles. The asking price of £6,000, to cover the machinery in the factory, was gladly paid. Soon after this in 1912 the company became a PLC (Public Limited Company) and with it a name change to the Villiers Engineering Co Ltd, with Frank Farrer becoming one of its shareholders.

From these small beginnings the factory expanded and now employed a workforce of thirty engineers, machinists and assemblers. But cycle component manufacture was soon to be replaced by something altogether different, for in 1911 an interest in motorcycle components had been established, with the manufacture of a multi-plate rear hub clutch and later a two-speed hub gear.

A TOUR of the VILLIERS WORKS

General Office

Drawing Office

THE VILLIERS COMPANY was established in the year 1898, for the production of higher grade Component parts for Cycles.

The Factory was equipped with the latest type of American Machine Tools for not only quality, but quantity production.

Page 3

From the time the Villiers Freewheel was first made it immediately created a good impression. At that period nearly all Cycle Manufacturers made their own Freewheels, but when they realised the superiority of the Villiers Clutch they were interested to carry out tests, and slowly many important firms discontinued making their own and fitted Villiers. So the output of Villiers Freewheels gradually increased, resulting in lower costs and selling prices.

Stamping and Forging Department

The secret of this success was entirely due to the Machinery that had been installed. Steadily the Works expanded, houses and buildings adjoining were pulled down or reconstructed and more plant added to meet the increasing demand for the firm's products.

From the early days the Directors of the Villiers Company were keenly alive to the possibilities of the Motor Cycle as a means of transport, and they carried out exhaustive experiments. It was only natural that the Villiers plant, capable of manufacturing articles

A Battery of Large Automatic Machines

Cutting, Welding and Assembling Silencers

Sand and Shot Blasting

It is interesting to record that before this date many Two-stroke Engines had been made, but had given much trouble because the Manufacturers were not properly equipped. There existed, in the minds of the public, certain prejudice against this type of engine but by Engineers it had always been recognised to very close limits should be suitable for the production of internal combustion engines, and in the year 1912 a small engine was designed for a Motor Cycle and put to test. In the following year, the Villiers Two-stroke Engine was placed upon the market.

Polishing Department

The Plating Shop

as the ideal type, because of its simple construction. Many Designers had been deceived by the simplicity of the Two-stroke Engine, believing that it could be manufactured in a cheap manner. Nothing was further from the truth, as a Two-stroke internal combustion engine actually requires more accurate manufacture than any other type of engine.

This the makers of the Villiers Engine realised, and they determined to concentrate on this type knowing full well that the British public ultimately would realise that the failure of the early engines was due to the poor workmanship.

It was necessary in those days actually to loan complete Machines to Motor Cycle Manufacturers for them to test the Villiers Two-stroke Engine. From that time the growth of the business has been miraculous. The increased

output of products necessitated working to the closest possible limits, because it is obvious that unless the parts assemble easily the output would soon be in chaos, and components would not be interchangeable. Accuracy and interchangeability of parts is a great advantage to the owner of a Villiers product, because he can purchase Spare Parts and fit them himself easily and without the aid of a skilled Engineer.

Part of the Engine Assembly Benches

The War caused many difficulties. The machinery had been specially installed for the production of Freewheels and Engines, but owing to the high reputation of the Villiers Company, they were put under Government control at a very early date, and the main productions were ceased practically at a moment's notice. Although they were allowed to manufacture Freewheels for Military Bicycles

Cylinder Boring Machines—No. 2 Works

This was maintained until the end of the War, after which it was not an easy matter to change back again to the manufacture of the regular products for which Villiers was renowned. It was no longer possible to purchase Magnetos for fitting to and Engines for Pumps, the majority of the plant was turned over to the manufacture of gauges for Shells, fuse parts, component parts for Aeroplanes, Lorry Governors and thousands of other delicate and intricate components in ferrous and non-ferrous metals demanding great accuracy.

Section of Machine Shop—No. 3

Machining Flywheel Magneto Components

the engines and, therefore, "necessity being the Mother of invention" Villiers immediately commenced to design a Magneto that would, if possible, give better results than had been obtained with Horse-shoe type Magnetos.

The outcome of this was the Villiers Flywheel Magneto, which has been a phenomenal success. Not only does it give an intense spark at high speeds, but also a much better spark at low speeds than had been possible with other types of Magnetos. The development of the Flywheel Magneto added another Department in the Factory, and this to-day is a very important section which grows annually.

Heat Treating and Hardening

Part of No. 2 Machine Shop

Walking through the Villiers Factory one marvels at the enormous quantity of Freewheels, Engines, Carburetters, Flywheel Magnetos, and Lubricators, produced hourly, and the accuracy in their manufacture.

Corner of Tool Room for making Jigs and Gauges

A Freewheel after assembly is placed on a mandrel and tested for truth and concentricity. Every engine when built is run and tested under its own power, and is not passed off test unless it develops a certain pre-determined power which is set as its minimum permissible performance. Every engine is put to a greater test on the bench than it ever receives in the hands of a Motor Cyclist.

Another very important factor is the quality and consistency of material. It was found that one consignment of steel varied from another, and similarly other materials varied, with the result that a Laboratory was built and placed under the charge of a skilled metallurgist whose duty it was, and is, to test and pass all raw materials and to carry out research work with various alloys to improve the products.

The British Government carried out exhaustive tests of Freewheels on their Post Office Bicycles, and it is gratifying to know that for many years now they have contracted for

Villiers Freewheels exclusively for their G.P.O. Bicycles, and find that with them they obtain longer life and are consequently cheaper in the long run.

Producing Bolts, Screws and other small parts

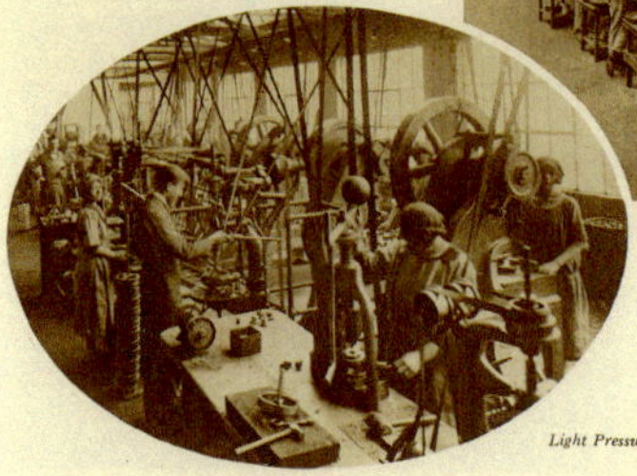

Light Presswork Section

Crankcase Section—Machine Shop No. 2

In the same factory where Villiers Freewheels are made, but in an entirely different Department, the Villiers Two-stroke Engines are manufactured in enormous quantities and as every Engine requires a Carburetter negotiations

Machine Shop—No. 3

A corner of the Coil-winding Room

Some of the Electrical Plant for testing Villiers Flywheel Magnetos

were commenced for the Mills Patent Carburetter, because on test it was found that this was the only automatic type of instrument which was really suitable for a Two-stroke engine. The Mills Patent was bought outright, and Carburetters

A gang of Milling Machines at work cutting sprocket teeth

have since been manufactured in the Villiers Factory.

As a Carburetter calls not only for accuracy in workmanship but also for high quality in material, a bronze foundry was laid down for the supply of castings for the Villiers Carburetter to ensure uniformity in material.

The Steel Stamping Department is a very interesting section where more than 30,000 Forgings are made each week. Nearby is the Heat Treating Shop, which is considered to be the most complete and up-to-date in the Midlands, each furnace being regulated by electric pyrometers to ensure correct temperatures.

Assembling Freewheels and Testing

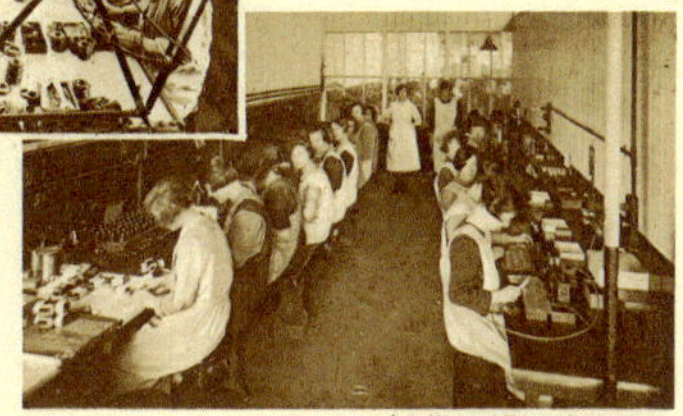

Assembling and Testing Condensers for Villiers Flywheel Magnetos

There is a busy atmosphere and a pleasant one throughout the whole Works. It has often been called a "Bee-hive"—probably due to the buzz of the machinery, and because everyone is so busily engaged. It is interesting to learn that many Workpeople have been with the

Packing Room

One of the Employees' Mess Rooms

firm since its inception, and that care, accuracy, and thought is their key-note. Cleanliness reigns supreme, and in some of the assembly Shops employees in overalls look as if they were in a Cake Factory rather than an Engineering Works.

It is felt that the reproduction of these photographs showing the activities of the Villiers factory, will be appreciated by many who have little knowledge of the skill and technique required in the manufacture of the Villiers products which they may be using.

2 The First Engine Units

By mid-1912 the Sunbeam Company, housed next door to the Villiers cycle parts factory, had entered into the realms of motorcycle manufacturing and it was to this market that the Villiers Engineering Co next looked. Not wanting to enter into direct competition, and tread on the toes of his father, Charles Marston decided to concentrate solely on engines, to feed the many fledgling motorcycle manufacturers of the day, the majority of which were sited on his doorstep. In this pioneering age it was only the large factories that made their own engines, and these were never sold to smaller competitors, being for the sole use in their own corporate designed machines. Villiers felt that there was a ready market for an independent engine manufacturer, to supply the smaller marques, many of which did nothing more than assemble a motorcycle from bought-in components.

The Sheffield Minor, 1920s

The first Villiers four-stroke engine, 349cc, 1911 -1912

Some engine manufacturers made nothing more than the engine itself, relying on an independent gearbox manufacturer, a carburettor maker and a magneto company to complete the package. And, it was for the provision of this complete package that Villiers assembled their first engine unit to supply the eagerly awaiting customers. This initial package was far from complete - lacking a carburettor and magneto - but in later years this shortcoming was addressed once the company had gathered together all the expertise and manufacturing machinery required for the production of the finite and fully equipped engine units within its own walls.

Prototype engine

Using nothing more than the same technology as other engine manufacturers of the day, Villiers produced a prototype engine in a relatively short period of time, designed and built by an engineer who was specially engaged for the job. The debut and the press release of the new engine was detailed in Motor Cycling dated 12th November 1912, in which it reported, 'The engine is a self contained unit comprising engine and two-speed gear on remarkably neat and ingenious lines.' The new engine unit was a four-stroke, with a bore of 74.5mm and a stroke of 80mm giving a displacement of 349cc. Valve gear was of the IOE (inlet-over-exhaust) design, popular at the time, with exposed springs and rockers, operated from the cams in the left hand timing chest. A platform mounted Bosch waterproof magneto was also driven from the timing chest by a train of six gears. The primary drive case was sited on the right hand side of the unit and enclosed both the clutch and drive chain.

Production figures of this first engine were very small, which resulted in a plea being printed in the January 11th 1951 issue of Motor Cycling when the Wolverhampton factory asked, 'If any reader can help, we are anxious to acquire an example of the first engine.' A year later one did turn up having been discovered in Australia.

Favourable reports on the new unit were received; with a comment in The Motor Cycle reporting a Brooklands lap of 46mph (74 kph) indicating that the Villiers engine was equal or better in performance than many of its contemporaries, and had it seemed come up with a winning design at its first attempt. Unfortunately, the reception from the all-important motorcycle trade was not so positive.

A rethink

The adverse comments from within the trade prompted Charles Marston to have a rethink. Criticism of the design even came from within the factory, for the workforce and managers alike viewed the prototype as being too revolutionary and overly complicated. Another factor involved was the factory machinery which was not suitable for this kind of work, and neither was the workforce, for they did not have the necessary skills to build the complicated design. A four-stroke flat twin design was looked into, but Frank Farrer wanted to build a two-stroke unit, possibly being influenced by the small Levis two-stroke made by Butterfields in near-by

MkII 269cc 1916 - 1920

Birmingham. Undecided, Charles Marston called a conference, which was attended by many outside experts, to give their opinions and advice as to the product that Villiers should next construct. The two-stroke concept was instantly rejected, on the grounds that it had been proved to be a failure, unable to deliver enough power - size for size - against the established four-strokes of the day.

The Flying Bedstead

Frank Farrer bombarded Charles Marston with two-stroke technology and requests to build his engine, In the end the exasperated Villiers boss relented and wrote the following note in the 'Work's Book', 'To oblige Mr Farrer, make him a two-stroke engine.' No one else was very enthusiastic about the project, but the design was passed to the tool room and a sample engine built. The completed engine was installed into a frame that was made from components acquired from the Chater-Lea factory, and put together by another small Birmingham firm. The completed bike, devoid of any name, was christened "The Flying Bedstead". When this machine was finally roadworthy, the anxious but excited Frank Farrer took it on its first proving run; using a 60 mile (96 Km) route from Birmingham to Bridgenorth and back, the same route used to test the Sunbeam cars. On his return to Birmingham, the ecstatic Frank Farrer immediately telephoned Charles Marston, to say that he would be able to sell thousands of them.

Production of the two-stroke engine began in 1913, becoming an immediate success. Exhibited alongside the four-stroke engine at the 1913 London Olympia Motorcycle Show, the two-stroke engine received many advance - both actual and prospective - orders, sealing the fate of the four-stroke design. As it was to be the first production unit, the four-stroke having since been scrapped, the two-stroke was designated as the Mk I, with all examples of this mark using the prefix O to the engine number. The engine was simplicity itself, having only three moving parts; the piston, the con-rod and the crankshaft. This fulfilled the design brief statement, 'production of a simple type, low cost, engine; to open up a large market for a very cheap motorcycle, within the pocket of the working man'.

The first two-stroke

This first engine was exactly that and not fitted with a carburettor or magneto, the choice of these components being left to the individual motorcycle manufacturer, but an exhaust system with transversely mounted double aluminium chambers was fitted. As already outlined the 'engine only' concept was far removed from the original 'complete package' idea, for Villiers was unable to produce the magneto and carburettor on the limited factory machinery. And it was only later that these shortcomings were to be addressed. With square bore and stroke measurements of 70 x 70mm and a capacity of 269cc, the engine featured a fixed head cast iron cylinder with a single transfer port to the rear and a single exhaust port, the induction port being on the right hand side of the cylinder. The crankshaft, which ran on phosphor bronze main bearings, was fitted with a roller bearing big-end and a cast iron deflector piston, the gudgeon pin of which ran in its own plain bearing and was held in place by a pair of split pins. The large outside flywheel and the inboard belt drive pulley was on the left side, with a chain drive, encased in an alloy cover on the right, to drive the magneto that was mounted on a platform at the front of the engine. This platform also doubled up as the hangers for the dual exhaust chambers.

A revolutionary feature

A revolutionary feature of Villiers first production engine was its lubrication system. Oil was fed to the crankcase by a hand pump that could be adjusted to the required rate, and in some cases a sight feed was also fitted. When oil entered the crank chamber it was directed to the main bearings by oil passages, the upper cylinder lubrication being taken care of by surplus oil dripping on to the crankshaft and being splashed onto the cylinder walls. Being versatile, Villiers could change the oil injection point to the inlet manifold, if the motorcycle assembler requested.

Fitted to pre-First World War lightweight motorcycles such as the Chater-Lea, Ixion and the Sun; the Mk I engine was used successfully for both touring and competitive events but enjoyed a production run of only three years, for in 1916 the factory was turned over to the war effort and all motorcycle engine work had to take a back seat.

This was then the small-scale beginnings of the Villiers two-stroke empire, which continued for a further five and a half decades, producing in excess of three million engine units before its final demise in the mid-sixties.

Ixion

Initially founded in 1901, the first Ixion Company was essentially a bicycle maker, who used De Dion Bouton and MMC engines - and according to unconfirmed sources - the French 1.5 hp Bichrome two-stroke, for their first venture into motorcycle manufacture. This small but early Birmingham based company only lasted two years and was terminated in 1903.

The second, bigger and better, Ixion Company restarted in 1906, lasting until 1923, during which time they used a wider variety of larger propulsion units from many sources. Abingdon V twins, Precision side-valve singles, Peco two-strokes and Villiers engines all played their part in the Ixion product, ranging in size from 269 to 670cc. When Ixion finally closed down, New Hudson purchased the pale green bike's trademark.

1913 Ixion fitted with the MkI 269cc engine

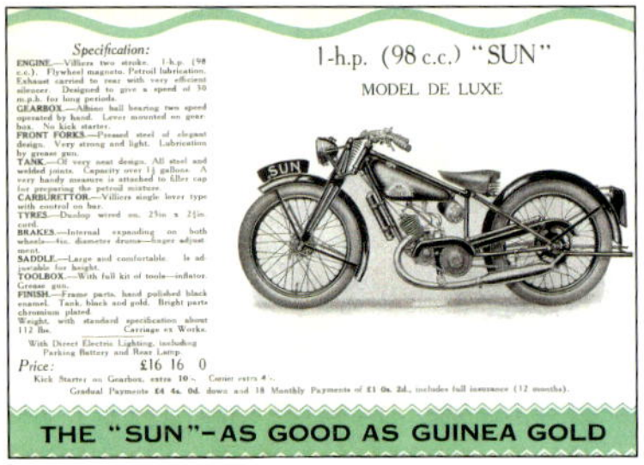

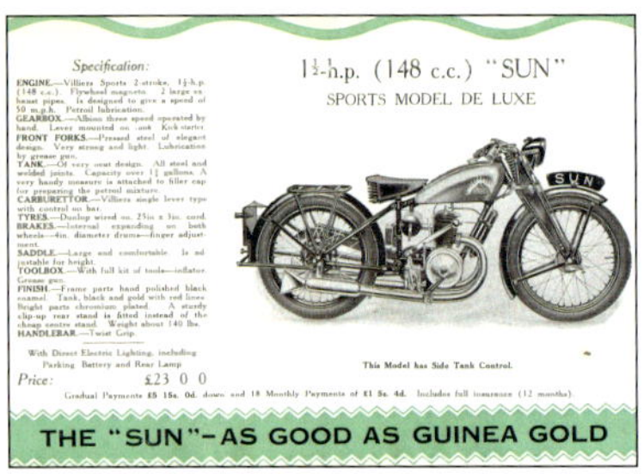

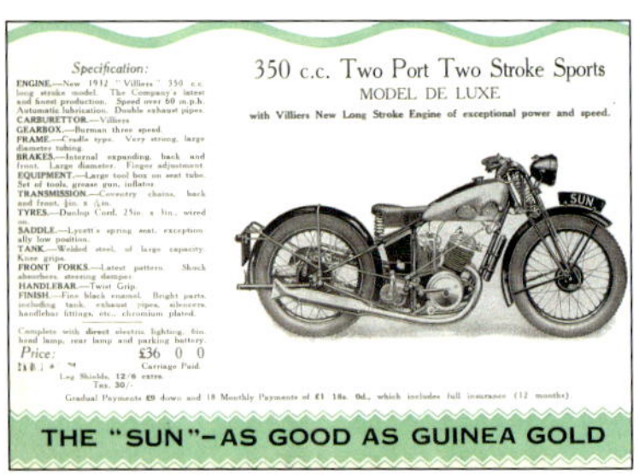

Sun

The Birmingham based Sun Cycle and Fitting Company Ltd - owned by the Parkes family - was one of the few concerns to use the first (inlet over exhaust) Villiers four-stroke engine, but they had been in business some two years prior to this. Originally makers of bicycles and cycling accessories at their Aston Brook Street works, Sun moved into motorcycle production in 1911 with a pair of Precision engined machines of 270 and 590cc respectively. The use of the original Villiers four-stroke engine in 1913 heralded an association with the Wolverhampton engine maker which was to last some five decades, until the final demise of the Sun company in 1961.

The Mk I Villiers two-stroke engine soon replaced the ill-fated four-stroke design and together with other engines from Blackburne, JAP and Vitesse, Sun produced a very healthy range of machines (98 to 650cc) to suit the needs of the post World War One motorcyclist. A lust for racing saw active participation in the post war TTs, but it was not the Villiers engine that powered the racer, for this machine was powered by the Vitesse VTS (Valveless Two-Stroke or rotary disc-valve) motor.

For the 1932 season Sun fielded only four models, three of them Villiers-powered, together with a solitary 350 JAP. The 98cc machine used the new Villiers Midget engine and retailed at £16.80, the 147cc model was equipped with the popular – and well-established - MkVIIIC, which was priced at £20.15. The final offering, the 350, was priced at £36.00.

Sun soon tired of motorcycle manufacture and for 1932 concentrated solely on bicycle production once again, but this was not the end of the firm's motorcycle days; the marque reappearing after the end of the Second World War, when it produced a range of machines exclusively powered by Villiers engines.

Chater-Lea

The London-based company - initially in Golden Lane and then in Banner Street - started its business as a supplier of lugs, castings and machined parts to the bicycle and fledgling motorcycle trade as early as 1890. Motorcycle manufacture commenced in 1900 but the Villiers connection was not established until 1913 with the advent of the Mk I engine.

The first Villiers-powered Chater-Lea was an up-market machine, equipped as it was with a two-speed gearbox, a very rare and novel feature for the early part of the twentieth century. The final drive of this machine utilised the standard toothed leather belt, a feature adopted by virtually every manufacturer of the day.

Production ceased in 1916 during the First World War and did not recommence until 1920 when the company tried to change its 'touring' image to one of a more sporting nature, with the use of the JAP 1000cc V twin and a home brewed ohc 350 single. The Villiers engine was not forgotten, and was once again pressed into use on the touring models. During the second venture into motorcycle manufacture initially using the 269cc Mk II engine and then the 247cc motor in the 1928 Sportette; after another factory move to Letchworth, Hertfordshire, Chater-lea terminated motorcycle production in 1936 and returned to general engineering.

Chater-Lea is not best remembered for its association with the Villiers Engineering Co, but more so for its sporting successes with the big V twins and the Blackburne engined 350 that became the first junior machine to take a Brooklands (100mph lap) Gold Star. Nevertheless Chater-Lea did figure in the early pioneering days of the first Villiers two-strokes, being one of only a handful of companies who opted to use the Mk I engine.

3 Between the Wars

Soon after the end of the First World War, extra production space was acquired, with the purchase of a farm that had been used as an allotment area during the conflict. On this land was constructed a drop forging shop, to which was added a machine shop and a foundry. The new buildings all fronted onto a new road, which the council named Marston Road, in honour of the work done by the Marston family for the Wolverhampton community. To this complex was later added a laboratory and then a new block to house the staff from Villiers Road. The laboratory was deemed necessary to test the products that were now built in-house, for prior to this time it had been found that some outside contractors' work had not come up to the exacting standards required by the Villiers company. Now the end product was under the direct control of the Villiers factory. Further expansion took place in 1933, when a new automatic machine shop was added to the complex, but 1938 saw even more expansion, with the take over of the adjacent Sunbeam factory premises, thus extending the Villiers empire to eleven acres.

A new management structure

These times of change had seen a new structure to the Villiers board, with Charles Marston becoming the Chairman of the company in 1919 and Frank Farrer taking on the post of Managing Director, both men holding these posts until 1946. In 1937 Frank Farrer's son, Leslie, was appointed to the board as Works Director and Geoffrey Jones became the Sales Director.

One of the first innovations to come out of the factory after the war of 1914-18, was the Villiers designed and built flywheel magneto. Having suffered at the hands of outside suppliers, and their inability to supply magnetos during the conflict, Frank Farrer set about thinking up ways to side step any further problems. Noting the large rotating mass of the external flywheel, he wondered if this component could be used to accommodate an apparatus to generate a spark. A team was set up to look into his idea, which became patented in 1919. Soon after, a new engineer joined the company, and one of his initial tasks was to develop the patent into a working proposition. By 1920

196cc Mk IE (61 x 67mm) 1928 - 1938

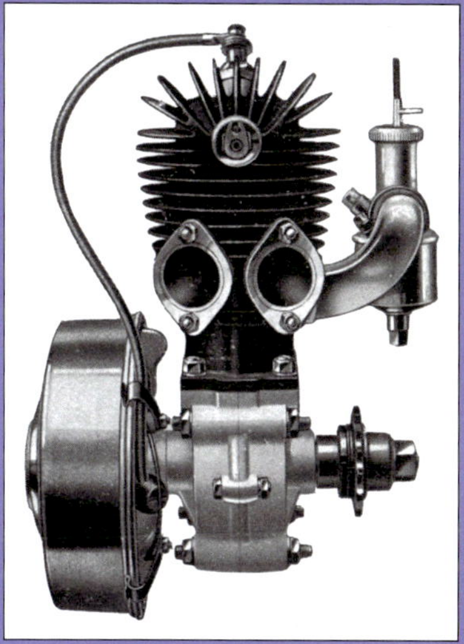

the new flywheel magneto was in production, to be offered as a built-in alternative on the later versions of the Mk IV engines, or easily fitted to the earlier production - standard magneto - Mk IVs of 1921. The young engineer responsible for this new design was Frank Pountney, and such was his faith in the final product, that he invested in the company as a shareholder before becoming a Director and later still the Chief Engineer.

The flywheel magneto

The flywheel magneto used a fixed spark advance point, unlike many magneto units of the time, and this was seen as a draw-back on the single speed engine units of the period. To counter this problem a simple advance and retard mechanism soon became available, which was nothing more than a moveable backplate that was rotated by the use of a long hand lever. This device allowed the engine to plonk along at very low revs, proving to be very handy in built-up areas.

The Mk II engine - built during the war years - was replaced in 1920 by the Mk III version; still using the original bore and stroke measurements of 70 x 70 mm, the revised engine featuring a new type of decompressor valve, which required yet another cylinder design and a modified casting. Changes were also made to the crankcases, main bearing bushes and drive shaft. The flywheel now featured a separate centre and a choice of chain or pulley drive was added to the specification. The magneto drive chain cover now became universal, enabling the magneto to be fitted to the front or rear of the engine, to give the motorcycle manufacturer a choice of mounting.

The Mark IV

The following year the 269cc engine unit was again further refined and designated as the Mk IV, with changes to the exhaust system. Halfway through the production run the drive shaft was altered to take the newly devised Villiers flywheel magneto. The flywheel magneto was placed on the right-hand side of the engine, utilising the drive shaft that, until then, had driven the chain to the external magneto. The large external flywheel on the left-hand drive shaft was now dispensed with. Kits also became available from the factory to enable users of the early Mk IV engines to update their machines, and fit the new flywheel magneto arrangement.

The Mark V

In 1922 the final version of the 269cc engine was announced. Coded Mk V, this differed from its predecessors in that the flywheel magneto was now equipped with lighting coils - to enable 'electric lights' to be used. To complement this new innovation, Villiers produced an Electric Lighting Set, which was also equipped with a dry battery to enable the use of parking lights, when the engine was not in use. A further kit also became available to bring the earlier Mk IV engines up to the same specification, which included a rectifier and an accumulator. At the same time alterations to the flywheel magneto were also made, with a modified points rocker arm and an improved high tension lead.

147cc MkVIII-C (55 x 62mm) 1924 - 1947

Having produced the 269cc engine for nine years, Villiers sought to widen its market, and in 1922 produced the same package type concept, but now it was available in three different capacity sizes. The Mk VI series of engines covered:

a) The one-fifty class with the Mk VI-C, a 147cc unit with a bore and stroke measurement of 55 x 62 mm.

b) The two-fifty class with the MK VI-A, a 247cc unit with a bore and stroke measurement of 67 x 70 mm.

c) The three-fifty class with the Mk VI-B, a 343cc unit with a bore and stroke measurement of 79 x 70 mm.

The use of the letter after the Mk number indicated the capacity class to which the engine belonged, and from this date onwards the vast majority of Villiers engines produced carried this identification letter. There were some exceptions to this rule, when an engine was given a name rather than a class letter. As the 269cc engine (roughly a member of the two-fifty class) was the first engine to be produced by the Villiers factory, this capacity class was designated as the type A, with the three-fifty being called the type B and the one-fifty being referred to as the type C. In later years this classification system was expanded to encompass all the remaining capacity classes.

The Mk VI series engines followed closely the design of the Mk V and were built to a similar pattern. Still using one-piece cylinders, the head finning now became 'Starburst', to increase cooling, instead of the original horizontal fin design. The single exhaust port cylinders, produced in the three different bore sizes, all utilised a forwards facing side-mounted carburettor and a cast iron deflector piston. All three Mk VI engines used similar style components, only varying in size dependent upon which unit they were fitted to. The ignition and lighting requirements were again taken care of by the new flywheel magneto, but now this was manufactured in two different sizes; the larger version of 9 inches (228 mm) diameter, being used on two-fifty and three-fifty, with a smaller, 7 inch (190 mm) version being fitted to the 147cc unit.

1923 Grigg 343cc Mk VI-B

A new face

A new face appeared at the factory in 1923, that of Geoffrey H Jones who had previously been employed on the editorial staff of the weekly magazine, Motor Cycling. Jones joined the staff of the Villiers Company to take over the Advertising Department, with a special role in the production of spare parts lists, instruction books and the publishing side of the factory's technical writing department. Having a flair for sales, he moved to that department and the following year embarked on a European tour, which included Austria, Belgium, Czechoslovakia, Holland and Germany, to visit established customers and to recruit new ones. For his expertise in the selling of Villiers wares, he was made the Sales Director in 1937. The same year saw Frank Farrer's son Leslie being appointed as the Works Director.

A Sports model

In 1924 the Mk VI engines became the Mk VIIs with only minor changes to the cylinders and exhaust system of the Mk VIIA, but that year also saw the introduction of a new 172cc motor. This unit was one of the exceptions to the class letter rule, being simply called the Sports, for that was its aim. Produced to capture sales in the increasingly popular sports/racing scene that was sweeping the country at that time, the Sports 175cc equipped motorcycle was a cheap - but fast - mount on which to race with the big boys. The Sports followed the same basic design as the Mk VII's, having a cast iron deflector piston in a cast iron fixed head cylinder, but now the cylinder was graced with double exhaust ports. With a bore and stroke measurement of 71.15 x 67mm (the 71.15 mm equating to 2 inch), the unit was fitted with a left hand side mounted, but rear facing carburettor, which was claimed to give 95 mpg.

Brooklands and the Super Sports engines

The following year the A, B and C range engines became the Mk VIII models, with the Mk VIII-C receiving a new piston and a gudgeon pin retained in the bore by a pair of brass end caps, instead of the split pins used earlier. The Mk VIII-A received a twin port cylinder with a new piston, which had a transfer port in the skirt and was fitted with an inertia ring to stop the build up of carbon in the top piston ring groove. By far the most exciting developments that year were the Brooklands and Super Sports engines. These new engines were super tuned versions of the previous years Sports engine, but now they were equipped with special flywheel magnetos, detachable alloy heads and racier cylinder porting. Some Brooklands engines were even equipped with special racing alloy cylinders. In this guise the Brooklands engine was specified as producing 8.25 bhp at 4,900rpm, with the Super Sports engine claiming to give 110mpg. The Sports engines were available with both petroil or automatic lubrication systems, but all the following Super Sports and Brooklands variants were entirely equipped with the Villiers patented Automatic Lubrication System.

Hermann Meier & Cliff Lewis

One racer who used a Brooklands engine to good effect in the 1930s, was two-stroke wizard Hermann Meier, who competed in grass track events, in conjunction with Weybridge Villiers dealer Cliff Lewis. Meier's Brooklands engined racer was fitted with a tapered expansion chamber designed by Cliff Lewis, who was considered to be the recognised two-stroke expert of that period. Hermann Meier learnt a lot from Cliff Lewis, and this expertise was called upon in later years, when he re-emerged as a tuning ace in his own right, during the 1960s.

196cc Super Sports engine (61 x 67mm) 1929 - 1940

247cc MkX-A (67 x 70mm) 1930 - 1932

Automatic Lubrication System

The Automatic Lubrication System was first seen on the Sports engines of 1924, setting a new standard, compared to the somewhat overkill provisions of the petriol oiling system used previously. The Villiers system used a pressure bleed from the crankcases, via drillings in the crank and a copper or occasionally flexible pipe, to pressurise the oil tank to 4 psi (0.27 bar), the pressure being regulated by a vent hole in the sight feed or filler cap. The vent hole was the lynch pin of the whole system, which had to be kept clean to ensure the correct pressure build up in the tank. The vent also gradually released pressure when the engine was stopped, ensuring that when the tank reached zero psi the oil would stop flowing. The system was automatic, in that engine revs dictated how much pressure reached the tank, delivering more as the speed increased and less as the throttle was eased off. The delivery rate to the engine was controlled by the rider, with the aid of a regulating screw, which was checked by the provision of a sight glass on some models.

A Knighthood

With the announcement of the 1926 New Years Honours List, the importance of the Villiers Empire had at last been recognised, with a Knighthood bestowed on Charles Marston, for his public and political services. In past years Sir Charles had devoted a lot of time and effort to the Wolverhampton Conservative Party, at local and national levels, as well as being a member of the Church Assembly representing the diocese of Litchfield, and a Justice of the Peace for twenty years. He also had a strong interest in archaeology and spent a lot of time and money on expeditions to the Holy Land; for Sir Charles thought that if the truth of the stories in the Bible could be proved as historical, it would lead to greater understanding.

A new engine capacity was introduced in 1926, this time a 122cc model, which was designated the Mk VI-D, the D suffix referring to the 125 class. The new unit followed closely the design of the Mk VIII-C one-fifty, but now used a bore and stroke measurement of 50 x 62 mm and was equipped with twin exhaust ports. The engine, rated at 1.25hp, did not find favour with the motorcycle manufacturers of the day, and was shelved the following year. This configuration was to be resurrected some ten years later, when the one-two-five class became popular, and carried on in various production guises for a further eighteen years.

More developments

During 1926 the two-fifty and three-fifty engines were renumbered to become the Mk IX-A and the Mk IX-B respectively. The 247cc version was equipped with an aluminium deflector type piston together with an external flywheel which aided smooth running at low engine revs. The last 247cc model was produced some four years later with the advent of the Mk X-A. Advertising played a large part in the sales of the Villiers product, which appeared in the weekly motorcycle magazines of the day. One such advertisement, in the 17th May 1928 edition of the The Motor Cycle, extolled the virtues of the Villiers equipped Francis-Barnett machines used in the London to Lands End race; praising them for their quietness and the gaining of seven Gold Medals. The advertisement also went on to say, 'After fifteen years of production, there were 200,000 Villiers engines on the road.' At that time there were five different Mks of engines available, which were being used by twenty well-known motorcycle manufacturers.

During this period many of the less expensive motorcycles employing the Villiers engine were not fitted with a gearbox, or a clutch for that matter. With roads being devoid of traffic a simple belt drive transmission was adequate for the average rider, who paddled off using the engine decompressor valve to aid engine starting. Villiers saw the need for a clutch to make the negotiation of road hazards and junctions easier for the rider, with the introduction of the Villiers Engine Clutch. This device was a simple system that used seven steel, and seven bronze plates, which were freed by a handlebar lever. The clutch mechanism kit sold for £2.75 and was easily fitted to any Villiers engine that was equipped with a flywheel magneto. The sales brochure eloquently described the method of operation thus; 'The rider has only to walk the machine a few yards until the engine fires when but a simple depression on the clutch lever is required to bring the machine to rest. The rider can take his seat, leisurely release the clutch lever, and the machine will glide away.'

As well as producing motorcycle engines and equipment, Villiers still manufactured the bicycle freewheel, marketed as the Model De Luxe Free-Wheel. To counter the competition from other manufacturers, Frank Pountney had designed and patented a new version that employed a single row of large diameter ball bearings, which ran truer and could carry a heavier load. Other freewheel builders used a double row of smaller bearings. Sales also progressed with the bicycle two-speed chain gear system, and when bicycle manufacturers asked about fixed hub sprockets, they too were researched into and produced.

Carburettors

Carburettors were the next venture into which the Villiers Engineering Co launched themselves. Having sold their engines without a carburettor, the choice of fitment was down to the motorcycle assembler. Various instruments were used, including Amac, B&B, Mills and Senspray. Continually being asked to recommend a suitable carburettor, Villiers, after much testing concluded that the Mills version gave the best all-round results on the various engines they produced. After negotiations Villiers bought the company, renamed the product the Villiers Carburettor, moving the manufacturing line to Marston Road. By 1927 the Wolverhampton factory was producing instruments for their entire range of engines. A modern version of the original carburettor was still being produced some four decades later, which only ended with the final demise of the company in 1967.

196cc Mk2-E (61 x 67mm) 1930 - 1940

Villiers

346cc MkXIV-B (70 x 90mm) 1931 - 1940

The 200cc class

The only new development for 1927 was the 344cc twin cylinder model, which is described in Chapter 9, but the following year the first two hundred class engine was announced. The 196cc unit was built on similar lines to the 172cc Sports engine, but now this new engine was categorised under a new numbering system. All reference to the Mk number (Roman numerals) was now forgotten, for this new class the number was now written in English, starting from 1 again. Designated the 1E, this engine became the forerunner of another long running range, ending in the 11E of the mid 1960s.

The new capacity class of 200cc was born of government legislation, which levied less taxation on smaller capacity vehicles using the roads. Many European countries during this period offered favourable road tax rates to small capacity machines, with Germany levying a zero rate on motorcycles under 200cc. Companies using the Villiers product asked them to provide suitable engines to meet these favourable taxation classes and Villiers responded to the challenge, for in line with the company policy of supplying cheap and affordable engine units, this was seen as the way forward. Some countries imposed weight limits on their motorcycle classes, and Villiers responded to this by producing lightened versions of its standard engine range to meet these needs. Not given any significant taxation relief in this country, the 196cc engine nevertheless soon became popular, due to its power output, reliability and good fuel consumption, seeing service in motorcycles, three wheeler cars, invalid carriages and industrial applications.

The 1E used a cast iron fixed head cylinder with twin exhaust ports, and a cast iron 61 mm deflector piston fitted with an inertia ring. The crankshaft had the same stroke as the 172cc Sports and was supported on a pair of phosphor bronze main bearings. A Super Sports version was announced for 1929, which used a detachable alloy cylinder head, a cylinder with larger fins and a deeper aluminium piston, which again used the inertia ring. This engine sold for the princely sum of £12.00, and that included the patented Villiers automatic oiling system. The 2E version was introduced in 1930, the only difference being the use of a single exhaust port. The 1E and 2E models used petroil lubrication, but the 1E could be specified with the automatic oiling system, which was a standard fit to the Super Sports version. All three engines carried on in production until the outbreak of the Second World War.

February 1934 Douglas advert for 148cc Villiers-based engine (mounted horizontally)

An ever expanding order book

At the turn of the decade the factory had expanded to provide additional production space, to meet the needs of the ever-increasing order book, with business looking very rosy indeed. And, in 1931 yet

Francis-Barnett Cruiser 250, February 1934

another engine size was introduced, to be used for the 100cc Autocycle market. Devoid of any Mk or class coding the 98cc engine was simply known appropriately as the Midget. Having a square bore and stroke of 50 x 50mm, the Midget used a cast iron, fixed head cylinder, with a single exhaust port, a single rear transfer passage and a side mounted Villiers Midget carburettor. The piston was again cast iron and fitted with an inertia ring. This engine led to the introduction of the 98cc Junior in 1934, with both units staying in production until the advent of the Second World War – when the Junior de Luxe was introduced - spawning another compete range of engines after the conflict was over.

The Junior engine employed an aluminium alloy deflector piston, a big-end bearing with alternating steel and bronze rollers carried on an overhung crankpin and a crankshaft that was mounted on ball bearings. A seal was also provided to prevent oil leaking into the clutch-case. The Midget had been just an engine, but now the single speed Junior was a complete engine package that had a primary drive and a clutch built in unit with the crankcases. The cylinder followed normal Villiers practice, with the cylinder head not being detachable, but strangely the finning of this horizontal unit was arranged diagonally. The right hand crankcase cover (or door) proudly proclaimed this newcomer to the Villiers range as the Villiers Junior.

A new three-fifty

1931 also saw the introduction of a new three-fifty engine, which had revised bore and stroke measurements of 70 x 90mm. This long-stroke engine, designated the Mk XIV-B, replaced its over square predecessor, staying in production until 1940. Available in three versions, the three-fifty was either petroil lubricated, equipped with the automatic lubrication system or water-cooled. An aluminium head was used on this engine, together with an alloy inlet manifold and an auxiliary flywheel. Used in the lightweight sidecar role, the XIV-B performed admirably, with plenty of low down pulling power and over all engine smoothness.

1930s Blue Diamond fitted with long-stroke 346cc Mark XIV-B

A new breed of two-fifty

The following year also saw the introduction of a new breed of two-fifty based on the same concept, which again could be equipped with automatic lubrication and/or water-cooling. The Mk XIV-A engines now had a bore and stroke of 63 x 80 mm and a capacity of 249cc, to capitalise on this popular class, and again stayed in production – being joined by the Mk XVII-A of 1935 and the Mk XVIII-A of 1939 - until 1940. The Mk XVI-A was the last 247cc engine and was produced from 1934 to 1940. The early versions of the Mk XIV-A had a choice of ignition systems. In some cases the flywheel magneto was used for both sparks and lighting, and in others a chain driven dynamo - fitted with a contact breaker set - was used to keep the battery charged, which then supplied power to the 6 volt ignition coil.

Bore and stroke measurement changes were the vogue during this period, and the same techniques were applied to the one-fifty engines, which became a twin port 148cc unit, with a bore and stroke of 53 x 67mm. This side carburettor, twin port engine, together with its successor the single port Mk XV-C of 1934, again stayed in production until 1940, alongside the earlier 147cc Mk VIII-C, which outlasted the war and carried on until 1947. The reason given for the change was one of versatility, allowing the motorcycle manufacturers a freedom to place the carburettor in the most convenient position, an array of different shaped manifolds being available for the purpose.

The 122cc Mk 8D

In 1936 the 122cc Mk 8D was introduced, the Mk number being intentionally printed in English script, a tradition that followed with the 9D of 1938. This renumbering was not universal, for later engines of other classes still continued to use the Roman numeral system. The 8D unit was the first true unit-construction motor, having an integral three-speed gearbox. And, at last the Villiers product approached the original design concept formulated by Charles Marston a quarter of a century before – the supply of a complete (totally Villiers built) power unit package for the motorcycle trade. Modern techniques were employed on this unit, for the crankshaft was supported on a pair of ball races, with outboard bronze sleeves to seal in the crankcase compression. A flat top piston, with fully floating gudgeon pin, was used in the twin exhaust port cylinder, which featured a detachable alloy cylinder head, a pair of detachable exhaust stubs and a side mounted carburettor. The primary transmission and clutch, fitted to the left hand side of the unit, was totally enclosed in its own oil-tight alloy case.

Using the same bore (50 mm) as the Midget and Junior engines, the 122cc 8D engine used a stroke of 62 mm, but its successor could be supplied with a capacity of 122 or 98cc, achieved with the change of a few components. Two years later the 8D was replaced by the 9D unit, which had an improved gear change mechanism and an 18 watt flywheel magneto. The 9D unit stayed in production until 1948, and saw valuable service during the Second World War.

More new engines

Before the war got under way in late 1939, Villiers produced two more engines that year, the 3E and the Mk XVIII-A. The 3E followed the lines of the 9D in that it was equipped with a three-speed gearbox, built in unit with the engine. The 3E had now grown in capacity, from 196cc to 197cc, using new bore and stroke dimensions of 59 x 72mm, a design configuration that lasted until the mid 1960s. The Mk XVIII-A used a new ball bearing mounted crankshaft that was equipped with spring-loaded glands to retain the crankcase compression. It was also only available with petroil lubrication.

The Villiers Engineering Co survived the boom and bust years of the 1920s and 1930s, ending these two decades with a large engineering factory capable of forging, casting and machining mechanical components for the motorcycle industry. With the clouds of war on the horizon - for the second time during the century - this engineering ability was again used to good effect.

Vincent HRD 1933 Olympia Show advert with new 249cc watercooled Villiers MkIXV-A

Vincent-HRD

Renowned for the production of extremely fast and well-equipped V twins, the Vincent-HRD (Philip Vincent and Howard Raymond Davies) company is not best remembered for the production of lightweight machines, least of all two-strokes. As long ago as 1932, HRD designed and built a lightweight machine to capture the lightweight market. Cheap and economic to run the machine also attracted lower tax and insurance prices.

Designed and built in 1932, the machine used a proprietary air-cooled Villiers 247cc engine and an Albion three-speed gearbox, but it was the total enclosure of the lower half of the engine and the gearbox, together with the advanced chassis design that appealed to would-be buyers. On sale for the princely sum of £39.50 the lightweight attracted few customers, and soon developed a bad reputation of seizing-up when pushed hard on a hot day. Two years later a redesigned model was ready for sale, this time equipped with the Villiers Mk XIV-A water-cooled unit and an Albion (positive stop & foot operated) four-speed gearbox. The massive frame centre section comprised a malleable steel backbone, onto which was bolted a tubular structure to carry the engine bearers, headstock and rear suspension pivots. The front forks were of the conventional Druid type, with a central spring and side-mounted friction dampers. Rear suspension followed the traditional Vincent-HRD cantilever design, pivoting on Timken roller bearings and having a single spring suspension unit mounted under the seat. The rest of the machine followed conventional practice, using Harvill 6 inch hubs and a Terry's saddle, but it was the total enclosure of the entire engine bay that gave it a purposeful image, a style that would be repeated on the Vincent Black Prince many years later.

The radiator for the thermo-siphon principle cooling system, was mounted transversely across the front down tubes, just below the nose of the fuel tank. Visible from the front of the quickly detachable engine covers, the radiator exhausted its warm air into the enclosure, from where it was then directed onto the rider's knees. The front of the engine enclosure, below the radiator, was formed by a large volume cast aluminium exhaust chamber, similar to the Francis-Barnett Cruiser of the same period, a tail pipe and small additional silencer led the gasses well to the rear of the machine.

A well documented example of this model is on display at the Sammy Miller Museum, painstakingly rebuilt by Ken Blake of Poole, Dorset, it represents a facet of the British motorcycle industry from the dark days of the Great Depression. This actual bike was ordered by motorcycle dealer EP Huxham of Bournmouth on 12th August 1933 and records show that it was personally tested by none other than Phil Irving, on 20th December 1933 and the sold to a Miss Price on 4th March 1934 for £49.50. It is certain that very few bikes were actually built, and believed that this machine is one of only two surviving examples of the innovative HRD lightweight model. The second example was on display at the National Motorcycle Museum, Birmingham, prior to the disastrous fire of September 2003.

Francis-Barnett

Born of a liaison in 1919 between Captain Gordon Ingoldsby Francis (the son of Graham Francis who was the Francis half of the Lea-Francis motorcycle company) and Arthur Barnett (the father of Gordon's war-time bride and owner of the Invicta motorcycle company), the Francis-Barnett company started - as did many others - with the use of proprietary engines from outside manufacturers. First models used the JAP side-valve 293 and 346cc engines and were built at the old Excelsior works in Lower Ford Street, Coventry. Running alongside - but always superior to - the Invicta, the new Francis-Barnett's soon became Villiers powered, with the use of the Mk II engine in 1920 and the Mk III engine the following year.

With the post-war motorcycle sales boom fading a decision was made to concentrate on the Villiers engine and low cost utility models, which heralded the arrival of the fully triangulated, straight tube frames, a bolted-up structure that could be easily repaired in the event of an accident. This model was first exhibited at the 1923 Olympia Show and earned the description, 'Built like a bridge.' Further advertisements advised, 'The frame can be packed into a golf bag.'

This advertising was not as insane as it first seemed, for this was the time of increased overseas sales and the ability to reduce the frame down to a bundle of tubes lowered shipping costs. Reassembly was simple, with two works fitters being able to rebuild the machine in as little as 20 minutes.

From the advent of the 1930s, Francis-Barnett relied on Villiers engines to power its range of bikes (the exception being the Stag which used a Blackburne four-stroke motor) a policy that stayed with the company until the latter years at AMC (see chapter 8). This policy continued throughout the 1930s with the use of the 122, 147 and 148cc engines, but by this time the company had started to go up-market again with the arrival of the Pulman, which used the 344cc Villiers twin engine, and the Cruiser range that utilised the 249cc single cylinder engine in air or water-cooled form.

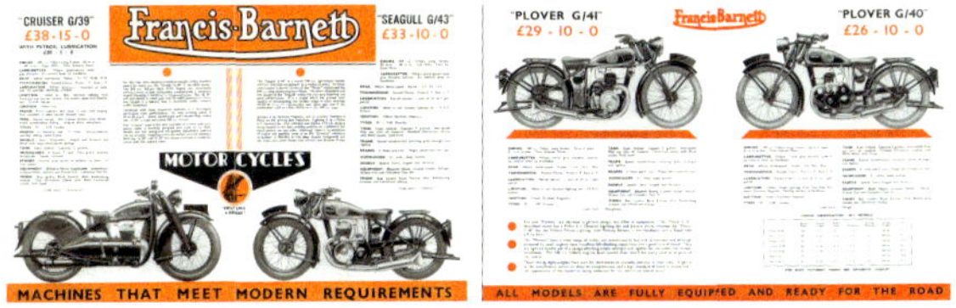

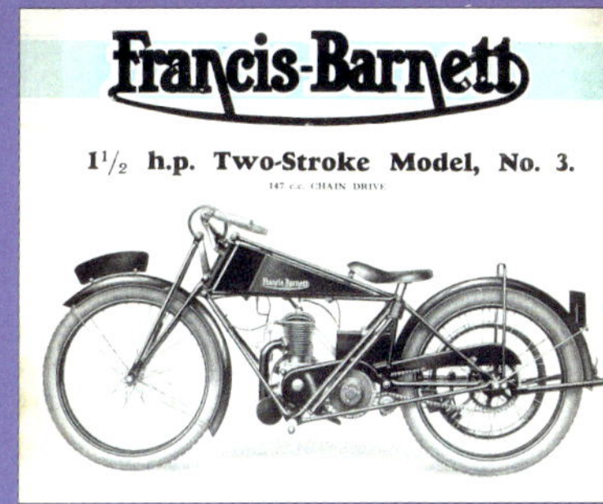

Built from 1933 to 1940 the Cruiser was designed by Bill King, a thoroughly practical engineer, who intended the machine to be a modestly powered all-weather model for use by the gentleman rider. The Cruiser was a big success, for the enclosed engine, leg shields and heavily valanced mudguards kept the rider clean and dry. The Cruiser departed from previous practice and used a frame built around a large I-section steel forging; with pressed steel frame members, engine covers and leg shields, together with a pair of King designed pressed steel fork blades. During the production period, the Cruiser received many specification changes, which included the four-speed gearbox - hand and later foot operated; magneto or coil ignition; air or water cooling; petriol or automatic engine lubrication.

The utility models were never forgotten, and during the same period Francis-Barnett continued to produce its bread and butter range using a mixture of forged and round tube frames and tubular girder forks, with single thickness pressed steel blades being used on the ultra lightweight models. This model range encompassed the 98 and 125cc Snipe, the 150 Plovers and the 250 Seagull.

With the beginning of the Second World War the factory planned to produce the Snipe for Army use, but when it was bombed this idea was shelved, as was any further production until peace once again reigned.

Tommy Meeten - and the Francis-Barnett racers

Francis-Barnett were never really interested in the competition side of motorcycling, but in line with other factories of the period, listed a TT machine in the 1924 brochure, the only reason being that everybody had to have a TT model! Prior to this Francis-Barnetts were listed as private entries in the 1922 and 1923 events and appeared regularly at the Brooklands track. George Brough even rode a Barnett in Midlands hill-climbs, at one time establishing a fastest 250 time and gaining a second fastest in the 350 event - on the same machine.

Tommy Meeten rode a Francis-Barnett to sixth place in the first 175 TT of 1924, but this machine was powered by an ohv Blackburne engine. Liking the machine's handling and having sampled a 147cc model, at the insistence of Gordon Francis, he became thoroughly hooked on the Coventry based machines.

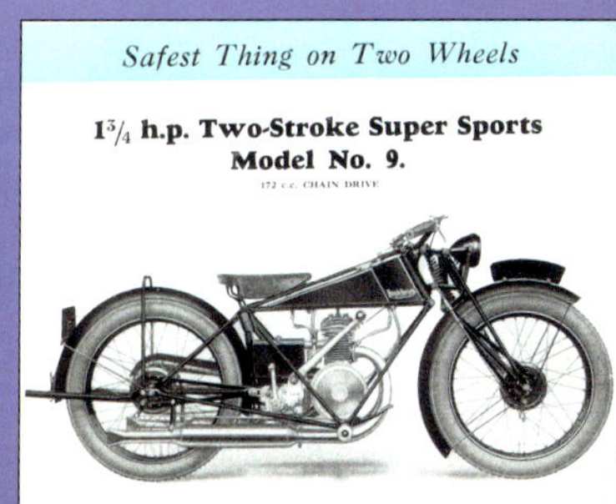

A racer was constructed at the factory for Tommy, using a specially tuned version of the new Villiers172cc Sports engine. The Meeten Francis-Barnett Sport engine used a pair of specially constructed exhaust pipes, with larger diameter chambers near to the cylinder exhaust ports, the chambers necking down to standard sized outlet pipes with fishtail ends. The cylinder had an additional finned alloy cooling ring shrunk on together with a special Villiers carburettor, on a short manifold, which stuck out into the airflow on the left hand side. A special flywheel magneto was also fitted to the engine, and it was on this machine that he regularly notched up

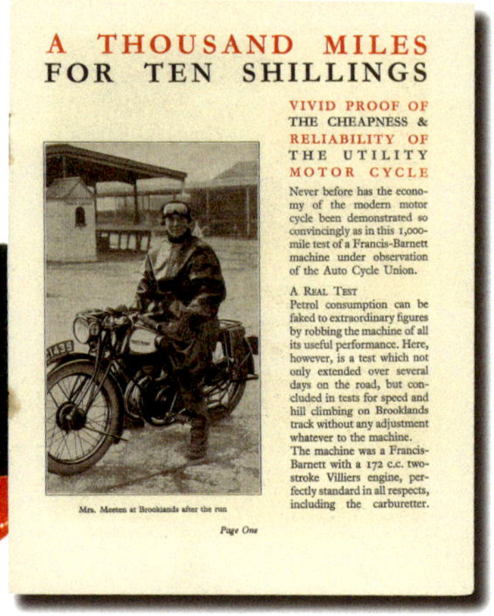

A THOUSAND MILES
FOR TEN SHILLINGS

VIVID PROOF OF THE CHEAPNESS & RELIABILITY OF THE UTILITY MOTOR CYCLE

Never before has the economy of the modern motor cycle been demonstrated so convincingly as in this 1,000-mile test of a Francis-Barnett machine under observation of the Auto Cycle Union.

A Real Test

Petrol consumption can be faked to extraordinary figures by robbing the machine of all its useful performance. Here, however, is a test which not only extended over several days on the road, but concluded in tests for speed and hill climbing on Brooklands track without any adjustment whatever to the machine.

The machine was a Francis-Barnett with a 172 c.c. two-stroke Villiers engine, perfectly standard in all respects, including the carburetter.

Mrs. Meeten at Brooklands after the run

Page One

October 1929 Mrs T G Meeten covered over 1000 miles riding a 172cc Francis-Barnett

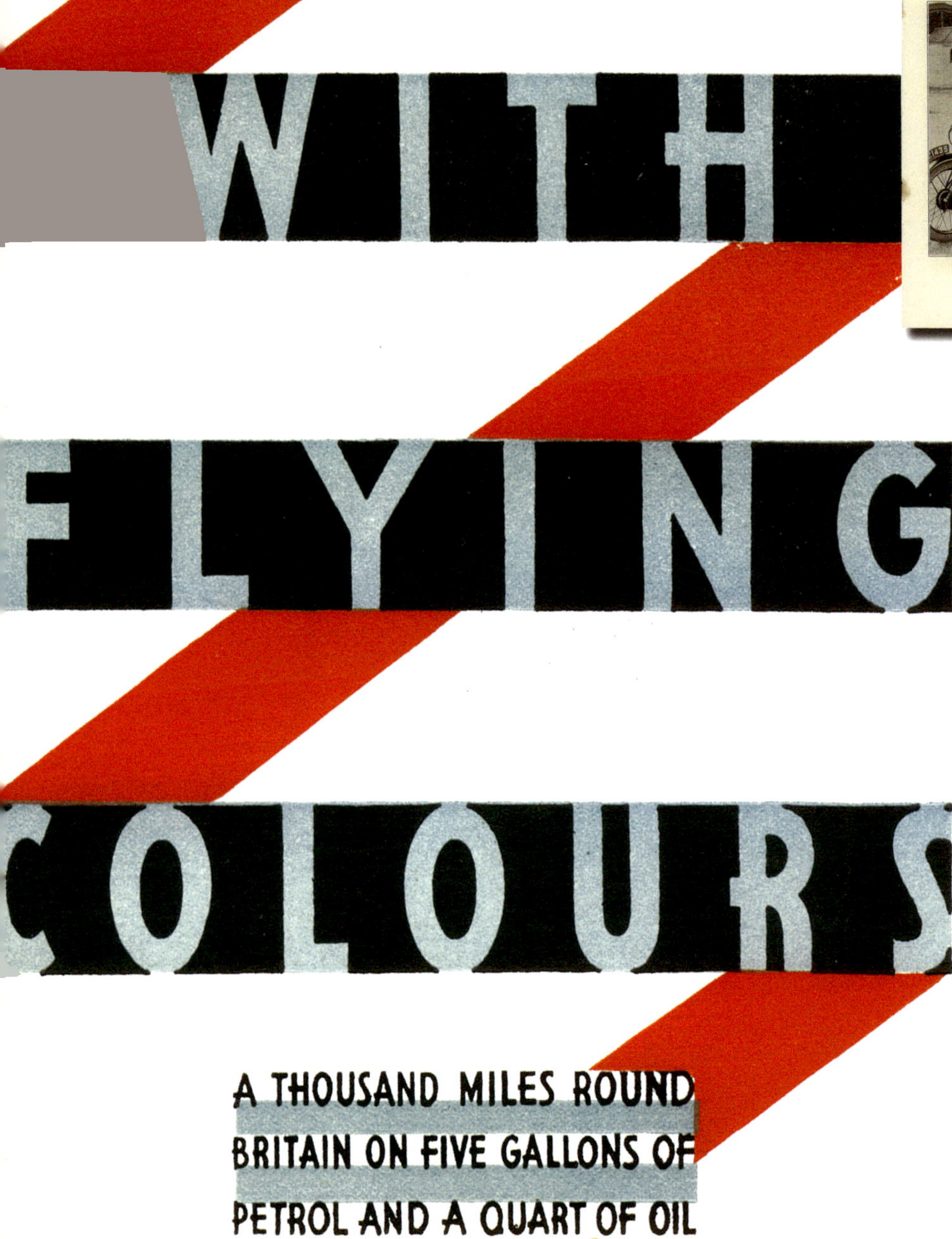

many class victories at the Brooklands banked circuit, as well as establishing the following world records:

51.24mph for 7 hours
51.87mph for 8 hours
51.75mph for 9 hours
50.84mph for 10 hours
50.52mph for 11 hours
50.27mph for 12 hours
50.06mph for 24 hours

In honour of Tommy Meeten and his world records, Villiers announced the super tuned Brooklands version of the Sports engine in 1925, followed a year later by the Super Sports TT version.

During the same period the French Monet-Goyon company also established many time and distance records - using the same Sports type engine - at the Montlhery banked track near Paris, one of which was the averaging of 52.05mph for 2,000 Km.

Tommy Meeten was a remarkable rider both on the tarmac and on the rough stuff, for he also regularly competed in the Scottish and the International Six Day Trials, not just as a solo rider but also as a sidecar driver – sometimes using the same 172cc machine!

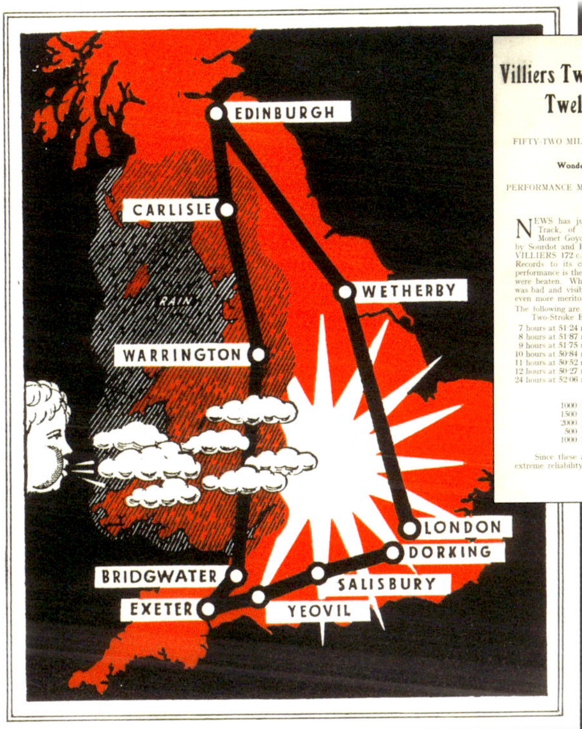

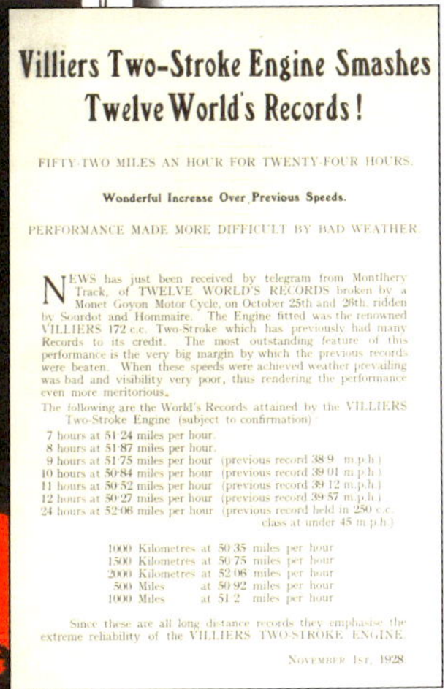

Villiers Two-Stroke Engine Smashes Twelve World's Records!

FIFTY-TWO MILES AN HOUR FOR TWENTY-FOUR HOURS.

Wonderful Increase Over Previous Speeds.

PERFORMANCE MADE MORE DIFFICULT BY BAD WEATHER.

NEWS has just been received by telegram from Montlhery Track, of TWELVE WORLD'S RECORDS broken by a Monet Goyon Motor Cycle, on October 25th and 26th, ridden by Sourdot and Hommaire. The Engine fitted was the renowned VILLIERS 172 c.c. Two-Stroke which has previously had many Records to its credit. The most outstanding feature of this performance is the very big margin by which the previous records were beaten. When these speeds were achieved weather prevailing was bad and visibility very poor, thus rendering the performance even more meritorious.

The following are the World's Records attained by the VILLIERS Two-Stroke Engine (subject to confirmation):

7 hours at 51·24 miles per hour.
8 hours at 51·87 miles per hour.
9 hours at 51·75 miles per hour (previous record 38·9 m.p.h.)
10 hours at 50·84 miles per hour (previous record 39·01 m.p.h.)
11 hours at 50·52 miles per hour (previous record 39·12 m.p.h.)
12 hours at 50·27 miles per hour (previous record 39·57 m.p.h.)
24 hours at 52·06 miles per hour (previous record held in 250 c.c. class at under 45 m.p.h.)

1000 Kilometres at 50·35 miles per hour
1500 Kilometres at 50·75 miles per hour
2000 Kilometres at 52·06 miles per hour
500 Miles at 50·92 miles per hour
1000 Miles at 51·2 miles per hour

Since these are all long distance records they emphasise the extreme reliability of the VILLIERS TWO-STROKE ENGINE.

NOVEMBER 1ST, 1928.

The tally of cups and medals won by Tommy included a Silver in the 1925-26-27 Scottish Six Days, on his 172cc machine, with a Gold in 1928 aboard a Pulman sidecar outfit. The following year also provided a Bronze Medal and a Meritous Performance award this time aboard the 172cc outfit. The 1930 Scottish also gained a Silver Medal, but this time he reverted to the larger Pulman outfit. The passenger on the 1929 and 1930 Scottish outings was none other than Mrs Meeten, an accomplished rider herself, and the only lady competitor in both these events.

The International Six Day Trial of 1926, that started from Buxton, Derbyshire, saw Tommy gain a coveted Gold Medal for his collection - again riding his trusty 172cc Francis-Barnett.

After this run of successes Tommy Meeten set up his own sales outlet - Meetens Motor Mecca, situated on the New Malden roundabout at Shannons Corner on the Kingston By-Pass - naturally retailing Villiers and Francis-Barnett products. He then branched out into manufacturing after taking over the SOS Company from Len Vale-Onslow. Being a two-stroke man at heart he kept abreast with current trends, and later he became one of the founding Members of The British Two Stroke Club.

The Famous
"JAMES"
MOTOR CYCLES
1936
W. H. JONES,
MOTOR CYCLE SPECIALIST
115 NORMANTON RD.
DERBY
THE JAMES CYCLE CO., LTD., LONDON & BIRMINGHAM

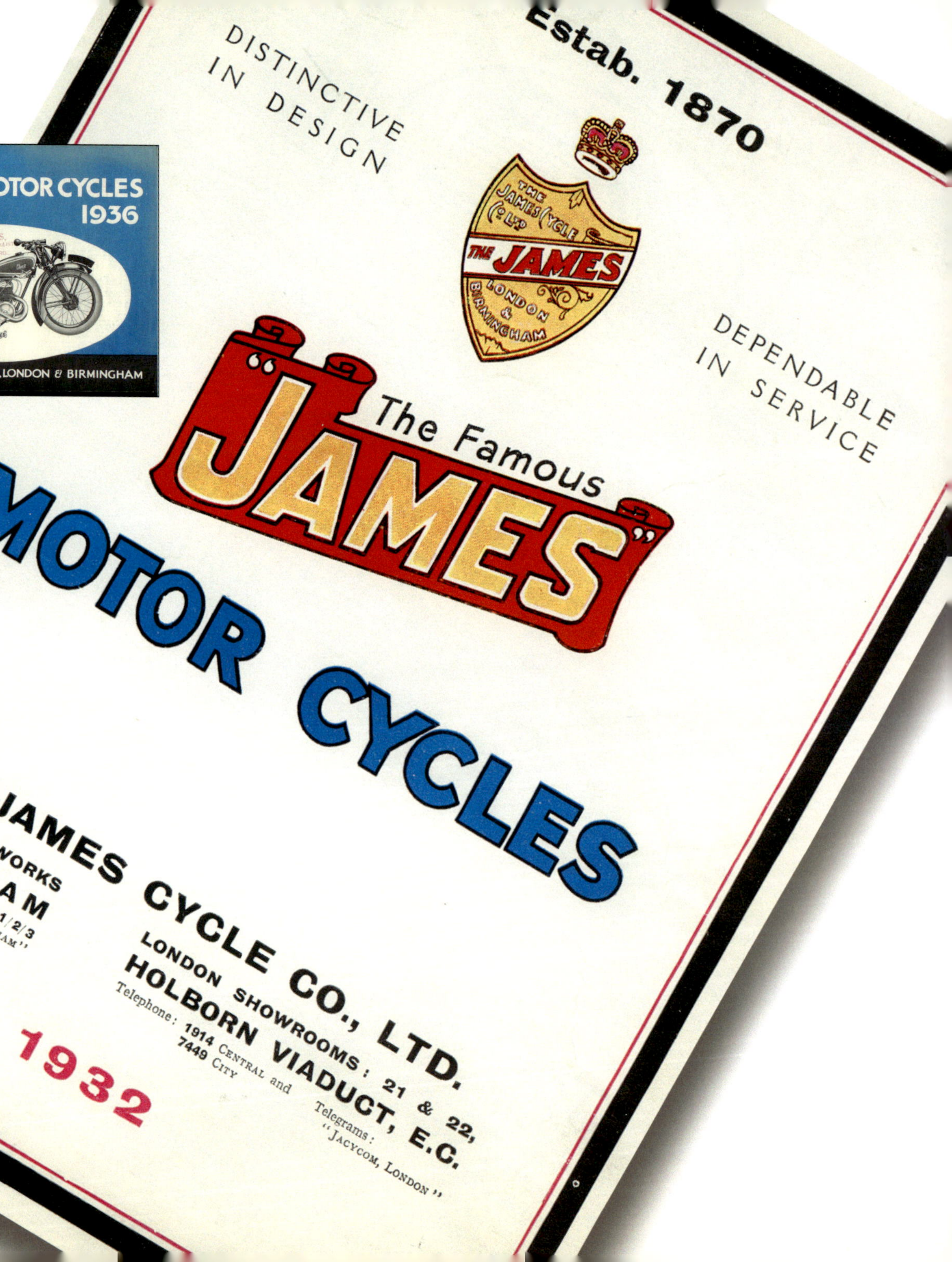
DISTINCTIVE
IN DESIGN
Estab. 1870
THE JAMES CYCLE Co. LTD
THE JAMES
LONDON & BIRMINGHAM
DEPENDABLE
IN SERVICE
The Famous
"JAMES"
MOTOR CYCLES
THE JAMES CYCLE CO., LTD.
HEAD OFFICE & WORKS
BIRMINGHAM
Telephone: VICTORIA 2211/2/3
Telegrams: "BICYCLES, BIRMINGHAM"
LONDON SHOWROOMS: 21 & 22,
HOLBORN VIADUCT, E.C.
Telephone: 1914 CENTRAL and
7449 CITY
Telegrams:
"JACYCOM, LONDON"
1932

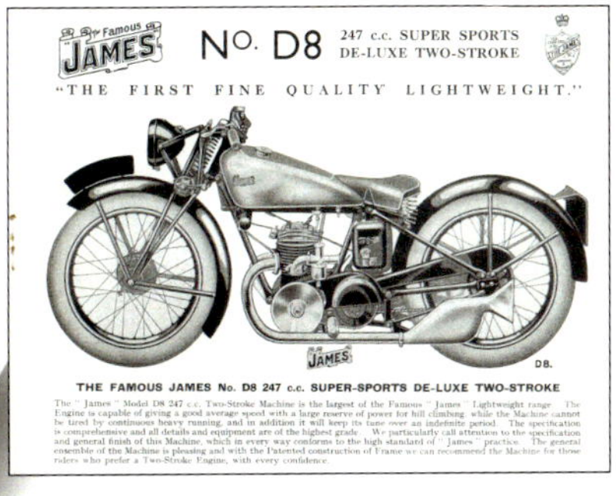

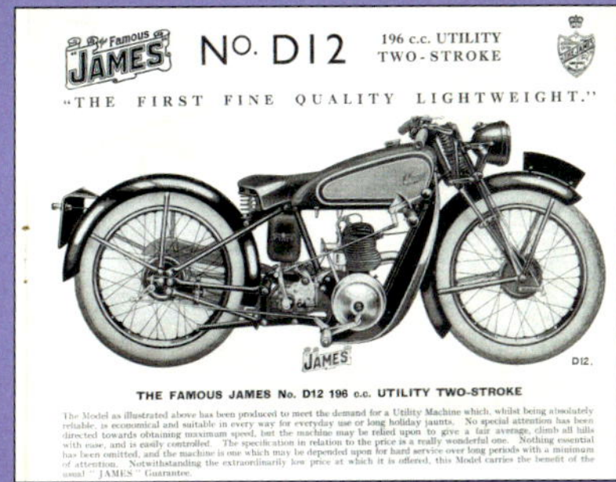

James

Bicycle manufacture was again the mainstay of this Birmingham based company, which was established in 1880 by Harry James, to produce the penny-farthing. Trade flourished and a move to larger premises in Sampson Road Sparkbrook was made some ten years later and the company went public in 1897. Harry retired at this time and installed Charles Hyde as managing director with Fred Kimberly as his deputy. It was the latter who urged the managing director to add a power unit to the James bicycle, as many of the local cycle factories had done to good effect. The first James motorcycle was announced in 1902 and comprised a typical - but strengthened - bicycle frame; with a Belgian Minerva engine clipped to the front down tube and a direct drive to the rear wheel pulley by a twisted rawhide belt. A second version featured the engine mounted within the frame, driving a friction roller that pressed against the rear tyre. The friction roller version was not a success and the following year the sales catalogue only listed the 2 hp Minerva engined Model T.

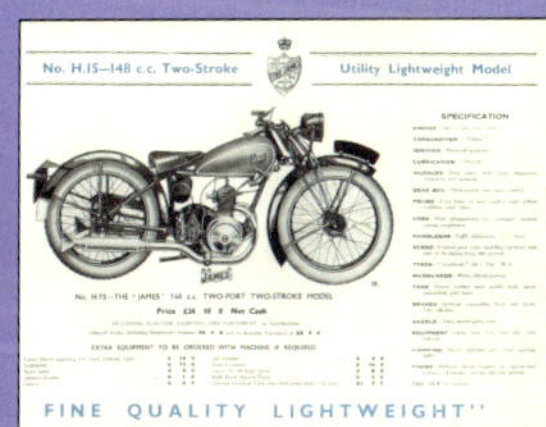

In 1908 the James company moved to the Greet works in Birmingham, a factory that they occupied until the ignominious and final crash of the mighty AMC empire in 1966. At the time of this move, James had started to produce their own engine, an 86 x 90 mm four-stroke with concentric valves, which was installed into the Safety model. This machine was very novel, for not only did it feature a low frame but was equipped with a clutch, wheels mounted on stub axles and internal expanding drum brakes. Unfortunately this radical machine was not a good seller, even though it incorporated some excellent engineering ideas; ideas that would become normal practice within the industry some years later.

Production continued after the First World War with high quality well-equipped single cylinder and V twin models for solo and sidecar work, but the early 1930s saw a decline in sales as trading conditions worsened prior the Great Depression. Having made their own two-stroke engine just prior to the Great War, James now installed the Villiers engine in its utility range, using the 150, 172 and 196cc packages. Gradually engine manufacture at the Greet factory was phased out and a policy of building lightweight machines with bought-in engines was instigated; naturally these were Villiers engines, the range encompassing the 98 to 250cc capacity classes. This move to building lightweight machinery saw the company spread its wings, when war was declared in 1939, with the introduction of the battle-field communications motorcycle – the 9D powered ML or Military Lightweight.

1930 Baker brochure

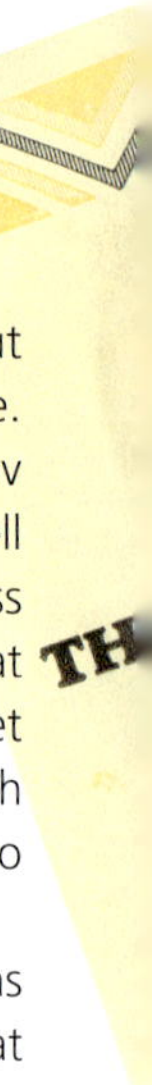

Jawa

During 1929 Czechoslovakian arms manufacturer Frantisek Janecek decided to branch out into motorcycle production and initially produced the German Wanderer machine under licence. This first production motorcycle (nicknamed the Rumbler) used a 498cc single cylinder ohv engine and shaft drive, to produce a fast but costly machine, which initially did not sell very well – for this was the beginning of the 1930s economic depression. Janecek's dreams of a mass produced motorcycle were dashed for the time being, but in 1930 he sent his son to Great Britain to study the world renowned British motorcycle industry. It was on this trip that he met George William Patchett, a motorcycle designer and racer who had learnt his trade at Brough Superior, McEvoy and FN. Janecek Junior eventually persuaded Patchett to return to Czechoslovakia with him, to become a designer for Jawa.

What Jawa were looking for was a simple, cheap and reliable lightweight machine that was capable of mass production, and Patchett having familiarised himself with Villiers products at McEvoy, soon came up with a design. Jawa management also realised that the little two-stroke was the right answer and due in part to George Patchett, Jawa soon started to import the Villiers 172cc engine, installing it in a chassis of their own design together with an Albion three-speed gearbox. The Jawa 175 was a considerable sales success, due in part to its remarkably cheap price tag; it being advertised as, 'A better machine for less money'.

The 1932 season saw the Jawa factory importing engines, gearboxes, hubs, brakes, magnetos, chains and even carburettors from Great Britain to complete the build of their 175 model. But, in 1933 these imports were reduced with many items being produced in-house, which included the Villiers motors that were now produced in the Jawa factory under licence.

The first year of production saw 3,020 Villiers engined machines produced, almost three times as many as 500cc Wanderer that it replaced, and the 175 remained in full-scale production until 1946, although its numbers were seriously reduced during the war years, due to the German war effort.

With the outbreak of war in 1939, George Patchett returned to England and spent the rest of the conflict designing arms for Enfield and other armaments companies, a job that brought him much fame and fortune. The introduction to the Villiers engine-by Patchett - set a trend that continued for many years to come, with Jawa being rated as the number one East European small capacity two-stroke motorcycle manufacturer, albeit – in the post-war years - using engines of their own design.

Czech Jawa factory imported Villiers 172cc engines and built licenced versions from 1933 onwards

1925 New Knight

Villiers-engined Triumph Model XVII

1931 SOS air-cooled 346cc Villiers twin-port single

SOS

In 1999, at the age of 100, SOS's remarkable founder Leonard Vale-Onslow was not only still riding motorcycles regularly, but was given the famous 'Red Book' treatment appearing as the special guest on the BBC's well-known This is your Life television programme.

This was a fitting tribute to the man whose company's name at first stood for 'Super Onslow Special' and later 'So Obviously Superior'. Vale-Onslow's motorcycles were considered to be more exclusive and of higher quality than the stock Villiers powered bikes so common in the 1930s.

Ironically, SOS originally employed a mixture of JAP four-strokes and Villiers two-stroke power units, but from the 1931 season only the latter were fitted, ranging from 172 to 346cc. In addition, Vale-Onslow manufactured its own 148 (53 x 67 mm) and 172cc (57.15 x 67 mm) engines with water-cooled cylinder and head and was always regarded as an upmarket brand due mainly to the fine finish of its products.

SOS machines were initially built at Hallow, near Worcester, but in late 1931 production was transferred to Vale-Onslow's home city of Birmingham. The company's most sporting model was the 172cc AA, later known as the Brooklands. This was available in track, road racing or trials guise to special order.

In October 1933 control of the SOS marque passed to Brooklands star and Villiers enthusiast Tommy Meeten, then based in Redhill Surrey; production however remained in Birmingham. During 1936 Meeten opened a dealership in South London, named Meetens Moto Mecca, which subsequently became the local agent for Villiers spares in Southern England for the next 50 years (later in post-war days trading as Meeten and Ward).

When the Second World War broke out in 1939, Tommy Meeten offered his services to the British government, but this offer was turned down. He closed the Birmingham factory, which was never to re-open. As for the original owner, Leonard Vale-Onslow, he continued as a motorcycle dealer in Birmingham.

Eysink

Eysink was a Dutch marque, which lasted for some 75 years. But for such a long standing company today they are largely ignored by motorcycle historians. DH Eysink founded the firm in 1886 and became interested in automobiles and motorcycles by the turn of the 20th Century. By the First World War, their 365 and 425cc singles were widely employed by the Dutch Army; there were also 366 and 409cc singles and a 774cc in-house V-twin.

After the conflict, in 1921 came a 702cc flat twin, but the 1926 range used a range of bought-in engines of between 147 and 1150cc. After the war, Villiers power units were normally utilised, and post 1926 the 147, 172 and 196cc units were being purchased directly from the

Dutch Eysink 125cc Villiers-engined racer 1998 Centential TT Assen

Eysink 125cc Dutch TT 1951

Wolverhampton concern to power the Eysink range. Later this list was expanded to include the 122cc units. The Amersfoort factory was closely connected to other European manufacturers of the period, with New Hudson, Sunbeam and the French Dollar factory supplying certain components to the relatively small Dutch concern.

Eysink was the only Dutch motorcycle marque to compete in road racing for many years – they also took part in the 1934 Isle of Man TT.

Then during the late 1940s, they became a leading contender for honours in the newly introduced 125cc class. In fact, in 1948 the twin exhaust Villiers 9D-based 125s were included in the Dutch TT race programme for the first time, with Eysink emerging victorious. The 9D type cylinder was chosen in preference to the single exhaust 10D cylinder, for it offered more scope in port modifications. This event attracted the likes of Nello Pagani and Rafaele Alberti from Italy (both mounted on Morini two-strokes) and a team of four Spanish riders on Montesas. There were a further 24 entrants on assorted machinery from the host nation.

But it was the Villiers-based Eysink of Dirk Renooy who emerged the winner, completing the 6-lap (62 miles) race at an average speed of 61.28 mph, compared to runner-up Pagani who managed 60.44 mph. Another Eysink was third.

The following year, 1949, saw the introduction of an official World Championship series, including the 125cc category. At the Dutch round the previous year's winner, Renooy, again Eysink mounted, led from the start, but fell at Bertelds Bocht – a hairpin corner 12 miles from the start. Although unhurt, the machine was too extensively damaged to continue. Eysinks were placed 6th, 8th and 11th out of twelve finishers.

Technically the Eysink 125 racer was interesting as the later engines sported a 'sun-burst' radial aluminium cylinder head, outside flywheel and magneto ignition. Additionally, but in early 1950s there was a duplex frame, swinging arm rear suspension and telescopic front forks. The later engines, although still retaining the twin-port exhaust, now had side, rather than front exiting header pipes. There were even experiments with disc-valves instead of piston port induction.

But as the 1950s unfolded Eysink together with the other two-stroke engined machines had to give second best to the latest breed of dohc four-strokes from the likes of FB Mondial, MV Agusta and NSU.

Eysink's final Grand Prix appearance came in the 1955 Dutch TT, when a solitary example came home 11th.

Later the Dutch company produced 98 and 250cc scooters and, until the late 1970s, offered tandem bicycles and sports mopeds.

Eysink's GP engine with their own cylinder head, flywheel and magneto

Dirk Renooy, winner of the 1948 125cc Dutch TT

1953 Dutch Sparta with 125cc Villiers engine at the Spanish Grand Prix

Coventry-
EAGLE
MOTOR CYCLES
DOF 960
Consistently Excellent

SIR MALCOLM CA
THE COVENTRY-EAGLE CYCLE & MOTOR C
EXN 2
Photograph above shows Coventry-Eagle's additional factory—Lincoln Street Works, Coventry, purchased from the Singe
HEAD OFFICE AND WORKS:
THE COVENTRY-EAGLE CYCLE & MOTOR CO. Ltd., BISHOPGATE GREEN WORKS, COVE
'Grams: "EAGLE, COVENTRY"
'Phone: COVENTRY 4017, 4018 and 4019

Late 1930s Coventry Eagle brochure showing various Villiers-powered models

1935 Coventry Eagle L3 Utility, fitted with the 247cc Villiers XVI-A engine recently restored by Peter Thorne

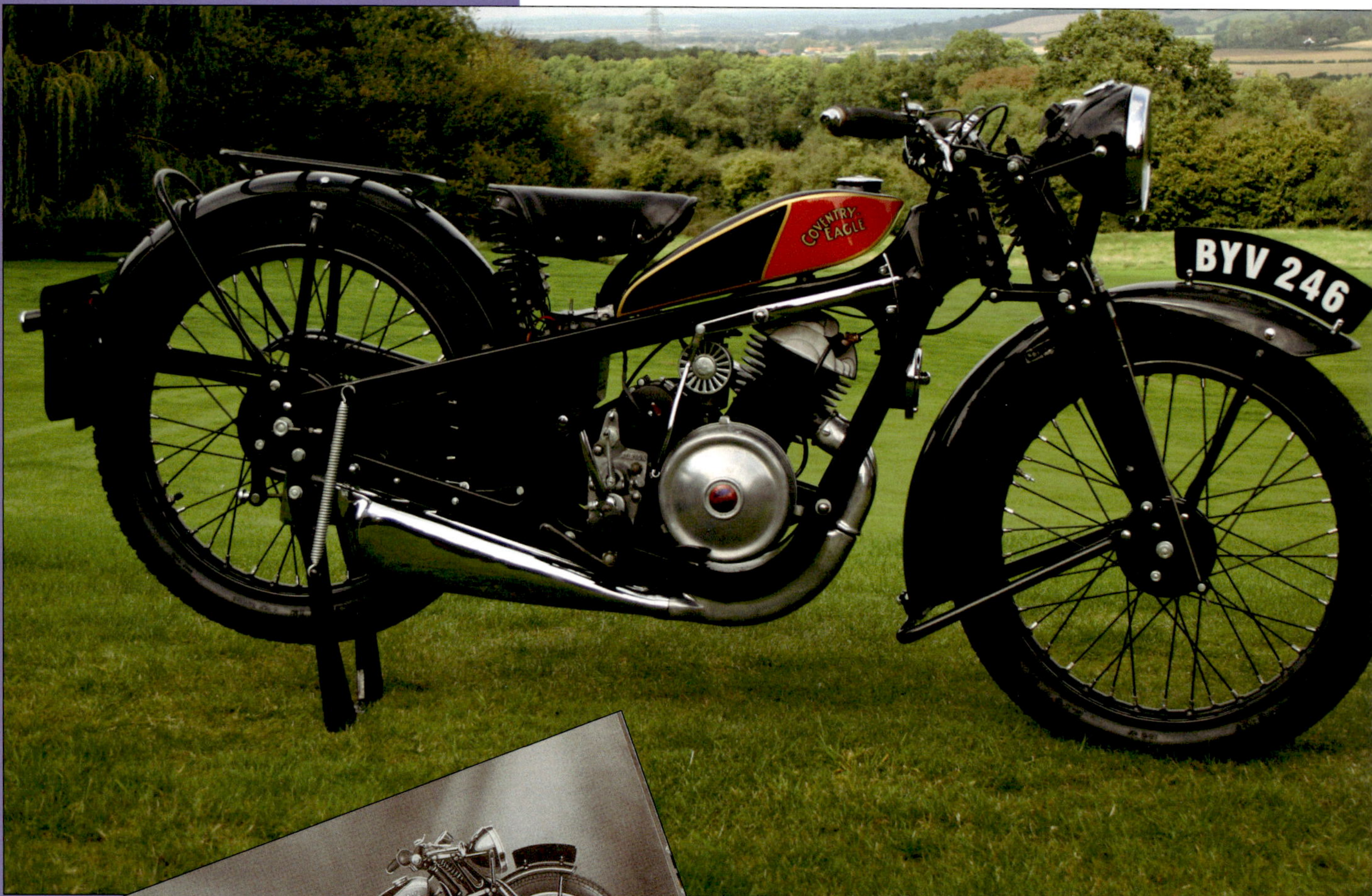

WOLF

MOTOR CYCLES 1938

WOLVERHAMPTON

WOLF VIXEN 148 cc.

12/- TAX.

WOLF UNIT 125 c.c.

12/- TAX.

WOLF 250 cc. SUPER SPORTS

22/6 TAX.

WOLF MINOR 147 cc.

12/- TAX.

'Excelsior'

FAMOUS THE WORLD OVER

Villiers

249c.c. Two-Port, Two Stroke SPORTS MODEL No. C.5

SPECIFICATION

ENGINE—New design Villiers two-stroke, two-port, 63 mm. bore × 80 mm. stroke, 249 c.c. Long stroke. Detachable aluminium alloy cylinder head. Aluminium alloy piston with inertia rings. Automatic system of lubrication. Full roller big end bearing. Extra long bronze gas-tight main bearing. Straight through twin exhaust pipes and two expansion chambers with fish tail ends, chromium plated.

FRAME—New design frame, constructed with taper gauge tubes of exceptional strength, giving great stability and low riding position.

FORKS—Girder model. Sports, incorporating link action and central spring under compression.

GEAR—3-speed hand controlled clutch and kick-starter.

TANK—Latest design, all steel welded saddle tank. Chromium plated. Petrol capacity, 1¾ gallons. Separate oil tank. Capacity 1 quart.

CARBURETTER—Villiers with twist grip control.

CARRIER—Stirrup handle only fitted on standard model. Carrier fitted as an extra. See special column for extra charge when fitted on standard model.

WHEELS AND TYRES—Best quality rims fitted with W.O. Dunlop cord tyres, 25 × 3.00.

SADDLE—Best quality Lycett "Aero" supple top.

BRAKES—Excelsior extra wide 5" internal expanding hub brakes front and rear, of improved design with great efficiency.

TRANSMISSION—Front and rear chains, ½" × $\frac{5}{16}$" heavy motor cycle.

HUBS—All steel hubs of exceptional strength, nickel chrome cones, $\frac{3}{16}$" balls.

MUDGUARDS—Of ample width and depth (dome section), rigid stays preventing mudguard vibration.

HANDLEBARS—Very neat "clean" type fitted by special clip to the steering head, adjustable, with twist grip control and external levers.

FINISH—Tank chromium plated and relieved with neat red side panels. All usual bright parts chromium plated.

EQUIPMENT—Kit of tools, inflator, chain punch, and a Tecalemit grease gun.

IGNITION AND LIGHTING EQUIPMENT—Ignition by H.T. flywheel magneto, separate Lucas 6-volt dynamo electric lighting and charging set. 7" headlamp incorporating ignition switch with illuminated ammeter. Dimmer switch and dip light operated from handlebar.

WEIGHT—Equipped, 226 lbs. (approx.).

Price No. C.5

Standard Specification, equipped with separate Dynamo Lighting and Charging Set (7" Head Lamp) with Dimmer Switch and "Diplite" Bulb, Licence Holder and Electric Horn **£31 - 10 - 0**

Model No. C.5 .. .. *Code Word:* "Villsior."

EXTRAS—See special column.

HIRE PURCHASE TERMS

Initial Payment	£8 0 0
12 Monthly Instalments of	£2 10 0

Insurance included in H.P. amounts.

MOTOR CYCLES 1933

Unique 1930 Berwick with transversely-mounted 250 or 350cc Villiers engine, both with shaft final drive

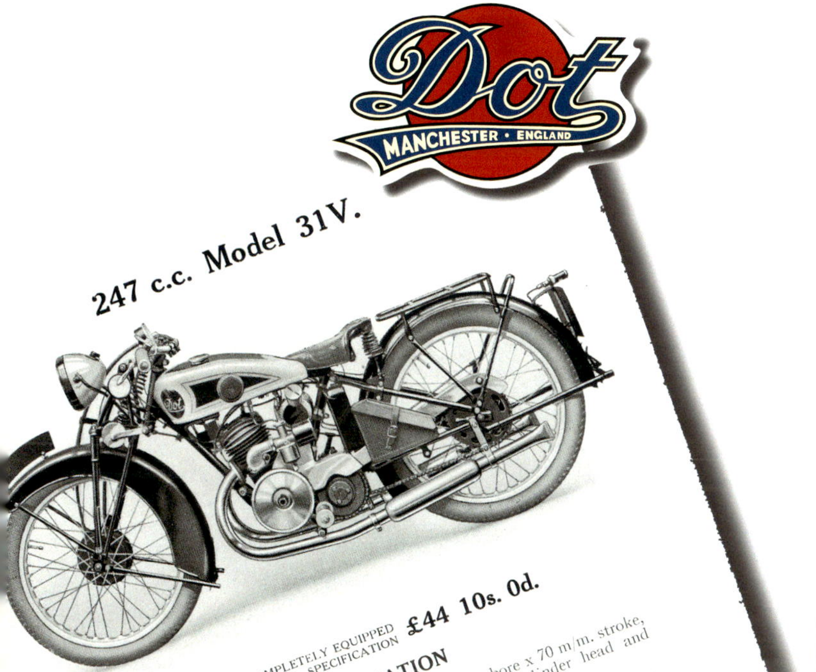
Dot MANCHESTER • ENGLAND

247 c.c. Model 31V.

Price COMPLETELY EQUIPPED AS PER SPECIFICATION £44 10s. 0d.

SPECIFICATION

Engine—247 c.c. VILLIERS Sports Engine, 67 m/m. bore x 70 m/m. stroke, roller bearing big end. Detachable aluminium cylinder head and aluminium piston and flywheel magneto.

Lubrication—VILLIERS Improved Type Automatic Lubricating system, operated by crankcase pressure forcing oil from tank to engine, bein distributed by means of crankcase suction direct to piston, two m bearings and big end. **Use Castrol XL Oil.**

Carburettor—VILLIERS, operated by Amal long sports twist gri with VILLIERS Air Cleaner.

Exhaust System—Two long exhaust pipes fitted with giving quiet running with a minimum of back pr

Frame—Constructed of weldless steel tubes where necessary, joints mitred. The Lu brazed to frame. Special lugs are accommodate pillion footrests.

Forks—Special Dot Brampton "Sp absorbers.

Steering Damper—Fitted a ebonite knurled knob

Transmission—Cover

Gear Box—Albio clutch and 4·8—8·2

Established 190

The Dot DEVOID OF TROUBLE Motor Cycle

MANUFACTURED BY

DOT MOTORS

ARUNDEL STREET

HULME

MANCHESTER

Telephone: Central 3160

Telegrams: DOTMOTA, Manchester

Codes: BENTLEY'S A.B.C. 5th Edition

SEASON 1931

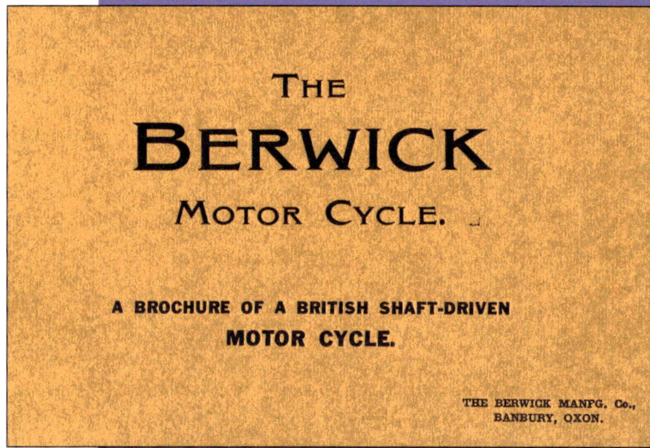
THE

BERWICK

MOTOR CYCLE.

A BROCHURE OF A BRITISH SHAFT-DRIVEN MOTOR CYCLE.

THE BERWICK MANFG. Co.,
BANBURY, OXON.

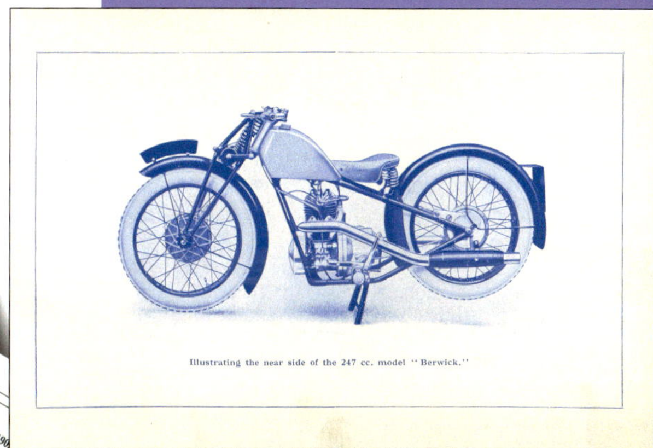
Illustrating the near side of the 247 cc. model "Berwick."

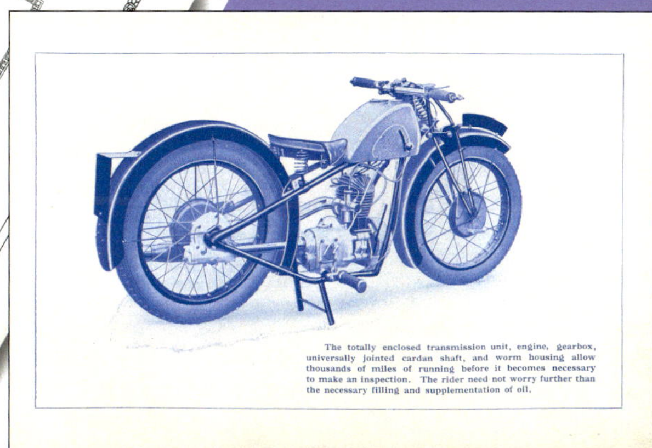
The totally enclosed transmission unit, engine, gearbox, universally jointed cardan shaft, and worm housing allow thousands of miles of running before it becomes necessary to make an inspection. The rider need not worry further than the necessary filling and supplementation of oil.

4 The War Effort

The war effort at the Villiers Engineering Co factory occurred on two separate occasions, firstly from 1916 to 1918 and then again from 1939 to 1945, when in compliance to the British government's directives it turned its production over to armaments and associated equipment. The first conflict of the century actually started in 1914 but Villiers were not drawn into armaments production until after the great shell scandal of 1915, when it was reported in the national press that gunners on the Western Front were limited to firing no more than ten rounds per day. Once this dire shortage became public knowledge, the Prime Minister, Lloyd George, stepped in and swiftly organised the British engineering industry into munitions production, with Villiers commencing their production quota the following year.

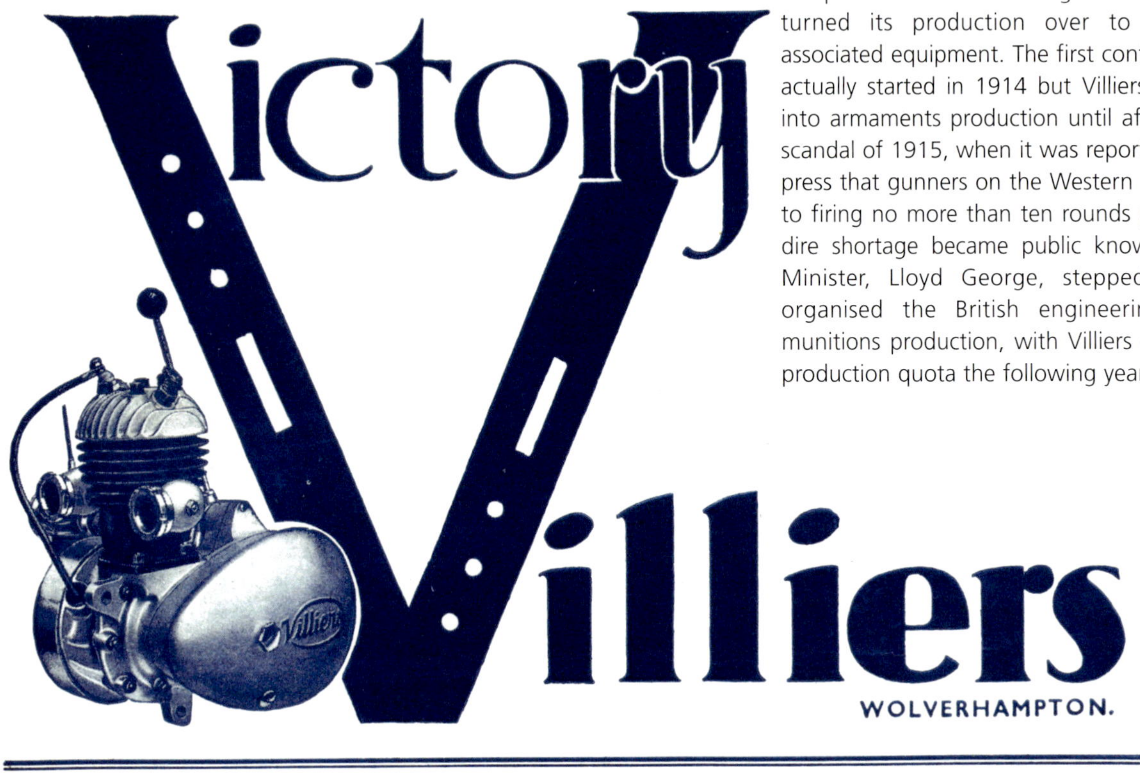

The First World War

The First World War saw the factory mainly making the various parts for the Vickers Munitions Company 75 mm high explosive shells, and small turned parts for the aero engine industry. But even so the Mk I engine remained in production until 1916, when it was replaced by the Mk II, albeit in limited numbers, throughout the conflict. The Mk II engine differed only slightly from its predecessor in having a new all-steel exhaust system, with a revised cylinder attachment. This change required a new cylinder to be cast, making the earlier version obsolete, and any rider requiring a replacement Mk I silencer was then saddled with the cost of not only the exhaust system but that of a new cylinder to go with it! The engine assembly line was not without its problems, for the preferred magneto for the Mk I engine was the German Bosch instrument. Being at war with that country posed a problem with the supply of probably the best magnetos available. Once British stock and a limited supply from France and Canada had run out, British motorcycle manufacturers looked elsewhere for a replacement instrument to fit to the Mk I and the later Mk II engine of their machines.

British magneto manufacturers filled the gap left by the Bosch instrument, but their products were not up to the same high standards as the German unit. Reliability improved as the war rolled on, but in the end the problem was solved by the Villiers factory itself, which produced its own specialised magneto, some two years after the armistice.

The Villiers Engineering Company never capitalised on the production of engines to feed the growing needs of the dispatch rider boom which started during the First World War, motorcycle manufacturers retaining their reliance on the larger capacity four-stroke power units. Certainly no British or Allied forces used Villiers powered bikes in any numbers, the only report being the use of 269cc Sun machines by a French Army unit based in Paris. Nevertheless the factory did contribute its engineering skills to the war effort when the country most needed them, a duty that was to be repeated some twenty years latter with the outbreak of the Second World War.

John Marston dies

The trauma of the war aside, it was still a great shock to the Villiers workforce when the death of its founder member was announced in March 1918, when John Marston passed away at the age of 82. Since the sale of the bicycle components manufacturing side of the business to son Charles, John Marston had concentrated on the Sunbeam factory, but still kept a fatherly eye on his son's fledgling operation. This great man was sorely missed by all who knew him both within the business and civil communities.

There'll always be an En

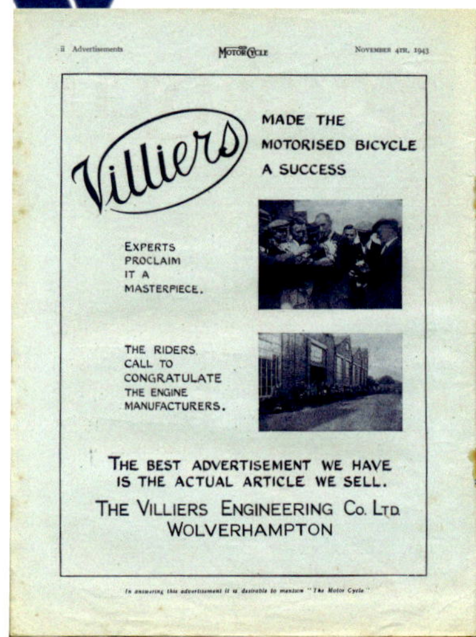

Villiers

MADE THE MOTORISED BICYCLE A SUCCESS

EXPERTS PROCLAIM IT A MASTERPIECE.

THE RIDERS CALL TO CONGRATULATE THE ENGINE MANUFACTURERS.

THE BEST ADVERTISEMENT WE HAVE IS THE ACTUAL ARTICLE WE SELL.

THE VILLIERS ENGINEERING Co. LTD.
WOLVERHAMPTON

land

The Second World War

Prior to the outbreak of the Second World War, the Polish army had evaluated many engines to power its home-built military motorcycle, but the contract was won by the Villiers factory, who had begun to supply large numbers of 9D units from the summer of 1939 onwards. The last batch of engines left the factory in late August; but unfortunately the ship carrying the consignment was captured by the SS Panzer Division in September 1939. This loss became the first casualty of the war.

Before the 1939 – 1945 conflict, the British Government had anticipated the need for engineering firms to contribute to the forthcoming war, having sent representatives out into the field to gather information on the expertise that abounded within the engineering industry as a whole. Villiers were visited and was told that as they performed so well in the first war effort, they would probably be asked to produce munitions components again, should the need arise. This need did arise in September 1939, with the declaration of war against Hitler's Germany. Shortly thereafter, the drawings for the "199" AAA (anti-aircraft-artillery) fuse arrived, with orders that they should be made as accurately and as quickly as possible.

The "199" AAA fuse was of a time-delay type, which exploded the shell at a specific time, and therefore at a specific altitude, the delay being preset prior to firing. For safety considerations the utmost accuracy in machining and assembly was required, with staff trained in the use of new machinery, quality assurance and building techniques, at the factory Training School. The guaranteed accuracy of this intricate work required the use of checking gauges at every step, and those were made to very fine limits by the Villiers factory tool room. The production gauges were themselves checked at intervals by master gauges, which were manufactured to an accuracy of 0.0001 inch (0.0025 mm), very fine limits indeed.

New machinery from the USA

The Marston Road factory was reorganised with new machinery, which arrived from the USA for this specific task, and the war effort got underway. During the height of the fuse production campaign the factory worked a six-day week, starting at 6 pm on Sunday to 6 pm on Saturday, with machinery running the full twenty-four hours each day. The working week was often extended to seven days during times of emergencies.

The work force was eventually increased to 2,500 to cope with this mammoth effort, and comprised mainly female operatives, who had to be trained in engineering skills, for many had never set foot in a factory before. With an obvious shortage of male staff in war time, the female staff coped remarkably well; practising their new skills alongside the duties of looking after families and homes, a process interrupted by the numerous Luftwaffe air raids and air raid drills. Morale was high amongst the female assembly-line workers and machinists, who had adopted the slogan: 'It all depends on ME'.

Designed and built in the VILLIERS Factory where nothing is left to chance.

Villiers engines are known throughout the world

Villiers
TWO·STROKE ENGINES

THE VILLIERS ENGINEERING CO. LTD. WOLVERHAMPTON

So successful was the Villiers fuse-building line, even in competition with the Royal Ordnance Factories - who had been making them for years, that the staff produced some six million fuses of different types during the period 1939 to 1945. The production figures for the "199" fuse alone indicated that the Villiers line produced the highest total throughout the whole country, a credit to the workforce who consistently cut the time taken to do their work, without compromising safety. The expertise and production of the type "199" fuse was noted by high authority in the War Office, and by way of a thank-you, the factory received a letter from Field Marshall Viscount Gort - Governor of Malta - in July 1942;

'Malta's anti-aircraft armament has recently warded off the heaviest scale of air attack the fortress has ever known, and for two months it was the guns alone which bore the brunt. The performance of the ammunition has left nothing to be desired and failures have been very few and far between. A short time ago, out of a flight of five, flying at heights exceeding 20,000 ft (6,000 m), three enemy bombers were destroyed and two others were severely damaged. This shows with what precision the fuses have been manufactured. The men behind the guns, therefore send a message of gratitude and greetings to the operatives at their benches. Signed – Gort'

The success of the '199' fuse-building programme led to further War Office contracts. The next fuse was the type '117' for artillery shells, which exploded on contact with the target rather than the time delay of the AAA variety. As war progressed, other types of fuses were produced, the '223' and the '370' being amongst them, together with rifle grenades and cannon shells. A measure of the efficiency of the workforce can be gathered from the production figures for the rifle grenades, which were produced and packed at the rate of one every three seconds.

Approximate munitions production figures for the 1939-45 war effort were as follows:

Artillery fuses	**6,000,000**
Rifle grenades	**3,000,000**
20 mm cannon shells	**5,700,000**
Explosive primers	**5,125,000**
Artillery shell and fuse components	**17,100,000**
Bomb components	**750,000**
Sterling bomber components	**525,000**
Steel forgings for aircraft, bombs, mines, vehicles	**7,300,000**
Non-ferrous castings for naval guns, aircraft, vehicles	**600,000**

Airborne Enfields
Royal Enfield
"MADE LIKE A GUN"
THE ENFIELD CYCLE Cº LTD Head Office & Works. REDDITCH.

Secret work

Other work carried out for the War Office by the Wolverhampton factory, was of a very secret nature, entailing speed with the utmost security. One example of this specialist type of work was a request from the Admiralty to produce castings for a secret project in 1943. On receipt of the drawings the cores and moulds were produced in three days and the castings despatched two and a half days later. The Admiralty Contractor was so pleased with the factory's work that he penned the following letter of appreciation:

'It gives me great pleasure to write and thank you and all the members of your staff and employees, for the excellent way in which they have worked to produce the castings that were so urgently required.

I am sure that everyone concerned will be delighted to learn that the job will be completed right up to schedule, and we feel sure our confidence in the efficiency of this produce will be justified when the trials take place next week.

Our combined efforts have produced for the Admiralty a prototype ready for trial on the day which, when originally given, seemed almost impossible.

Thanks to your initial efforts, we have been able to deliver the goods.'

During this time the engine production facility at the factory was not idle. The production and sale of leisure motorcycles had ceased, but a need to provide transport for the workforce engaged on essential duties still existed. Public transport still ran on defined routes; but some workers and personnel, who worked odd hours and in out of the way places, had to have their own transport. They were given permits to purchase new Autocycles. This form of cheap and reliable transport suited the workers who had their rounds to follow, and is best illustrated by the District Nurse, who was often seen - skirts flying - travelling the country roads to see her charges. The mobile mid-wives of the Queen Charlotte Maternity hospital were even equipped with Autocycles, a fleet of forty such machines being issued to them.

The sales of new motorcycles up to 150cc for the period March to July 1940 reached 9,570, with the vast majority of these being Autocycles. To meet this demand Villiers put into production the 98cc Junior de Luxe engine in November 1940, to supply the new Autocycle manufacturers of the day. Based on the Junior before it, the new engine now featured a flat top piston and redesigned cylinder porting to suit, adopting the Schnurle system of loop scavenging), together with a roller bearing big-end and floating gudgeon pin. The cylinder head now became detachable and made in light alloy, with the cylinder finning running vertically.

The success of the Junior de Luxe engine can be gauged by the number of Autocycle manufacturers who used the engine to power their models. Coventry Eagle, Excelsior, Francis-

Barnett, James and Norman took up options straight away, with Rudge, New Hudson and Sun following suit in 1941 the latter two manufacturers, who had fallen by the wayside during the depression, seizing the opportunity to re-establish themselves in the expanding Autocycle market. The price of motoring freedom, bearing in mind the meagre war-time petrol ration, was relatively cheap, with all the above models being priced at around £22.00.

For communications duties on the battlefield a small air-transportable one-two-five motorcycle was devised to be used by the Army, to take the place of the heavy dispatch riders machines. Having folding kick-starters and footrests, these lightweights were equipped with sealable fuel tanks, for air transportation, and were packed into steel crates which were then parachuted in with the airborne forces. Both James and Royal Enfield produced similar mounts to fulfil this role, but it was the James ML that used the Villiers engine unit, with Enfield using a motor of its own manufacture. Both models used a Villiers carburettor to ease the maintenance and stores holding problem. The James ML was equally at home on internal communications duties, but saw service in many diverse theatres of operations, including the European fronts, the Western Desert, British airfields and stores depots. Used by all three branches of the armed services and the many civilian organisations, such as the Civil Defence and the Fire Service, the lightweight one-two-fives performed admirably, both on and off-duty.

The "Clockwork Mouse"

The James ML or Clockwork Mouse as the forces called it, used the pre-war hand-change Mk 9D engine unit which Villiers produced in their thousands. Alongside the 9D unit, Villiers produced it first four-stroke industrial engine, which did sterling work, together with the two-stroke stationary engines, pumping water for both fire fighting and drinking, supplying emergency power for hospitals, charging batteries and even inflating aircraft tyres.

Many companies within the industrial sector made great efforts and sacrifices during those troubled times, whilst some failed to survive. But it must be said that the Villiers Engineering Co, who started as a cycle parts manufacturer, contributed the lion's share of the effort required to supply the fighting and emergency services with the equipment they needed for their various tasks.

The James ML

During 1941, the Mechanisation Board of the Army High Command issued a directive to the motorcycle industry, for a lightweight machine that could be used for communications duties. The requirement was for a machine smaller and lighter than the DR machines that were currently in service with the armed forces. This new machine was to have the ability to be air dropped, be easily manhandled over obstacles and have an all-terrain cross-country capability, a run-about rather than a long distance high-speed machine.

Of the machines tested by the army, the final choice fell between the Royal Enfield and the James 125. In the end the army placed orders for both in late 1942, finding that riding under adverse and difficult conditions was far easier than with standard issue machines of three times the weight. The first prototype James was actually taken on charge by the army on 23rd January 1943, and was quickly followed by a further twelve "improved" pre-production machines. When production got going at the James factory the ML was coming off the line at the rate of some 400 units per month.

The James ML (Military Lightweight) was the heavier of the two contenders, weighing in at 160 lbs compared to the 134 lbs of the Enfield, most of this weight increase being due to the use of the heavy brass flywheel of the Villiers motor. But, nevertheless, this still resulted in a top speed of some 42mph, a speed that enabled averages of 30mph to be attained easily. Tests to prove this were carried out as far afield as the Yorkshire Moors and the soft sand of the North African Desert, both conditions that the lightweight machine revelled in. Fuel consumption at its cruising speed of 38mph resulted in well over 100 mpg.

The engine of the ML was the 122cc Villiers 9D unit, installed with a pronounced forward tilt, which featured a flat top piston, a built-in three-speed, hand-change, gearbox and a Villiers flywheel magneto that supplied both sparks and lighting power. The twin port exhaust system fed into a transverse silencer mounted at the front of the frame, with its outlet running back along the left hand side. The tubular frame, with a rigid rear end, featured Webb-type pressed steel girder front forks and a 2.25 gallon fuel tank. Little in the way of carrying capacity was afforded, for this was a communications mount, the rider carrying his despatches in his haversack and his weaponry over his shoulder, but a canister was fitted to the frame – below the seat – in which to carry any tools required for en-route maintenance.

Wheels were of 19 inch diameter and equipped with a 4 inch brake drum at the front and a 5 inch brake at the rear. Shod with narrow section Universal tread tyres (2.75 inch) the bike was capable of traversing any type of soft going, foot assistance sometimes needed due mainly to its light weight.

The lightweights were often ridiculed by the heavyweight DR riders of the day, but in private they were rather fond of the Enfield and James machines, for they were far less exhausting to handle over rough going than their big BSA and Norton DR machines. Production figures for the James ML indicate that some 6,353 army examples were produced, which were put to good use on the many battlefields of the conflict. The James MLs, known originally as the "Mechanical Sheepdog" were used in their hundreds for the June1944 D Day assault on the Normandy beaches and were a main factor in controlling and handling of logistic supplies and manpower on those beaches. This action alone resulted in the ML being affectionately given a new nickname and henceforth it became known as the "Clockwork Mouse". The ML also saw action with the famous 6th Airborne Division at Arnhem, but its forte was in the assault and commando units rather than airborne use, which was more suited to the Enfield "Flying Flea" and its specially designed air-drop cage.

Villiers

3E 197cc (59 x 72mm) in production 1939 - 1940

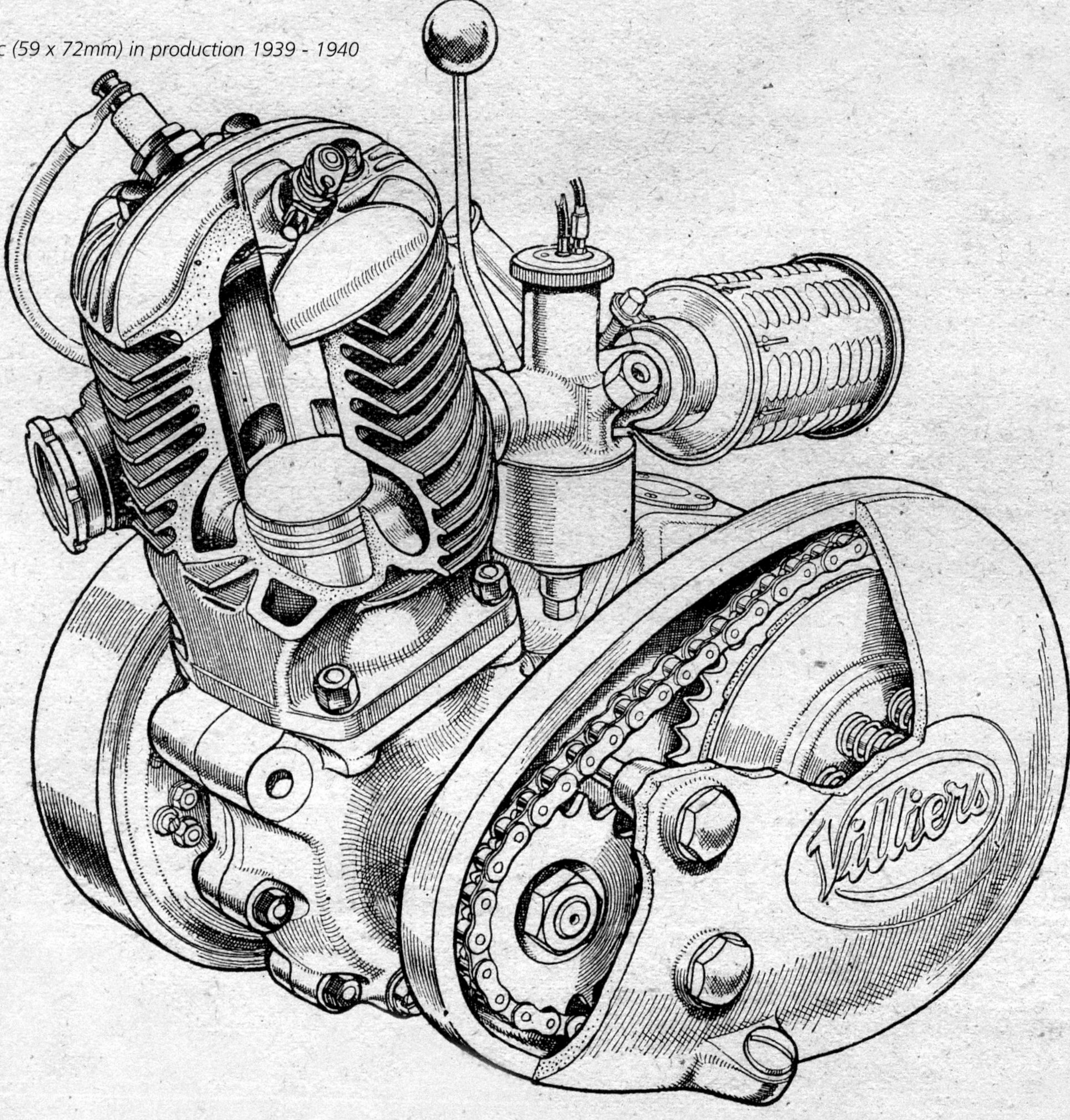

The ML was seen as a much more robust and mechanically reliable machine than the more flimsy battlefield expendable Royal Enfield, which resulted in the tried and tested "go-anywhere" lightweight ML being resurrected after the war and sold as a utility machine on the civilian market to get the masses moving again. This move was due in part to the last big army order of 3,000 units in 1944, which was cancelled half way through, as the war drew to a close. Apart from lengthened mudguards, a revised tool box, rear carrier and a smarter civilian finish, the post-war ML was the same as that supplied to the army, and in all, military versions included ,26,000 examples of this remarkable lightweight machine were built.

The Excelsior Welbike

The need for greater mobility on to the battlefield was addressed in 1943 when Excelsior produced the Welbike. This machine was designed by Lt-Col JRV Dolphin, with the prototype being built at the Military Research Establishment at Welwyn Garden City, from whence it derived its name (Wel as in Welwyn). Its main function was to equip airborne forces with a means of rapid assembly, advancement or even withdrawal after landing at a drop-zone. Parachuted in with the paratroopers, the bike was carried in a 15 inch (380 mm) diameter container, and on landing could be assembled in minutes; requiring only the seat, handlebars and footrests to be extended. To meet the container packaging requirements, the Welbike used 12 inch wheels, a horizontally mounted Villiers 98cc Junior de Luxe engine and weighed in at less than 80 lbs. The bike was considered to be battlefield expendable, and to this end little thought was given to rider comfort or off-road capabilities. After the war JRV Dolphin took his design to Brockhouse Engineering, where the machine was put into a civilian guise and marketed as the Corgi, but the new model used an engine of Excelsior manufacture.

The single-speed army version was very basic and had but a single brake on the rear wheel, and a clutch, but no compression release valve. Fuel was supplied from a sealed pannier tank and had to be pressure fed to the engine by the use of a hand pump. The frame was a simple tubular affair with no springing at all, and the front forks were of the bicycle type. The handling was not that good, some even going as far as saying they considered it 'dire', with the handbook advising that a certain amount of care was needed when riding the machine.

Excelsior fulfilled three Army supply contracts; S789 for 1183 machines, S1649 for 1400 and S1946 for 1340, but many of these bikes remained unused and were sold off after the war, still packed in their containers. The Welbike did not conform to the British roadworthiness standards, having been designed as purely functional battlefield transport, but nevertheless they provided a lot of off-road fun for their new owners.

5 Civilian Life Returns

Post-war Great Britain of the late 1940s saw many shortages, the main one being a lack of cheap and reliable transport. This situation was brought about by two distinct factors; the vast numbers of demobbed servicemen who needed transport to resume their civilian occupations and a severe shortage of suitable machinery that had actually survived the war. At the onset of the war many motorcycles were sold to raise cash, disposed of for the National Scrap Metal Appeal, commandeered for the war effort, or even simply dumped. In 1945 those machines that had actually survived the war were either very old and tired or very second-hand and of little use to the workforce.

A new breed of machine

What was needed was a new breed of machine, with a view to getting the masses mobile again, and to feed the needs of ex-servicemen who had savoured the delights of motorcycle riding/maintenance whilst in the military. Some of the established motorcycle manufacturers did not survive the war and those that did found it very hard indeed to get back into peace-time production. The country was in a poor way, paying heavily for the war effort and material shortages were rife. The best materials available were earmarked for the export market, a move found necessary to reduce the National Deficit. The established motorcycle manufacturers rose to the occasion, and produced many large capacity models, most of which were exported to the USA, for they were in a better post-war condition than Great Britain was.

With the upsurge of worldwide trading and the export-orientated determination of the British motorcycle manufacturers, the import of bikes into the United States took off, to feed the needs of the eager American public. In contrast to the rest of the world, the Americans came out of the war in better shape than they had entered it. They did not suffer ground fighting or aerial bombing, instead they had vastly expanded their industry to meet the war effort. After the conflict unemployment was low and overtime high, the workforce having fat bank accounts with which to finance their leisure activities. The major British producers all contributed to this requirement, with the likes of BSA, Matchless, Norton and Triumph all heavily involved in the export drive. To add to this the American marque importers actively encouraged the racing of British machinery, which was superior in many ways to the average American product.

The Transatlantic Boom

The transatlantic large capacity sales boom did help the National Economy, but it was of little use to the Villiers factory or the British worker who needed cheap and reliable transport to get to work; what was required here was a small capacity economical motorcycle, that was simple both to ride and maintain. The expertise for such a machine already existed, for the Villiers factory had been manufacturing an ideal power unit which had been used by various companies' autocycles, during the conflict.

During the war many of the Villiers motorcycle engine designs had ceased production - the 148, 196, 197, 247, 249 and 346cc models all having been axed in 1940 - but by the time peace resumed, the company still had on offer the 98cc Junior de-luxe and the 122cc 9D. Having made these engines for the autocycle manufacturers and the lightweight military motorcycle contracts, they were very quickly civilianised. The 147cc Mk VIII-C was resurrected and soon followed, these engines forming the basis of the new breed of ride-to-work motorcycle to meet the needs of the workforce. Many manufacturers took up the option on these engine units to power their post war range, but times were still difficult, the supply of sufficient raw material being a major problem. The Villiers company did however have an advantage over many of the other firms; they continued to supply spares and complete engine units to countries that had been untouched by the war, for these nations still had a strong economy and could afford to import. Being an exporter, Villiers did not fully experience the material shortages in quite the same way as other manufacturers did.

Villiers pre-war customers carried the firm out of the immediate post-war period, together with the demand for transport from other countries that had been affected by the war. Former enemies did not contribute to this buying spree, for they did not have the necessary capital to purchase the power units needed to revitalise their trading economy, preferring to build their own with the help of American cash and machinery. This rebuilding programme of the former Axis forces homelands did not at first have much effect on the British motorcycle industry, but twenty years later its effects virtually brought it to a standstill. One country that did contribute to the Villiers export drive was Australia; untouched by the war but contributing heavily to it, the Australians still needed power units to prosper and turned to the Wolverhampton concern for the necessary hardware.

Charles Marston dies

On the 21st May 1946 the Company Chairman, Sir Charles Marston, died at the age of 79. The Chairmanship of the Villiers Engineering Co Ltd was now handed over to Frank Farrer, for Sir Charles had no sons and his only son-in-law, George von Harten, a gifted concert pianist, had died during the war. This responsibility was not new to Frank Farrer, for he had been at the helm for a number of years, when Sir Charles had started to take an increasing interest in Public and Church affairs. Sir Charles had been created a Knight of St John, was a Justice of the Peace and a Fellow of the Society of Antiquaries. He had also written many books on his religious and political convictions, financed or taken part in archaeological expeditions at home and the Holy Land and made a lasting impression on the politics of his native Wolverhampton. The death of Sir Charles saw an end to the Marston family involvement - at managerial level – in the day-to-day running of the Villiers Engineering Company. Two years later a further loss was felt by the factory, when Frank Pountney - the Works Director and Chief Engineer - died on 30th August 1948.

1949 Swallow Gadabout scooter with 10D 122cc (50 x 62mm) engine and 3-speed gearbox

A seventeen and a half acre site

The immediate post war period saw new machinery installed in order to improve the quality of engines and bicycle freewheels; with the Villiers empire occupying some 17.5 acres of the Marston Road and Sunbeam Street complex, which now included a Medical Centre (staffed by a sister and five nurses) and a flourishing Sports and Social Club. The company prided itself in the welfare of its workforce, a Marston family aim, that included not only good working conditions and the superb in-house training school but also after-hours activities. The Marston Road complex was a family concern in more ways than one, not only on the management side of the company but also within the workforce itself, with fathers, mothers, sons and daughters all working under the same roof. The Villiers Engineering Works was the place to be employed in those bleak post-war years. The workforce were looked after, and they respected it and guarded their jobs jealously, giving their all to the company. And it repaid them by providing relatively well-paid, secure employment.

The three engine range of 1945 was increased to four in 1946, with the introduction of the 5E, a model that was almost exclusive to the Ambassador company. This new post-war 197cc engine was not a rehash of the war-time 3E (there was no 4E) but a completely redesigned unit. Still using the bore and stroke measurements of the earlier engine (59 x 72 mm) the 5E did not feature the unit construction gearbox of its predecessor, but now used a separate box with foot change bolted to the rear of the crankcases by four long studs. This method of gearbox production and attachment set a trend that was to last to the very end of engine manufacture at Villiers. The essence of the design was that when bolted together the engine gave the appearance of being a unit-construction module, but with the gearbox being readily removable a change from three to four-speed boxes could be carried out without a major engine redesign. On the maintenance side this design proved to be very popular, in that remedial work or even ratio changes could be carried out without dismantling the engine. The following year the 147cc Mk VIII-C engine, which was initially introduced in 1924, was finally dropped from the list.

Industrial operations at the Villiers works during the 1950s

The three remaining engines continued unaltered until the 1949 season, when the 1F and 2F units replaced the Junior de-luxe, the 10D replaced the 9D and the 5E was superseded by the 6E. The new F range engines now had a bore and stroke measurement of 47 x 57 mm and a swept volume of 99cc to cater for the continued popularity of the Autocycle. Figures issued in 1948 indicated that a total of over 100,000 Villiers-engined Autocycles had been sold. The 2F engine introduced at the November 1948 London Earls Court Motorcycle Show was a logical progression from the Junior de-luxe, but now incorporated some well tried improvements to increase its efficiency. With a power output of 2 bhp at 3,750rpm it was a single speed unit with the magneto and primary drive on the right hand side. The primary chain and clutch were enclosed in an alloy casing, the clutch driving a countershaft with the final drive sprocket positioned on the left, as per normal practice. The cast iron cylinder used a pair of transfer ports and a single exhaust port, equipped with a flat-topped piston and alloy cylinder head. The pressed up crankshaft employed a parallel crank pin and three ball race main bearings.

The 1F was a two-speed version of the 2F engine and was practically identical, the sliding dog gearbox being housed in the same compartment that held the countershaft of the single speed unit. Other differences were a modified carburettor and no provision for the decompression valve. This engine was rated at 2.8 bhp at 4,000rpm and was, Villiers sources claimed, able to return 140 miles per gallon.

A complete redesign

The 10D motor was another complete redesign with a separate foot-change gearbox and a single exhaust port, and followed very closely the configuration of the 5E launched three years before. At the same time the 197cc engine was redesigned to become the 6E. Both the 10D and the 6E units were interchangeable in respect of the frame fixing lugs, and although the gearboxes were identical, the larger engine used a primary chain of 1/2 inch pitch against the 3/8 inch pitch of the 10D. Apart from bore and stroke measurements and carburettor sizes, both engines looked very similar, the 6E cylinder being fatter and having one extra fin. Power output figures indicate a claimed 4.8 bhp at 4,400rpm for the 10D and 8.4 bhp at 4,000 for its bigger brother. Both engines could be supplied with direct or rectifier type lighting sets. A set of wide ratio gearbox internals were soon to become available for these engines, giving a bottom gear ratio of 3.25:1 - as opposed to the 2.55:1 of the standard box - so that riders could indulge in a bit of competition work at weekends. The year, 1949, was probably significant in that the introduction of the competition gear ratios coincided with the launch of BSA Bantam, for BSA had seen fit to offer a competition version of this machine alongside the standard roadster, to take on the Villiers engined competition machines. Five years later Villiers surprisingly ended production of the of the 122cc engine altogether, leaving that class wide open to the BSA Bantam – and foreign imports.

197cc 6E-engined Monet-Goyon, French built under licence in the mid 1950s. Note the major difference of Morel ignition rather than the normal Villiers flywheel magneto

At the turn of the decade the Villiers Engineering Company was 52 years old, but this did not mean that the company was going to slow down. quite the contrary, the following year saw the signing of an agreement to build engines in Spain.

Expansion

In 1952, the management policy was again one of expansion, the aim being to bring the Villiers Group up to eight companies by the end of the decade. This they did with the formation in 1952 of Villiers Australia Pty Ltd at Ballaarat, Victoria, where thousands of engines were being produced every week to feed the growing demand for powered machinery in Australia.

Still expanding, in 1956 Villiers acquired the Wednesfield steel pressing firm of Robert Harris Ltd. The following year a new factory was also built there to house the newly created company of Villiers (Tool Developments) Ltd, who had already established a reputation as producers of special-purpose precision tools, not only for the Villiers group but for some of the biggest names in the British aircraft and motor industries.

The Two-Millionth Engine

On the 26th September 1956 the two-millionth engine rolled off the assembly line at 12.15 pm. Built by Ken Sherratt of the motorcycle engine assembly line, the 224cc 1H unit was presented to Mr CF Caunter of the Science Museum for permanent display as a milestone of British engineering. Before taking the engine away, it was fitted to a Francis-Barnett Cruiser Model 75 and ridden around the local area by Villiers/Francis-Barnett expert Tommy Meeten, as part of the celebrations.

JAP are acquired

The next acquisition was that of the JA Prestwich Industries Ltd, which brought with it Pencils Ltd, after JAP got into financial difficulties during 1957. The news was given to the motorcycle fraternity with a brief announcement relating to 'a merger of interests' appearing in the June 20th edition of Motor Cycling. A further two years on saw the Diamond Jubilee of the Villiers Group, celebrated with a lavish exhibition featuring no less than 350 Villiers and JAP exhibits at the Royal Horticultural Society's New Hall, Greycoat Street, Westminister, London, SW1. The Souvenir Brochure for this event listed the companies that were then part of the Villiers Group:

THE VILLIERS ENGINEERING CO LTD - Wolverhampton
VILLIERS AUSTRALIA PTY LTD - Australia
JA PRESTWICH INDUSTRIES LTD - London
ROBERT HARRIS LTD - Wednesfield
VILLIERS (TOOL DEVELOPMENTS) LTD - Wednesfield
PENCILS LTD - London
JA PRESTWICH-VIRTUE PTY LTD - Australia
HISPANO VILLIERS SA - Spain

J·A·P

Geoffrey Jones' statement

The 1950s had been a good decade; not only had the group taken control of the above companies, but they had also set many production records. The summer of 1957 had seen a giant leap forward in the production of two-stroke engines, so much so that the joint Sales and Managing Director – Geoffrey Jones – gave the following statement to the Motor Cycling of 27th August 1957: 'During the four complete weeks of July we dispatched to motorcycle, scooter and three-wheeler manufacturers a greater volume of engines than for any four-weekly period in the past. This not only further emphasises the steadily growing popularity of motorcycles of 250cc and under, but what is more gratifying it also proves very conclusively that at long last the British scooter industry is getting well and truly under way. The demand from British scooter manufacturers, however, has come very suddenly and our order books suggest that scooter enthusiasts are now "Buying British" whenever possible.' A year before this only one manufacturer was building a scooter fitted with a Villiers engine but at the time of the statement, the figure had grown to seven.

The production record mentioned by Geoffrey Jones further added to the very impressive running total of engines built by the Wolverhampton facility, which now stood at over two-and-a-half-million units, two million of which were produced after the Second World War. With the Villiers product revered throughout the world, many of these units were destined for overseas customers, for Villiers had seen fit to establish direct trading accounts in no less than 140 different countries.

The emerging British scooter industry

The needs of the emerging scooter industry in Great Britain contributed to the growing range of engines, which in 1958 had reached eight capacity classes. For this season many of the units had the option of being equipped with the SIBA Dynastart and fan cooling, specifically aiming them at the scooter and light car industries. The Dynastart, as its trade name implies, was both an electric starter and a dynamo; being able to fire up the engine in forward or forward and reverse directions, this latter system proving to be popular in the light car and invalid carriage markets. The main feature of the system was that it had the ability to generate 12 volts, a voltage generally used on cars of that period, which was needed to operate the extra lights and starter windings of the large heavyweight flywheel.

1946 civilian version of the wartime 125cc James ML fitted with 9D 122cc engine unit

"Go-anywhere Lightweight"

The Guarantee of a fine Lightweight

1952 Bown 122cc Tourist Trophy model optimistic to say the least!

Villiers supplied engines to service the needs of the scooter and microcar market, with a bewildering number of modifications. The specification of many of these engines could include a combination of any of the following; electric starting with unidirectional or reversible operation; optional kick starter (even if an electric starter was fitted); 6 or 12 volt generators (even 12 volts on the non electric start models); three or four-speed gearboxes (with normal or wide ratios, direct change, optional gearbox driven speedometer drives and neutral light switch), together with blower cooling (the fan being driven from either left or right hand side of the engine), higher ratio primary drive and a strengthened clutch and clutch lifter mechanism.

Other modifications

Other modifications used included an ingenious half compression device for the electric start 35A engine for the Bond Minicar. In order to get the Dynastart to turn over the motor, some form of decompression device was required to relieve the initial compression pressure in the cylinder, this being normally achieved by the decompression valve. When activated the oil laden mixture was dumped to atmosphere, which usually meant that it was sprayed over the cylinder head fins. The cable operated half compression device simply allowed the mixture to vent into a sealed chamber, which had the same volume as the cylinder head.

The 1950s also saw the Villiers company take note that its products were being used in competition, and they started to offer mildly modified competition versions of the standard roadster units, for use in clubman's type events. The competition engine of that period meant nothing more than a trials unit with wide ratio gears and a heavy flywheel, with possibly the fitment of a high compression head. Scrambling was in its infancy, and no serious thoughts as to participation in this high-speed discipline were entered into at this time. This was to come later.

November 1953 Earls Court Show

The first competition units

The first competition units were announced for the 1953 season, with the introduction of the 11D 122cc unit. The 11D was a derivative of the new 12D roadster engine, introduced at the same time. The 12D was again a refined version of the 10D, and was now equipped with rubber crankcase oil seals (replacing the spring loaded bronze glands formally used) and a new big-end assembly that used twelve $1/4$ x $1/4$ inch rollers with six bronze spacing rollers. A cylinder head gasket was also fitted – first seen on later versions of the 10D. The primary chain case was also redesigned, now featuring the Villiers logo over four horizontal stripes, instead of the original "wing" design. A utility version of the 12D was introduced at the same time, using the 12D bottom end it was fitted with the original 10D cylinder. This model was designated the 13D.

The 11D competition engine used the refinements of the 12D unit, but it was equipped with a special cylinder with a detachable inlet manifold and a type S24 carburettor normally fitted to the 8E 197cc unit. A high compression cylinder head (10:1) was also fitted, together with a high performance ignition coil and a special contact breaker cam. The power output was quoted as being 6.1 bhp at 4,600rpm. By far the most exciting development was the introduction of the four-speed gearbox for this unit, which altered its designation to Mk 11D/4. The new box - of Albion design - was available in both close and wide ratio versions, to enable it to be used in both trials and scrambles activities.

Refinements to the 197cc engine

At the same time the 197cc engine received the same refinements as the 12D, the larger engine retaining its original bore and stroke measurements of 59 x 72 mm, the only difference being the big-end bearing, which utilised 26 1/4 x 1/4 inch crowded rollers. The roadster version of the

197 was designated the 8E, and featured a new cylinder with a short integral inlet manifold, the rest of the engine following the lines of the 12D. In line with its smaller brother, the 8E variant was also available in competition form, this was the 7E. All that distinguished the competition engine from its roadster brother was a new cylinder; similar to the detachable inlet manifold 6E component (but a different part number) and a cylinder head with a compression ratio of 8.25:1. The power output of the 7E was rated as 9.3 bhp at 4,300rpm. In line with the competition version of the 122cc engine. The 7E was also available with the Albion type four-speed gearbox, again fitted with either close or wide gear ratios. Two years after their introduction the 7 and 8E were joined by the 9E, an updated and modernised 197cc unit that was to set the trend for the next eleven years. Villiers had had a serious rethink and saw it was necessary to move with the times.

The same year also saw the introduction of the 4F two-speed Autocycle unit, which replaced the discontinued 1F engine. Basically a cleaned up version of its predecessor, the updated 4F now featured an enclosed flywheel with the contact breaker assembly moved to the near side of the engine. As with other engines introduced in 1953, the 4F now featured the superior rubber crankcase seals.

A 150cc makeover

The following year it was the turn of the 150cc range to get its makeover. Still retaining the original bore and stroke measurements of 55 x 62 mm, the newly introduced engines gained a cleaner external appearance similar to that of the 12D unit of 1953. The redesign included a new cylinder that now utilised a flat-top piston, two transfer passages and a single exhaust port. In line with D and E range engines the one-fifties again had a choice of three or four-speed gearboxes. The standard three-speed roadster engine, designated the 30C, had a compression ratio of 8.25:1 and delivered 5.4 bhp at 4,300rpm. Its competition variant, designated 29C, had a larger S25 carburettor, a compression ratio of 10:1 and was quoted as delivering 6 bhp at 4,500rpm, but this unit was fitted with the four-speed gearbox.

The 224cc 1H

For what seemed to them good reasons, Villiers showed considerable reluctance to produce an engine of more than 200cc, but a compromise was arrived at with a completely new breed of engine which was unveiled at the 1953 London Earls Court Motorcycle Show, ready for the 1954 season. This was the 224cc 1H unit. Entirely different in its appearance from any of the previous Villiers designs, the 1H set a new precedent on the cosmetic imagery of the Villiers engine package, a factor used on the later twin cylinder engines right up to the end of the factory production.

The streamlined – or "air smoothed"- unit appeared to be built as a single unit, but in fact it followed earlier practice of using a bolt-on gearbox. It was the faired in primary chain case and the long magneto/gearbox cover, together with the carburettor cover that produced the streamlined shape, or as some called it the 'egg shape'. The new cast aluminium engine side covers were a step in the right direction, for prior to the 1H, the timing side of the Villiers engine was quite unsightly. Early units had the flywheel covered by a pressed aluminium "saucepan" shaped cover, and on some units no cover at all. Four mounting lugs now held the 1H engine unit in the motorcycle frame or engine plates, two at the rear and two at the front, instead of the more usual three.

Full-circle flywheels

The 1H was entirely new internally as well, for the engine now featured full circle flywheels instead of the "hammer head" cranks used in all previous designs, and was supported on four ball bearing races. The flywheels followed the BSA Bantam practice of using a riveted-in sheet steel disc to blank off recesses in the crank wheel, these recesses being needed to effect the correct balance factor of the pressed up crankshaft. The big-end bearing came from the 8E and comprised a total of 26 1/4 x 1/4 inch crowded rollers.

The 1H set new engineering standards to the entire Villiers engine range and many of the newly introduced components became a standard fitment to the later engine units, with some of these items lasting until the very end of the Villiers motorcycle engine production. One new component that was introduced on the 1H was the small diameter flywheel magneto; so small

was this item that there was no room for the internal HT coil or contact breaker points, the HT coil being located under the tank (an energy transfer system) and the points being relocated in the right-hand engine cover. Another novel feature was the key operated ignition "kill" facility, the switch being positioned in the right hand magneto/gearbox cover.

With the 224cc unit being quoted as delivering 9.6 bhp at 4,500rpm, the original two-plate clutch of the 8E would not have been good enough, and a brand new four-plate assembly was designed especially for this engine. The new clutch was such an improvement that it was adopted – with various spring arrangements – for use in all the subsequent single and twin cylinder engine units. Initially built with a primary chain tensioner mechanism, to stop the chain hitting the primary drive case, it was discarded because of the noise made by the chain running over it, the gearbox being spaced out a further 0.015 inch to compensate. Another change was the gearbox; again entirely new and capable of transmitting the power that the 1H developed; the box seeing extended service with the twin cylinder units described in Chapter 9. Up until this point Villiers had never built a four-speed box for themselves, having relied on the hand change Albion product for the pre-war designs and the foot change version for the post-war competition units; from this point Villiers were to become self-sufficient. The new gearbox utilised a rotating cam barrel with a superior positive stop mechanism and an external gear position indicator, together with a speedometer drive taken from the layshaft.

A popular engine

The 224cc 1H was a popular engine. Being the largest power unit built by the Wolverhampton factory in the mid 1950s, it was used by many of the British commuter motorcycle producers to power their top-of-the-range machines. Ambassador, DMW, Francis-Barnett, Sun and Tandon all used this motor in preference to other engine manufacturers products. The engine did not exactly revolutionise the design of the motorcycle itself, but manufacturers did take full advantage of its streamlined looks, and produced machines with cleaner and sleeker lines. This had a knock-on effect and created an increased demand for machines using this engine. The 1H was never intended to be anything other than a touring/roadster engine, but one intrepid Belgian rider did score a continental motocross victory, when he rode his specially tuned 1H equipped Salira to first place against keen British and continental opposition in 1955.

The 9E engine is introduced

1955 saw the introduction of the 197cc 9E engine, a design that changed the fortunes of the Villiers company and spawned a new generation of competition power plants, which are described in Chapter 6. But development on the more mundane roadster engines still continued, with the 99cc unit being uprated to the 6F the following year, with the introduction of a foot change mechanism. A 6F/H unit also became available, which reverted to the cable operated gear change, similar to the 4F. A final version of this range became available in 1959. This was the 9F, which was principally designed for kart use. Utilising a cylinder head with a compression ratio of 9.15:1, revised cylinder porting and an S19 carburettor, the 9F gave superior performance over its roadster brothers.

A year after the introduction of the 9E came an entirely new 148cc unit that replaced the 29 and 30C, but they continued in production for a further three years. Having a new nearly square bore and stroke measurement of 57 x 58 mm the newcomer was designated the 31C and closely followed the external appearance of the 9E. The 31C was also available with the new three or four-speed 9E type gearbox, with official Villiers sources claiming 6.6 bhp at 5,000rpm.

Bore and stroke changes became the vogue again in 1957, when a new 174cc unit was announced. The new unit - designated the 2L - was basically a short-stroke version (59 x 63.5mm) of the 9E, but used an S22 carburettor and developed 7.4 bhp at 5,000rpm. Available with a combination of three or four-speed gearboxes, kick or electric starting and fan cooling, the engine was aimed at the fledgling British scooter market. The 2L was uprated in 1960 to become the 3L, which featured fan or turbo cooling, and remained in production to the very end.

The streamlined 1H received a big-bore cylinder (66 mm) to become the 246cc 2H unit of 1957, but in uprating this engine many more modifications were incorporated, which produced an engine capable of delivering 11 bhp at 4,500rpm. The big-end now used the 9E Sport caged roller bearing, and the crankshaft was supported on three roller and one ball race, held in the crankcase by no less than six circlips. The same flywheel generator was fitted but now the low tension current to the external HT coil was provided by a single charge coil, instead of the pair of charge coils (connected in parallel) found on the 1H. The 2H was not as popular as its smaller brother, being upstaged by the introduction of the twin cylinder 2T the previous year, and in just one year its popularity waned even further with the introduction of the versatile, lighter and more powerful 246cc A-range family of single cylinder motors. Even so the 2H continued in production until 1964.

The 50cc Moped engine

At the very end of the 1950s Villiers had a quick dabble into the 50cc Moped engine market, with the production of the 3K engine. This two-speed engine, similar in concept to the 99cc Autocycle engine, utilised a bore and stroke of 40 x 39.7 mm, and incorporated a pedal starting mechanism. Phillips, Norman and Ambassador all built it into their products, but by 1960 the popularity of the Moped was in decline and the 3K was axed. Years later the Moped was to be resurrected, with the market being flooded with fast but fragile Oriental and Italian machines, to suit the needs of their sixteen-year-old riders. By the time of the Moped's second coming Villiers had long since ceased motorcycle engine production.

During the production run of the 3K engine, experiments into electronic ignition systems were under way, with some of the initial work being carried out on the 50cc unit. Much in the way of testing was carried out, but Villiers remained steadfastly loyal to their original, forty-year-old principles, with electronic systems not becoming available until the industrial engines of the NVT era.

DOT tradesman's vehicle 1930 - 1948

1958 SEASON Dot MANCUNIAN

The MANCUNIAN is supplied fully equipped as illustrated.

THERE ARE NO EXTRAS TO THESE INCLUSIVE PRICES

MODEL	List Price	Purchase Tax	Total Price
MANCUNIAN 3 SPEED	£139 0 0	£34 8 0	£173 8 0
MANCUNIAN 4 SPEED	£144 0 0	£35 12 10	£179 12 10

DOT CYCLE & MOTOR MANUFACTURING CO. LTD., MANCHESTER, 15

One piece of government legislation of 1961 did nothing but good for the Villiers company. This was the introduction of the 250cc limit for learner riders. Banning the use of motorcycles over 250cc for provisional licence holders it was aimed at saving the lives of young riders, but this restriction was not passed on to the four-wheeled world, which still allowed youngsters to drive, albeit under supervision 150mph sports cars. This legislation brought about a sudden increase in the sales of quarter-litre machines, with the inherent demand for engine units. Villiers geared up for this eventuality and willingly supplied the ensuing demand placed upon them by the motorcycle manufacturers.

The 35A Minicar unit

Another new engine that appeared in 1962 was the 35A Minicar unit. Utilising the new slim line crankcases of the 36/37A sporting engines, these units were pressed into use in the fledgling scooter and new minicar market. This specialised unit was designed to feed the needs of the three-wheeler market; a market epitomized by the Bond Minicar. The 35A featured many novel ideas, but was never intended to be a sporting motor, even though many of the uprated components used in it were pressed into use on the scrambles tracks of the period. The gearbox received its own special set of wide gear ratios, together with a beefed-up clutch lifter mechanism, which featured a radial thrust bearing, a modified clutch arm and a strengthened bridge. This arrangement was deemed necessary to cope with the extra thrust imposed by the use of the 1H double clutch spring. Being destined for the minicar market, the gearbox did not feature a kick-starter, for now the engine was equipped with an electric starter.

SIBA Dynastart

The electric start facility was supplied by a SIBA Dynastart, a combined rotor/stator arrangement that not only cranked the engine over, but also supplied 12 volts from its generator windings. The rotor was so heavy that it needed an extra timing side main bearing to support it, the right hand crankcase being specially designed to accommodate it. The Dynastart cranking action was strong, but it needed a decompression device to allow the engine to turn over fast enough. This was achieved in one of two ways; initially the engine featured a valve that allowed compressed gas to escape to atmosphere via the exhaust port, but in later years this was replaced by a simple chamber, screwed in to the decompressor hole, which when opened halved the compression ratio. The refinements of the 35A were incorporated into the 11E; an engine specified by the Ministry of Pensions, used to power the many invalid carriages popular with the disabled drivers of that period. Derivatives of the 11E later saw service in the kart-racing world.

The late 1950s and early 1960s was a hectic time at the Wolverhampton factory, and one major reason for this was the popularity of the product. To ensure that this product was at the peak of its performance, Villiers set up a new dealer service network in 1961, selecting and approving 500 dealers to the service scheme. Each dealer had to set aside an area specifically

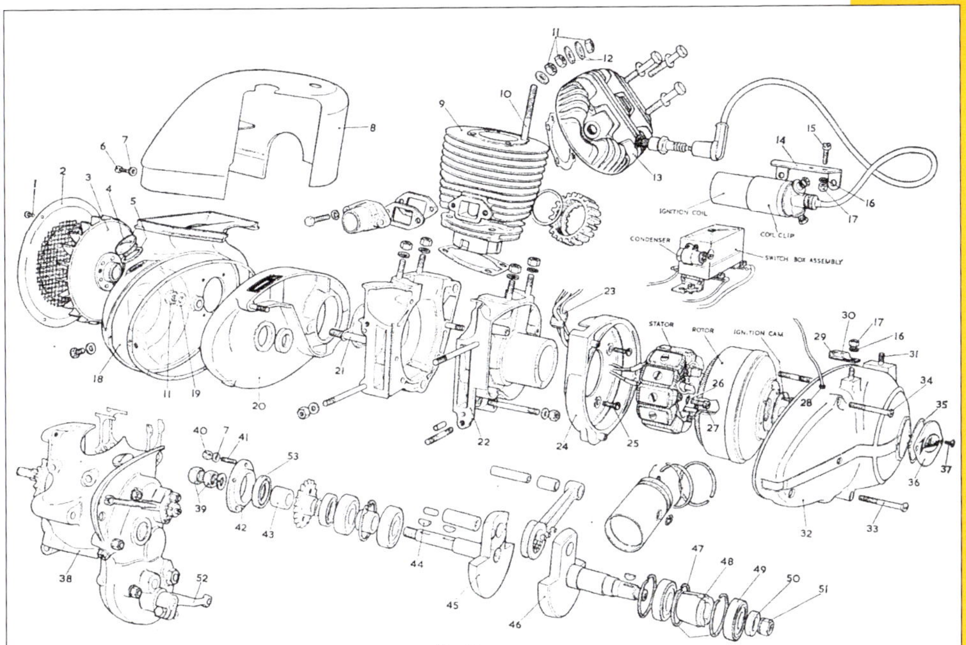

Fig. 10
Blower-cooled. Siba-equipped engine.

Carburettor S.25/8

V.2146D	Body	V.1951E	Spindle, strangler
V.1952E	Top disc	V.1950E	Cable stop, strangler
V.1308D	Throttle No. 3	V.586E	Return spring, strangler
V.1948E	Screw, throttle stop	V.234B/HO	Cable, throttle
V.749E	Spring, stop screw	40028	Cable, strangler

BLOWER-COOLED ENGINES WITH ELECTRIC-STARTER/GENERATOR

The following additional and alternative parts fitted to engines with the fan on the left-hand side.

Illus. No.	Part No.	Description
1	E.12028	Screw, fan-cover and gauze (3)
—	M.2707E	Washer, shakeproof (3)
2	C.10417	Cover, fan-and-gauze
3	25709	Fan/hub assembly
4	E.11116	Plug, chaincase-filler
5	E.8261	Washer, chaincase filler-plug
6	1022 x 4E	Screw, top-cowl (2)
7	E.5257/1	Washer, cowl and adaptor screws and studs (7)
8	80027	Cowl, 9E
or	A.10617/1	Cowl, 31C
or	80028	Cowl, 2L
9	D.11032	Cylinder, 31C
or	D.11505	Cylinder, 2L
10	E.11724	Stud, cylinder-head, 9E
or	E.10932	Stud, cylinder head, 31C and 2L
11	E.834	Nut, cylinder head and bottom cowl studs (4)
12	E.11162	Washer, cylinder head stud (2)
13	D.11599	Cylinder head, 9E
or	B.10424	Cylinder head, 31C
or	60104	Cylinder head, 2L
14	Quote Engine No.	Bracket, ignition-coil
15	E.478	Screw, ignition-coil bracket (2)
16	E.1430	Washer, spring (4)
17	E.2539	Nut (4)
18	A.10376	Cowl bottom and outer chaincase
19	E.373	Washer, bottom-cowl stud
20	D.10740	Chaincase, inner half
21	E.10619	Stud, cowl-bottom
22	B.9530	Crankcase R.H. (supplied only with A.9077)
23	M.2806E	Grommet (rect. 3 hole)
24	B.9536/1	Housing, stator
25	M.2673E	Screw, stator-housing (4)
26	M.3166E	Washer, shakeproof (3)
27	E.10008	Screw, stator (3)

9E engine with SIBA Dynastart - stator and rotor assemblies

for the Villiers product, posses the correct specialist tools and carry out the work to a stringent standard. Those dealers picked for the scheme were readily identified by a large red and gold sign, proclaiming "approved Villiers service".

Reliability and dependability

Reliability and dependability were two watchwords used a lot by the Villiers Company, for they had built up a reputation on these two factors over the preceding decades. As the 1950s drew to a close the standards previously achieved were never eroded, if anything they had become stricter. Quality control played a big part in the day to day running of the factory, with materials being stringently checked in the factory's own laboratory on receipt from the metal suppliers, to ensure the correct grade and material specification, with further checks being carried out during and after the machining and heat treatment phases. With the continuing move to self-sufficiency Villiers left nothing to chance and manufactured virtually everything in house, with the exception of spark plugs, control cables and pedal rubbers. To have everything under one roof, a very large roof that spanned some 20 acres, meant that every part of the manufacturing process could be followed closely, checked by the quality assurance operatives and controlled by the progress chasers. Making 99% of the engine package in-house meant that the problem caused by the inability of outside suppliers to deliver on time was now effectively eliminated.

By the 1950s the Marston Road site had increased to 20 acres

The austere post-war period

The immediate austere post-war years were not too bad for the Villiers factory, but it was the 1950s that saw the biggest leap forward in terms of innovative designs, the number of models offered and above all the quality and quantity of units produced. But, it was the following decade that saw the move into the sporting arena, with the production of purpose designed sporting power units, which saw many successes in off-road activities. This final period of Villiers engine manufacture, a span of only six years, saw the Wolverhampton company rise to the dizzy heights of propulsion unit suppliers to World Championship leaders, but it also saw the final and ignominious end to a once great manufacturing organisation.

DMW

Founded in 1945 by Les "Smokey" Dawson, to produce competition suspension systems, Dawson Motor Works (Wolverhampton) was initially not intended to be a motorcycle manufacturer. Having competed in grass track events immediately after the war, Dawson built a few JAP engined machines for the grass, but concentrated his efforts in the suspension department, marketing a range of bolt-on front and rear telescopic spring units. As most bikes available in that period were pre-war rigid roadsters, his ideas in modernising unsprung machines were highly thought of and sought after. Dawson was an engineering ideas man, but lacked the business expertise to expand these ideas. Wanting to sell up and emigrate to Canada, the firm was put on the market.

A later buy out by the Metal Profile Engineering Company in 1947 and a move to Sedgley, established DMW as a bike manufacturer and another Villiers engine user to market complete machines for the suspension specialists with a range of bikes for road and off road activities. The range naturally used MP forks but also Girling brakes, as well as the full complement of Villiers engines.

Harold Nock, of the rival suspension manufacturers MP, had been keeping an eye on his successful competitor, and when the time came he snapped up the Dawson Company. Both firms continued under one roof making and marketing their suspension systems, under the MP banner. When MP wanted to go into the manufacture of motorcycles the DMW name was used for this purpose, in order not to offend the rival established concerns to whom MP supplied suspension components.

Production of the DMW roadster range was announced in 1948, with ex BSA engineer Michael Riley being recruited as head of machine development. With a competition background, Riley was the ideal choice to develop the trials mount that was announced in 1950, but which had been tried out (in disguise) at the Scottish Six Day Trial over the previous two years.

In the early fifties DMW became a force to be reckoned with in the competition field, establishing themselves as contenders for the lightweight crown. Using 125 and 197cc Villiers engines they gained many successes in trials, scrambles and even the International Six Days Trial. Development continued throughout the 1950s, resulting in many more successes for the company, and the acquisition of Ambassador Motorcycles in 1962. This same year saw a change in tradition and a redesign of the famous square tube frame, which was now manufactured in round tube.

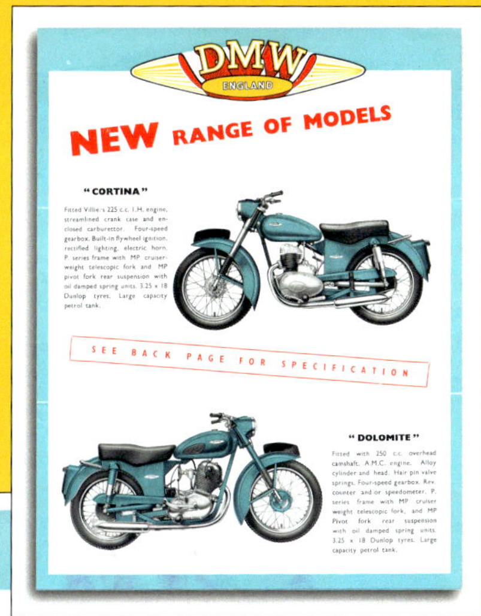

DMW ENGLAND

NEW RANGE OF MODELS

"CORTINA"

Fitted Villiers 225 c.c. I.H. engine, streamlined crank case and enclosed carburettor. Four-speed gearbox. Built-in flywheel ignition, rectified lighting, electric horn. P. series frame with MP cruiser-weight telescopic fork and MP pivot fork rear suspension with oil damped spring units. 3.25 x 18 Dunlop tyres. Large capacity petrol tank.

SEE BACK PAGE FOR SPECIFICATION

"DOLOMITE"

Fitted with 250 c.c. overhead camshaft. A.M.C. engine. Alloy cylinder and head. Hair pin valve springs. Four-speed gearbox. Rev. counter and/or speedometer. P. series frame with MP cruiser weight telescopic fork, and MP Pivot fork rear suspension with oil damped spring units. 3.25 x 18 Dunlop tyres. Large capacity petrol tank.

1954 DMW brochure

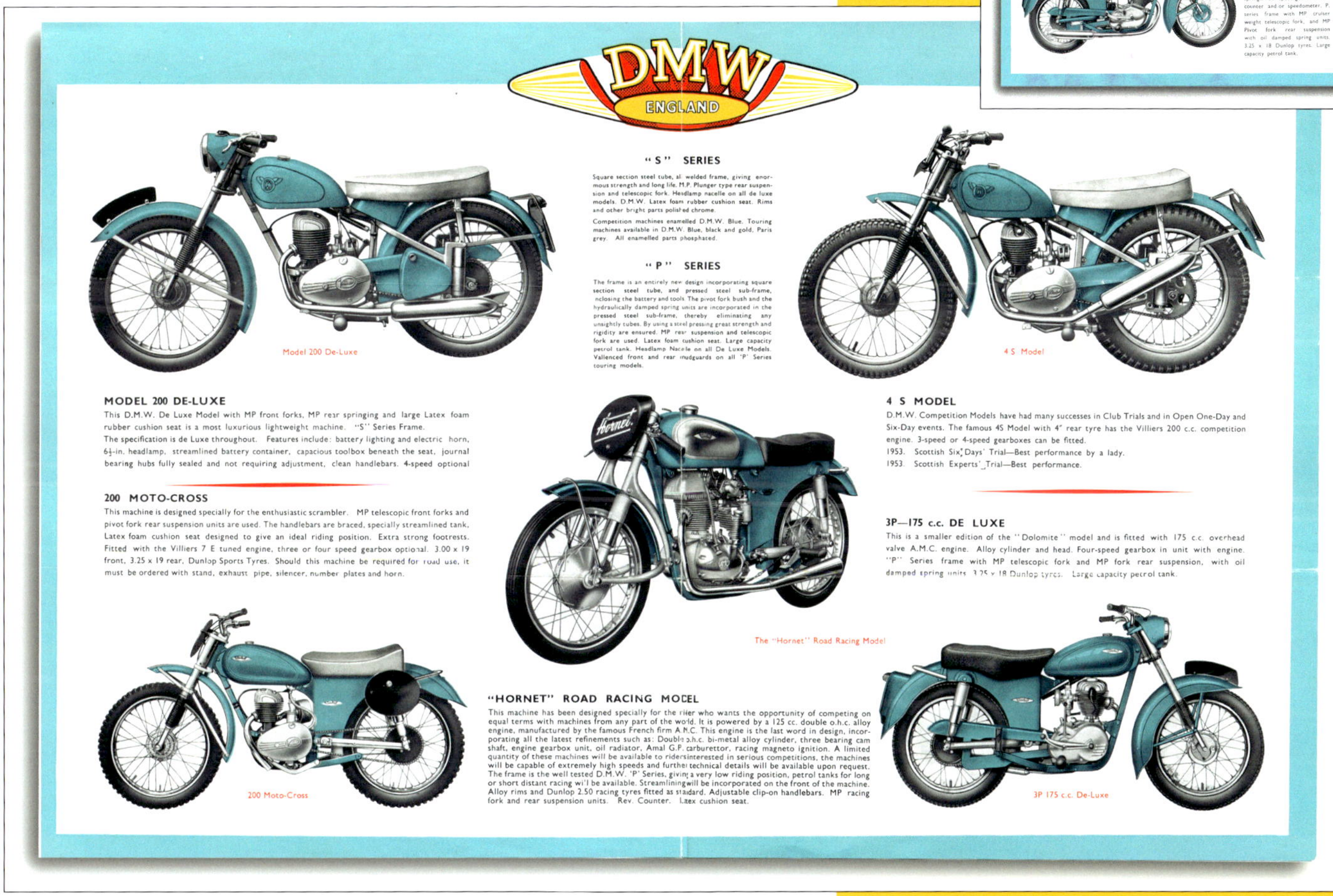

DMW ENGLAND

Model 200 De-Luxe

"S" SERIES

Square section steel tube, all welded frame, giving enormous strength and long life. M.P. Plunger type rear suspension and telescopic fork. Headlamp nacelle on all de luxe models. D.M.W. Latex foam rubber cushion seat. Rims and other bright parts polished chrome.

Competition machines enamelled D.M.W. Blue. Touring machines available in D.M.W. Blue, black and gold, Paris grey. All enamelled parts phosphated.

"P" SERIES

The frame is an entirely new design incorporating square section steel tube, and pressed steel sub-frame, enclosing the battery and tools. The pivot fork bush and the hydraulically damped spring units are incorporated in the pressed steel sub-frame, thereby eliminating any unsightly tubes. By using a steel pressing great strength and rigidity are ensured. MP rear suspension and telescopic fork are used. Latex foam cushion seat. Large capacity petrol tank. Headlamp Nacelle on all De Luxe Models. Vallenced front and rear mudguards on all 'P' Series touring models.

4 S Model

MODEL 200 DE-LUXE

This D.M.W. De Luxe Model with MP front forks, MP rear springing and large Latex foam rubber cushion seat is a most luxurious lightweight machine. "S" Series Frame.
The specification is de Luxe throughout. Features include: battery lighting and electric horn, 6½-in. headlamp, streamlined battery container, capacious toolbox beneath the seat, journal bearing hubs fully sealed and not requiring adjustment, clean handlebars. 4-speed optional

200 MOTO-CROSS

This machine is designed specially for the enthusiastic scrambler. MP telescopic front forks and pivot fork rear suspension units are used. The handlebars are braced, specially streamlined tank, Latex foam cushion seat designed to give an ideal riding position. Extra strong footrests. Fitted with the Villiers 7 E tuned engine, three or four speed gearbox optional. 3.00 x 19 front, 3.25 x 19 rear, Dunlop Sports Tyres. Should this machine be required for road use, it must be ordered with stand, exhaust pipe, silencer, number plates and horn.

4 S MODEL

D.M.W. Competition Models have had many successes in Club Trials and in Open One-Day and Six-Day events. The famous 4S Model with 4" rear tyre has the Villiers 200 c.c. competition engine. 3-speed or 4-speed gearboxes can be fitted.
1953. Scottish Six Days' Trial—Best performance by a lady.
1953. Scottish Experts' Trial—Best performance.

3P—175 c.c. DE LUXE

This is a smaller edition of the "Dolomite" model and is fitted with 175 c.c. overhead valve A.M.C. engine. Alloy cylinder and head. Four-speed gearbox in unit with engine. "P" Series frame with MP telescopic fork and MP fork rear suspension, with oil damped spring units 3.25 x 18 Dunlop tyres. Large capacity petrol tank.

The "Hornet" Road Racing Model

200 Moto-Cross

"HORNET" ROAD RACING MOCEL

This machine has been designed specially for the rier who wants the opportunity of competing on equal terms with machines from any part of the wo-ld. It is powered by a 125 cc. double o.h.c. alloy engine, manufactured by the famous French firm A.M.C. This engine is the last word in design, incorporating all the latest refinements such as: Double o.h.c. bi-metal alloy cylinder, three bearing cam shaft, engine gearbox unit, oil radiator, Amal G.P. carburettor, racing magneto ignition. A limited quantity of these machines will be available to ridersinterested in serious competitions, the machines will be capable of extremely high speeds and further technical details will be available upon request. The frame is the well tested D.M.W. 'P' Series, giving a very low riding position, petrol tanks for long or short distant racing will be available. Streamliningwill be incorporated on the front of the machine. Alloy rims and Dunlop 2.50 racing tyres fitted as standard. Adjustable clip-on handlebars. MP racing fork and rear suspension units. Rev. Counter. Laex cushion seat.

3P 175 c.c. De-Luxe

Sun Avenger with Villiers IH 224cc (63 x 72mm)

Sun

During 1946 Sun reinstated the motorcycle side of its business, this time producing a range that was totally powered by the Villiers product. Starting with the Junior de-Luxe powered Autocycle the range was soon increased to encompass the capacity classes covered by the Wolverhampton engine producer. The first true motorcycle was introduced in 1949 and used the two-speed 1F engine. The early 1950s saw an explosion in capacity classes with the launch of the 122 de-luxe, the 150 and 197 Challenger and the 225 Cyclone. The mid 1950s saw even more variants, with the 9E powered Wasp, the 2T powered Wasp twin and finally the Overlander twin.

As the seasons rolled by the Sun motorcycle was gradually updated, plunger rear suspension being introduced for 1951, which again gave way to swinging arm suspension two years later. The front suspension received just as many changes, with the original telescopic forks being replaced by Armstrong type leading link types in 1954. A move to Earles leading link forks was made at the same time, but this change was only applied to the 197 Scrambler.

As with other manufacturers of the period, Sun delved into the sporting side of motorcycle riding, producing both trials and scrambles mounts. Not in the same league as Cotton, Dot, Greeves and James, the Sun competition bikes provided many fledgling riders their first tastes of off-road trials and scrambling, using nothing more than the standard Villiers competition motors. The competition bikes were never made in great numbers, the production scrambler lasting only one year. With little to distinguish the Birmingham lightweight from the other Villiers-powered machines of the day, it can only be said that it was the high quality paintwork and gold lined maroon fuel tank that put the marque one step above its drab contemporaries.

The rigid trials version of the Sun competition machine did better once the 6E engined Challenger was equipped with the four-speed gearbox, but it was the arrival of the 9E engine and a completely new swinging arm frame for the Wasp model of 1955 that put Sun on the trials map. It was fitted with the Armstrong leading link forks and full-width Metal Profile hubs.

Motorcycle production ceased in 1959 but the Villiers 2L powered Sun scooters carried on for a further two years until powered two-wheeler production closed down for good. The factory - and the Sun trademark - was acquired in 1961 by Nottingham-based Raleigh Industries who continued to produce Sun bicycles for many more years to come, the Sun marque ending as it began.

1912 Sun Motorcycles 1952
BRITAIN'S PREMIER LIGHTWEIGHTS
SUN CYCLE & FITTINGS CO., LTD. Aston Brook Street,
BIRMINGHAM, 6

November 1958 Sun introduce the 2T-powered Overlander model

1953 Sun 197cc 6E Twin Seat model

Greeves

The Greeves motorcycle company of Thundersley in Essex was founded by Bert Greeves in 1954 as an offshoot of the Invacar company, to produce utility go-to-work machines powered by the popular Villiers engines of the day. But the early fifties was a time of relative austerity with the aftermath of the Second World War and the Korean War still being contested. Great Britain was still in the process of getting back on its feet, and needed transport to become mobile again. Before Invacar diversified into motorcycle production, the concern built their well-known invalid carriage using an off-the-shelf Villiers engine to cater for the needs of the many disabled former servicemen who needed transport.

Because of the post war shortages of good quality materials, most motorcycle manufacturers used whatever they could get hold of to build their bikes, which led to problems when put under pressure. Top quality steel tube for frame building was unavailable at the time, it being for export only, which led Bert Greeves to the idea of constructing his frames from a mixture of aluminium and steel. Having witnessed frame breakages on the racetracks of the day, and the plentiful supply of aluminium due to the continued melting down of wartime Lancasters and Spitfires, these two factors contributed to the design of the traditional Greeves composite frame, which became a trademark of the Essex based marque for the next 15 years.

The Greeves Motorcycle Co products soon became noticed, for not only did they gain successes in trials and scrambling, but they also came to the fore in road racing. These high publicity competition successes earned the company a well deserved niche in the annuls of Great Britain's motorcycling history, which rubbed off on the less publicised – but still highly regarded roadster range that included single and twin cylinder models. These machines used the tried and tested cast aluminium front frame members, the Greeves leading link front forks – with a smaller bottom loop for the roadster sized front wheel – and the competition machines brake drums, to produce agile and superb handling road orientated examples. Components such as larger steel fuel tanks, dual seats and valanced mudguards on the earlier machines all played their part in the cosmetic appearance of the roadsters.

GREEVES Motor Cycles
Model 20D
Photograph by courtesy "Motor Cycling"
First time at Earls Court
SEE US ON STAND No. 17
and examine our full range, including the NEW Super
with the velvet smooth
Designers and
Manufacturers:

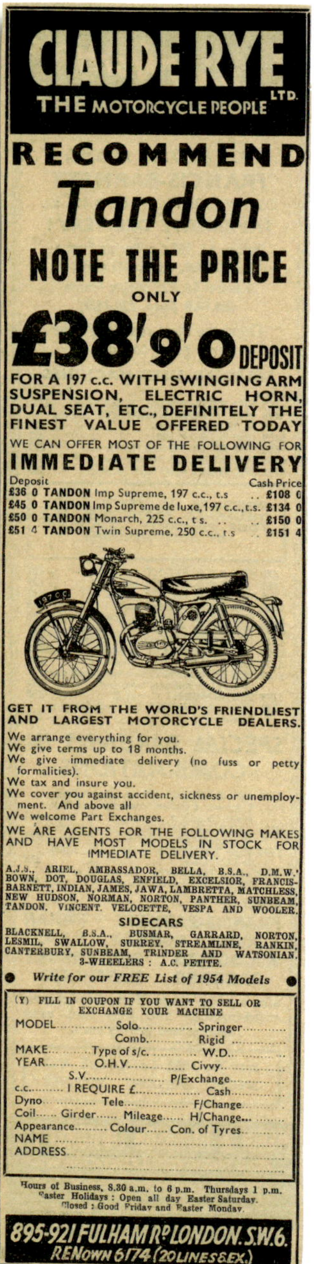

Claude Rye Tandon advert April 1954

Tandon

The Tandon Motorcycle Co entered the market place in 1948 with the Special, a lightweight machine that was powered by a Villiers 9D unit. This initial offering set a precedent in the use of Villiers products, that was followed until the end of production in 1959, only broken by the use of the Anzani twins during 1954 and 1955.

Produced on the upper floor of a warehouse in Watford, Hertfordshire, and brought to street level by a lift, the Tandon used the same technology and bought-in components that most of the other lightweight producers of the era used. The first machines of either 122 or 197cc capacity, used a rigid rear end but in 1951 - with the introduction of the 6E powered Superglide Supreme - a swinging arm rear suspension layout was utilised. This new suspension system was not controlled by standard spring units, but by a rubber block in compression, which worked remarkably well on the lightweight machine. During this period rigid rear suspension was still the vogue in the trials discipline and Tandon produced the rigid 122cc Competition Kangaroo to cater for its traditional competitors. By 1953 even the competition machine was equipped with swinging arm rear suspension and the Villiers 197cc 6E engine.

The 1953 season also saw the introduction of the Imp and Imp Supreme models. The standard Imp was initially equipped with 10D 122cc engine unit but this was changed to the 12D the following year and then to the 147cc 30C unit in 1955. The Imp Supreme was the bigger brother, which used the 6E 197cc engine that was changed to the 8E once it had become established in 1954. During the same period the Scrambler was produced, initially using a tuned 8E engine unit, this was changed to the 7E competition engine in 1955. The front forks of these models were also changed, with Earles type forks being a standard fit to the Scrambler and Armstrong leading link forks being fitted to the Imp Supreme Special of 1955.

When Villiers announced the 224cc 1H engine in 1954, Tandon were quick to build a machine to utilise it. This was the Monark, the largest single cylinder model of the entire Tandon range. Larger machines were made however, with the 242cc Anzani engined Twin Supreme and its bigger brother the 325cc Viscount.

By the end of 1955 all production at the Watford warehouse ceased, but six months later limited production was restarted with the Imp Supreme Special and the Monark. Both models were updated and used the same frames, which were now equipped with 6 inch brakes instead of the original 5 inch type. Production carried on for a further three years, but in 1959 everything ground to a halt and Tandon was consigned to the history books. The reason for the final demise of the marque was one of fashion, for the days of the simple utility machine were fast drawing to an end. Other companies carried on producing small capacity machinery, but Tandon saw fit to call a halt then, rather than to carry on and risk a humiliating financial disaster.

"Tandon" Leads Again!

125 C.C.

DE LUXE

Tandon

LUXURY LIGHTWEIGHT

NEW SUPAGLID SUSPENSION

- TELESCOPIC FRONT FORKS are spring loaded for Main and Rebound Springing, giving an added comfort to the rider.
- CHROME MOLYBDENUM STEEL is used throughout the TANDON Motor Cycle.
- WHEELS are fitted with DUNLOP 3.00 × 19'' RIBBED and UNIVERSAL treads to the front and rear respectively.
- Solid steel STAYS give extra strength to front and rear mudguards.
- LIGHTING—LUCAS 7'' Headlamp, type MU. 42, incorporation Switch and Ammeter.
- THE HORN is operated by a special 6 Amp. Accumulator.
- WIRING is connected to a Junction Block, which is neatly placed in the petrol tank recess.
- TOOL KIT is also stored in the Petrol Tank and is out of the way. It is covered over by chrome plated petrol tank plate.

- ENGINE—The engine is a VILLIERS 10D 1950 Model, three speed foot change.
- FINISH in various colours of Polychromatic Stove Enamel, also black, to suit your choice.
- Every Machine is BONDERIZED for protection against rust.
- All NUTS and BOLTS are heavily CADMIUM plated for rust prevention.
- CHROME plate Handle Bars, Tank Top and Exhaust Pipe and Silencer, etc., add extra finish to the Motor Cycle.
- WHEEL RIMS are also CHROME plated, centres are enamelled and lined to match.
- CENTRE STAND is fitted with patent spring. Either wheel can be lifted from the ground with ease.
- SPEEDOMETER—Smith's Speedometer.

…junction box is neatly …nged at the rear of the … in the Tandon tank.

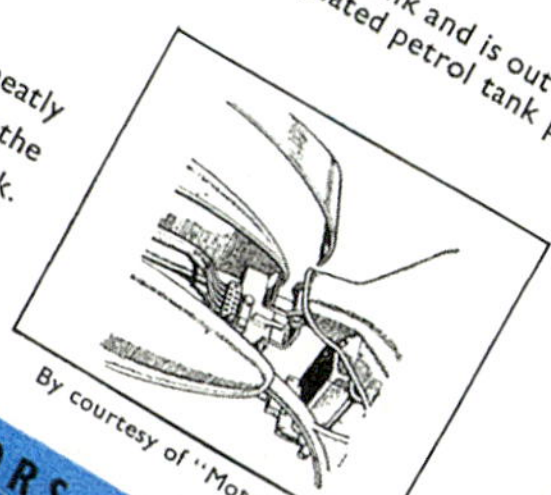

By courtesy of "Motor Cycle"

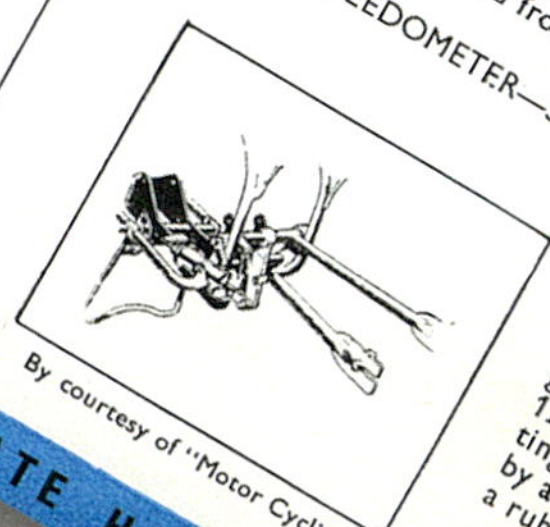

By courtesy of "Motor Cycling"

Simple, ingenious "Supaglid" suspension of the new 125 c.c. Tandon. The piv… ting chainstays are … by a bell crank an… a rubber-buff…

…DON MOTORS LTD. 29 LUDGATE HILL

Tandon Imp with 10D engine November 1952

FOR 1959
NORMAN
MOTORCYCLES & MOPEDS
The NORMAN
AUTO
CYCLE
WE ARE
NORMAN
DEALERS
AND
GIVE
SERVICE AFTER SALES

Leading racer Derek Minter was closely involved with the Norman marque

Norman

The Ashford, Kent based Norman Motorcycle Ltd concern first produced Villiers engined machines at the end of the 1930s, with the Midget powered Autocycle and a utility lightweight that used the 9D unit. Many Norman machines were in general use during the war, but none so famous as the 122cc Lightweight ridden by Wing Commander Guy Gibson, the leader of the legendary 1943 Dambuster raid. The 617 Squadron commander used his bike (GKT 315) for daily transport on and around the airfield, in preference to his staff car, when the weather permitted.

The Autocycle side of the business was a legacy from a buy-out in 1937 of the small two-stroke division of the Rudge factory, which ceased production at the beginning of the war. Production waned during the war years, and resumed when the hostilities ended, but now the Autocycle was powered by the Junior de Luxe, which in turn gave way to the 2F powered Model C when the engine became available in 1949. The two-speed 1F powered Model D Autocycle was introduced the following year. The lightweight motorcycle had disappeared in 1948 but was then reintroduced as the B1 for the 1949 season – powered by the new 10D unit.

The Norman concern used many bought-in components in the construction of their bikes, as did other lightweight manufacturers of the day. This was a typical practice, for most of the manufacturers and component makers were based together in the British Midlands, but Normans were made in rural Kent - miles away from the traditional centre of the trade. The geographic location made little difference to production, and Norman went on to build many fine roadster and competition models, which from 1949 were fitted with their own designed hydraulically linked front forks.

Early machines had all been fitted with rigid rear ends, but in 1952, with the advent of the B1S and B2S "Springer's", rear springing was added. In an effort to add the rear springing without altering the main frame, a novel Dunlop designed and patented system was employed. The rear fork was pivoted on a spindle pressed into a frame lug and its movement controlled by a pair of diagonal or laid-down spring units that ran from the wheel spindle to another frame lug under the seat. Two years later these models were equipped with more orthodox rear springing arrangements, as were the remainder of the range. By 1953 the 122cc engine of the B1 range was phased out in favour of the 147 and 148cc engine units. All the remaining singles became the B2 197s, initially with the 6E, then the 8 and 9E units in both the road and competition models – the 7E being used solely in the 1954 B2C.

Villiers

The mid 1950s saw a move to twin cylinder engines, with the advent of the 242cc Anzani engined TS of 1955 to 1957, but this was soon axed in favour of the superior Villiers 2T unit that first saw service in the B3 of 1958. The twin concept carried on, and at the beginning of the 1960s the B4 and B4 Sports were introduced. All the twin cylinder machines, and subsequent single cylinder machines, were equipped with the Armstrong leading link front forks. The competition B4 machines of 1960 now used the 246cc single cylinder engines, the trials bike being fitted with the newly introduced 32A and the scrambler using the specialised 34A unit. These competition models only lasted for a year, being axed in 1961, but the B4 twins carried on for a further year before all factory production ceased.

During its production years Norman Motorcycles were the Villiers southern area parts distributors and in 1959 alone sold more than £1 million worth of components. When during this time Villiers was stricken by strikes and industrial action, the Norman workforce spent weeks dismantling complete engines in order to gain spares and keep sales flowing.

Prior to the ending of motorcycle production, Norman had seen fit to enter the 50cc Moped market, and offered a range of single and two-speed machines as early as 1955. Initially using the Sachs, Mi-Val and then the Villiers 3K engines, the Nippy and Lido Moped models remained to the end.

Despite the acquisition of the remains of the German Achilles factory in the late 1950s, the Norman brothers Fred and Charles, saw fit to retire and sold the Ashford factory to the mighty Raleigh Industries Group of Nottingham, who at the time had promised to keep motorcycle production going. This promise was not honoured, and Raleigh closed the Ashford factory doors for good in 1962. The name lived on in the manufacture of bicycles at the huge Nottingham site, but from that day on no new motorcycles were ever produced.

Norman Nippy moped produced between November 1955 and early the 1960s - Mival, Sachs (shown) and Villiers used

1952 - 1953 Francis-Barnett Merlin 122cc 10D engine

Francis-Barnett & James

After the war, Francis-Barnett and James both re-entered the civilian manufacturing market, with surprisingly similar offerings. In 1947 Francis-Barnett was amalgamated with AMC, with James following suit in 1951; from that point the two firms – still operating independently from their original factories – produced machines that used many common components. Some models became virtually identical - apart from the tank badges and the colour schemes – but the two concerns did retain their independence from the Woolwich headquarters, producing some individual mounts, especially on the competition side.

Post-war production of the Villiers Junior de Luxe engine prompted both companies to produce Autocycles, with Francis-Barnett building the Powerbike and James constructing the Superlux. Both machines featured centrally sprung girder forks, rigid rear ends and side panels that enclosed the engine. Both companies continued Autocycle production until the mid 1950s, with James building the Comet 1 from 1949 to 1955. This machine initially used the 1F motor but in 1950 this was uprated and was fitted with the 4F unit. In 1955 the Comet 100 was announced which now used the 4F engine and was fitted with telescopic forks and swinging arm rear suspension. This model only lasted for two seasons, for the Autocycle by then was beginning to become outdated. On the other hand Francis-Barnett had seen the light earlier and terminated Autocycle production in 1952, when the Powerbike 56, which again used the 2F unit but was equipped with girder forks and a rigid rear end, was axed for good.

The 125 class was catered for by the civilian version of the wartime James ML, and in 1946 the Francis-Barnett Merlin 51, both machines using the 9D motor. With the advent of the 10D for the 1949 season, both firms again advertised machines that were powered by it, James producing the Cadet in 1949 with girder forks and rigid rear end, which received telescopic forks in 1950 and a plunger rear end in 1952. The equivalent Francis-Barnett machine was the Merlin, which was equipped with telescopic forks from its inception in 1948. The Merlin became the Kestrel in 1953 with the fitment of the 13D engine unit, but this was soon changed to the 147cc 30C unit in 1954. Further chassis changes resulted in the announcement of the model 73 Plover the following year and the model 78 Plover in 1956. James followed suit using the 13D unit in the 1953 Cadet and the 30C engine in the L15 Cadet some two years later.

The introduction of the Villiers 197cc 6E engine unit for the 1949 season saw both manufacturers producing new models; Francis-Barnett introduced the Falcon, a rigid rear end roadster that set the seal on a run of successful 200cc class machines, with James bringing out the girder forked Captain. Both models were gradually uprated to use telescopic forks and swinging arm rear suspension, and used the 8E motor from 1953, only to be replaced by the upright cylinder 10E engine in 1958. By now the two companies were controlled by AMC and the products offered to the buying public were very similar.

1953 also saw the introduction of yet another capacity class machine, this time the 225, with Francis-Barnett bringing out the model 68 Cruiser and James launching the K12 Colonel, both using the new Villiers 1H engine. These models were the largest capacity post-war machines yet produced by the AMC two-stroke division, but they wanted something even bigger and the introduction of the Villiers twin cylinder 2T seemed to be the answer. This avenue was not open to them, for AMC wanted sole user rights to this engine, but Villiers vetoed the deal. In retaliation AMC produced its own 250cc engine for fitment to the Francis-Barnett Cruiser and the new James Commodore models, but this move saw nothing but trouble and lost AMC much of its street credibility.

Common sense prevailed when AMC at last relented and started to buy in the 2T engine units for its top-of-the-range models in 1961, but this deal was for the twin cylinder engines only, with the single cylinder models still being powered by the AMC produced units. This was not the end of Villiers single cylinder engine unit usage, for in an effort to regain some of the competition successes of the past, AMC reverted to the use of the specialist Villiers trials and scrambles motors, but by then it was too late, and AMC went bust in a big way in 1966.

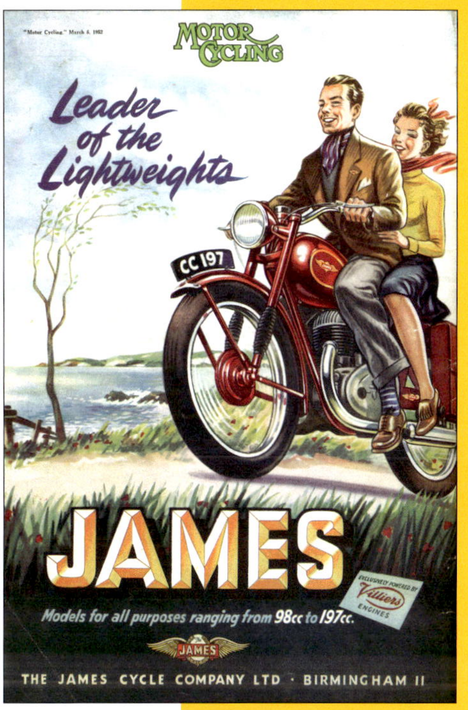

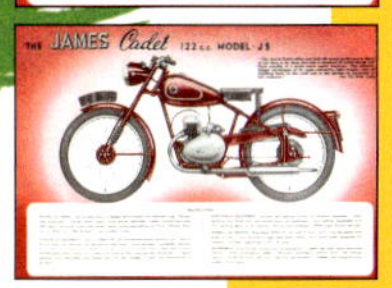

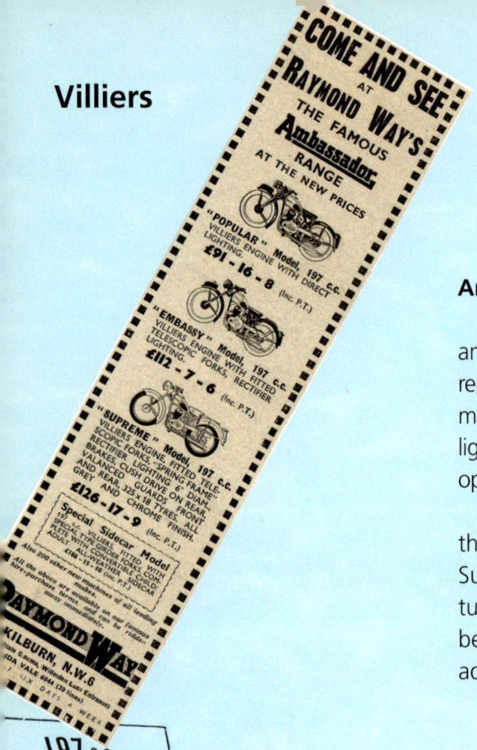

Ambassador

Pre-war record breaker Kaye Don, in the 1930s held both land and water World records. He ran an American Pontiac car and Zündapp motorcycle importing business which was turned into a vehicle repair depot during the Second World War. But once hostilities had ended he turned his hand to motorcycle production. With the experience gained mending motor vehicles, the building of simple lightweight motorcycles was no problem for the Ascot, Berkshire, based engineer - who named his operations base The Pontiac Works, turning to the Villiers factory for his power units.

Initial production centred on the use of the 197cc engine units, with the Series I of 1947 using the 5E engine and the Series III of 1948 using the 6E. Later came the Popular, Series V and Supreme models, again using the 6E. The first machines used a simple brazed-up single down tube frame with bolted-on engine plates, a rigid rear end and Webb girder forks. The frame became a single loop tubular structure the following year, with plunger rear suspension being added to the Series V in 1953 and telescopic forks to the Popular in 1955.

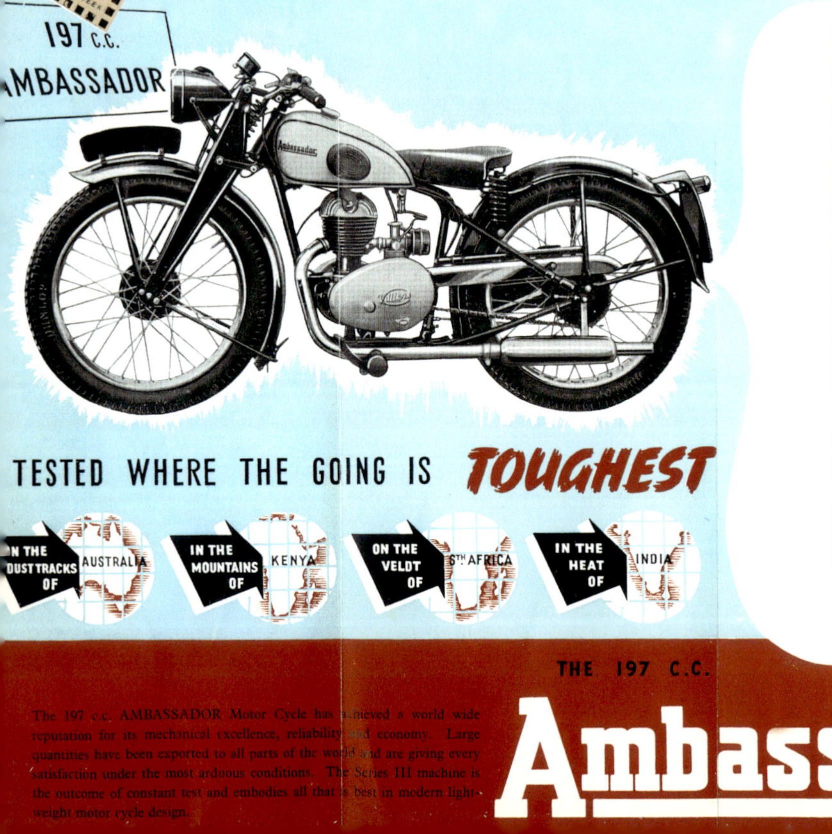

The Supreme model introduced in November 1953 used the new 225cc 1H engine unit and was the first Ambassador to feature swinging arm rear suspension and the larger 6 inch brakes. In August 1956 the capacity of the Supreme was increased with the adoption of the Villiers 2H 246cc engine, but two years later this model was discontinued.

This second generation of machines encompassed not only the Supreme but the 8E powered Envoy, the 9E Envoy/Popular/3 Star Special and the 30C powered Popular, all of which were equipped with telescopic forks, swinging arm rear suspension and 6 inch brakes – except for the earlier 8E Envoy which used the original 5 inch stoppers. As an addition to this model range, a 148 and 174cc version of the Popular also became available with either three or four-speed gearboxes. The 174cc 2L engine was also fitted to the Statesman Model of 1957 to 1960 with the fan cooled electric start 3L version being fitted to the Ambassador Scooter that was announced in November 1960.

From 1956 the Ascot factory used the Villiers 2T twin engines in a four-bike line up, which included the Statesman, Super S, Super Sports and the electric start Electra 75 model. These models featured deeply valanced mudguards and a neat rear enclosure, the exception being the Sports models that used abbreviated mudguards and rear fairings.

On the retirement of Kaye Don in October 1962, the rights to the Ambassador machines were acquired by the Metal Profile factory and manufacture was relocated to the Dudley works. The Ascot factory remained open but was turned over to precision engineering sub-contract work. The take-over resulted in Metal Profile hubs, Girling brakes and DMW cowls being fitted to a reduced Ambassador range. The following year the range received the DMW square tube frames, fibreglass rear enclosures and restyled fuel tanks with new badges. During 1964 the range was yet again reduced down to three models, the 9E powered 3 Star, the Super S and the Electra 75, the twins now being fitted with the 4T twin cylinder engines. The acquisition of the Ambassador rights by DMW was not enough to save the marque, for later that year it disappeared for good, with the DMW factory concentrating on its own models.

Ambassador 197cc Series III of November 1948

Cotton

The famous company of Cotton Motorcycles was founded by Frank Willoughby Cotton after the First World War, to fulfill the transportation needs of the British public. His first machines used a triangulated frame of straight tubing that gave his products great strength and exceptional handling characteristics, which naturally led to the marque being used on the race tracks of the day. Prominence in the TT races of the 1920s, with riders like Stanley Woods, proved to be a sales winner and the company flourished.

The company failed to survive the Second World War, when Cotton was requisitioned to manufacture armaments for the government, and disappeared from public view. The company was re-formed in 1954, when Pat Onions and Monty Denley commenced production at the Vulcan Works, Quay Street, Gloucester, under the E Cotton banner – the E standing for Elizabeth, the wife of the original founder.

The E Cotton factory production initially encompassed but one machine, the 197cc Vulcan, a utility roadster that utilised Metal Profile telescopic front forks and a frame that used four straight tubes running from the headstock to the rigid rear end with duplex loops under the engine unit. The engine unit for this first machine was the three-speed 8E, but the following year the 9E Vulcan was introduced, with a three or four-speed gearbox option. A new single loop swinging arm frame was produced for this machine, but it still used the Metal Profile forks, that were replaced by the Armstrong leading link type in 1958. Mudguards for this machine were heavily valanced and the machine was fitted with a large rear enclosure to protect the rider from road dirt, a move made popular by Triumph with the advent of the "bathtub" models.

This extra equipment resulted in an all up weight of some 255 lbs, but in 1960 a Sports Vulcan was produced that was fitted with aluminium mudguards and an abbreviated midriff enclosure, which resulted in the weight being reduced to 245 lbs. The 197 Vulcan, with its 6 inch Motoloy full width aluminium brake drums, remained in production until the very end of the Villiers era in 1968, but was always eclipsed by the sportier twin cylinder roadsters and the fearsome competition mounts.

Being a competition orientated company, Cotton concentrated on this area producing many fine race machines, but it must not be forgotten that racing successes alone do not pay the wage bill. The bread and butter roadster range provided the day to day finances of the firm, with the building of some equally attractive machines, especially the quarter litre Anzani and Villiers twins.

Excelsior

The manufacture of Penny Farthing bicycles saw the beginning of the Excelsior Company in Birmingham during 1874. Owned by the Walker family of Coventry, the factory produced its first powered two-wheelers at the turn of the century, and as with many other fledgling manufacturers used bought in engine units. Minerva, De Dion and MMC engines graced the first machines, but in the 1920s and 1930s Blackburn, JAP and Villiers engines were pressed into service.

Between the wars the company built up a good name for its products, many of which were of a sporting nature, and sales flourished. Racing soon followed with the use of the potent JAP 173 and 248cc engines; but it was the ingenious four-valve 250cc Mechanical Marvel – designed by HJ 'Ike' Hatch - that started the trend for building of World class racing machines, after gaining two TT victories in the lightweight category. Capitalising on these successes, Excelsior went on the produce the ohc Manxman racer in 250, 350 and 500cc forms.

The pre-war reputation that Excelsior built up did not help them through the conflict, which was spent building Autocycles and the army Wellbike. The first Autocycle was built in 1937 using the Villiers Junior engine, and this started a trend that carried on well after the ending of hostilities in 1945, but this was all that persisted, for the four-stroke models did not survive the war.

In the austere initial post-war period production was focused on utility machines, with the 1946 range featuring just two models, one of which was the 98cc Autobyk. Using the single-speed Villiers Junior de Luxe engine, the Autobyk was very basic indeed, using neither any form of springing nor engine panels. The following year a new version was produced which used sprung front forks, but from then Excelsior shunned the use of the Villiers 98cc engine, preferring to use those of its own manufacture, with production carrying on until the mid 1950s. Alongside the Autocycle was the Universal, another utility machine that this time used the Villiers 9D engine. The Universal again used a rigid frame equipped with girder forks. The hand change lever of the 9D unit was sited in the centre of the fuel tank, rather than on its right hand side, as on other models; but this feature was abandoned in 1949, when the engine unit was replaced by the foot-change 10D engine.

Even with manufacture of Excelsior's own 98 and 123cc engine units – which started in the late 1940s – the company still used Villiers products of the same capacity right through to the early 1960s, producing an extensive range of light weight models to cover the 100, 125, 150 and 200cc classes. Always overshadowed by the Talisman twin cylinder models, which used an engine of Excelsior manufacture, the singles did not prosper even with the use of plunger rear suspension in 1953 and a swinging arm system the following year. The "no frills" single cylinder machines had little to offer the young bloods of the period, for they were aimed extensively at the commuting worker, with sales in this area reflecting company policy.

Twin cylinder engine production maintained the financial status quo, with units also being built to service the emerging Minicar market. This part of the company flourished and the standard Talisman engine was enlarged from 243 to 328cc as demand for the units increased. The engine was again increased in capacity (492cc) with the addition of a third cylinder, specifically for the Berkeley four-wheeler Minicar. But it was this engine that brought about the final demise of the company.

Berkeley cars – along with other manufacturers used the 328cc twin to power its three-wheeler, but when a sportier four-wheeler was announced, a move to BSA power was also muted. To counter this rumour, Excelsior built the three cylinder engine, which Berkeley accepted and used in its roadsters, circuit racers and rally cars with much success. Berkeley soon got into financial difficulties that resulted in them going bankrupt, with Excelsior as its major creditor. The money troubles of Berkeley affected Excelsior to such a degree that they too went under, and late in 1962 the doors finally closed on what had once been one of Great Britain's most respected motorcycle marques of the first half of the 20th century.

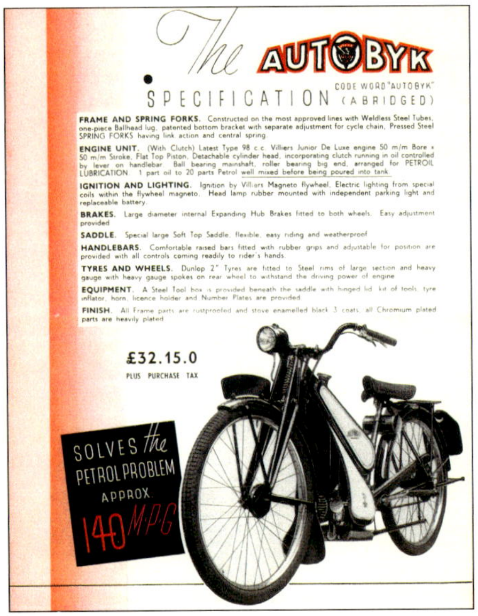

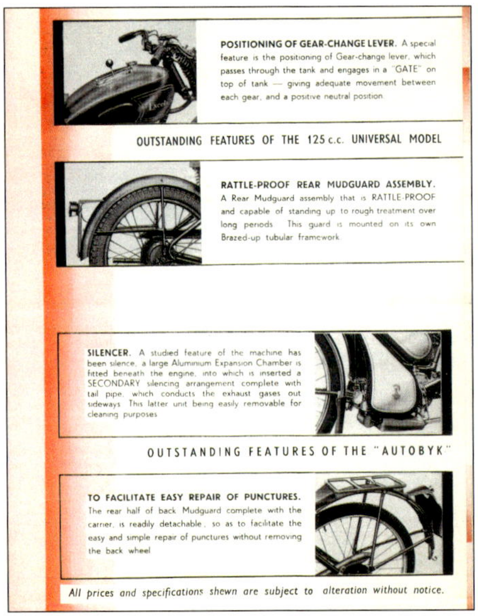

MODELS
by
June 3, 1948.
MOTOR CYCLING
AUTOBYK
Safe simple speedy—
THE 48/VI AUTOBYK
The cheapest mode of motorised travel, the Autobyk is as easy to ride as a bicycle. It is light in construction and handles well at all speeds. Complete with all accessories—ready to ride away.
MODEL DESCRIPTION PRICE
48/V1 Standard Autobyk. Villiers Engine £45
48/S1 Autobyk de luxe. Excelsior "Spryt" Engine .. £47.10
48/G2 Super Autobyk. Excelsior "Goblin" Engine—2-speed gear unit £55
(Purchase Tax extra to above prices)
The Excelsior 125 c.c. Universal Model Lightweight Motor Cycle is available in very limited quantities.
Excelsior
THE EXCELSIOR MOTOR COMPANY LIMITED, KINGS ROAD, TYSELEY, BIRMINGHAM 11
L.G.B.
Excelsior
MORE MILES PER GALLON
Consort
98c.c. Model CA9
Skutabyke
98c.c. Model SB1
Write for main illustrated catalogue containing full technical data and detailed specifications.
Name
Address

Bond

The Bond Aircraft and Eng Co (BAC) of Longridge in Lancashire was the domain of Lawrence Bond, a designer famous for the conception of the Bond Minicar and a rotary valve conversion for the JAP speedway engine - he was also responsible for a rotary valve conversion tried on the legendary Manx Norton - but during the late 1940s he delved into small capacity utility motorcycles.

During 1949 the Minibyke was introduced to the public by an enthusiastic Mr Bond. This futuristic machine was based on well proven aircraft construction techniques and used 18 gauge pressed aluminium panels that were lap jointed and pop riveted to form a stressed skin. The main frame member was of an oval shape and tapered back from the steering head to the rear wheel axle, the wheel being covered by another pair of mudguard pressings welded together and riveted to the frame member. The engine – a two-speed Villiers 1F or a JAP 125 unit – was under slung on a flat strip steel cradle. Front forks were at first just tubular legs, but after adverse comment by the motorcycling press, springing was added. The designer initially specified solid front forks, for the large section tyres fitted were 4.00 x 16 inch and said to offer a degree of comfort without extra springing. The tyres were fitted to split rims – of Bond design – and equipped with 4 inch diameter brakes. One of the main attributes of this machine was its lightness, for the dry weight of both models was under 100 lbs.

Originally produced and marketed by BAC, the Minibyke production line was taken over by Ellis of Leeds in 1950 and marketed under the Bond label. The Minibyke gave excellent weather protection with its heavily valanced mudguards and built-in leg shields, but was a little too radical to attract volume sales and despite a change to a tubular engine mounting cradle, production of the 98cc version ceased in January 1953. The JAP engined variant also ceased production later that year in August.

During this period BAC continued to produce their own machines, but these offerings were of a more conventional design. Again using the Villiers 1F or the JAP 125 engine units, the Lilliput was, as its name implied, a small scale machine with a single loop, rigid rear end, tubular frame and telescopic front forks of Bond design. The Lilliput failed to gain market sales and by 1952 both models had disappeared. In their place came the Gazelle scooter. These used the Villiers 1F or 10D engine units.

The Gazelle followed conventional scooter practice in the use of small wheels and leg shields but the engine, in front of the driving wheel and under the seat, was exposed. Instead of using a large steel pressing to cover the engine, the Gazelle used a protective cage of six horizontal bars from the footboard to the seat base, allowing airflow and easy access. As in the Italian scooter the fuel tank was placed above the rear wheel, but again this was exposed and of an odd motorcycle shape. The Gazelle lasted only one year before production ceased, the design being taken over by Projects and Developments of Blackburn who did little more than move the fuel tank, but this had little effect and the scooter disappeared into obscurity.

Even though Bond delved into the manufacture of lightweight motorcycles, by far the largest production figures were for the Bond Minicar, a simple runabout that aimed at simplicity of construction and economy in operation. Conceived in 1948, after a couple of years development, the three-wheeler Bond was a relatively inexpensive mode of transport that would stretch the meagre petrol ration that was in operation during the austere post-war period.

The three-wheeler was another design by Laurie Bond but was built at Sharps Commercials Ltd of Preston, who continued to develop the model. The first Minicar was the Mark A of 1948 which used a 122cc Villiers engine unit that gave a top speed of 40mph and a fuel consumption figure of some 100 mpg, but with performance in mind this was soon changed to the 197cc 6E unit when it became available for the 1949 season. The Mark A was devoid of any frills and was a very basic vehicle, a pressed aluminium body with a perspex windscreen, low pressure balloon tyres and no suspension.

The Mark B of June 1951 saw many significant modifications to the original model, and included such refinements as a curved triplex glass windscreen, front suspension with an hydraulic damper, independent rear suspension, an improved rack-and-pinion steering system and smaller wheels. The engine starter of the Mark B was a simple pull handle in the cab, connected by wire to the engine's kick starter lever, but this was further improved to electric starting during its manufacturing run. The electric starter system consisted of a motor mounted above the cylinder head that drove a free-wheel on the engine's flywheel via a V belt. A larger battery was also fitted to cope with the motor power requirements.

After some 2,000 Mark A and 3,000 Mark B models were produced, the Mark C made its

Villiers

Gordon 3-wheeler - 1961 Bond advert - mid-1950s Bond Model C

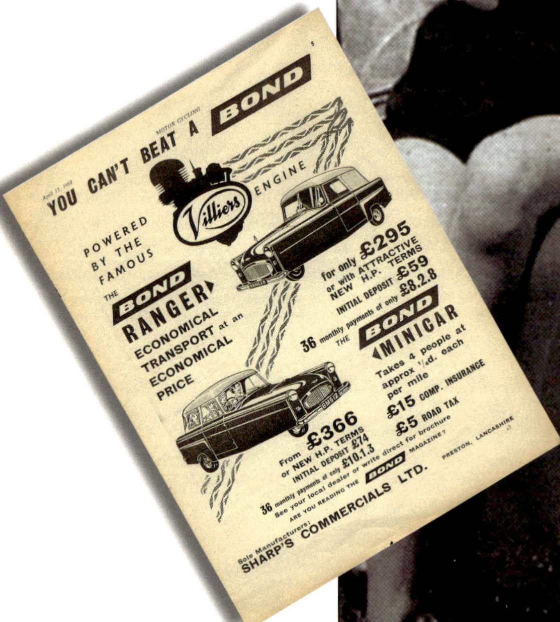

appearance in January 1953. The body of this model was completely restyled as a two or four seater and used a trailing arm rear suspension mounted on bonded rubber flexitor units, together with a worm-and-sector steering system and brakes on all three wheels. The Mark C received the Villiers 8E engine unit fitted with a high output generator in November 1953, but in May 1956 this was replaced by the Villiers 9E engine, when the Mark D was introduced. This new model offered some improvement in the car's electrics for the engine was equipped with the SIBA Dynastart, which used a 12 volt system. The Dynastart could also be activated in either direction, enabling the driver to start the engine backwards to reverse the vehicle into parking bays etc.

December 1956 saw the introduction of the two-seat Mark E, which had received another complete redesign of its longer aluminium body shell. The Mark E was complemented by the Mark F which was the four-seater variant that now used the 246cc Villiers 31A engine. Both models still used the electric starter first seen on the 9E engine unit.

The next model was the Mark G of 1962, which used the much improved Villiers 35A engine, a unit that had been specifically designed for Minicar use, but this was soon superseded by the twin cylinder Mark G of March 1963 that used a Dynastart version of the Villiers 4T engine unit. The final Bond Minicar was far from being a mini car for this was the Bond 875 and the Ranger 875 that was fitted with the Hillman Imp four cylinder car engine.

Many Villiers engined Bonds are still around today, being looked after by an owners club which has been in existence since 1950, when a small group of enthusiasts started the first club in Blackburn. The Villiers engines used in these vehicles were of a specialised type, in that they used many strengthened components to deal with the rigours of three wheel motoring. These components have since been put to good use in motorcycle competition and kart racing. Strengthened clutches are today sought after by kart racers and scramblers whilst the wide ratio gearbox internals now find their way into trials bikes. The development put into these Minicars by Laurie Bond and his team enabled many an impoverished motorcyclist to sample the weather cheating properties of car ownership at an affordable price.

1956 New Hudson Autocycle with Villiers 2F 98cc engine (47 x 57mm)

New Hudson

Initial production of New Hudson motorcycles commenced before the First World War, with Bert Le Vack, the famous record breaker, and Fred Hutton as both designers and riders in sporting events. The name came to the fore in the 1920s with Le Vack breaking many Brooklands records, with this activity leading to the production of some fine ohv sporting models and further sporting successes in the hands of riders such as Jimmy Guthrie and Tommy Bullus. The company became yet another victim of the Great Depression and motorcycle production was terminated in 1933, but the factory stayed open with engineering production carrying on, the factory becoming the sole manufacturer of Girling brakes.

After the Second World War the name was resurrected, but now as a member of the BSA Group, when Autocycle production was restarted in 1946. The first offering was a fairly basic utility machine that used the Villiers Junior de Luxe engine as motive power. This initial machine, produced from 1946 to 1949, used a lady's-type open bicycle frame from which the engine was hung and the fuel tank positioned between the frame tubes to give the machine a traditional Autocycle image. Bicycle type front forks were initially used but these were changed to the pressed steel girder pattern in 1948, when engine panels were also added.

The following year the main frame was changed to a single loop type, which ran under the new single-speed Villiers 2F engine unit that became available at the same time. The new model remained in production, virtually unchanged, for the next seven years, apart from a colour change – black fuel tank with gold-lined red panels and a strengthened centre stand in 1952. During 1956 the model was again altered with the addition of tubular girder fork legs, another styling change and a general brightening up of the finish that included more chrome plate and a gold lined maroon fuel tank.

New Hudson Autocycle production went the same way as other manufacturers products during this period; fighting off the onslaught of imported Mopeds of half the size, the battle became rather one-sided and the assembly line was shut down in 1958, but the name lived on with the building of the New Hudson bicycles.

The Name to Remember when buying your New Machine.

Panther

Originally known as the Phelon & Moore – The Perfected Motorcycle – the name Panther gradually crept in, but it is hard to say when this became the official title of the Cleckheaton factory. Jonah Phelon and Richard Moore started motorcycle production at the turn of the Twentieth Century with Phelon designed engines that were fitted to frames made by the Beeston Humber company, and by the 1920s were offering a complete range of machines from 250 to 600cc, the first two-stroke model being the Villiers 247cc engined Panthette of 1928.

Between the wars Panther also built many trials machines which became popular in the sidecar role, but it was the racing 500s of the 1920s that captured the imagination of the buying public, with many victories in the hands of Tommy Bullus, Count Ashby and HM Walters. These successes ensured that the company survived the Great Depression, but in the mid 1950s the factory went into receivership and carried on for a further ten years in a limited capacity. This later period was renowned for the 600 and 650 slopers, and these provided sterling service to the sidecar brigade, but it also saw the reintroduction of the Villiers engined models.

The first post-war two-stroke was the 10/3 of 1955 which used the three-speed 197cc 8E engine unit, but a four-speed model was soon introduced with the 9E powered 10/4. These two models required the use of two different frames to accommodate the differing mounting points of the 8 and 9E engines. But in 1956 a 10/3A model was launched that used the three-speed 9E, which eased the frame building problems. The all-welded single down tube frames were equipped with Armstrong controlled oval-section swinging arm rear suspension mounted on Silentbloc bushes and Earles type leading link front forks which used Girling units. All models used deeply valanced mudguards, a well-panelled central area under the dual seat and 18 inch wheel rims fitted with 5 inch brake drums, but the brakes of the 10/3A were increased to 6 inch in diameter during 1957 to bring it into line with the faster twin cylinder models that appeared during that year.

Finished in the traditional maroon with a gold-lined fuel tank the Panther two-stroke singles remained in production until 1962 when the singles were axed in favour of the twin cylinder models. One further single was the proposed model 25, which was to have used the Villiers 2H engine, but this machine did not go into production, production being concentrated on the more powerful twin cylinder range.

The twins were soon the only two-stroke models available, with the model 35 and 45 taking Panther from the early to mid 1960s, when production finally finished, this part of the story being recounted in Chapter 9.

SANGLAS

Spanish Sanglas with a German Zündapp engine (shown) was also produced with a Villiers 2T unit during late 1950s - early 1960s

The Spanish Connection

British visitors to Spain during the years following the end of the Second World War would have been surprised to find a large number of Spanish marques of motorcycles and three-wheeled commercial runabouts powered by Villiers engines. The engines however were not built at the Villiers factory in Wolverhampton, but were manufactured under licence by Hispano Villiers SA of Barcelona. Nonetheless, they conformed strictly to the design and quality of the British-made Villiers engines – of 122 and 197cc – which were the main production. However ,later during the 1960s the 249cc 2T/4T and the 324cc 3T twins were also built in Spain. The origins or the Spanish operation had come via the efforts of ex-pat Harry Walker.

Originally, Villiers had been represented in Spain by Autocesorios Harry Walker SA – the concern taking its name from the founder who had left Britain shortly before the First World War to become a highly successful "British" manufacturers representative. As regards motorcycles Harry Walker was instrumental in several British marques – notably Norton and BSA – having their bikes imported into Spain during the 1920s and 1930s. However, first came the Spanish Civil War (1936-1939) and then the Second World War which Spain was not involved, but they still restricted imports of foreign goods during the period.

After the conflict, however, came other problems. There was a host of international trading difficulties and Spain like many other countries was forced to impose import restrictions. As time went on import licences for motorcycle engines became scarcer and scarcer and early in 1951 investigations into the possibility of building Villiers engines under licence in Spain were begun at the instigation of Harry Walker's company, together with some of the Spanish manufacturers of Villiers engined motorcycles.

Approval for the idea was given by the Spanish Government of General Franco and negotiations were begun with the directors of the Villiers Engineering Company on 3rd August 1951. When full approval to the formation of Hispano Villiers SA was subsequently given, the contract was officially signed at the Wolverhampton factory on 14th September 1951.

Before going ahead with the erection of a factory a team of Spanish technicians made an extended visit to Wolverhampton, where they made a comprehensive study of the requirements involved in the manufacture of two-stroke motorcycle engines. During this visit they not only learnt the basic essentials of quality production so far as it affected engine manufacture, but also of the rigid quality control exercised at the Wolverhampton factory over raw materials and all the manufacturing processes.

Whilst this survey was being carried out, back in Spain a suitable factory site of 10,000 sq meters ($2^1/2$ acres) was obtained in the San Andres quarter of Barcelona. Plans for the factory were drawn up; building work commencing in February 1952 with completion in March the following year.

During the building operations technical details of the Villiers 122cc motorcycle engine were studied by the Hispano engineers, who had decided that this was the engine most suited to the needs of the Spanish market. The necessary machines, jigs and tools were installed, and by May 1953, the factory was equipped for production.

The next stage was to engage and train a labour force, an operation which naturally delayed production, but which was still speedily achieved. This phase and all other assorted problems having been completed, on the 1st September 1953, the first Hispano Villiers 122cc two-stroke engine went on the test bench, and proceeded to give a completely satisfactory account of itself.

As production got into full swing more and more Spanish manufacturers became interested in the engines. By the end of July 1954 production had reached 300 engines a month and by the end of that year this figure was above 400.

For 1955 the factory planned an output of 5,000 units and had also decided to extend the range to include a 197cc engine – again identical to the comparable unit produced at Wolverhampton. However, before the year was half-way through, demand had outstripped the above figure, and plans had been approved to extend the factory building and to step up production to 10,000 engines per annum.

For the remainder of the 1950s the Spanish Villiers operation continued to expand, helped by a close liaison between the British and Spanish factories, regular visits being paid to Barcelona by Villiers methods engineers to advise on production techniques, whilst an equally frequent visitor to Wolverhampton was Dr Ramon Pinto Oliveras, managing director of Hispano Villiers.

The formation of Hispano Villiers did not sever the link between Villiers and Harry Walker. In fact this was strengthened, with sales of Villiers agricultural and industrial engines for Gibraltar and Tangier still handled by Autocesories Harry Walker SA, who was also responsible for the actual sales of Hispano Villiers engines in Spain. A number of directors, too, were on the boards of both companies, amongst them being Dr Pinto Oliveras and Don Enrico Colomina, who had become managing director of Autocesories Harry Walker SA, upon the death of its founder in 1951.

During the late 1950s Hispano Villiers supplied engine units to some 16 Spanish motorcycle builders, but by the early 1960s the operation was suffering from increased competition. Although there was a ban on imports of under 500cc motorcycles (which effectively kept out the Japanese and Italians), Montesa had been joined by Bultaco and Ossa. Not only this, the larger Italian companies had done a Villiers, and set up their own Spanish operations, notably Ducati (Mototrans), Moto Guzzi (Moto Hispania) and MV Agusta (Avello).

Many of the smaller Spanish marques that had used Villiers engine units began to fall by the wayside. However, the gap this left was plugged by the sales of engines for use in the small 3 and 4-wheelers then prevalent in Spain, plus the continued industrial engine work.

Spanish Huracan 197cc Hispano-Villiers engine - 1957 - 1959

6 The Sporting Era

The turning point of the Villiers factory sporting fortunes came with the introduction of the 197cc 9E engine of 1955; an engine which many other factories used to power their production competition machines. The unit was an instant success with in excess of 60,000 units being produced. I quickly began to gain awards on both the trials and scrambles scene. With the eventual build up of both user, factory and rider tuning experience, the far-from-exotic 9E continued to gain favour, for with a good rider on board a lightweight 197cc powered machine could be a match for even a 500cc, a point proved time and time again by the Greeves and DOT machines that ruled the roost in the late fifties and early sixties. It is often wondered if Villiers realised what an instant and profound effect this motor had on the competition world, for it took a number of years for the factory to capitalise on its early sporting successes.

Trials successes

The glory attached to the scrambling successes came after the initial introduction of the competition variants of the D, C and E ranges, these engines being then aimed predominantly at the trials discipline. Many trials wins were achieved with the small capacity power units, for in the early 1950s riders began to look for a cheaper alternative to the large capacity four-stroke trials irons which dominated during that period. This trend was started by Bill Lomas, on his works 197cc James, when he won the prestigious Travers trial of 1951. The James factory trials activities had started some four years previously, when the three Normans – Hooton, Moore and Palmer – competed on standard military ML models, in the British championship qualifying national trials. Seen as a publicity exercise rather than a serious onslaught on the trials scene, the riders however notched up many class wins. This led the James factory to state in their advertisement during 1949, 'Our models are the most successful of all lightweights in trials.'

The 9E enters service

The first 9E entered service in 1955, which again only delivered 8.4 bhp, but this was soon increased to 9.3 bhp at 4,300rpm for the very mildly tuned competition version, which used a new cylinder head with a compression ration of 8.25:1. The competition engine was basically similar to the roadster unit with either a three or four speed Villiers gearbox, but in order to obtain additional power, the specification varied in several respects. Available as a trials or as a sports motor, the specification was similar with the exception of the magneto, the trials being fitted with a heavier flywheel in order to obtain smoother torque at low speeds. The standard roadster version of the 9E continued in service to the very end of the Villiers Empire in 1967, but another version, the 10E, was introduced to the range in 1957. This unit utilised a vertical cylinder instead of the normal 8 degree forward slope which was produced for motorcycle manufacturers who had a penchant for vertical cylinder engines. The 10E used the same crankcase as its predecessor, the only alteration to the engine being that the stripes on the primary drive and magneto covers were realigned to give the desired effect.

Brian Stonebridge

Within the confines of the Greeves factory the 9E was worked on by Brian Stonebridge, who had learned the art of two-stroke tuning from Hermann Meier when working on the BSA Bantam scrambler project. Stonebridge built up the "hammer head" crank to full circle - with brazed-on steel sheet. He also modified the main bearing arrangements. The ports were enlarged, with the exhaust and inlet timings lengthened. The cylinder head was welded up and remachined with a $1^3/_{16}$ inch Amal Monobloc carburettor added to a tuned length inlet pipe. Stonebridge also tested a variety of exhaust systems, but opted for a plain pipe of 18 inch length, which gave the best all round results. By 1957 the Stonebridge 9E was developing some 15 to16 reliable bhp, almost double the power available from the standard Villiers motor.

Villiers fails to take the lead

Why then did Villiers not do a similar job? For it would seem that this would have been a simple exercise, given the facilities available in the Wolverhampton factory. Bert Greeves was asked the same question, but remarked, 'They did not want to know. They claimed that the 9E was at the very peak of its development.' Private owners were treated in much the same way, with any requests for tuning advice being turned away. The only reply that would-be tuners got was a curt reminder that the warranty would be null and void if any tuning work was carried out.

Villiers must have taken some notice, for later on they ventured into 9E kart motors, with units being supplied by the factory to service the needs of the karting fraternity. Several specifications were available with the 246D being the top of the range. This engine unit used the competition cylinder, with an extra half a thou piston clearance, an Amal 389/63 Monobloc 1 3/16 inch carburettor and was reported as delivering some 15 bhp in this form. The kart engines were derived from the motorcycle competition engines.

Alternative barrels

Now three types of cylinder barrel became available from the factory for the 9E; standard, Super Sports and Kart, together with an array of cylinder heads, which featured a choice of compression ratios and compression release valve arrangements. Efforts were being channelled into the production of more power, but little development work was being carried out in other areas, namely the original "hammer head" crank.

As the tuning expertise of the riders grew, so did the failure rate of the engines, with the 9E being nothing more than a road engine being thrashed mercilessly every weekend. It was at this point that the after-market goodies manufacturers stepped in to save the day, but they were aiming for a full 250 engine, rather than the continued use of a 200, which gave away 50ccs to the competition. Firms such as B and C Pearson Ltd, who produced the popular Ajax alloy cylinder conversions and Vale-Onslow who made a cast iron cylinder type, showed Villiers that a full 250 was needed. Greeves too had jumped on the bandwagon, producing their own 250 alloy cylinder as far back as 1958.

The 2H engine

At this time Villiers did produce a full 250cc engine, the 2H, but this unit was large and heavy and not suited to the competition role. What was needed was a slim, lightweight and versatile unit, which would lend itself to service within the two differing worlds of trials and scrambles. There was one such unit already in production, a unit that had received much in the way of development by outside organisations, a unit that would stand the rigors of competition work; this was the 9E.

1955 Sun Trials model with 197cc 8E and Albion 4-speed gearbox

Tony Bryant with his 1954 Francis-Barnett 197cc Falcon Trials model

The 30-series two-fifty engines

Villiers soon hit back and produced the 246cc 31A roadster/trials unit in 1958, but this was only a big bore (66 mm) version of the 9E, which inherited all the problems that an increase in size - and therefore power - gives when allied to a standard roadster motor. The situation got slightly better when the next generation of 246cc engines was introduced in 1960. Now sporting caged big-end roller bearings, first used on the competition 197s. The 32A roadster/trials and the 33/34A scrambler units featured a 5.5 inch connecting rod and a thicker cylinder barrel flange. Power outputs had now risen to 12.4 bhp at 5,000rpm for the roadster unit and 19 bhp at 6,000rpm for the scrambler. The extra "umph" that these engines delivered benefited the trials riders, but only led to further failures on the scrambles track.

The new 246cc engines continued to use the same four-speed gearbox, which had first seen service on the 9E, instead of the more robust version available from the 2H, a choice that did give some trouble with the overworked scrambles engines. The gearbox continued relatively unchanged right through to the end, apart from the casting changes for the 36/37A units and the introduction of an improved gearchange mechanism for 1962. The new mechanism now employed a set of redesigned selector pawls, that could be recognized without stripping by the deletion of the large external nut which held the selector spring stop in position. The new gearchange system was also used on the later twin cylinder engines, which were retrospectively modified, with a similar mechanism appearing in the brand new Starmaker engine of 1963.

The factory did recognize the fact that the 9E gearbox was not as strong as it could be and built a number of experimental single cylinder competition engines during the early 1960s, which used the stronger internals from the 1H/2H/2T engines. These internal gear sets were available in both wide and standard road ratios, but that is as far as the exercise progressed, the factory reverting to the instant availability of the many ratios of the versatile 9E gearbox.

Six different gearbox ratios

The gearbox may have had its drawbacks, but its versatility far outweighed any problems in this area. Villiers saw the need for versatility and produced six differing ratio sets, from close to standard, with wide and special wide ratios. In later years the versatility of the gearbox was further enhanced with the availability of even more specialist ratios. The primary drive line was again standard 9E, but in an effort to transmit more power, the clutch spring arrangement was strengthened up by the use of three extra small springs, one being inserted into every third larger spring in the clutch centre. An alternative heavier spring arrangement was available, this being the original double spring set up of the 1H, which proved to be too heavy in normal use - but it did stop clutch slip in the heat of battle and many scramblers converted to this arrangement.

With the need for extra power the square alloy cylinder became the vogue. Producing anything up to 25 bhp they were made by Cotton, DMW, DOT, Greeves, Marcelle and Parkinson,

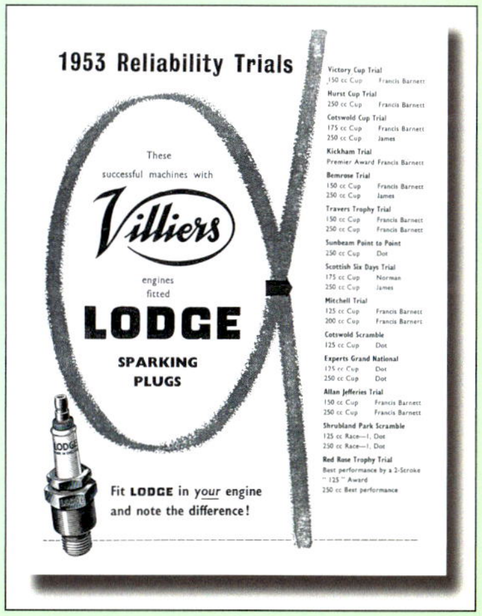

with most manufacturers using the Hepolite 66 mm piston. These new high performance cylinders, some of which started life with a chrome-lined bore, began to put the pressure on the standard Villiers crankshaft, which was nothing more than a standard 9E item with a caged roller big-end bearing. To counter this new problem the Alpha company came up with a full circle crankshaft, which featured an oval section streamlined connecting rod and a superior big-end bearing. The Alpha crank was universally accepted by all the works trials and scrambles teams of the early sixties, for it gave them better cylinder filling, reliability and the ability to extract even more power from the engine without the crank twisting that plagued the Villiers shaft.

Parkinson & Alpha

Once the crankshaft reliability problems had been solved, the next item to give trouble was the crankcase itself, and this now became the weak link in the chain. The crankcase problem was solved in two ways, firstly by the Parkinson company of Marks Tey, Essex, who manufactured a pair of special crankcase halves which incorporated heavy strengthening webs. At the same time Alpha made a set of crankcases, but this time they were to be used in conjunction with a new Alpha crankshaft that ran in caged roller bearings directly on to the crank mainshafts.

The next engines to come from the Villiers factory were the 36A scrambles and the 37A trials units. These new engines used a redesigned crankcase which did not feature the fairings behind the magneto, primary drive cases and carburettor pocket. They were of a neater appearance and allowed cooling air onto the main bearing housings, a problem often solved on earlier engines by drilling or cutting away the fairings. The replacement crankcases were complimented by a new gearbox case, which again did not feature the now extraneous fairings and a primary chaincase of smaller, slimmer and neater appearance. The chaincases were used by many works trials teams on their earlier engines, for they were much narrower and consequently avoided the scenery in tight trials sections. The new castings not only looked better but allowed the ingress of cooling air. Unfortunately many users believed them to be inferior in strength because of the absence of fairings. This doubt was never proven. Apart from gearbox ratio changes, the two new engines shared identical bottom halves, but the scrambler was equipped with its own, smaller flywheel cover.

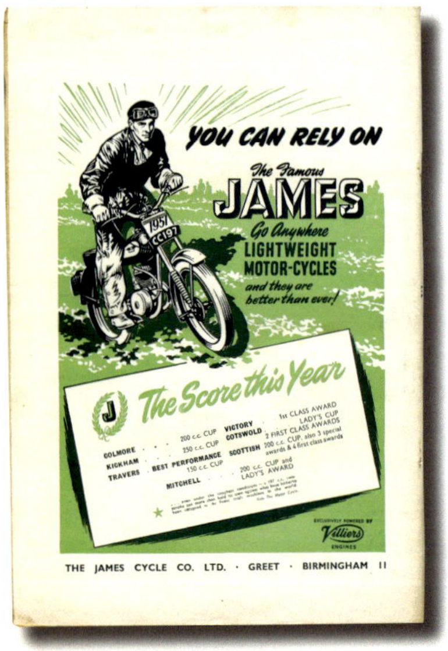

Different carburettors

To produce the trials unit a 32A cylinder and Villiers S25 carburettor were used, whereas the scrambler was fitted with the 34A cylinder and an Amal 1$^{3}/_{16}$ inch Monobloc carburettor. Good as they were, the new engines were still fitted with the original bob-weighted "hammer head" 9E crankshafts, but many user companies specified the superior Alpha product to increase the unit's reliability. The new scrambles engine saw limited service for it was soon to be ousted by another new Villiers design, the Starmaker, but the trials unit carried on to the end, seeing service in the vast majority of British two-stroke powered trials machines.

For decades the Villiers company had supplied nothing more than commuter engines to the motorcycle manufacturers, who then modified them by fitting items made by the peripheral manufacturers who had sprung up to fill this void. Villiers could have done the job themselves but chose not to. The expertise was on hand at the factory and an uprated 250 could have been made, which would have had a better reliability factor than the products on offer. In 1962 this state of affairs finally came to an end when Villiers at last shook off their conservative cloak of relative respectability and produced their first true competition engine. This was the exciting Starmaker, which is dealt with in Chapter 10.

1966 - 1967 Sprite Monza trials (with Starmaker engine)

Sprite

The Sprite was born of government taxation regulations, in that any new motorcycle sold was subject to the payment of Purchase Tax - but there was a legal loophole providing a way of avoiding payment. If the bike was sold in kit-form it was tax exempted, but the term kit-form was very vague. In essence most of the machinery sold in this way simply required the fitment of the wheels and engine package, a task that would have taken the average spanner man an hour or two, but it saved a tenth of the total purchase price.

The Sprite was the idea of Frank "Hippy" Hipkin, a motorcycle dealer and weekend scrambler from Handsworth in Birmingham, who strived to build a competitive bike that incorporated all the features he liked. The result was a hybrid, which used a Cotton Cougar duplex chassis - converted to triple front down tubes - Norton telescopic forks and a Villiers 36A engine, the latter featuring a re-ported Greeves cylinder barrel. An Alpha full-circle crankshaft was also fitted, to cope with the power output of the tuned engine. British Hub Co - Motoloy - full-width aluminium hubs were employed for the same reason.

An initial production run of just six bikes sold instantly, which prompted a move to bigger premises in Smethwick, which saw increased output and a new 32A powered trials machine together with a 500cc Triumph powered scrambler. The following year saw another move, to Eel Street, Oldbury and the fitment of home designed leading link front forks, the stock of forks from Bracebridge Street having been exhausted.

The Starmaker engine was the next unit to be fitted, with the introduction of the Monza scrambler in 1966, but this association with Villiers was soon to end when they ceased manufacture and new owner Manganese Bronze steadfastly refused to supply any other outside organisations.

The Sprite story does not end here, for Frank Hipkin had seen fit to establish links with Maico and Husqvarna for the scramblers and Sachs for his trials machines. The results of this was a new range of bikes, with improved frames and long-travel suspension, but best of all the big scramblers were now powered by copies of the 360 Husqvarna - built by Sprite Developments Ltd. A further move was needed to cope with increased production with Sprite again setting up a factory in Stourbridge Road, Halesowen.

Production soared with a contract to supply thousands of 405cc Goldfinger scramblers to the USA for the American Eagle company. But, when American Eagle collapsed so did Sprite. Frank Hipkin soldiered on for a while, fulfilling his lesser contract obligations, but dwindling sales forced him to call it a day in 1974.

Butler

During 1963, Chris Butler built himself a trials bike to contest (with good effect) the numerous events held in the Midlands and Eastern ACU areas. Chris was an expert in the manufacture of fibreglass accessories for off-road motorcycles and his wares sold well to the trade as well as to private owners, with Sammy Miller using examples on his legendary lightweight 500 Ariel HT5. The first Butler machine used a homemade square-section frame and leading-link forks (based on the steering head angles and frame geometry of the Greeves Scottish) and naturally featured many of the Butler fibreglass products, together with a 9E Villiers engine which was fitted with a Parkinson 250 conversion kit.

After being asked to build numerous replicas of his successful trials prototype, Chris decided to enter the manufacturing arena and after further refinements, marketed frame kits for the 1964 season. Initially the Butler was sold as a kit, to which the owner only had to add a set of wheels and an engine package to end up with a handsome and competitive machine. Later came complete machines, not only for the trials rider, but now the scrambler rider was also catered for. Three trials machines were listed; the Tempest that used a standard 32A engine, the Fury that was fitted with the alloy Parkinson cylinder conversion, and the Spitfire that utilised the Starmaker engine. Now being a motorcycle manufacturer in his own right, Chris Butler exhibited his product range at the London Earls Court Show in November 1964.

To prove these new models, Midland Centre trials expert John Lee joined the Butler factory as a works rider, with Olga Kevelos helping to spread the fortunes of the marque by giving sterling performances in both the 1964 and 1965 Scottish Six Days Trial. Both trials and scrambling activities continued during 1966, with John Lee notching up some very good feet-up results. During the August of that year a works bike was entered in the Swedish run International Six Days Trial, in the hands of Brian Bonny. But alas, the forth day saw the rear wheel of the Butler break up and put Brian out of the event, a tragic end to such a meritorious effort, for up to that time he was in the running for a coveted Gold Medal – a creditable feat on such a difficult event.

The take-over of the Villiers empire by the Manganese Bronze company and the turmoil which ensued, spelled out the end of Butler motorcycle manufacture with Chris Butler reverting to his fibreglass products and accessories. During the 1980s the product range was once again increased, this time to include ocean-going yachts. Being a man who wanted to prove his products, as he had initially demonstrated with the trials bike, he went on to win three Transatlantic single-handed yacht races in craft of his own manufacture.

Greeves – The Scrambles Scene

In the early days the relatively standard Villiers motor was bolted straight into the frame of the competition machines, but once a keen interest in scrambling was reached, a certain amount of engine tuning was carried out prior to fitting. Villiers would not, and indeed strongly advised against, any engine tuning, saying that their product was adequate for its job, but this did not include competition work. With the works teams fighting it out every weekend on the scrambles tracks, every last ounce of power was needed, but with the standard Villiers motor this led to disaster, as it just wasn't strong enough to sustain the continued hammering it was given. Many firms came up with tuning goodies to increase the power output, whilst others produced replacement parts to sustain power and it was to these companies that Greeves turned to ensure that they had the edge over their competitors.

The new Greeves scramblers started to make a name for themselves during the mid fifties, but it was the arrival of Brian Stonebridge in January 1957 that saw the fortunes of this small factory change for the better. Stonebridge had been a works rider for BSA and Matchless, and during his time at the former had learned the art of two-stroke tuning from Hermann Meier, who was working on the quick 150cc Bantam project. Within a few weeks the power output of the Greeves scramblers was nearly doubled, with the modified engines being tested on a home-brewed dynamometer made from a Ford lorry axle. The device was a crude but effective piece of apparatus, designed by Bert Greeves who had learned the dyno trade as a draughtsman with Heenan and Froude in the 1930s, before his Invacar days.

Dave Bradley with the 1951 Greeves experimental XP1 scrambler - 122cc 10D

Many early experiments used Bantam technology as well as parts which looked like they came from a Bantam, for example the early Stonebrige engines sported central plug cylinder heads that were nothing like the Villiers heads. The Vale-Onslow 250 conversion was also tested, being used by Stonebridge during the 1958 season. Later a Hermann Meier expansion chamber exhaust system was even tried, which led the team to try other systems, but at that time the two-stroke expansion chamber shape was an unknown art, and regular use was made of the low slung ultra noisy flat megga as it gave a couple of extra bhp over the short open pipe still favoured during the earlier part of the period.

In 1958 the first square section alloy cylinder was produced, which became the forerunner of the MDS component. This original cylinder featured detachable transfer ports, to ease development, and a hard chrome plated bore which was applied by the Van der Horst company in Germany, for at that time no English firm could carry out the work to the standard required. The cylinder was a direct replacement for the Villiers cast iron component, even using the original holding down studs for the four long alloy sleeve bolts. The studs used a Whitworth thread in the crankcase and a fine cycle thread for the cylinder nuts; but this thread proved to be unsatisfactory in the alloy sleeve bolts, the specification being later changed to all Whitworth studs. As this cylinder was a 250 conversion for the 197 motor, it used a new 66 mm piston developed by Hepolite. The new piston used a pair of thinner rings, which delayed the onset of ring flutter way above the maximum rpm of the original 197 motor, enabling even higher speeds to be attained.

The production cylinder was cast in the Greeves works own foundry and was a direct descendant of a prototype detachable transfer-port iron cylinder, which had first been seen at the Welsh three day trial of 1958. The alloy cylinder was used on the works bikes for the ISDT, held that year in Austria, Stonebridge gaining a gold medal for his efforts. The square alloy cylinder was refined, re-ported on a number of occasions, given a corrugated cast in iron liner (for Bert Greeves did not want to be dependent on a foreign supplier) and became a standard fitment on the MCS and MDS motocross models, although it was available as an optional extra on other machines.

Attempts by British firms to chrome-plate the cylinders on a commercial scale were totally unacceptable, which led Greeves to utilise its own foundry to cast the alloy muff onto the cast iron corrugated liner. This casting technique was another compromise, for a chrome bore would have equalised the expansion rates between the piston and cylinder, which would have allowed an even smaller running clearance.

1952 Greeves XP4 (the fourth experimental Prototype) trials with 6E 197cc 3-speed engine

The Worlds most potent production 250 cc. Scrambler ! !

Greeves **Proudly Present**

The 250 cc. Moto Cross Special Model 24MCS

DEVELOPED FROM THE MACHINE THAT WON DAVE BICKERS THE 1960 250 cc. EUROPEAN MOTO CROSS CHAMPIONSHIP

The need for a full 250 scrambles engine had been felt by Brian Stonebridge earlier and in 1957 he had experimented with the new twin cylinder 2T Villiers unit. Although it looked promising on the dyno, it proved to be a handful on the track as its power delivery characteristics were all wrong. The factory did make a twin scrambler in 1958 but this was no better than the Stonebridge machine and only 32 were sold, but it did find favour with the street scrambler fraternity in the United States, who wanted the looks and noise of an off-road machine without the necessary performance.

For the 1959 Coupe d'Europe Motocross championship series, Stonebridge decided that an engine which delivered more low to mid range power would have the edge over the two-strokes high but narrow top end power band performance, constructing himself an NSU Max powered Hawkstone to prove his point. Bert Greeves was not happy to find out that his employees had been messing about with the company's product and nearly sacked mechanic Bob Mills on the spot for being involved in the project, but Brian Stonebridge saved the day by convincing the boss that it would work. The hybrid was finally approved when Bert Greeves pointed out that the heavier engine would test his frame design to a higher degree and thus ensure the safety of the average rider. The Max was not used on every round of the championship, for Stonebridge reverted to the detachable transfer port Greeves cylindered engine when the track suited its characteristics.

Greeves SAS scrambler with later SCS rear hub

1960 Greeves 24 SCS Hawkstone Scrambler

The competitions successes of the Greeves factory in 1959 were short lived, for in the October of that year Brian Stonebridge was tragically killed. Whilst returning from a visit to the Hepolite factory, the car in which Stonebridge and Bert Greeves were travelling was involved in a head-on collision, which left the factory boss with only minor injuries but the star rider was killed outright. The Greeves concern carried on as best it could, launching the young and inexperienced Dave Bickers onto the European motocross scene. Bickers, who had been an apprentice to Stonebridge, did not disgrace himself and took on his new role with increased enthusiasm, going on to gain European titles back-to-back in both 1960 and 1961.

The Villiers company finally realised that there was a real need for a 250 competition engine, after witnessing the upsurgence of the after-market conversions and introduced the 31A (a 246cc engine of 66 x 72 mm bore and stroke) road and trials engine in 1958 together with the 33A scrambles motor. By 1960 Villiers had introduced the 32A that Greeves used in its trials bikes, and the 34A for scrambles duties. The new "over-the-counter" Greeves high performance alloy cylinder, stated as producing 21 bhp (but the works engines produced more) was fitted to the top of the range machines, but this began to put a strain on the standard Villiers bottom half. To counter this problem the factory began to use the Alpha full circle crankshaft, which had just become available, but this variation to specification was only available to the works riders. The use of the Greeves cylinder and the Alpha crank enabled Dave Bickers to take the 1960 and 1961 European Motocross Championships, as mentioned above.

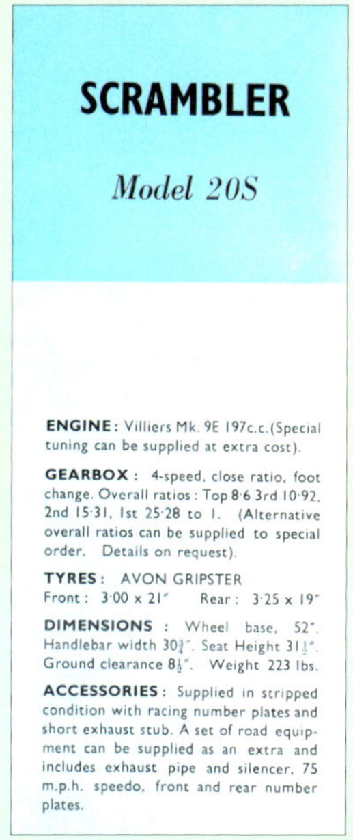

SCRAMBLER

Model 20S

ENGINE: Villiers Mk. 9E 197c.c. (Special tuning can be supplied at extra cost).

GEARBOX: 4-speed, close ratio, foot change. Overall ratios: Top 8·6 3rd 10·92, 2nd 15·31, 1st 25·28 to 1. (Alternative overall ratios can be supplied to special order. Details on request).

TYRES: AVON GRIPSTER
Front: 3·00 x 21" Rear: 3·25 x 19"

DIMENSIONS: Wheel base, 52". Handlebar width 30¾". Seat Height 31½". Ground clearance 8½". Weight 223 lbs.

ACCESSORIES: Supplied in stripped condition with racing number plates and short exhaust stub. A set of road equipment can be supplied as an extra and includes exhaust pipe and silencer, 75 m.p.h. speedo, front and rear number plates.

Factory fresh 1963 RAS Silverstone

Greeves Road Racing - the Silverstone era

During the winter of 1961-1962 other developments were taking place outside the Greeves factory, this time on the road race scene. Having sampled the delights of racing a 2T powered roadster in the production class, on loan from Chelmsford-based dealer Derek Cornell for the 1961 season, privateer Reg Everett decided to build a single cylinder Greeves based racer. Reg liked the road holding of the roadster that he subsequently modified for 250 class racing, but wanted a faster engine to mix it with the big boys, so was born the idea of using a modified motocross engine.

Reg had met up with Greeves competition shop engineer Bob Mills whilst preparing his twin for the Silverstone 1,000 kilometer race, and later contacted him at the factory about the single cylinder racer project. At first Bob said it could not be done, and could not help as nothing was suitable for a road racer, but then changed his mind when he realised that the idea was feasible. On an unofficial basis, Bob organised the parts that Reg required to complete his racer. The new machine was assembled in Reg Everett's front room and comprised a roadster frame and forks, a motocross alloy tank, Manx Norton seat and full-width Motoloy hubs laced to alloy rims and shod with Avon racing tyres. The $1\frac{9}{32}$ inch Amal GP carburettor, which came from a BSA Gold Star, was fitted to a home-brewed stub with a remote mounted float chamber.

Tom Phillips, Greeves 246cc RAS Silverstone, Lightweight TT 1963

The 1962 racing season saw the Everett-Greeves Special gain a host of wins at both club and national level against many established riders of the day. It was at Snetterton in August 1962 that Brian Woolley had a look at the motocross based engine with a view to changing the power delivery characteristics. He suggested a few modifications could be carried out, but at this stage he did not become involved with the project. The only tuning done during that season was when Bob Mills presented Reg with an expansion chamber, during one of his many unofficial trips to the factory. Reg Everett has nothing but the highest praise for the late Bob Mills, for he was the only contact at the Greeves factory, and without his enthusiastic help the project would have been doomed.

It was after the internal inspection of the Everett Special that Brian Woolley entered into a long correspondence with Bert Greeves, to sow the seeds for a need for a road race variant. This resulted in a visit to the factory to finalise the plans for the new Greeves racer, to which Brian contributed specific recommendations on porting, carburettor and exhaust dimensions. This involvement resulted in Brian Woolley being taken on as a freelance development engineer from 1963, and a happy association with the marque for many years.

The father of the Greeves Silverstone, Reg Everett on the machine he built and raced during 1962

At the early stage of the Everett Special's development it is not certain whether Bert Greeves knew about it, but when Reg began to gain results he must have known, for the special achieved much publicity. In the October of 1962 Bert Greeves tested the Everett Special at Brands Hatch, putting in a lap time of 69 secs on the Indy circuit, and this heralded the unveiling of the all-new Greeves built Special at the Earls Court show in November that year. The new bike was built as a trainer for beginners to racing, but showed its motocross pedigree by using a high level expansion chamber. The rest of the bike was pure road racer. The engine was a Greeves modified 34A Villiers unit, that used an alloy cylinder and a 1¼ in Amal GP carburettor. The one-off special led to the production 24RAS Silverstone, which employed the new Villiers 36A motor with a much modified alloy cylinder, and a 1⅜ ins GP carburettor, this producing an impressive 31 bhp at 7,400 rpm.

The production 24RAS Silverstone used a low level expansion chamber, and a total of 94 models were built before it was dropped from the range in May 1964. At 250 cc club level the new Silverstone proved to be a very competitive racer, and was responsible for introducing many riders to the thrill of road racing, as well as gaining the 1963 ACU 250 Star in the hands of Tom Phillips.

The first production RAS Silverstone (No 102) went to the famous Guildford tuner, Francis Beart, who prepared it for Joe Dunphy to ride, the combination achieving considerable success. This alliance only lasted for the 1963 season, but during this time both Beart and Dunphy fed back much useful data to the factory, used to develop the Mk 2 Silverstone. Number 103 went to Brian Woolley and was ridden by Horace "Crasher" Crowther, who was equally successful, once the two stroke's fickle technique had been mastered. The early season debut of the RAS was marred by seizures and ring breakages, but once the critical mixture and ignition settings had been found the RAS Greeves began to fly and set a pattern that no other British factory could emulate. Reg Everett took over the Woolley RAS (Horace having crashed and injured himself again) after he had written off the factory prototype at Mallory Park, due to the bad handling which he always complained of, saying that, 'My special handled better than the factory prototype'.

The 1963 TT saw no fewer than six Greeves entered for the Lightweight race, but only one was to finish; entered by Reg Orpin and piloted by Rhodesian Allan Harris. Orpin was a confirmed four-stroke man, the only contact with two-strokes being his lawn mowing on Sunday afternoons, so why the sudden change? During a track testing day at Brands Hatch in early May, Greeves director Derry Preston-Cobb invited Reg to try the Silverstone, but Reg declined and suggested that his rider Allan Harris have a go. During the morning Allan put in a dozen fast laps coming within half a second of the class lap record, but in the afternoon he dropped it in a big way. Reg being a man of honour approached Preston-Cobb, cheque book in hand, and purchased the damaged Silverstone, saying: 'As my rider dropped it, I'd better buy the damned thing.' Once rebuilt the Orpin/Harris Silverstone put up some very creditable performances on the main land tracks, prior to the TT, where he finished eighth at an average of 81.47 mph.

The original one-off Greeves-built Special prototype as displayed by the company at the 1962 Earls Court Show

Greeves Trials – Scottish & Anglian era

During the intensive Challenger and Silverstone development period, the trials bike took a back seat, but nevertheless it too received its fair share of modifications to make it one of the best machines of its day. Starting with the first true Scottish (the 20TA in 1958), the trials bike was developed from a clubman mount to become an international winner, which only ceased when the supply of Villiers engines dried up. The 20TA Scottish used a standard 9E Villiers trials specification engine, which differed from the road engine in having a long induction stub, wide ratio gears and a weighted flywheel. Later an S version was added to the range, the S denoting the use of a mildly tuned engine. In 1959 the first 250, the 24TAS, was announced, which used the new 31A Villiers engine, but this was basically still a road engine. The same can be said about the 32A engine that powered the TC and the TD variants. But with the next machine, the 24TES of 1962, the Villiers motor was transformed by the use of the scrambles developed alloy cylinder, which put the Essex factory on the road to many successes.

The square cylinder used on the trials bikes differed in that it did not use the symmetrical combustion chamber shape found on the scrambles and road racing engines. Instead the shape reverted to a hemispherical chamber to the rear of the cylinder, with a broad squish band to the front. Externally the head was readily identifiable, as the plug was positioned slightly to the rear. Porting changes were made to the cylinder, and this allied to a lower compression ratio, a Villiers S25 carburettor and a heavyweight flywheel, ensured that the engine would plonk away at tickover and accelerate smoothly to its maximum operating rpm. Exhaust arrangements differed on the TES models; with the Mk 1 having an expansion

Greeves pre-production 24TFS trials

1956 Greeves 20T trials two years before the Scottish model name was introduced

chamber positioned over the magneto and exiting behind the rear sub frame. The Mk 2 used a square section pipe and silencer box that tucked in tightly over the primary drive casing, again exiting behind the sub frame. This was by no means the only exhaust system used on the trials machines, for the bikes used for six day events originally employed the up and over systems of the TA - TC range, and then a simple round pipe and Peco type silencer, tucked in tightly on the left side of the machine.

When the Challenger engine was created the same cylinder holding down stud spacing as the Villiers engine were used, which enabled the new cylinder to be used on the second generation of trials engines. The 24TFS of 1965 used a Villiers 32A trials specification engine with a Challenger cylinder fed by an S25 carburettor. This specification continued on the 24 TGS Anglian trials bike for the 1966 season, but by then the Villiers 37A bottom end was being used. The TFS again used an expansion chamber type exhaust on the right hand side of the machine, but the new Anglians used a round exhaust pipe, and a small silencer mounted at 45 degrees, tucked in very close on the left side of the bike. This system was first seen on the development TFS that was campaigned successfully by works rider Don Smith during the period. Carburettor arrangements had also changed, for the TGS Anglian used the Amal Monobloc whereas the model H and J Anglians used the new Amal Concentric instrument.

The Anglian was the last - and the best - Villiers based trials machine ever produced by the Greeves factory. It enabled Billy Wilkinson to win the Scottish Six Day Trial in 1969, the only time the factory won it, but they had been close to it on several previous occasions. By now the Spanish trials machines were showing their worth, and over-shadowing the Greeves Anglian. What was needed was a new generation of bikes to beat them. Don Smith proposed a Challenger engined machine based on his experiences with his development machines, but Bert Greeves vetoed any such idea having doubts as to the market value of such a machine. The final blow came with the take-over of the Villiers Empire by Manganese Bronze, and the supply of engines dried up for the Anglian range. A replacement trials bike was hurriedly put together, this time using an Austrian Puch engine, but after a long wait for production to start, the bike failed to impress trials riders. The six-speed engine thrived on revs, had little or no flywheel effect and used a crankshaft-mounted clutch, its characteristics totally alien to the job for which it was intended. All was not lost, for the Puch engined Pathfinder did find favour on the enduro scene, a job to which it was much better suited.

TRIALS

Model 20T

ENGINE: Villiers Mk. 9E 197 c.c. (A tuned engine can be supplied at extra cost).

GEARBOX: 4-speed, foot change, wide ratio. Overall ratios: Top 7·45, 3rd 9·99, 2nd 17·89, Ist 26·83 to I. (Alternative overall ratios can be supplied to special order. Details on request).

TYRES: DUNLOP TRIALS UNIVERSAL Front: 2·75" x 21" Rear: 4·00" x 18"

DIMENSIONS: Wheel Base, 52". Handlebar width 30¾". Seat Height 31½". Ground clearance 8½". Weight 233 lbs.

ACCESSORIES: 75 m.p.h. speedo, bulb horn and front and rear number plates.

Norman

Prior to the 1952 season the Ashford, Kent-based Norman Motorcycles concern never offered a competition mount to the general public, but as many other lightweight motorcycle manufacturers did, they fielded a semi-official works trials team. Two years previous to the launch of the BC (Model B Competition) a works trio of Karl Pugh, Ian McIntyre and Alan Grant entered the Scottish Six Day Trial. Running with the James team as the only lightweight contenders, the Norman team all ended with awards, which they continued to gain during the subsequent British championship season.

The first production competition mount – the B2C of 1952 – was fitted with the three-speed 6E engine unit, but this specification could be changed to the 10D unit on special order. From 1954 the Albion type four-speed gearbox could even be specified, a gearbox that was tried and tested by the works team in the Scottish some two years beforehand. Initially using a rigid rear end, the competition mount gained (on special order) a swinging arm rear suspension system the following year and used in conjunction with 2.75 x 21 inch front and 4.00 x 19 inch rear tyres (a novelty on the smaller bikes then) this combination proved popular. At the same time the opportunity was taken to fit the improved 7E competition motor, equipped with the three or four-speed gearbox.

The 1956 season saw many changes to the B2C, which now became the B2C/S (Model B, 200cc, Competition, Springer) that used the trials specification 9E engine unit. Following fashion, the Norman factory now fitted the Armstrong leading link front forks and full-width 6 inch brakes, a retrograde step in the eyes of some riders who considered these items to be too heavy for trials use. This was factually correct, for the competition machine now weighed in at 237 lb instead of the 190 lb of the old rigid mount, despite the use of alloy mudguards and a 1.75 gallon fuel tank. The Norman was a little heavier than its rivals, but this slight disadvantage was far outweighed by the results it obtained in experienced hands, and it was most certainly one of the prettier lightweight machines available during the period.

As Norman was a small company, production line space for the building of the roadster range was always at a premium, and the B2C was terminated in 1960. But, with the advent of the 246cc Villiers engines, the competition Normans began a new lease of life. After a short break the B4C was introduced, this dual purpose machine being supplied in either trials or scrambles form. The difference was mainly in the engine package, with the trials specification 32A engine being fitted to the trials mount and the 34A scrambles specification motor being used in the scrambler, the only other major difference was in the tyre fitment. The B4 competition model was now using the roadster frame, which gave an amazing 9 inch ground clearance, even though the rear wheel diameter had been decreased to 18 inch. The B4C, arguably the best competition Norman, was to be the last, for in 1961 the whole competitions range was axed followed one year later by the factory itself. In 1962 Norman Motorcycles Ltd of Beaver Road, Ashford, Kent, ceased to exist, the factory gates having closed for the final time.

Maker of History
COTTON
The Motorcycle Masterpiece

The COTTON Trials Model "SPECIAL"

Bill Jackson (250 Cotton) Cotswold Scramble 29th June 1963

Cotton

When E Cotton recommenced motorcycle manufacture in 1954, initial production was based on Villiers powered roadster models, as was the range of many other smaller manufacturers of this period, but by 1956 a trials model was also included in the line-up. The first competition machine used the 9E engine, Metal Profile front forks and wheel hubs and Girling rear suspension units. Weighing in at 250 lbs the new trials machine was merely a modified roadster with all the inherent penalties of such a move. By 1959 the trials model had gained Armstrong leading link forks – but had shed little of its weight – and was joined by a new scrambles machine that used the newly introduced Villiers 33A 246cc engine unit. This motor was soon replaced by the uprated 34A scrambles unit in 1961. During the same year a duplex cradle frame was also introduced, together with a Cotton designed cush drive system for the rear hub.

The trials machine was uprated at the same time, receiving the duplex frame and the 32A engine unit, but even with the larger motor, this model had shed some 5 lbs in weight over its 197cc predecessor. To further enhance power and weight-saving, the trials model was offered with the Villiers 36A motor fitted with a Parkinson alloy top end during 1963. Motoloy alloy hubs were also specified at the same time.

The second generation scrambles machine, the Cougar, was introduced in 1961. This used a lighter and lower duplex frame, smaller Italian wheel hubs and the radical Cross alloy top end. This machine led to the introduction of the third generation scramblers that were to be powered by the brand new Villiers Starmaker motor, with the introduction of the Cotton Cobra in 1962.

Time was beginning to run out for the Villiers engined machines and Cotton now looked into the fitment of the Triumph twin in order to keep up with the Rickman Metisse models which had become top dogs on the scrambles tracks. The Triumph powered machines were developed by Arthur Lampkin and marketed in kit form to avoid the payment of purchase tax. Before the final demise of the Villiers power units, Cotton put into production the 37A Trials model. Using the latest Villiers 246cc engine, this machine was probably the best of the trials machines, with its lighter and longer wheel base frame. Forks, with 7 inch movement, now came from Metal Profile and the total weight of the package was down to an incredible 198 lbs.

The Manganese Bronze buy-out of the Villiers empire did not stop production at the Gloucester factory straight away, for they had seen fit to establish links with the DMW factory in the supply of power units to tide them over for another couple of years. In 1967 the Cossack scrambler was in production, using an Alpha bottom end with a DMW cylinder and head. This last scrambler was also equipped with Metal Profile forks, a fact noted by the motorcycle press, who stated that the Metal Profile company were now manufacturing more of the Cossack's components than Cotton themselves. On the trials side, Cotton continued to use the DMW built 37A motors, but soon this supply dwindled and they had to look further afield to acquire suitable power units, ending up with the Italian-built Minarelli engine.

From 1968 no further Villiers engined machines were made at the Vulcan Works, but Cotton soldiered on, using Minarelli engines in the trials mount, until 1976 when, in financial difficulties, operations ceased. The company was finally swallowed up by CCM during October 1980. The name did reappear some time later, but this time it was on a Rotax powered road racer.

1961 Cotton Cougar scramble with 34A engine with Cross top-end conversion

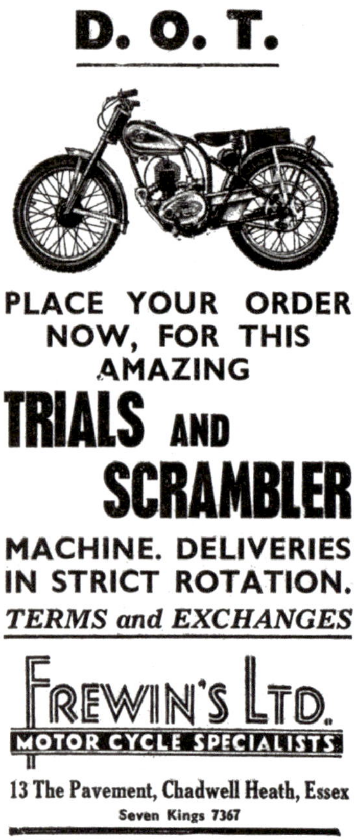

DOT

Formed in 1903 by Harry Reed, the Manchester based DOT Cycle & Motor Manufacturing Co Ltd of Arundel Street, Hulme, used early proprietary engine units to power its machinery. A TT win in 1908 and further results in the 1920s ensured the fortunes of the company, but in March 1926 they were forced into voluntary liquidation due to mounting debts. In August 1926 the company was re-established this time with Thomas Sawyer at the helm, but the Great Depression of the 1930s became its downfall and the company again fell on hard times and ceased motorcycle production in 1934.

Although the manufacture of motorcycles had ceased, the name lived on when Burnard Scott Wade took over as the new boss at the Arundel Street factory, but now production was limited to bicycles and handcarts. One steady seller was the three-wheeled Pedal Truck – a tradesman's truck for carrying the tools of his trade – which at times was adapted to meet the needs of ice cream salesmen, window cleaners and milkmen.

When the war started a need for a small economical motorised truck was established, and during 1940 the DOT Pedal Truck was converted to the Motor Truck with the inclusion of a Villiers 122cc engine unit. Production was once again resumed, with the building of these tradesmen's three-wheelers, many of which were exported.

Motorcycle production restarted in 1949 with the introduction of a pair of utility models that used rigid rear ends and girder forks. The 125 – in production for one year only – used the 10D engine unit, whereas the 200 model was equipped with the 6E unit. The 200 stayed in production for four years, receiving telescopic forks in 1951 and a swinging arm rear end in 1953.

The first post-war competition DOT arrived in 1950, this being the 6E powered scrambler, which featured telescopic forks, but as then it utilised a rigid rear end until replaced by the swinging arm system in 1953. For the 1954 season the 8E was the preferred engine unit, with both a trials and scrambler being offered; the trials machine being supplied with a rigid rear end, as an optional extra to suit the traditionalist rider.

DOT did not only build off-road competition machines, for in 1951 they entered a three-man team in the newly introduced Isle of Man Ultra Lightweight (125cc) TT. Using highly tuned 10D motors that were tilted forward in the square tube frames, the trio won the Manufacturers team prize for the Manchester company, even though they were outclassed by the works FB Mondial and Montesa opposition. The DOT entries finished 7th, 11th and 12th, ridden by EVC Hardy, G Horn and G Newman. The following year, 1952, Hardy came home 10th in the same event, but Newman was forced out through mechanical troubles. The mounts this year were upright cylinder versions of the previous year's racers, but now they featured reverse cylinder heads, Albion racing gearboxes and a rotary inlet valve sited behind the cylinder.

Pride in Achievement
with the

PIVOTING ARM FRONT FORK

Dot

ENTHUSIASTS, COMPARE THIS SPECIFICATION

- ★ Lightweight frame of immense strength and lateral rigidity. Tubes of manganese molybdenum.
- ★ Pivoting arm suspension, front and rear. $4\frac{1}{2}''$ rear wheel displacement and over 6″ front wheel displacement. Hydraulically controlled spring units.
- ★ Tuned high-compression engine with 3 or 4 speed gears (wide or close ratio).
- ★ Journal bearing hubs with 6″ diameter brakes, oscillating brake plates on front gives unrestricted fork action (patent applied for).
- ★ Long dual seat standard on all models.
- ★ Reinforced unbendable handlebars, dural mudguards, and centre and prop stands.
- ★ Tyres fitted with security bolts on both wheels.

DOT CYCLE & MOTOR MANUFACTURING CO. LTD.

ARUNDEL ST. and ELLESMERE ST. WORKS, MANCHESTER 15

Telephone : Blackfriars 5472

DOT works rider Bill Barugh - 1955

With the introduction of the competition model line up for the following season (two standard trials mounts, two standard scramblers, plus a pair of special works replicas), all models featured the DOT type leading link forks, first seen on the previous years Mancunian roadster, together with 21 inch front wheels and 19 inch rears - the trials works replica being fitted with a 400 x 18 inch rear tyre.

During the 1950s DOT enjoyed a virtual monopoly in the field of motorcycle competition riding, building both trials and scrambles machines that won many major events in the hands of works rider Bill Barugh. Even holding this monopoly, DOT did not stand still and developed many further winning Scott Wade designs, to become the top competitions factory of that decade.

For the 1959 season a move was made to use the Villiers 246cc single cylinder motors, initially using the 31A motor for the trials mount and the 33A for the scrambler, these units were superceded by the 32A and the 34A the following season, when another six model line-up was announced – the SH, SCH and SDH scramblers together with the THX, TDHX and the Works Replica trials mounts.

The 1962 season saw the introduction of the Demon scrambler, perhaps the best remembered and most feared of all Dot competition mounts. This machine used the newly introduced square tube frame that was fitted with a Marcelle equipped 34A engine, later to be re-equipped with a similarly equipped 36A for the 1963 season, and an Alpha/DOT engine unit for the 1965 season, when it was renamed the White Strength. Soon after the first showing of the Demon, the Demon International was launched, using the new Villiers Starmaker engine unit. In the meantime the Trials 250 and the Works Replica trials mount were still in production, only to be phased out in 1968 due to the drying up of the Villiers power units. During this period the Manchester concern was fighting a head-on battle with its southern rival Greeves, fielding riders such as Eric Adcock, Alan Clough and Pat Lamper to fly the flag for this northern company.

By 1965 DOT were only building competition machines, the roadster range having been phased out in 1960, and fielded only four models; the Trials 250, the Works Replica Trials, the Demon and the Alpha/DOT Demon Special. But in 1967 these were joined by a 360 Demon (78.7 x 74 mm) – first seen at the Blackpool show of May 1965 - which again used an engine unit of Alpha/DOT/Albion manufacture that was again named the White Strength in honour of its white and silver finish. Initially this machine was envisaged to be sold alternatively as a 350 (77.5 x 74 mm) but this idea was shelved. The same year saw the fitment of the 37A engine into the Trials 250 but one year further on witnessed the end of Villiers involvement.

DOT followed the lead of other ex-Villiers users who had been left high and dry by the Norton Villiers consortium and looked for alternative power plants, entering the 1970s using a mixture of Husqvarna and Minarelli engines, but by 1977 even production of these machines had ceased.

When the production of motorcycles finally ended, DOT Motorcycles continued with the manufacture of DOT Armstrong shock absorbers from their Ellesmere Street premises - the Arundel Street factory having been bombed out in 1942. Today the company with a staff of four is still in existence, under the guidance of Michael Wade, making DOT cycle parts to service the needs of owners worldwide.

1963 DOT Demon Scrambler

DMW 200 Moto-Cross 1954

DMW Competition model with the 197cc engine, 1954

DMW

When the Metal Profile Co bought out the rights to DMW suspension components, it was seen as an ideal opportunity to use the newly acquired name to promote MP sporting products. To this end, DMW Motorcycles was formed and Michael Riley, BSA development engineer and competition rider, was brought in to design a significantly different, but easily recognisable, mount that would do justice to the company. The first Riley design used a butt-welded lugless plunger suspension frame, constructed from Talbot square section tubing, and was an all-round competition mount. First competition outings for the design were in 1948 and 1949 at the Scottish Six Day Trial and by 1950 DMW had an official works supplied clubman team in the International Six Day Trial, held that year in Wales.

Motorcycle production now got underway, with the Competition model – available with a 122 or 197cc engine – coming on line for the 1951 season. Again used in the 1951 and 1952 ISDT, the DMW lightweights started to gain credibility, which was further enhanced by the achievements of Jack Walton, who was responsible for many successes on the scrambles tracks of the Midlands.

Like rivals DOT, DMW entered the road racing arena in 1951. The Motor Cycle of the 8th February that year reported, 'Four private entrants for the 125cc class in the TT have ordered DMW frames. In all DMW are to make twelve special frames for this particular class in racing. The frames will be of square-section tubing, weighing only 10 to 11 lbs.' HA Grindley finished 8th in the 1951 TT, averaging 56.9 mph for the 2-lap 75.46 mile race.

The first mount offered for competition was the plunger frame 4S, which was available with either the 10D or 6E Villiers three-speed engine units, but in 1954 this machine was dropped in favour of a pair of purpose designed machines which both used the new 7E competition motor. Available with three or four-speed gearboxes, these were the 4S trials and the Moto-Cross 2, but they only stayed in production for two years. With the advent of the 9E competition motor, DMW launched a further pair of machines, the Mk6 MX and the Mk7 Trials. These bikes now sported swinging arm rear suspension systems and a box section rear frame spine, with the MX using MP manufactured Earles leading link forks (first seen as an option on the 4S).

With the Mk8 and Mk9 models being roadsters, the next competition mount was the Mk 10 of 1957. Using the Villiers 2T twin, the Mk 10 was a dual-purpose machine, for it was available with close or wide ratio gearbox internals and the appropriate tyres. The potential as a trials machine was overshadowed by its weight, which was given as 288 lbs, and on the scrambles circuit the power delivery characteristics of the "snappy" twin cylinder engine did not endear itself to its riders. Even though this model remained in production until 1961, it soon lost its appeal with the advent of the Villiers 250 single cylinder competition motors.

1967 DMW Highlander fitted with Cotton frame, MP forks and 37A trials engine

For the 1959 season DMW launched the Mk 12 series with the new Mk 12 MX and Mk 12 Trials machines. Still available with 9E motors as an option, the new trials mount used the 32A motor with the MX being fitted with the 33A scrambles unit. The MX machine certainly benefited from this engine fitment, for it instantly lost 10 lbs in weight and gained an extra 5 bhp. The trials variant only lost its weight penalty.

With the advent of a new frame that featured a large square top tube and a tapered square section down tube, first seen on JC Bodenham's ISDT mount, a new generation of DMW competition mounts was announced in 1961; these were the Mk 14 MX, which used the 34A and for its final year of production the 36A motor, together with the Mk 15 Trial which retained the use of the functional 32A unit. The frame of the Mk 15 still used engine cradle plates, but by late 1963 even this feature had disappeared when a conventional round tube duplex cradle frame was introduced.

This frame became the standard fit to the Mk 16 MX, but now it housed a Starmaker engine and was again equipped with Earles forks. The Mk 18 MX was again Starmaker powered, but the Mk 19 of 1964 reverted to the use of the 36A engine, produced mainly for the American off-road market, Being equipped with lights, this machine was christened the Overlander. This machine was the last MX type machine to roll out of the factory gates.

Towards the end of production, the next trials bike was the Mk 17 of 1963 to 1965, when the building of complete machines finished. Dwindling sales and the onslaught of Spanish trials bikes put an end to the DMW competition range, but a discovery of a tax loophole meant that the sale of cheaper kit-form bikes carried on for a few more years. The Mk 17, which also used the tubular frame and Earles forks together with the new Highlander – the last production DMW trials machine - were sold in this way.

The Highlander used the 37A type engine to which had been fitted a cylinder and head of the company's own manufacture, that had first been seen on the Mk 17 in 1963. It also used a Cotton-built frame with MP Ceriani-type forks and MP lightweight hubs.

With the demise of the Villiers empire and the subsequent purchase of the 9E/37A rights, DMW carried on production, but by then it was too late. Nevertheless, DMW continued development and were still using the Highlander machine through to the mid 1970s, but now the engine used an Alpha bottom end and the DMW wide-fin top end. DMW carried on longer than their rivals, only because they had the engine manufacturing facility, but by then long-stroke engines had lost their charm and become outdated.

7 Aftermarket Manufacturers

It was not until the mid fifties that the average motorcyclist, who lusted after a little more in the way of motive power, began to tire of the staid products of the Wolverhampton engine manufacturer. The biggest motorcycle power unit available from Villiers at the turn of the decade was the 197cc Mark 6 E series engine, with a power output of some 8.4 bhp at a meagre 4,000 revs. It was not until 1953 that anything else was available with increased power. A renewed interest in motorcycle sporting activities prompted the building of an updated version of the 197 in 1953, with the introduction of the 8E and its sporting derivative - the 7E - that now produced 9.3 bhp at 4,300rpm. Even this 10% increase in power output was not enough for the rider who used his bike to ride to work during the week and indulged in a bit of sporting action at the weekends. What was needed was a conversion that brought the engine up to a full 250cc to take on other riders in the lightweight class, unleashing a little more power into the bargain.

The two hundred class was born of the Government's motorcycle taxation classes, where the 197cc machine attracted a lower duty rate, with the insurance companies following suit and levying a favourable premium on these small capacity machines. Because of the popularity of these cheaper to run machines, many sports promoters of the day included a class for them in their programme, but again once up against the bigger machines in the two-fifty class, a full 50cc was given away to the opposition.

The Ajax conversion

One of the first companies to offer a full 250cc conversion was B & C Pearson of Wilson Works, Warwick Road, Knowle, Birmingham, who marketed the 'specially Tuned Ajax Alloyclad Conversion' for the 6/8E engines, the price in the late fifties being £14.00. Also available was a conversion for the 9E and alloy cylinders for the 30C and the Villiers 2T twin cylinder engines. Aimed mainly at the Bond Minicar owner who used the 6/8/9E versions of the 197, the Ajax conversion utilised a 66 mm piston to give a swept volume of 246cc. No power output figures were available, but it must be assumed that these conversions delivered in the region of 12 to15 bhp, a figure that the standard A series Villiers engines delivered in non-sporting form.

The conversion was a straight bolt-on accessory, which required nothing more than a piston, head and cylinder change to give the extra capacity and performance that owners yearned for. The cooler running alloy cylinder, with iron liner, was a near copy of the original cast iron Villiers component, which utilised the original inlet manifold and exhaust pipe, but the cylinder head was completely different. Instead of vertical head fins the Ajax head was equipped with horizontal fins, cast at the same pitch as the cylinder fining.

B & C Pearson where quick to realise the need for the cooler running standard and larger capacity cylinders, offering them to an eagerly awaiting public, for nothing else was available at the time. Villiers could have capitalised on this market, but lagged behind in the production of larger capacity engines, producing their 225cc 1H engine in 1953 and the 246cc 2H engine in 1957. Even when the 246cc 31A engine appeared in 1958 it still used the heavyweight low power cast iron cylinder. It was not until 1963 that the first - original fit - alloy cylinder became available, on the Starmaker engine.

Frank Darrieulat

The only other alloy cylinder for the 8E type motors came from sidecar star Frank Darrieulat, which again was a direct replacement for the standard iron component. Manufactured by the Chesterfield, Derbyshire, company of Sheepbridge Engineering, the coarse-finned cylinder featured a three-bolt exhaust fitting, thicker base flange and a chromium plated bore. The chrome plating was applied by the German Mahle process, which Sheepbridge carried out under licence. First seen in 1956 the alloy cylinder range was expanded to include a narrow fin variant the following year.

Vale-Onslow

Another 250 conversion was developed by Hermann Meier and marketed by the Harold Daniel (of Norton TT fame) concern at Forest Hill, South East London. This was the Vale-Onslow conversion, which featured a cast iron 66 mm cylinder and a special (in that it was shorter than the Villiers item) Hepolite piston, together with a cast-in inlet manifold that was tailored to suit the Amal 1$^{3}/_{16}$ inch Monobloc carburettor. The cylinder was identified by the use of heavily interrupted fining that featured two cutaways, one either side of the transfer passages, the fins on the transfer passages being extended to help cool this area. The conversion was available in two forms, a trials conversion with a normally finned head that incorporated a decompressor and a heavily finned squish type head for scrambling, road racing or even roadwork. It was one of the latter that Brian Stonebridge used on his works Greeves during the 1958 scrambles season, alongside his NSU Max engined special.

Later during 1966 Vale-Onslow produced another 66 mm cylinder, but this time it was of all alloy construction and did not feature any interrupted finning. Fitted to Ernie Greer's DOT scrambler, the unit showed promise, but as this was fast approaching the time of the Villiers factory demise, it too faded away.

During this period Villiers were quite happy to churn out mundane roadster engines, oblivious to the fact that their engines were now being used in anger on the weekend clubman's scrambles scene. The torture that these engines were subjected to resulted in many component failures, but the garden shed tuners persevered and tried their hardest to increase both power and reliability. Villiers were not interested in this form of weekend activity and any owner who contacted the factory to enquire about tuning was politely rebuked by the standard company reply, 'The Villiers engine is quite adequate for its intended role and any form of tuning will invalidate the company's warranty.'

On the fledgling trials scene of the early fifties Villiers did recognise the need for a specialised engine, equipping the competition engines with wide-ratio gearboxes and heavy flywheels to suit the sport. Some engines were even treated to an uprated ignition coil but nothing else in order to increase the power output, other than a high compression head.

High compression cylinder heads

When the Villiers Engineering Company talked of high compression heads they considered 8.25:1 to be high, for the standard roadster engines were only 7.25:1, but the need for something even higher was required for the weekend racer. To fulfil this need various companies produced heads for the 197 with compression ratios as high as 9:1 or even 12:1. One company that supplied high compression heads was The Kelston Engineering Co Ltd of Fishponds, Bristol, who manufactured heads for the D, C and E range Villiers engines, as well as 9:1 and 10.5:1 heads for the Vale-Onslow 250cc conversions that could be equipped, with or without the decompressor fitting. These cylinder heads were marketed under the GT 100 label, and by 1960 were sold exclusively through George Todd at his Bristol address. Fred Launchbury took over this business when George took up the position of Deputy Development Manager at BSA.

With the arrival of the Villiers 246cc scrambles engine, designated 33A and introduced in 1958, an increase in power was noted. Received well by the sporting fraternity, the new engine delivered 19 bhp at 6,000rpm but was still hampered by the heavy cast iron cylinder. What was needed here was even more power and a reduction in weight. Villiers could not - or would not - offer this option and so it was again up to the after-market manufacturers of the period to offer an alternative.

Marcelle

Along with after-market cylinder heads came complete top end kits from the various designers and manufacturers of the day. The Marcelle conversion was another tuning aid to increase the power output of the humble Villiers motor, with a compression ratio of 11.5:1, this one was reported as giving 23/24 bhp at a phenomenal 6,500 to 7,000rpm. Designed by Derek Brown of Cromwell Motors, Colchester, this conversion was unique in that it utilised a chrome plated bore (to a depth of 0.0035 inch or 0.09 mm) applied directly to the alloy cylinder and continuing 0.25 inch (6 mm) inside the radiused ports. Both the exhaust and transfer ports had a 50% increase in cross-sectional area - over the 33A - at their entry points, but the transfer ports in the cylinder wall remained as standard, resulting in a higher transfer velocity. Another novel feature of the porting arrangement was that the piston crown uncovered the inlet port by 1/16 inch (1.5 mm) at BDC (Bottom Dead Centre), allowing mixture to flow across the top of the piston, as well as though its skirt and transfer ports in the normal two-stroke fashion. The extra large exhaust port was responsible for this, as the exhaust gases escaped at very high velocity and caused the cylinder pressure to drop to approximately 12 psi (0.8 bar) below atmospheric.

The cylinder and head was of a square shape with wide pitch fins to prevent mud clogging, and held in place by four long sleeve bolts (of L65 alloy) which attached to the existing cylinder flange studs. A steel induction manifold was bolted to the rear of the cylinder - in preference to using a cast-in alloy stub - to reduce heat transference to the carburettor and to prevent distortion of the bore due to expansion.

This conversion was not to every rider's liking, but when the DOT works riders tried it out it proved to be successful and was adopted by the works team and pressed into use. Versions were available that bolted onto the short con-rod 9E and 31A together with kits for the 32/33/34A engines with the longer con-rod. Using a 66 mm piston (or 59 mm for the 197 kart engine conversions) the 2.5 inch (63 mm) high heavily finned head employed a squish type combustion chamber with a centrally mounted spark plug.

During 1964 Marcelle looked into the building of complete engines with a view to going into complete machine manufacture. One machine was built, and ridden in the 1964 Experts Grand

1960s DOT Demon with Marcelle conversion

National by ex DOT rider, Pat Lamper. The debut did not, and was not expected to turn many heads, for it was still in the very early stages of its development and was completed only hours earlier, but nevertheless it was very interesting. The frame was of a single down tube type with Norton forks, square section swinging arm and Motoloy full-width brakes, but the main interest lay in the engine package. Using the previously marketed Marcelle alloy top end, the motor was equipped with new crankcases, a neat primary drive case, AMC gearbox and a Femsa ignition system. This was as far as Marcelle got, for the prototype faded away, as did many other innovative projects of this era.

Parkinson

Another alloy cylinder conversion from the Essex area was the Parkinson, this time made at London Road, Marks Tey, Essex. Used by several motorcycle manufacturers; James, Francis-Barnett, Cotton and Scorpion to name but a few, the MT1 conversion followed normal practice in using an iron liner and big wide fins. The fin area was quoted as being some 400 sq inch (2,580 sq cm) for the cylinder head and a massive 500 sq inch (3,200 sq cm) for the cylinder barrel. The inlet manifold for the Amal Monobloc carburettor, was this time cast in with the cylinder, which sat on a 6 mm Tufnol spacer, to prevent heat transference to the crankcases.

DMW

Also available at the same time was DMW's own light alloy cylinder barrel for fitment to the Villiers 250 single. The new cylinder used a Laystall Cromard liner with a dull chrome inner surface. Used with the Hepolite scrambles specification piston, it was said to reduce the running in period and increase the power as well as augmenting reliability. As with other alloy cylinder makers of the period the fins were of a square shape and widely spaced to stop mud build up. Four long through bolts secured the head (which used a centrally mounted spark plug) to the crankcases, a method employed by other manufacturers. The new cylinder gave the extra surge to ensure that the DMW's stayed up at the front, although no figures were given the power output was an improvement over the Villiers heavyweight iron cylinder, that was fitted as standard to the 33, 34 and 36A scrambles motors.

The Cross/Cotton conversion

The most radical of all the replacement cylinders available during 1962, for fitment to the 246cc Villiers engine, was manufactured by combustion experts Cross of Bath, Somerset, who had been making linerless alloy cylinders since the 1930s. This conversion was produced in conjunction with, and in sole use by, near neighbours the Cotton factory at Gloucester. The alloy cylinder barrel had neither a steel nor chrome plated liner, but used a special piston, with a seven stage interlocking ring and steel slipper plates riveted to the piston skirt. The piston ring assembly comprised two spiral rings each of seven turns; the first ring, when fitted to the piston formed a multiple knife-edge contact with the cylinder, with the second ring acting as the ring lands. Expensive to produce and of limited success, the Cross conversion was not in production for long.

Pacemaker

Jack Heath of Wolston, Coventry, was the next company to develop alloy conversions for the Villiers scrambles engine. The Pacemaker conversion he marketed was similar to its predecessors in that it used big, wide-spaced cylinder and head fining, with a cast-in inlet manifold for an Amal Monobloc carburettor. The 66 mm cylinder sleeve was externally ribbed and made of spun cast iron, onto which was cast the LM4 alloy, to form a good heat transfer path. The cylinder was unique in that it employed a triple exhaust port, 169 degrees around the cylinder wall and removable 'spiral twist' transfer port covers, to simplify cleaning, tuning and piston inspection. The cylinder was available with either straight or angled exhaust ports to suit the various frame layouts. The cylinder head was made of heat-treated alloy and featured a two-plane squish band.

Development of the Pacemaker conversion was carried out by Les Hughes. with one of the first production units being fitted to Joe Johnson's Cotton scrambler, with good results. As a natural progression from the two-fifty conversion, Jack Heath built a 351cc Senior class engine, using a cylinder of 78.5 mm bore, which retained many of the features of the 246cc conversion. Fitted to a pair of modified Alpha crankcases that Alpha Bearings had advised should 'be restricted to 6,800rpm' the 351 Pacemaker was installed into a Cotton scrambler frame and first blooded by Dave Bickers in the 1963 Winter BBC Grandstand Scramble Series. This machine was fitted with a coil ignition system that employed a twin plug head with a three-plane squish band.

Greeves

Marcelle, Parkinson, Pearson and Vale-Onslow were not alone in the production of powerful cylinder conversions for the Villiers 197 and 246cc engines, for Greeves had been using their own square cylinder since 1958, which had been put into good use in their trials, scrambles and road racing engines. The development of the Greeves cylinders and ultimately their own complete engine is detailed in Chapter 8.

By the early sixties the square alloy cylinder barrel had become the vogue with the weekend sportsmen, for it offered an increased power to weight ratio which was useful on both the scramble tracks and the trials courses of the day. But, this increase in power was not without its problems.

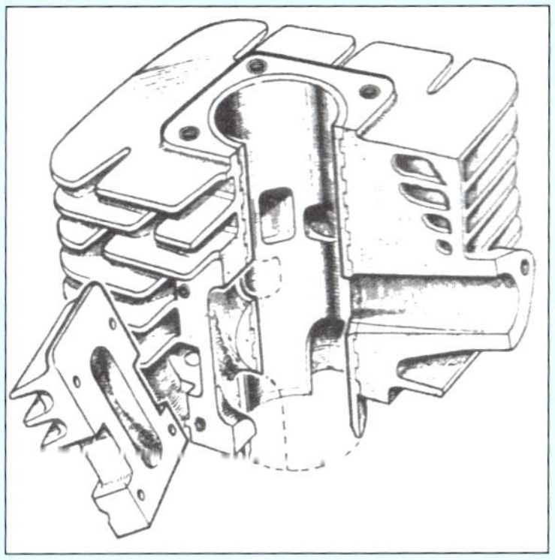

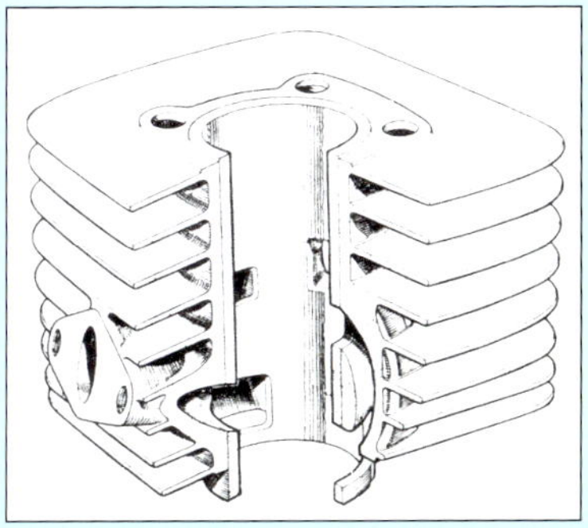

Greeves pre-production alloy cylinders

The Alpha crankcase has no room for the flywheel magneto

Alpha involvement

Adequate for its normal roadster role, the Villiers crankshaft cried enough when used with the powerful alloy cylinder conversions and subjected to sustained high speed and increased power outputs. Villiers had seen fit to uprate the big-end bearing on the sports 9E, when the 26 x $^1/_4$ x $^1/_4$ inch crowded roller bearing big-end was replaced by the caged bearing which contained 9 x $^1/_4$ x $^5/_{16}$ inch rollers and it was this big-end assembly that was inherited by the later 246cc competition engines, albeit with 1 thou (0.025 mm) extra clearance. An alternative was at hand, for Alpha Bearings of Dudley, West Midlands, produced a streamlined replacement con-rod with a superior big-end bearing that could be pressed into the Villiers crank. This rod, available in a length of $5^1/_4$ inch (133.3 mm) to suit the Mk 9/10/11E and 31/35A engines, or $5^1/_2$ inch (140 mm) in length to suit the Mk 32/33/34/36 and 37A engines, used a caged bearing which contained 8 x $^1/_4$ x $^5/_{16}$ inch bearings.

Good as it may have been, the Alpha rod utilised the original Villiers crankpin dimensions, i.e. 0.8 inch (20.3 mm) diameter, and when used with the flimsy Villiers 'hammerhead' crank, this combination was still unable to cope with drastic power increases. The Villiers shaft was notoriously weak and twisted quite badly at the first hint of a power increase. A measure of this flexibility can be gained from the factory maintenance & repair manual, in which it states, 'If reconditioning the original flywheel assembly, a 1 thou oversize (0.025 mm) crankpin and rod must be used.' Presumably this was to take up the slack in the elastic flywheels, a sad state of affairs that would be not tolerated in today's high speed two-stroke motors. A further note is contained in the Villiers maintenance manual, which advises owners not to apply a spanner to the engine sprocket nut when tightening the flywheel nut, for this again may twist the crank.

Same engine showing belt drive conversion

John Wood's 250 Alpha engine - note the Suzuki single-ring piston

The Alpha Mk2 full circle crankshaft

The Alpha crankshaft

To counter this problem Alpha came up with a superior replacement crankshaft assembly which fitted straight into the Villiers crankcases. Having stronger full-circle flywheels, this rigid assembly was used quite extensively by many works teams of the sixties, for it solved the twisting problems. The first Alpha shaft had full circle flywheels with reduced crankcase wall clearance which not only added rigidity but also increased the primary compression ratio, which in turn aided cylinder filling. In the trials application with the flywheel and the extra weight of its additional ring, the better cylinder filling increased plonkability markedly. With the Alpha shaft came a streamlined con-rod (of both lengths) and a superior racing type big-end bearing that contained 10 x 3/16 x 3/8 inch rollers, but the small end remained bushed as in the Villiers rod.

The very early rods had a big end width of 0.5 inch (12.5 mm), and a single diameter pin of 0.925 inch (23.5 mm), which ran in parallel full-circle flywheels. The rod width was later increased in width to 16 mm on the Mk 2 crank, the flywheels being machined away around the big-end to accommodate the wider con-rod and the new stepped crankpin (22 to 25 mm), larger bearing (25 x 32 x 16 mm) and thrust washers. Much of the increased rigidity came from the larger crank pin of the early imperial type and the later stepped metric crankpin, which was needed to accommodate the larger big end bearing. When replacement for the Mk 2 was needed it could be, and often was, substituted with the superior silver plated cage type INA KZK bearing of the same size. This size was the same as that used on all Greeves Silverstones and Challengers, with good results.

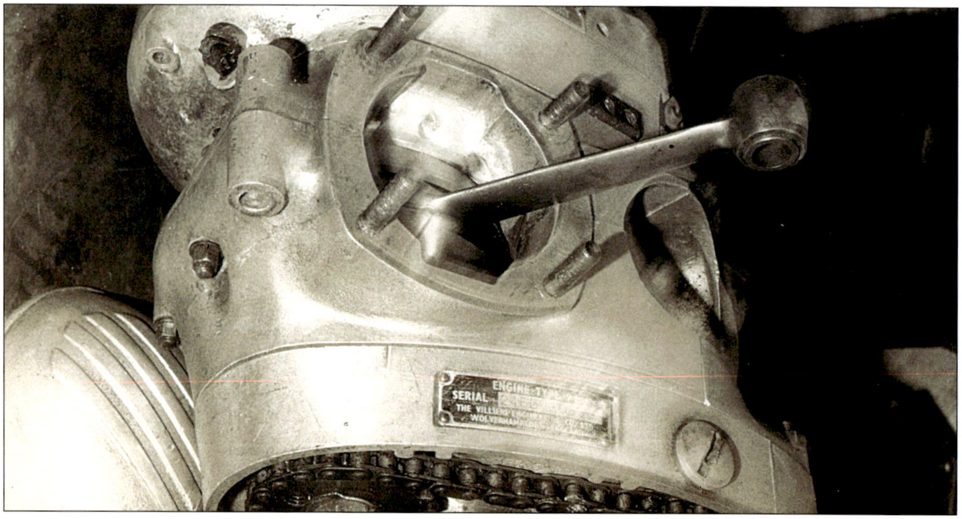

Alpha streamlined con-rod

Replacement crankcases

The Alpha crankshaft reigned supreme during the classic period, when the Villiers engine ruled the roost on the scrambling scene. But, with high power cylinders and rigid crankshafts, the problems associated with this predominantly roadster orientated engine simply moved to other areas. Now the weak link became the crankcases themselves, which again were adequate for their original role, but they simply could not stand the rigours of competition riding. Two companies rose to the challenge and produced beefed-up castings, but in two differing directions. Parkinson produced a nice pair of heavily fined cases, strengthened in the right areas, which complemented their alloy cylinder conversion. The Parkinson cases were designed to accommodate the standard Villiers, or the Alpha 'replacement' full circle crank, but Alpha Bearings went one stage further and produced a complete bottom end which could be used in the Villiers product.

As power outputs continued to creep higher, this then began to put the pressure on the flimsy Villiers crankcases, the principal problem areas becoming the main bearing housings and the gearbox mounting lugs. To combat this new problem, Alpha then turned their attention to the crankcase castings, coming up with a heavily finned pair, that were beefed-up in the appropriate places. Instead of the standard two ball and single roller main bearings, Alpha opted for the use of one ball and two roller bearings. The rollers (a single row on the driving side next to the ball and a double row on the timing side) ran in hardened steel sleeves in the cases, but directly onto the crank drive shafts. As the crank was factory balanced, the heavy brass magneto was not required, nor was there any room for it, as the contact breaker ran straight onto a cam ground on the shaft end. The cases were intended solely for racing use, and the application of a simple total loss battery coil ignition system was deemed to be the most reliable method of generating sparks at that time.

The Alpha bottom end did see service – not only as a replacement – in the DOT White Strength scrambler of the mid sixties. Using an Albion gearbox and a DOT designed head and barrel the White Strength - a name derived from the machine's colour scheme and a popular brand of washing powder - was built to take on the Greeves Challenger that used a similarly designed engine. A 360cc engined White Strength scrambler was also built, being shown to the public for the first time in May 1965.

Watford motorcycle dealer Jim Bound's Villiers powered 125cc EMB Special pictured at Silverstone in 1960, EMB was derived from his wife's initials, points to note are, magneto ignition and two carburetors, one on either side of the cylinder

Carburation needs

With Villiers insistence of using a carburettor of their own manufacture on the roadster engines, this naturally kept the power down to an acceptable figure, a figure that was acceptable to the Wolverhampton factory, but not to the average red-blooded youth of the period. To gain more power a bigger carburettor was needed, and this was available in the form of the Amal Monobloc or the Wal Phillips Fuel Injector, but both these instruments had a flange fitting, against the Villiers stub fitting. To counter this mismatch, various carburettor inlet manifolds were produced in cast aluminium, not only for the various single cylinder engines, but also for the 2T twins. These manifolds were marketed by such companies as Flynns and The Speed Shop, with claims of increased power and flexibility; fulfilling the needs of the rider who required that extra edge over his riding companions. The inlet tract lengths were long by modern standards to increase acceleration, but they did increase power outputs; probably not as much as the manufacturers specified, for it was all down to the expertise of the owner in tuning in the new carburettor to suit the engine.

Crankcase compression

The really adventurous owner, in the need to extract the last ounce of power, could fit a pair of crankcase stuffers to increase his crankcase compression. The stuffers were cast aluminium blocks that were screwed and glued into position in the lower transfer passages, and in some cases featured projections that protruded vertically to occupy the space underneath the piston crown. The transfer passages in the Villiers crankcases were very old fashioned, in that the floor of the passage was well below the rim of the flywheel, which resulted in the gas transfer having a torturous route over the flywheel rims before moving up the transfer passages. Smaller stuffers were also available that simply filled in the lower transfer passages to the level of the flywheel rim, blending in the crankcase passages up to the cylinder joint face.

Another area that was highlighted to increase crankcase compression was the space between the drive-side main bearings. Villiers simply provided a small diameter steel distance tube to space the bearings apart, but large diameter aluminium spacers became available to take up more of the crankcase volume. These crankcase modifications were a good idea, based on tuning practice of the day, but they needed to be used in conjunction with the Alpha full circle cranks and transfer passage stuffers to gain the maximum benefit. However, the continued use of the Villiers hammerhead crank simply negated any gain in this area.

Crankcase stuffers in position

Summary

The after-market equipment available in the sixties could virtually double the power output of the Villiers single cylinder competition motors, but that was not the end of the development on these engines. Years later when the 197cc unit found favour on the karting scene, this venerable design was uprated even further, to produce yet higher power output figures.

At one stage, due to the availability of after market components, it was possible to construct an E or A range single cylinder engine without using any Villiers components at all, utilising parts sourced entirely from the alternative component manufacturers. But, when adding the primary drive and gearbox some Villiers parts had to be used, for there were no substitutes available or needed. This situation nicely illustrated the lack of interest, by the parent factory, in the engine's development programme, development that could have easily gained extra credibility and sales for the company.

Early efforts at an aftermarket exhaust system to cut down noise - Villiers 34A with a Greeves top end

8 Design Derivatives

During the 1960s the original Villiers design concept was copied by various companies, in some cases to gain sales, but mainly to try and improve upon the basic inadequacies of the Wolverhampton product. Some companies were successful, but others were not so fortunate.

Prior to the mid-1950s there was no need of such high performance engines, or bolt-on equipment for that matter, for the average rider was just that - an average rider who only wanted a motorcycle for transportation purposes. If the quest for speed was that overwhelming it was a simple enough exercise to buy a larger machine. The two-stroke technology of the day was not that far advanced, and anyone contemplating serious sports riding or racing would immediately opt for an established four-stroke competition machine rather than an under powered two-stroke. On the commuter front the Villiers engine unit was quite acceptable, being relatively economical, reliable and producing enough power to cope with the job in hand. Villiers had a virtual monopoly over this market, for there was very little else available and they became quite complacent. By the 1960s and the subsequent explosion in the competition side of the motorcycle scene, the inadequacies of the basic Villiers unit soon became apparent.

AMC-engined James trials machine; circa 1960

Villiers was adamant that there was nothing wrong with their design, refusing to believe that anyone was actually racing any of their commuter engines in anger, but this was not the case. This refusal to improve on the basic design of the roadster and even the competition variants left no alternative and many concerns, both large and small, set about building a superior product to go racing. The racing envisaged was from club level scrambling to Grand Prix road racing. The basic 1960s E and A range engines, even when kitted with after market equipment, still failed at an alarming rate when ridden by top-notch works riders. Power outputs had risen with the advent of the alloy cylinders, with the resulting crankshaft problems soon eradicated by the use of the Alpha crank, but other components still failed. New problem areas were the crankcases, primary drive and the gearbox. From the design and development of the engines listed below, it will be seen that the builders addressed these problems, albeit in their own differing ways, and with their own differing results.

AMC

The once proud Associated Motorcycle Group (AMC), even with its extensive resources, started to fall into decline during the early 1960s, but prior to then - in an effort to regain some of its credibility - started to produce its own brand of two-stroke engines to power the lightweight James and Francis-Barnett range. These engines were not designed or produced with performance in mind, for in this case AMC wanted nothing more than an alternative to the Wolverhampton product. Designed by the Italian engineer Vincent Piatti and initially built in France, the range originally consisted of the 17T (59 x 62.7 mm) 171cc unit; the 20T (59 x 72.8 mm) 199cc unit; the 25T (66 x 72.8 mm) 249cc unit; and latterly the 15T (55 x 62.7 mm) 149cc engine.

When AMC took over Francis-Barnett in 1947 and then the James concern in 1951, they then became the largest Villiers motorcycle engine customer, to feed the ever-growing demand for their lightweight motorcycle range. These two once great names - and traditional Villiers engine users - were integrated into the AMC empire and built from similar parts, so started the AMC trend towards badge-engineering.

Mick Dismore pictured in Edinburgh prior to the start of the 1961 Scottish Six Days Trial with an AMC-engined Francis-Barnett trials model

AMC-engined Francis-Barnett 1962 100 mile scramble, Purbright, Surrey

The AMC lightweights used a wide selection of Villiers engines, from 98cc to 225cc, but AMC always wanted something bigger, and when the Villiers 2T twin was announced in 1956 they deemed that this was the motor to power their updated Francis-Barnett Cruiser range. Plans were drawn up and AMC approached Villiers to demand that as they spent the most cash they should be the sole user of the new twin. Villiers did not give in to this corporate blackmail and quite rightly refused the deal. In retaliation (sour grapes?) AMC decided to develop their own, in-house, Piatti designed power units, and with the huge AMC factory resources available to them this seemed a cheaper and more sensible approach to motorcycle engine production at Woolwich.

The 249cc 25T single cylinder engine unit was the first to go into production in 1956, its overall external appearance being very similar to the Villiers 1H which it replaced, but internally it was quite different and technically more interesting. Using the Villiers bore and stroke measurements of 66 x 72 mm (the stroke being increased to 72.8 mm), a bolt-on gearbox and a Lucas alternator, the 25T had some novel features. Built to Piatti patents, the cylinder barrel did not have transfer ports cast into walls as in the conventional two-stroke engine, but used deeply machined grooves with the piston forming the port's inner walls. The engine transferred the compressed mixture from the crankcase though windows in the piston to the combustion chamber via the transfer passages and a pair of deep cut-outs in the piston crown, to a matching pair of deflectors in the cylinder head. The 17T and the 20T engines that followed, again used this same transfer passage principle, but the 15T engine, introduced in 1959, reverted to the more normal method of transfer ports cast into the cylinder.

The 15T again looked like a unit (or semi-unit) construction engine, but the design of this motor allowed for three different engine configurations; with the AMC three-speed gearbox being bolted to the crankcases via a multi position welded steel cradle plate, to give a vertical cylinder, an inclined cylinder or a horizontal version for the James scooter. When the Villiers four-speed gearbox was used on the Francis-Barnett Fulmar Sport, a specially made aluminium casting was positioned between the engine and gearbox to retain the unit construction image of this upright cylinder engine.

The Piatti engines

The Piatti designed engines, in theory, should have been far superior in performance and reliability to the Villiers products, but in practice this was not the case. The new engines suffered from crankcase condensation, but more seriously poor assembly techniques and even poorer quality control, which gave them a bad reputation throughout the motorcycle world. Engine noise, piston ring breakages and seizures long after the running-in period was over further enhanced this reputation.

The AMC two-stroke was a disaster, it was very wide, heavy, under-powered and its reliability did irreparable damage to AMC's reputation. On the competition side the use of the engine

AMC 149cc 15T engine

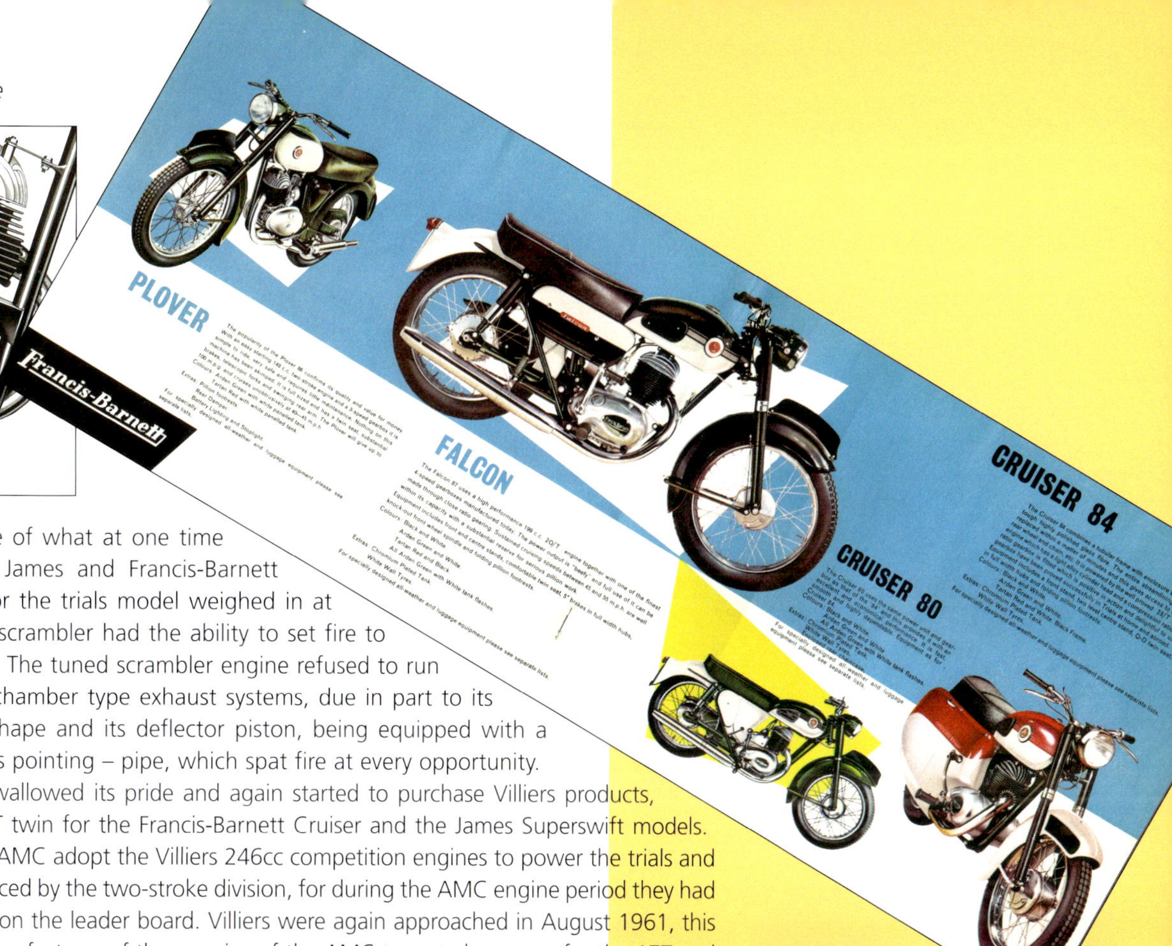

virtually halted the sale of what at one time was a top seller, the James and Francis-Barnett competition models, for the trials model weighed in at some 300 lbs and the scrambler had the ability to set fire to the track undergrowth. The tuned scrambler engine refused to run on long or expansion chamber type exhaust systems, due in part to its combustion chamber shape and its deflector piston, being equipped with a very short – downwards pointing – pipe, which spat fire at every opportunity.

During 1961 AMC swallowed its pride and again started to purchase Villiers products, namely the powerful 2T twin for the Francis-Barnett Cruiser and the James Superswift models. The following year saw AMC adopt the Villiers 246cc competition engines to power the trials and scrambles models produced by the two-stroke division, for during the AMC engine period they had slipped ever backwards on the leader board. Villiers were again approached in August 1961, this time to become sole manufacturer of the remains of the AMC two-stroke range, for the 17T and the 25T had been finally abandoned and now all that remained was the 15T and the 20T. Villiers gladly accepted this task, safe in the knowledge that this deal spelt a final and well deserved victory for them and the new motors proudly carried a new logo – Villiers AMC. The Villiers built AMC engines were noticeably better in build standard and reliability than their predecessors, which resulted in a considerable lessening of warranty claims, as there were far less problems.

After 1962 Francis-Barnett finally vacated its traditional home in Coventry and amalgamated with the James factory at Greet in Birmingham, but such rationalisation did not halt the downward spiral of the once great AMC company, and in August 1966 they crashed with dire consequences. From the ashes of this empire emerged the Manganese Bronze controlled Norton-Villiers company, who in turn managed a subsidiary concern that looked after the two-stroke interests of the consortium. This company, AJS, carried on the task of two-stroke engine production, taking the remains of both AMC and Villiers into the next decade. But of all the inherited designs, only the Starmaker survived.

Alpha

Alpha Bearings of Dudley started in 1946 in the West Midlands, as many firms do, making hard to source items for the engineering industry. From this start the company expanded to include components to service the motorcycle trade and specialised in the supply of bearings (both main and big-end), connecting rods, valves, guides and currently now even control cables. The company is still very much in existence and able to supply the above mentioned items off the shelf for the majority of old British machines. Their replacement big-ends are famous world wide. It is gratifying to note that Alpha is in good health and still capable of making one-offs, to service the needs of the classic motorcycle restorer.

Alpha came to the forefront as two-stroke performance equipment manufacturers during the late fifties and early sixties, which coincided the beginning of the Villiers 197cc 9E becoming popular as a competition engine. As the power outputs of the 9E increased, so did the failure rate of its standard components. The advent of the high performance alloy cylinders - and 250cc conversions - put so much pressure on the standard crank that it cried enough far too regularly. Frank Cutler, then managing director of Alpha, decided to make good the basic inadequacies, a job that should have been tackled by the makers. First item to come out of the factory was the Mk 1 full circle crank and streamlined con-rod, but replacement rods for the standard Villiers crank had been available for some time. The metric Mk 2 crankshaft soon followed, setting a standard that was hard to improve upon.

The second experimental single with rearward facing carburettor

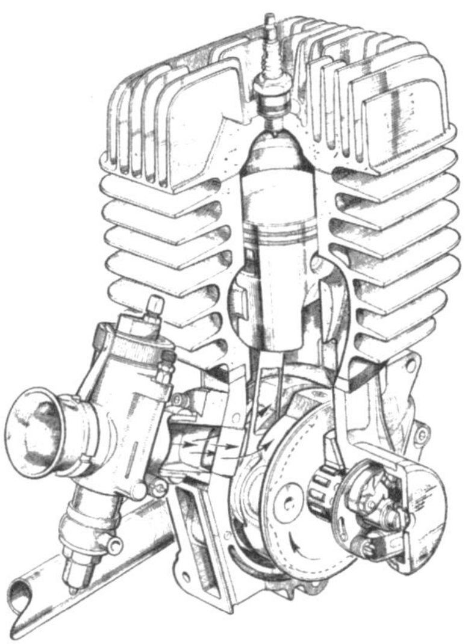

The Alpha singles

Not content with making replacement parts, Frank Cutler turned his attention to a complete motor. The first engine was based on the Alpha bottom end, and in an attempt to provide a better induction cycle, used a rotary valve. The inlet port was positioned on the right hand side crankcase at the front, with a machined cutaway on the ultra close fitting crankshaft, acting as the valve. A vertically mounted Dell'Orto carburettor, square alloy cylinder and a Villiers gearbox completed the specification of this motor, which was installed into an elderly DMW frame for testing purposes.

This engine was soon replaced by the Mk 2 version, which placed the induction tract, and the Amal GP carburettor at the rear of the cases. The crankshaft again acted as the valve, but this time the cutaways were machined on the circumference of both flywheels, and fed by a bifurcated inlet tract. A third transfer port was added to the rear of the cylinder, which connected to the underside of the piston, situated in the area vacated by the repositioning of the inlet port. The crankcases followed the same design as the Alpha 'replacement' cases and even used the same main bearing and ignition system arrangement. Employing positive oil feed to the main bearings, the engine also used petroil to lubricate other areas, at a leaner ratio. Installed in a pair of Royal Enfield frames, the single cylinder engines revved well but failed to come up to racing

A pair of works development Centuri road racers, Snetterton 1965. Mike Cutler (29) DMW/Alpha, Don Wolfindale (39) Royal Enfield/Alpha, tuner Fred Hadley centre (in cap)

Mike Cutler 250 Alpha Centuri, Cadwell Park, CRMC, 1985

expectations, in that they would not rev to the required limit. The road legal versions, equipped with lights and a silencer, were clocked at a steady 101mph(162 kph) but the expected 120mph(193 kph) of the racing version was not achieved. Even though both Royal Enfield and Scorpion showed an interest in the design for their production racer projects, the disc valve single was shelved. Was it due to the failure to produce the required rpm, or the demise of the two racer projects that persuaded Frank Cutler to drop the single development in favour of a twin?

The Centuri twin

The twin, called the Centuri, employed a bore and stroke of 54 x 54 mm, with a pressed up crank that used a pair of inboard discs to collect the mixture from a centrally mounted single carburettor. As the disc controlled inlet periods of less than 180 degrees, this system was deemed as perfectly satisfactory for the state of tune prevailing some thirty years ago. With modern high performance engines having an inlet period of truly wild proportions, this system would not have been adequate, reuiring a change to twin carburettors. Conventional ball races supported the centre of the full circle crank, with caged rollers being used on the outer ends, again running in steel sleeves but directly on the crank drive shafts. A new set of cylinders were sand cast (the development cylinders coming from a Velocette Viceroy scooter) and fitted with spun cast iron liners. The new liners featured not only the main transfer ports but an extra pair of auxiliary ports placed between the main transfers and the exhaust port. This method of gaining an increase in gas transfer was a full five years ahead of Japanese two-stroke wizards Yamaha, who adopted the same idea for the TD2 racers of 1969.

The rest of the engine was quite conventional, except for the massive star burst cylinder head finning, which replaced the Bantam cylinder heads used during the initial development. Employing battery coil ignition and an Albion HG 5 speed gearbox, the motor revved well over 10,000rpm and produced an excellent power curve. The choice of the somewhat suspect Albion HG 5 gearbox was purely political, as Alpha was part of the E&HP Smith empire who owned Albion. The gearbox was soon changed when Albion came up with their new barrel-cam five-speed box.

The Centuri power output was gradually increased to some 48 bhp, but in this form it became very fragile, the output being lowered to 44 bhp in order to make it more reliable. The increases came from the use of a new set of seven port cylinders, a bridged exhaust, four transfers and an extra transfer through the piston. The production engines, which would have been on sale to the general public had the project carried on, only gave 36 bhp, which was enough to be competitive against its nearest rival, the 32 bhp Greeves Silverstone. When asked what the difference was between the production and the works engines, Mike Cutler said it was 'works tuning by port wizard Fred Hadley'.

Don Wolfindale, 250 Alpha Centuri, 1965

The definitive Alpha Centuri engine with big-fin heads and single Dell'Orto carb, 1967

Dave Browning and Don Wolfindale, 1967

Alpha finally abandoned the Centuri altogether and went back to making crankshafts and connecting rods for the run of the mill motorcycle market, after receiving an edict from E&HP Smith in 1968, which put a stop to what Smiths called 'costly race development'. All the work put into the Centuri (much of it being after hours at a reduced cost and well below budget) was lost, for the ruling stated, 'No further engines or spares to be sold.' Even the engine sold to privateer John Kirkby was re-purchased, thus Great Britain was deprived of yet another project that could have blossomed, or at least kept abreast with the rapidly improving Japanese hardware.

The sad fact is that when the Centuri project was wound up, Frank Cutler had already completed the drawings for a water-cooled, gear driven primary, six-speed, disc valve twin that would have beaten the TZ Yamahas into production by several years. Frank Cutler even had ideas of a four cylinder 500, but that is another story. In all, it's a sad reflection on those who were in a position of power during the final days of the once great British motorcycle industry.

Another project did blossom from the ashes of the Centuri program, when it was terminated on the orders of the Smith group, this was the Hadley Starr 125. Built by Fred Hadley (an unpaid helper on the Alpha Centuri) the 125 was half a Centuri twin engine with a side mounted 28 mm Dell'Orto carburettor, which had began to show some promise, but again was never fully developed.

Alpha development twin engine in roadster frame, early 1965

Alpha Centuri big-fin engine

Bert Greeves on the works hack 360 Challenger sidecar outfit

Greeves – Bert Greeves and the Challenger project

With the continued use of the modified 36A engine in the RAS Silverstone, Greeves had to buy a complete standard motor from Villiers, for they would not sell part motors. This was a costly exercise, as major items such as the crank were replaced by an Alpha unit, with the cylinder heads being replaced by Greeves manufactured items. The gearboxes were even rebuilt, using specially hardened pinions, and the carburettor replaced by an Amal. This situation soon led to a wasteful stock of unused Villiers spares building up at the factory, which were sold off at knock down prices, redundant iron cylinders being retailed at £1.50 each. This situation was noted by Brian Woolley who suggested to Bert Greeves that if the factory was to produce a set of crankcases and use an Albion gearbox, the need for any Villiers involvement would be ended, and a saving of many thousands of pounds would be made. This suggestion was duly noted.

During late 1963 and early 1964 the creative genius of Bert Greeves had been at work, and by March 1964 the Challenger motocross machine was launched. The Challenger engine was a totally new design, which utilised new components that were manufactured with the Villiers failure points in mind. The crankshaft was made by Alpha, to Greeves specification, retaining the 72 mm stroke, but the main bearings were replaced by a combination of ball and roller races. On the drive side a single ball race was used to give the crank a positive location, being backed up by a single unlipped roller bearing. On the timing side a large twin row roller bearing was used, rotating in a pressed-in ground steel sleeve. The con-rod was typically Alpha using a streamlined shape and a caged roller big-end. The new crankcases, cast in the Greeves foundry, were of massive proportions when compared to the Villiers components which they replaced, and of course were much stronger.

The Challenger engine was treated to a new cylinder and head, again of increased size, providing some 50 per cent greater fin area over the original square cylinder, but at a cost of only a 25 per cent weight increase. This figure included the cast-in induction manifold. Much time was spent in developing the new cylinder and head, but as no real power boost was obtained from the various squish band trials that were carried out, this development was channeled towards the cylinder. An Albion four-speed gearbox was bolted to the rear of the crankcases, and a clutch from the same concern handled the single row primary transmission chain. The ignition department also came in for a radical change; gone was the heavy Villiers flywheel magneto, replaced by a Swedish Stefa unit of half the size and weight.

Mike Philpot with his RAS Greeves Silverstone, Ramsgate Sprint, May 1963

Previous Villiers engined motocross models used a steel plate engine cradle, but the new Challenger engine was deemed to be so strong that this cradle was deleted, the engine becoming a stressed member. This structural change gave an unexpected bonus when it came to adjusting the tension of the primary chain, a job that had to be carried out at all too regular intervals until the chain was replaced by a duplex type. With the Villiers engines the adjustment was carried out by adding more gaskets between the engine and gearbox, which required the engine unit to be removed from its cradle. With the Albion gearbox, which had its oil contents sealed in, all that was required was to slacken the four gearbox mounting bolts, lever the two units apart, and insert horseshoe shaped shims to arrive at the correct adjustment.

The Challenger motocrosser carried on for five years, with as many model changes, mainly in the gearbox department, for the earlier models suffered badly due to the limited choice of boxes offered by the Albion concern at that time. The final Challenger, the MX5, broke away from the long-stroke layout, and used a 70 mm piston with a 64 mm stroke crankshaft. This motor was destined to be the forerunner of the next generation of Greeves engines.

The RBS Silverstone

In May 1964 the factory launched the Challenger-engined Mk 2 Silverstone, designated the RBS, which used an Albion five-speed gearbox. The cylinder had similar porting to the RAS, but a lot more work went into the round section expansion chamber which made the engine more tractable, with useable power coming in at 3,000rpm and having a power band from 6,000 to 8,000rpm when it was quoted as delivering 31 bhp. Much of the actual development work on the Mk 2 was carried out by two men, race shop mechanic Bob Mills and Brian Woolley, who was then acting in a consultancy role. The new engine produced no more power than the earlier RAS, but it was easier to ride due to the additional mid range torque and the five-speed gearbox. Early tests of the RBS on the Isle of Man prior to the 1964 TT found that the engine had a chronic misfire at 7,000rpm which baffled the experts, until Brian Woolley cured it by simply removing the carburettor bellmouth. The initial figures that determined the inlet tract length had been calculated wrongly, which upset the airflow at this rpm, once the bellmouth had been removed the engine accelerated cleanly right up to its maximum rpm. When TT practice started Bob Mills, Brian Woolley and Reg Orpin were on hand to lend assistance to the many Greeves riders who had entered, but this turned into a nightmare during the early practice with broken machinery, rebuilding engines, transmissions and gearboxes, evening practice sessions saw a repetition of the work with much burning of the midnight oil.

1965 Lightweight Manx GP winner, Dennis Craine Greeves Silverstone

The Orpin watercooled conversion

The 250 TT was a disaster for Greeves, as every rider save Reg Everett dropped by the wayside. Reg was riding an old RAS works hack with a top speed of only 90mph(145 kph) but he did manage to average 77.42mph(124.5 kph) to come home last. In fact he was so disappointed with the bike's lack of speed that he called it a day and transferred his allegiance to the Ted Broad Yamaha twins. Later in the year the RBS redeemed itself by winning the Manx Grand Prix in the hands of Gordon Keith. Prepared and fettled by Bob Mills (who was on the Island as part of his annual holiday) and Reg Orpin, the Orpin-Greeves fell foul of the MGP no advertising rule, but this was smoothed over and the Orpin logo removed from the tank. After 32 pre-practice laps and the practice itself, Gordon was instructed not to use the clutch except for starting, not to over-rev and go for a finish. Starting the race at number 64, by the third lap he was third on the road and leading the field by almost a minute, finishing at a record average of 86.19mph(138.7 kph). This success resulted in the Silverstone winning the Motor Cycle News Machine of the Year award, the first time a competition machine had won this accolade.

Reg Orpin

Reg Orpin continued his association with the Greeves factory during the 1966 racing season, with a tubular framed RDS ridden by Peter Williams, which they built jointly. Having licence to construct the bike to their own specification, the Orpin/Williams Silverstone sported Italian Ceriani forks and Oldani brakes, but the biggest change was to the engine, which now featured water-cooling. With the steady increases in power output had come an increase in piston seizures and to counteract this the team had opted for liquid cooling. Reg would have liked a brand new water jacket cylinder with a central exhaust port, but as the motocross team were top priority he had to wait. With the help of Bob Mills they converted a production cylinder by machining away the fins and welding on an alloy jacket, the cylinder head remained air cooled however. The 5.5 pint (3.1 lt) radiator which was placed behind the engine came from a Velocette LE, courtesy of the L Stevens Velocette dealership of which Reg was the boss. Limited success was gained by the team, with Peter Williams achieving a second at the North West 200 meeting, but the spin off was the sale of water-cooling kits for Silverstones, for the princely sum of £45.00 (around a sixth of the cost of a new Silverstone).

Mervyn Stratford, East Fortune, Bob McIntyre Memorial Meeting 18/19th June 2005. 1967 Greeves RDS water-cooled conversion

Dave Simmonds, 1964 Greeves Silverstone RBS

The RCS Silverstone

The Silverstone had been updated for the 1965 season to become the RCS, and it was in that year that Brian Woolley started a successful association with Trevor Burgess. With the assistance of Bob Mills (who was then in charge of the race shop) they embarked on a development program that resulted in many short circuit victories. One of the first modifications carried out by Brian Woolley was to convert to battery/coil ignition, for he had seen all too many instances of the Stefa magneto shearing the main shaft. This modification reduced flywheel effect, made it easier to time and added reliability. Other modifications included a top hat combustion chamber shape and a squish band of 30 thou (0.76 mm). Allied to slight alterations to the inlet timing, it all added up to an increase of 500rpm. The RCS used a duplex primary chain and a new Albion five-speed gearbox, together with porting changes and a full fairing. As the Silverstone concept became older the modifications became fewer, the RDS receiving a new splined clutch and a fairing that lost the controversial perspex nose bubble. When the last Silverstone - the RES - was produced in 1967, the might of the Japanese Yamahas and the Spanish Bultacos was beginning to be felt. Being 25 per cent down on power against its rivals ,the Silverstone was due for the chop. With a good Yamaha TD1C or Bultaco TSS producing at least 40 bhp, the Greeves with only 32 bhp was hard pressed to keep up. The RES received only minor changes over its predecessors, the most significant being a change of colour (silver frame with red tank) but now they were built under strict supervision by service manager John Millward and track tested at Brands Hatch. Production of the Silverstone finished in April 1967 with 58 RES models being made, which gave a total of 304 Silverstones built during the period. What started out as a trainer, or a beginners machine, blossomed into an international contender but was quickly overtaken by the larger factories who had bigger budgets. During its production time the relatively inexpensive Silverstone achieved numerous successes and allowed many fledgling racers their first steps to stardom.

The ill-fated 1966 record attempt

One episode in the life of the Silverstone, which the factory wanted to be kept quiet, was the ill-fated 1966 attempt on the 4, 6 and 12 hour speed records, together with the 500 mile and the 1,000 Km speed records. The attempt was masterminded by Charles Mortimer Senior, who ran the Mortimer racing school, equipped with Silverstones. The idea of going for the records came about when Charles found that the records established in the thirties still stood, and he considered that the time was ripe for the school's Greeves to break them. The factory was enthusiastic about the project and loaned chief road race mechanic Bob Mills, rider Peter Williams from the Greeves drawing office and a brand new RDS Silverstone. The second rider was Ron Eldridge. By way of a practice run before any officially observed run, the team went to the French banked track of Montlhery 15 miles south of Paris, scene of many record attempts.

1965 Greeves Silverstone (Norton Dominator front brake) ridden by Jeff Bing, CRMC Snetterton, 26th May 2003

Each rider put in half a dozen laps at 95-98mph(153-157 kph) on one of the school's well used RAS's - the 1,000 Km record being 75.75mph(121.88 kph). As the RDS was 15mph(24 kph) faster, it was decided to use it for the practice attempt and this was the next bike out, but after $2\frac{1}{2}$ hours a misfire set in.

The first pit stop saw the plug changed, then on the second stop the points were adjusted, but still it misfired. On the next stop the coil was changed and the misfire was cured, but after a further two laps the seat fell off. At the $3\frac{1}{2}$ hour point the engine stopped dead and Peter Williams coasted into the pits to discover that the magneto shaft had sheared. At this point the attempt was aborted, for it was realised by all that the Silverstone was not a long distance record breaker. Bob Mills summed it up, 'The Silverstone was a club racer that was made for 20 minute short distance dashes, not the hour after hour pounding that the team expected of it.' His brief for the trip had not included much information on what to expect and therefore both he and the bike were not ready for if it. Had he known, he would have prepared the bike to counter the vibration problems exacerbated by the concrete surface of the French speed bowl by using split pins, locking wire and lock nuts.

The sheared magneto shaft was a known problem to him and he could have eliminated this by running a battery coil system, as many of the fast Greeves riders of the day had done. Bob was not happy with the lack of preparation for the practice attempt and let his feelings be known. The final outcome was a flat refusal by Bert Greeves to sanction any further official attempts to ensure that the factory would not be made the laughing stock of the motorcycle industry, if the bike was to again fail in mid stream.

The 360 motocrosser

In 1965 the factory began experimenting with a 360cc engine to contest the 500 motocross class. The need to build such an engine was brought about by an FIM ruling that outlawed the use of over bored 250s in the World 500 championships. The rule was not aimed directly at Greeves who were using 252cc Challengers to good effect, but it sought to bar machines of under 351cc from contesting the event. The new engine was based on the 250, but with a redesigned crankcase to take a ring of studs to hold down the 80 mm cylinder, instead of the four sleeve bolts used on the smaller 250. As the new cylinder bolted directly to the crankcase, the new head was attached to the cylinder with six studs. Because of the enormous size of a single exhaust port, and the problems that would be associated with it, Greeves opted for the use of a split port and two separate exhaust pipes that linked to a common expansion chamber. The new 360 came into production in 1967, listed as the 36MX4, it gained many wins on the race track and went from success to success.

Brian Wooley and the 350 road racer

In line with the new 360cc motocross machine, the factory built a 350cc road racer for the 1968 season. Based on the 36MX4 engine, it kept the same bore but used a reduced stroke crankshaft (68.5 mm) to achieve the required size. The prototype 350 racer was rapid and reliable, and fitted with a new Greeves clutch that replaced the Albion unit of the 250s. But this motor was stolen when the competition shop was burgled. The prototype 350 motor was the brain-child of Brian Woolley who did all the early development work on it, giving the factory all his notes and drawings to be used when production went ahead. A disregard of the Woolley specifications and an uncorrected drawing office error led to the production cylinders being inferior to the original design, for the fault was neither recognised nor rectified.

The 350cc 35RFS Oulton racer could have enjoyed the success that the Silverstone had five years before, for it was aimed at competing against ageing Nortons and AJS 7Rs that dominated the class at that time; but the first batch of machines were far from impressive. Advertised as developing 40 bhp at 7,500rpm the production racers were hard pressed to achieve this figure and were far from reliable. The chassis and cycle parts also came in for some criticism. Being basically a dated RES frame with a larger engine and fuel tank, it was not up the job of handling the extra weight, power and speed of the Oulton. Doomed to failure the last Oulton left the factory in August 1968 after a production run of only 21 units.

The 410 and 500cc engines

Alongside the 350, a larger 410cc racer was built, but this was the work of Bob Mills and Reg Orpin. The new engine had a bore and stroke of 85 x 72 mm and was constructed to take on the Manx Nortons and the Matchless G50. It was reasoned that if the 350 was capable of delivering 40 bhp, then a larger motor should be good for 45 - 46 bhp, and with a superior power to weight ratio, be a match for the 500cc four-strokes. Reliability was not its strongest characteristic, and it was discarded following a capacity increase to 498cc (91 x 76 mm) and the use of a geared primary drive. This 498cc engine was a direct descendant of the 498cc motocrosser that the factory built to exploit the 500cc open class, but never went into production. The 500 motocross engine, which dated back to 1971, proved to be too much for the frame and an improved frame was built for the following season, but this also proved to be too much of a handful on the rough.

The road racing machine passed into the hands of Brian Woolley and was raced by Bob Stevenson as the Selva. The twin port 500cc motor was housed in a Spondon frame with Spondon brakes, and was destined for production in 1972 when all the problems with the

Frank Ball's 500cc Greeves prototype built from a MX unit, 498cc (91 x 76mm) first raced August 1971

motor had been ironed out. Spondon never perfected the package, and the engine was passed on to Wisbech farmer Frank Ball who did further development work on it to make it more reliable and enable it to actually finish races.

A 500 Greeves racer was not a new idea, for in 1967 Bob Stevenson had constructed a twin housed in a Spondon frame. Unlike other attempts at constructing a twin from two separate motors, the Stevenson engine featured a completely new set of crankcases to accommodate his own crankshaft and separate cylinders. The spline coupled cranks ran in roller bearings and used piston ring type chamber seals. A gear drive was used to transmit the power to a countershaft but a chain was used to take the drive to the clutch. Much Greeves technology went into the construction of the twin, but it never got beyond the prototype stage, even though a Mk 2 version was constructed at a later date.

The motocross machines

During 1968 a brace of new motocross machines was tested by Arthur Browning and Vic Allan. At first called the "tubular" Greeves by the motorcycling press of the day, for they had an all tube frame, for now was gone the trade mark alloy beam which Greeves had used since 1954. These new machines, later called the Griffon, used engines of basically the same design as the Challenger and Villiers units before, but they were refined in many ways. The best feature was the use of an all Greeves gearbox, the factory having suffered enough jibes at the Albion box that was used throughout the Challenger production run. Now Greeves decided to enhance the reliability of the new machines and also to reduces the reliance on outside suppliers, by making their own gearbox. The new 250 engine retained the shorter stroke of the last Challenger, but the open class machine had its capacity increased to 380cc by the use of a new 82 mm piston.

It was at about this time that Bert Greeves decided to go into retirement, and left the day to day running of the factory to the team he had built up. From this date the factory started its steady decline from being at the top of the league, to becoming an also ran. The decline was not directly attributable to the loss of its leader, but more likely to the infiltration of Japanese bikes onto the American off-road market, where Greeves exported the majority of its products. With this market lost the factory was doomed.

Bryan Wade, Greeves Griffon, West Lake Village, California, December 1968

Greeves – the final years

With the arrival of the 1970s, the future for Greeves did not look too rosy. Roadster and racer production had finished, and by 1971 so had the trials machines. This only left the motocross models. During 1971 the QUB 380 was introduced, a product of the cooperation between the Thundersley factory and the Queens University Belfast. The new QUB 380 developed 44 bhp, a gain of 5 bhp over the original 380, but this was not enough to enable the Greeves factory to carry on production, and they went into a period of withdrawal, but development and racing carried on. As far as production machines go, no more were made until 1975, and even this was on a low key with only the QUB 250 and 380 models being manufactured. The end of motorcycle production came in 1977 with the 380 QUB Mk2, which featured an updated frame, but this was not enough to secure sales. Originally intended for a run of 250 machines, production ceased after only 40 units had been made.

Greeves 380 Griffon reed valve cylinder, tested in 1975

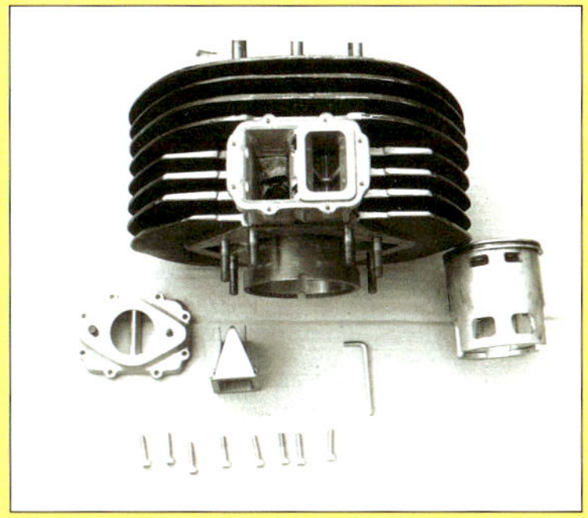

During the period in which motorcycle production ceased, the factory started experimenting with reed valve induction. With the assistance of Bernard Hargreaves, the acknowledged expert in this field, a 250 and a 380 were converted to take a pair of double-sided reed blocks. Ridden by Dick Clayton, the reed valve Griffon works racers proved to be fliers, but never did achieve the success expected of them, and the modification was never embodied when bike production restarted.

The last new design to come out of the factory was in 1974, when the Ministry of Defence invited manufacturers to tender for the BSA B40 replacement. The bike that Greeves put together was a heavily modified Griffon called the Saxon, and then renamed the Gauntlet. This used a unit construction engine with a geared primary drive. The cylinder and porting was left as standard Griffon, which gave shattering performance, but made it totally unsuitable for the army's needs. An attempt was made to civilise the beast by reducing the compression ratio, but the MOD was not impressed, neither was the Jordanian army who had also been looking for a replacement machine. Although tooling for production had been set up, only two or three bikes were made, of which only one is known to survive.

Greeves 380 Griffon

Even when bike production started again in 1975, the factory was on borrowed time, for the year previously the Ministry of Pensions had axed the invalid carriage, giving its users a mobility allowance instead. This meant the end of the Invacar, a bread and butter product that the factory relied upon to ensure the wages of the work force. With the loss of the Invacar, Greeves moved into the marketing of motorcycling accessories, but even this was not enough to stop the firm going into receivership in January 1979. From humble beginnings the Greeves factory had become known worldwide, its giant-killing activities of the fifties and sixties will never be forgotten. At its height, Greeves was the most prestigious and respected sporting concern in Great Britain, and its name lives on today thanks to the efforts of the Greeves Riders Association, who promote the product of this truly remarkable company. As a lasting tribute to the late Bert Greeves and his enthusiastic team, many of the company's products still do the job that they were intended for; on the road, on the trials field, on the scrambles track and the road race circuits, both in Great Britain and overseas.

John Hartle and Geoff Duke with the prototype Villiers Starmaker powered Royal Enfiels GP5.

Royal Enfield – The GP5 project

During 1964 a new name entered the road racing field, that of Royal Enfield, with the freshly announced GP5. Enfield, a long and well established company had little previous experience with high performance two stroke engines, putting their faith in four-stroke singles and twins. Delving into the commuter market before the war, they had produced both 150 and 225cc two-stroke mounts in limited numbers. After 1945 came a 125cc model, originally developed for the Dutch market and used during the war, known colloquially as the Flying Flea in the forces. The next machine to be marketed was the Turbo Twin, a Villiers 4T engined sports tourer, which used the Crusader Sports frame and cycle parts. From these humble beginnings the swing to high performance race machinery was made.

The racing project came about as a direct result of Greeves sales successes with the RAS Silverstone in 1963, which set Enfield's managing director Leo Davenport, a past TT winner, thinking along the same lines. This resulting in the building of a four-speed Starmaker engined prototype. John Hartle and John Cooper rode the early version in 1964, but because it was uncompetitive they decided to concentrate on their own 350 and 500 mounts. The TT debut of the Starmaker engined prototype ended on the first lap of the 1964 event, when Griff Jenkins retired it. All three riders condemned its lack of power and poor overall performance. Disillusionment soon set in when it was found that little or no extra power or reliability could be extracted from the motor, and alternative avenues were explored.

1965 production Royal Enfield GP5 racer, designed by the German engineer Hermann Meier

At that time Enfield were part of the E&HP Smith Engineering Group, which also controlled Alpha Bearings and Albion Gearboxes, so it seemed logical to use the combined talents of these companies to produce a superior racer. All that had to be done was to bring together the existing expertise, and this task was put into the hands of two-stroke genius Hermann Meier. During the late 1940s Meier had worked with Erich Wolf, the Chief Designer at DKW, and during 1947 he designed an expansion chamber exhaust system for the DKW 125 RT, which was used on both the road and race track with good results. When he moved to BSA in 1954, Meier used the similar type of exhaust system on the Bantam, again with good results. The extra power unleashed by the exhaust system, and Meier's tuning expertise, enabled BSA rider, New Zealander Barry Stormont to lap the MIRA test track at 78mph for one whole hour. Later Meier was responsible for the Harold Daniell-sponsored Ariel Arrow racer that finished in a very creditable seventh position in the 1960 Isle of Man 250 TT.

Geoff Duke

Geoff Duke made the initial approach to Hermann Meier on behalf of Royal Enfield, early in 1964; asking, 'Could the performance of the Starmaker based racer be improved by 10 per cent.' Meier's answer was yes and he was hired immediately. When taken on it was implied that he would have a free hand in the design of a replacement engine for the Starmaker, but this was not to be. Soon after starting work he was told that he was to use existing E&HP Smith products, which included the Alpha 72 mm stroke bottom end. He had planned the use of an ultra short stroke design, with a view to using high revs to gain the required power output. The change to his original design posed no problems, as he had used the Alpha product on an engine he was building in conjunction with Vale-Onslow, prior to his employment with Royal Enfield.

When the GP5 appeared, it was assumed to be another contender for the clubman racing scene, to compete against such established mounts as the Cotton Telstar, DMW Hornet and the Greeves Silverstone, but Enfield had their sights set higher. The new machine boasted a Ken Sprayson designed frame, with leading link forks, and an all in one seat and tank unit that gave an excellent riding position. By far the most radical departure from the norm was the engine unit. Designed by Meier, the unit used an Alpha bottom end and five-speed Albion gearbox, but was fitted with an entirely new top end, using Meier's experience and up to the minute ideas.

The new engine followed the usual piston port induction system, even though its designer would have preferred to use a disc valve and a shorter stroke. As the project had to be completed in a relatively short period of time, management decreed the use of the Alpha cases with its 72 mm stroke crankshaft. Company policy of using in-house equipment, also played a part in this decision. The bottom end was a standard Alpha unit, except for wider spaced front cylinder studs and the name Enfield, which appeared on each crankcase half. A duplex drive chain transmitted the power to the Albion clutch, housed in an alloy chaincase of typical RE design, using a one piece sealing strip and single attachment bolt. The bike had a long wheelbase, long by the standards of other Villiers engined racers, which required the engine to be placed further forward in the frame to ensure the correct weight distribution. To achieve this, a cast alloy spacer was inserted between the crankcase and gearbox, clamped together with long through bolts.

Hermann Meier

Hermann Meier had many years of two-stroke tuning experience behind him, covering such diverse motors as the Bantam and Ariel Leader, from which he extracted well above what was considered to be their maximum horsepower. This experience he put to good use in the design of the GP5 cylinder. The development alloy cylinder used, in the first instance, a detachable chrome-plated alloy liner that was a sliding fit when cold. This practice enabled the port shapes to be easily altered during the testing phase. Once the optimum port shapes had been determined, the production cylinders were cast onto a ribbed steel liner.

Another departure from normal practice was to corrugate the top of the liner, in order that it bit into the cylinder head, thus eliminating the troublesome head gasket. Four long sleeve bolts tightened down onto the short crankcase studs, clamping the whole assembly in place. Vertical as well as horizontal fins adorned the head, which used a classic top-hat shaped combustion chamber. The cylinder ports, as can be expected of a performance engine, were on the large side, requiring the use of an exhaust port bridge to prevent ring trapping. Meier's masterpiece was the use of four transfer ports. Behind the normal pair lay a second smaller pair, open to the crankcase, but with small windows half way up the port, matching with corresponding windows in the piston at BDC. This configuration took gas from directly below the piston crown, aiding cylinder charging, and greatly increasing the power output. The use of the extra transfer ports was originally intended by Meier, with his first four transfer port cylinder giving 34 bhp on test. But, someone in authority at Enfields dictated that it should only have two, because the Greeves and Villiers engined racers only had two. A hurried redesign was carried out and a new two-port cylinder was made, but this only developed 31 bhp on test. At the insistence of Geoff Duke the four port cylinder was quickly reinstated, but valuable development time had been lost.

The new engine was fed by an Amal 3GP2 carburettor, of 1$^1/_2$ inch (38 mm) choke that delivered 34 bhp at 8200rpm, a shade up on its rivals in the clubman class. But this figure was later increased to 36 bhp and even further to 39 bhp, to establish its presence in the GP class. No match for the Japanese multi cylinder machines of the day, it still fared well, Percy Tait being clocked at 132mph (212.3 kph) in the 1965 North West 200, and Neil Kelly coming within two seconds of the Manx Grand Prix lap record.

When the GP5 was ready to race in anger, it was launched with much publicity, with Geoff Duke chosen to run the works team of John Hartle and Percy Tait, later to be joined by Gordon Keith. Day to day management of the team was put into the hands of Jack Booker, an ex road racer and trials rider of some repute. The recruitment of Gordon Keith caused some tension within the ranks of Enfield's middle management, for at this time Rhodesia, his home country, declared UDI, and Harold Wilson masterminding a sanctions plan against it. It was feared that the many ethnic Indian workers at the factory would revolt against the enlistment of the Rhodesian, but in actual fact they could not have cared less.

Fast but fragile

The GP5 was a flyer in the right hands, but had a habit of blowing up if over revved, and at one stage catching fire. Riders were under strict instruction not to rev the engine over 8,000rpm, which was checked by Meier, matching the exhaust note to a mouth organ. This check led to the discovery that the rev counters were in fact under calibrated, hence the high-recorded speeds and blow-ups. Early outings were marred by piston seizures, due to a faulty exhaust pipe labyrinth seal, but this problem was eradicated when the seal was redesigned. Royal Enfield was not without its bizarre one-off problems either, for at the TT, Percy Tait's machine caught fire and completely burnt out, due to a faulty ignition switch. The 1965 Manx GP saw seven Enfields entered for the Lightweight race, but due to reliability problems, only one bike finished, down in 53rd position. This was enough for the furious factory management, and the plug was pulled on the racing side. Hermann Meier was given his marching orders at the same time, leaving to take up a position with Kawasaki in the United States.

As befell the majority of British motorcycle manufacturers in the mid sixties, Enfield began to feel the pinch, due to reduced roadster sales, a direct result of the Japanese invasion. Economics dictated the closure of the Redditch factory, and the GP5 project had to go. The short lived entry into GP racing saw a rapid development, a chequered history and a quick decline, with only about 20 machines being built. The outcome of the project was beyond the wizardry of even Hermann Meier, for the financial constraints were out of his hands. He had built the engine to the brief given to him by the management, but in an effort to extract the power required for GP successes, he had to use a higher compression ratio, which shortened the life of the big-end. The works machines differed from the production versions in that they had positive oiling to the big end in an effort to combat problems in that area. Negative crankcase pressure sucked oil from a frame mounted tank via a non-return valve and directed it into the right hand main bearing. From there it passed via a machined groove and centrifugal force to the hollow crank-pin. Having no escape it entered the pin and exited through a hole to the big-end bearing. Petroil was still used, albeit at a lower ratio, to lubricate the remainder of the engine.

The GP5 was quicker than the Greeves Silverstone (as it was intended to be) but it was far less flexible, with a narrower power band. This was as expected because all increases are hard won to the detriment of others in the racing game. Given more time, Royal Enfield may have come up with a stronger big-end bearing and stronger transmission, notably the weak primary chain, to enable the use of higher revs and therefore more power. But this attractive, fast, well-braked and powerful machine had to be sacrificed in order that the company could carry on, selling roadsters for a few more years.

Cowies buyout

With the end of the GP5 the remains of the competitions shop was sold off in March 1967, to Cowies of Sunderland. Two further GP5s were completed from spares by Cowies, but in the main the remains of the competition stock was sold off at knock down prices, to enthusiastic special builders of the day.

The GP5 also showed its metal on the drag strip, in the hands of master sprinter George Brown who had purchased a pair of ex TT motors from Geoff Duke. Turning out 44 bhp at 7,000rpm on the dyno and using a fully faired, minimally tubed chassis and a battery powered dual spark head, he set two national and one world record, over a cold and wet October

Standard Villiers 9E crank (left) and Alpha full circle replacement (right)

weekend, on the runway at Greenham Common airbase in 1966. For the record these were the Standing Start Kilometer in 26.89 sec, an average of 83.18mph(133.4 kph) and national record, the Flying Start Kilometer in 18.26 sec at an average 122.45mph(197.02 kph) and national record, and the Standing Start Quarter Mile at 14.49 sec at an average 62.63mph(112.03 kph), adding another world record to the CV of the then 54-year-old master sprinter.

Merlin

The roots of the Merlin design are attributed to the world of 200cc kart racing of the mid sixties. To go one better than the Villiers based engine producers of the day, Chris Merlin of Motor Karts Ltd of Kingston-on-Thames, used a rotary disc valve to control the induction phase. Having looked at piston port induction engines Chris saw a need for asymmetric port timing to develop the power he needed, opting for the disc valve configuration which gave him the degree of control he wished for.

The Higley-Merlin road racer

To produce the 200cc Merlin kart motor, based on the 9E, a complete Villiers engine/gearbox package was used as a starting point, but the cylinder and right hand crankcase were substituted by Merlin's in-house produced items. When the move to a 250 conversion was made, the same formula applied, but this time a modified Greeves Mk 2 Silverstone cylinder was used. Production figures were low, with Motor Cycling of 6th May 1967 reporting the completion of twenty-seven 197cc units and only five 250s, of which the prototype was delivered to Berkshire racing sponsor Frank Higley. The prototype 246cc engine was installed in a Dennis Evans frame, with Ceriani forks and Oldani brakes, to produce the first Higley-Merlin, the forerunner of an intended production run by the Reading based engineer.

The first 246cc engine used a 32A drive side crankcase, with a Merlin cast timing side case complete with the rotary valve housing. The stainless steel disc valve of 32 thou (0.81 mm) thickness ran in a 50 thou (1.27 mm) chamber, and was fed by a 1 3/16 inch (30 mm) Amal. As with any Villiers based performance motor, an Alpha crankshaft was used, but with a modified timing side shaft to drive the disc. Retaining the usual Villiers dimensions of 66 x 72 mm bore and stroke, a modified Greeves RBS cylinder was used. To suit the rotary valve timing, the transfer ports were lifted and the exhaust lowered, the original inlet port having been blanked off. No provision for a flywheel magneto (the disc valve taking its place) meant the use of a total loss battery/coil ignition system. A minicar gearbox and primary drive completed the specification.

Merlin claimed 39 bhp at 8,000rpm, but on its initial test in the Higley frame, it only managed to rev to 7,000rpm. The test carried out at Silverstone by Tony Godfrey and Bruce Main Smith, proved the worth of the disc valve engine, revealing a generously wide power band. The bike

Trio of crankcases; top, full stuffers in position; middle, transfer passages smoothed out; bottom, standard transfer passages, all 9E type

Standard AE replacement piston, fat rings 250cc

was purposely over-geared but the tractability of the motor ensured a smooth and effortless passage with good results. The four-speed gearbox was initially thought to be a handicap, but with the good spread of power, fewer changes were needed to keep the motor on the boil. Compared to a Starmaker engine (for that was what it was intended to compete against) the Merlin had twice the usable rev range, with power coming in at 3,000 and increasing steadily to 5,000. A second surge of power came in at 5,000 to the natural peak at 7,000. Both riders commented on the unfussed way the motor performed, not needing to rev it like the Starmaker, using higher gear ratios out of the Silverstone corners.

As the development of the 250 Merlin continued, a break-away from the Villiers dimensions was made, with the later motors using 68 x 68 mm bore and stroke measurements; an ultra short stroke motor was even made to exploit the free revving nature of this configuration. Of the five 250 engines produced, two went to the States, the remainder staying in England with only the Frank Higley Merlin flying the flag at UK events. Rod Scivyer rode the Higley-Merlin two or three times, but it was not fast enough for him and the machine was then loaned to Tony Godfrey for a year. A New Zealander then rode the Merlin for a further year before it was bought back by Dennis Evans in a rough and sorry state. The machine was then sold on with the promise that it would be restored, but it never was and has failed to surface since.

Classic Racing

With the upsurgence of Yamaha two-stroke power, the Higley-Merlin was laid to rest and the project forgotten about, until a motor came to light in Scotland during the early 1980s. Scottish 200 kart racing champion Bill Logan was selling the engine, numbered MD1002. It was snapped up by Peter Crew who wanted to return to classic racing. On contacting Dennis Evans a spare Higley frame was unearthed, and the Merlin project was reborn. To bring the engine up to a modern specification, Fahron Engineering made a new sleeve for the Greeves shape central exhaust port cylinder, which incorporated an extra pair of transfer ports. This modification allied to a disc with 200 degrees of opening and a 38 mm Amal Mk 2 Concentric, together with electronic ignition, unleashed much more power, but to the detriment of the tractability experienced with the prototype.

After a visit to dynamometer expert Leon Moss, the Merlin now produced 29 bhp at the rear wheel, with a usable rev range from 6,000 to 10,000rpm. The 68mm Villiers piston originally used was not up to this sort of speed and was replaced by a Yamaha YZ 250 motocross component. The same problems beset the Villiers/Alpha big-end, which turned blue with every race meeting, this too was replaced with a Honda CR 250 rod and a modified crank pin. This extra power also showed up the inadequacies of the standard Villiers clutch and gearbox, which

Hepworth replacement piston with Dykes top ring

has now been replaced by a six-speed unit and Starmaker clutch. The new clutch drum misaligned the primary drive chain, but a longer Starmaker drive side crankshaft drive shaft was pressed into service to restore the chain line.

Peter Crew continued to develop the Merlin motor, and with the help of Dennis Evans has extracted a degree of power with reliability hither to undreamed of in its early days. The Merlin was used regularly in CRMC events resulting in winning the 1992 Race of the Year and the 1993 250 championship.

A 350 Merlin

To complement the 250, a 350 Merlin was also built. Originally designed by Dennis Evans and based on Merlin experience, also made by Dennis for free, with Frank Higley paying for the parts. It originally produced 44 bhp on Frank Higley's dyno, but suffered constant piston and primary chain troubles. Development slowed down and then stopped when Frank's dyno split in half, due to the water freezing up one cold winter night. Shortly afterwards the engine was given to a local rider to play with. The remains of the 350 unit was tracked down and bought back by Dennis Evans in 1989. A second 350 unit has since been unearthed at a breakers yard in London.

The 350 was rebuilt and ridden for a while by Peter Crew but it was still unreliable, suffering piston problems, even though this had been changed to a Suzuki component. The problem was traced to the third transfer port in the rear of the cylinder, which employed a window in the rear of the piston. When the port was redesigned to use a conventional duct up the rear of the cylinder sleeve and a windowless Suzuki RM 400 motocross piston, the problem was solved. The 80 x 69 mm engine now uses a Yamaha rod with a needle roller small end, and produces 35 bhp at the rear wheel, but fine tuning increased this figure even further. The 1996 racing season was used to evaluate the modified Higley/Evans Merlin engine, which has so far resulted in two class wins and numerous top three places, but further planned improvements are in the pipeline. The motor will eventually revert to the use of a Gardner carburettor, for one was fitted as standard to the original design.

Both the 250 and 350 Merlins were regularly used in classic racing events, with Peter Crew gaining many wins. The fast but fragile engines are now proving - in the light of modern day technology - to be faster and more reliable, and this, allied to Peter's aggressive riding style, ensured the combination is the formula for continued success. The Merlins have now ceased serious racing, but are still active within the classic racing scene.

Alpha replacement crankcases with no room for a flywheel, showing contact breaker points

Scorpion

The company Scorpion Motorcycle Developments may be remembered not as a developer of high performance two-stroke motors, but more predominantly as a motorcycle manufacturer. Scorpion Motorcycles survived only a few years, but during that time made a lasting impression on the sixties competition scene, with its seam-welded sheet-steel chassis, made to Formula One car standards. The idea of applying car technology to a motorcycle frame came from Paul Wright, at one period a Lotus racing car chassis designer and weekend trials rider. The high strength low weight concept of the car chassis appealed to him and after much thought he decided to construct a trials mount along these lines.

Scorpion

"RACER 250 G.P.5"

Trials riding acquaintances and sidecar racers, Bob Robinson and Ted Young, who ran a sheet metal and car body repair business (Arch Motors of Tottenham), joined Paul in the Scorpion venture, to produce motorcycles for the trials and scrambles disciplines. They again were not new to this chassis building technique, having gained experience in the construction of Lola and Lotus racing cars, and the building of their own sidecar outfits. Butler Laminates boss, Chris Butler, also joined the enterprise, designing and supplying the fibreglass mouldings for the tank, seat and mudguards.

The prototype chassis

On the prototype machine the chassis was constructed of thin gauge sheet steel welded to form three boxes. The first was the top frame rail, the second acting as the seat pillar, and the third supporting the rear suspension, seat and mudguard. To this main frame was added a bolt on square section engine loop (later to become duplex) and swinging arm. Armstrong leading-link type forks, Motoloy hubs and the Butler cosmetics completed the rolling chassis. Motive power was the Villiers 197 or 246cc unit, fitted with either the Marcelle or Parkinson alloy cylinder conversion. The bolt on engine loop could be replaced, which allowed the use of the BSA four-stroke C15 or B40 engines. Italian Parilla high camshaft power units were also considered.

The complete machine, even with the heavy iron barreled Villiers engine, weighed in at less than 91 Kg (200 lb), which gave the bike an edge over its similar engined trials rivals. Ridden by development riders Chris Cullen and Air Force pilot Jon Tye, the prototype bikes were entered in the 1963 Scottish Six Day Trial and other national events to good effect. Once the concept was proven the team went into production, adding a 197 and a 246cc scrambler, with or without an alloy cylinder conversion. Interest in the new machines was shown internationally, with agents recruited in Vancouver, Ontario, Reno, New York and even Australia.

The road racing engine

The Scorpion company has been included as an engine developer, for in 1965 they intended to expand the range to encompass road racing, and on the drawing board was the design for a 250 two-stroke 5-speed road racing machine. The machine, named the GP5, broke away from the sheet steel chassis idea and used a tubular frame. A single large diameter tube ran from the headstock to the swinging arm pivot, with a smaller tubed subframe to support the seat and suspension units, which were of Girling manufacture. Ceriani telescopic forks looked after the front-end suspension, with Oldani 200 mm brake drums fore and aft. Initially intending to use the Starmaker, the engine fitted was referred to as Scorpion designed; using a bore and stroke of 66 x 72 mm with an Alpha crankshaft (rumoured later to be modified to include a positive oil feed to the big-end) and Albion 5-speed gearbox. The alloy engine castings bore scant resemblance to the Villiers unit it was intended to replace, designed with some help from the Cromwell Motors foundry at Colchester, who were responsible for the Marcelle 9E conversions, for Scorpion had seen fit to establish links with them in the supply of alloy cylinders for their off-road machines. As soon as the motorcycle press of the day caught wind of the project, the headline "Another British Worldbeater" appeared, and blew the project out of all proportion. The press, even motorcycle journalists, love a scoop, and this story was over enthusiastically reported, the inclusion of the letters GP in the name conjuring up thoughts of Grand Prix successes. The GP5 was merely intended to be another club racer in the same vein as the Hornet, Silverstone or Telstar.

The Worldbeater story

The Worldbeater story stemmed from the reported input of £300,000 to the Scorpion company, by an anonymous Northhamptonshire businessman, his idea being to bring a world road racing championship back to Great Britain. His belief that racing success breeds roadster sales, much in the same way that the Japanese big four operate, led him to opt for an attempt to dominate the two lightweight (125 and 250) classes. When the story broke in mid 1964 the design of the 250 contender was underway, with Ron Herring being recruited as the head of development. Originally it was intended to use an Alpha rotary valve engine for the GP challenger, but secrecy surrounded a press statement which declared this was not to be the final choice. The Worldbeater image began to fade by the end of the year, as Scorpion got on with the more sensible approach of building the production racer first, before entering into cut throat and expensive realms of world class racing. The rumour was revived at the Earls Court Show, when the company exhibited the one and only GP5 production racer, even taking orders for the 1965 season.

The bubble bursts

The bubble finally burst the following year, when the decision was made to scrap the Scorpion attack on the world championship. Full reasons were never given, but it seemed that internal wrangles ended the project. It was at this juncture that the final intended engine specification was revealed. The works racing machines were to be fitted with a disc valve three cylinder two-stroke motor, the outer cylinders being horizontal with the middle cylinder at 45 degrees. The one-piece crankshaft that ran on split roller bearings was to be housed in an oil-cooled crankcase, with air-cooled cylinders and heads. The triple motor had been envisaged to run at 15,000 - 18,000rpm and would have needed an eight-speed gearbox to keep it on the boil. With the GP project terminated, Scorpion intended to carry on with the single cylinder production racer, but worse was to follow. The basic manufacturing ideas were sound, but before production could commence the company closed its doors for good, following the AMC crash of 1966 and the Manganese Bronze buy-out, which effectively stemmed the flow of Villiers engines for the bread and butter off-road motorcycle range.

9 Multi Cylinder Engines

The 344cc twin

Single cylinder two-stroke engines were the bedrock product of the Villiers factory; but during the many years spent supplying the motorcycle trade the Wolverhampton company did diversify and at times built twin cylinder engines. The first twin was the 344cc unit of 1927. Using the same dimensions as the 172cc Sports engine (which had then been in production for three years) the 57.15 x 67 mm twin now used three large plain bearings on the fore-and-aft crankshaft, with a front mounted magneto. The unit-construction motor featured alloy pistons and a worm drive to the gearbox, which then used a normal chain final drive to the rear wheel, a la Douglas. The lubrication system was again automatic, as were many other engines of that period, but now the lubricant could be individually regulated to each cylinder.

The twin did not prove to be a popular engine, lasting only two seasons, even though it received favourable comment in the motorcycle press. Four companies took up the challenge and produced machines to utilise the new motor. Francis-Barnett built the Pullman with Sun building a similar model. The French Monet-Goyon Company and the Belgian La Mondiale concern were the only other takers.

AMC at last gave in to pressure and offered the James Superswift, probably the best of all the 2T-engined models. Francis-Barnett produced the more conservative Cruiser Twin

One reason for the twin's downfall was the price, with a Francis-Barnett Pullman commanding some £68.25, which was expensive compared to the BSA and sportier Velocette 350 singles of the day.

When testing the Pullman, the motorcycle press praised it for its smooth running, ease of starting, comfort and acceleration; 'The engine resembled that of a four-cylinder car engine – but without the mechanical clatter of the valve gear.'

A 500cc version

Following the 350 in-line twin, Villiers went on to design and build a 500cc version in 1930, but this time the cylinders were set across the frame. Horizontally split crankcases were used on this design, together with separate heads and cylinders (from the Mk X-A 247cc single) and a flywheel magneto on the right hand end of the built up crankshaft. Examples of this engine were sent to Len Vale-Onslow of SOS, George Brough of Brough Superior and the Monet-Goyon factory in France, in order to gauge interest.

Very nice, but not entirely original Norman B4 Sports

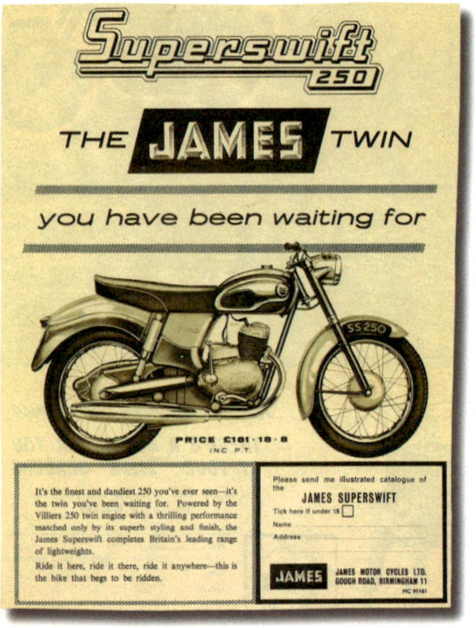

Only Brough and Monet took up the offer and built bikes to evaluate the power plant. Much correspondence was exchanged between Villiers and Monet with reference to the 500cc twin, but in May 1931 – when Monet requested a second unit – they were politely informed, 'Our factory is completely occupied by the production of the 98cc engines at the moment, at this time demand is extremely high, and for the moment we find it necessary to abandon plans to produce a 500cc model. Under the circumstances we would be pleased to know if you still require a second two-cylinder engine. We would be happy at the moment not to have to provide one, but should you require one we will make every effort to build you one.' It can only be assumed that Villiers did eventually supply that second engine, for in recent years a Monet-Goyon 500 twin has been unearthed in France, together with the remains of a spare engine.

The one and only Brough Superior 'evaluation' twin however, has been recently rebuilt and put on public display.

The new 2T twin

After a break of twenty-five years, Villiers once again embarked on the production of another side-by-side twin cylinder engine unit. Based on the cosmetic appearance of the 1H and 2H engines, the new 2T twin of 1956 retained many of the single cylinder unit's specially developed features. Utilising the same four engine mounting points of the singles, the twin was a direct replacement, and able to be bolted straight into the singles mounting cradle. But now the new engine was equipped with rubber bushed mounting points, to insulate the high frequency vibrations of the twin from the rider. The single's four-speed gearbox, four-plate clutch and even the all-enveloping side covers and carburettor covers were pressed into use to give the twin a pleasing overall streamlined package concept, often referred to as the "Power Egg".

The engine side of the package was now a 180 degree twin with separate crankcase chambers inside the vertically split crankcase. The cylinders being very close together – to promote the single cylinder look – left little room in the crankcases, which resulted in the use of only three main bearings and three main crankshaft seals. The crankshaft, with a stroke 63.5 mm, used a pair of full circle inner flywheels; pressed on to a central shaft which carried the single central main ball bearing race and a single oil seal in the right hand chamber. The outer flywheels were not of the full circle variety, reverting to the traditional Villiers hammer head crank configuration, supported on a ball race at the drive side and a roller bearing at the timing side. The big-end bearings used caged rollers, similar to the type used on the 9E Sport. The crankshaft being the heart of the engine was a massive assembly (compared to the singles) which also carried the inner crankcase chamber dividing wall. The dividing wall, referred to as the centre-plate, was an interference fitted on the central main bearing (it also carried the central oil seal), and was fitted to the crank assembly during the pressing up phase.

Dick Wyler, Greeves 25DC he shared with Griff Jenkins, 1961 Thruxton 500 mile endurance race

A narrow crankshaft

Because of the narrow crankshaft – a design requirement dictated by the use of the 1H gearbox and primary drive – the cast iron cylinders were equally closely spaced to speed up the airflow between them, but this configuration significantly reduced the space available for the transfer ports. To counteract this problem the ports were moved from their more conventional side positions to a point further forward, just aft of the front cylinder mounting studs.

The cylinders - with a bore of 50 mm - were fed from a single Villiers-made S22 carburettor, mounted on a bifurcated cast iron manifold, both hidden from view under the carburettor cover. Purpose designed alloy cylinder heads held in place by short sleeve bolts again, enhanced the single cylinder look. In essence, the twin can easily be mistaken for its single cylinder cousin, but on closer inspection it should be noted that the cylinder block and heads are oval in shape, and are in fact two separate items. The give-away is, of course the twin exhaust ports.

The 2T engine was never intended to be anything other than a touring type motor, for it only developed 15 bhp at 5,500rpm, but with a bit of tuning it could be made to perform better. Only DMW, DOT and Greeves were brave enough to market a competition machine that was powered by the 2T, but these machines were never sold in great quantities, for the power delivery characteristics were all wrong for trials and scrambling – a fact noted by Brian Stonebridge when he tried to develop one for the Greeves scrambler. Some engines did find their way on to the road race circuits, but only in the hands of under-funded clubmen. At one time a double-engined 2T dragster was even seen on the British quarter mile strips. The 2T and even the 3T engines were pressed into use as propulsion units for boats, being used mainly by amateurs and for experimental purposes, nothing serious in the way of production ever resulted.

Many of the smaller British motorcycle manufacturing companies immediately took up options on the new 2T engine, producing some fine quarter-litre scooters, touring and sports machines, the notable exceptions being Francis-Barnett and James (as explained in Chapter 8). For those manufacturers who chose to fit a full rear chain enclosure, an alternative gearbox and inner primary casting was available, which completely covered the gearbox sprocket, for this was an area that was normally open to the elements.

During the year 2004 the Chairman of the Francis-Barnett Owners Club commissioned the manufacture of 'look alike' aluminium cylinder barrels for the 2T engine. The new cylinders used a rubber mounted S25 carburettor and upped the capacity of the engine to 300cc, giving a boost to power and torque, at the same time reducing the overall weight of the engine unit.

The larger 3T version

Two years after its launch, the 2T was enlarged to produce the 324cc 3T twin. With nothing more than the use of 57 mm pistons and different con-rods the new engine now produced 16.5bhp at 5,000rpm, and was pressed into use by both motorcycle and light car manufacturers.

The Ambassador Electra 75, featuring the SIBA Dynastart with 12 volt electrics

Cotton 325cc Messenger of 1958

After the initial batch of engines, the primary drive ratio was raised, when the engine sprocket was changed from its original 20 tooth sprocket (the same as a 9E) to a 25 tooth component which was borrowed from the 8E. Why the choice of 57 mm pistons (probably from the 148cc 31C) was made has never been made clear; for during this period the 174cc 2L was in production, which also used a stroke of 63.5 mm, but utilised the 59 mm 9E piston. By using the 2L/9E pistons and 9E con-rods a full three-fifty could have been produced - a path which Adrian Armson took many years later when he raced a 3T with the VMCC (Vintage Motor Cycle Club). The problem was probably one of space; for the 3T used the original 2T crankcases with the closely spaced 50 mm bore cylinders, and to expand these bores to 59 mm may have further limited the area available for the transfer ports, as well as making the cylinder walls intolerably thin.

The 4T

After seven years in service, in 1963 the 2T was uprated to become the 4T, with both engine units remaining in production to the very end of the Villiers motorcycle engine building empire. Originally designed to power the new Bond Minicar, the correct designation of this new engine unit was, rather confusingly, the Type 225T-2, a designation thankfully only used by the factory, with owners simply referring to it as the more well-known and universally accepted Mk 4T.

The job of uprating the 2T to become the 4T was placed in the hands of Bernard Hooper; the design brief dictating that as many parts as possible be used from the old 2T. This included not only the primary drive and gearbox but also the engine bottom half. The redesign endeavoured to extract more power from the dated twin, but because of the constraints within which the engine had to be produced, no major gains were made. Given that the bottom end of the engine should not be changed, this component using a crankshaft of ridiculously narrow centres by modern standards so much so, that it adversely restricted the size of the transfer ports. In order to obtain more port area, a change to four ports with piston windows was made; with the original crankcase transfer passages feeding one pair of ports and a pair of windows in the piston feeding the second pair of ports. This modification, being bang up to date and possible due to advanced cylinder casting techniques, only gained 2 bhp and 500 revs, but it was to the detriment of the old 2T's tractability and smoothness. This point was duly noted by the motorcycle press testers of the day when they road tested the new twin.

Diagonal finning

The new 4T cylinders took on a squarer shape and utilised a pair of central plug heads to match, these heads featuring extended diagonal finning instead of the original fore and aft variety of the 2T. Other improvements in this area were oval exhaust ports for easier ring life, the use of a Villiers made S25 carburettor - on a new manifold - and a revised method to hold the exhaust pipes (with more efficient silencers) in position. The new silencers were specifically

Royal Enfield 250 Turbo Twin with Villiers 4T engine

designed for this engine, using Starmaker technology. Special attention had been paid to the harnessing of pipe and silencer resonances, using precisely calculated perforated discs and a series of tubes to achieve the desired results.

Still using the four rubber bushed mounting points of the 2T, the 4T found favour with motorcycles and scooters as well as minicars. To service the needs of the latter, the unit was available with a combination of the following specifications; electric starting, reverse operation, blower cooling, stronger clutch springs and wider gear ratios. A larger 25 tooth engine sprocket could also be specified to raise the primary drive ratio, a necessity when used with the small road wheels of the minicar and the scooter.

The Hooper fan-cooled 500 twin

The next twin Hooper was asked to design was a fan cooled 500cc unit for the Bond Minicar, but he was lumbered with an axial cooling fan left over from a flat twin engine developed for the Rootes group. This was completely inappropriate for the 27 bhp vertical twin Bond unit. Needless to say, the Bond twin never reached the production stage. The earlier Rootes engine and gearbox had been designed and built at Wolverhampton and was originally destined to power the first Hillman Imp, and comprised a rubber mounted flat twin ohv engine of similar design to the Citroen 2CV and BMW Coupe, which the Imp was to compete against in the market place. In the end, the production models utilised the four-cylinder baby Coventry Climax motor, when the Hillman design team was taken over by a new boss with sporting aspirations. This change in direction led to some bad feeling at Wolverhampton, with the Villiers team considering themselves to have been "used" by the Rootes group.

After many other such upsets Bernard Hooper handed in his notice and left the Villiers factory in 1965 to take up consultancy work with colleague John Favill. But, the following year the pair returned at the express wish of the new Norton Villiers management, to carry on the development work on the Norton twin cylinder engines, a task that resulted in the eventual production of the Atlas and then the Commando. Hooper also became involved with the revolutionary NVT Wulf, a stepped piston twin cylinder two-stroke power unit which used inter-cylinder transfer porting and stratified charging, to meet the needs of the export markets.

The Bill Hindes V4

A four-cylinder experiment was explored by engineer Bill Hindes in 1963, but instead of the more usual method of chaining a pair of 2T engines together in a square configuration, this time the cylinders were arranged in a V4 formation. The engine was designed and built by Bill, with the intention of using as many 2T parts as possible, the only major deviation from this plan being the wider than standard crankcases with the extra cylinder flanges. The crankshaft, made from standard 2T components, employed longer crankpins to accept a pair of con rods each side, which were separated by a hardened steel washer. To use a pair of pistons in a V formation on a common

The Bill Hindes Villiers V4, four 2T cylinders on a common crankcase, now on display at the Sammy Miller Museum

crankcase meant that the normal method of crankcase pumping was lost, as the crankcase volume had to feed two pistons at very irregular and inopportune intervals. In order to get over this problem a Shorrocks supercharger was used at 1.18 times the engine speed to deliver the mixture to the crankcases. The aim was not to supercharge the engine to gain power, but to gently feed the primary pumping chambers to ensure good cylinder filling. This was borne out by the pressure gauge that indicated zero boost at 4,000rpm. The ignition system was converted to total loss battery and coil, as the magneto had been removed to make way for the supercharger drive belt. The points were housed in the standard cover, but now there were four, courtesy of the Ford Motor Co.

The engine was accommodated in a Douglas Dragonfly chassis, in order that the two front cylinders could lie between the widely spaced front rails. The completed machine was so professionally built, that Villiers actually purchased it for evaluation purposes, but once it had been inspected it was stored away in the company cellar. When the NVT company closed down and the assets sold off in 1978, the machine came to light again. The late Bob Currie viewed the rediscovered bike, and quite understandably thought it to be some sort of factory prototype, later he realised his mistake and gave praise to its original creator. The machine has since been restored to its original specification and is now an exhibit in the Sammy Miller Motorcycle Museum.

Tait Triple

Intrigued by the DKW racing triples of the mid-1950s, way before the Japanese Honda NS400 road going triple was conceived, design draughtsman Bob Tait decided that he wanted a two-stroke triple to ride on the road, but where could he get one? This was in 1967, when only relatively mundane two-strokes were available and certainly with nothing more than two cylinders.

A chance conversation with Cyril Quantrill, then editor of Motor Cyclist Illustrated, resulted in the decision to build his own. As a design draughtsman, with access to machining equipment, the project became a viable proposition, but the crankshaft production would have to be farmed out. When the crankshaft design had been formulated, Bob contacted the world-renowned crank specialists, Alpha Bearings of Dudley, who were only too pleased to accept the work, but at a price.

Having chosen a bore and stroke of 59 x 60 mm (which gave a total displacement of 492cc), to use products that were readily available, the crankshaft was manufactured and assembled by Alpha. It utilised four roller main bearings, with grooved outer rings to accept split rings which located the crank in the horizontally split crankcases, together with dowels to prevent turning. This method of crank location predated its use by most Japanese multi cylinder machine makers by many years. A fifth bearing, this time a ball, was positioned outboard of the primary drive sprocket, and located in the outer primary chaincase to act as an outrigger. Crankshaft seals posed a problem, for the rubber seals of the day were not very reliable, and therefore piston ring type labyrinth seals were chosen for the inner crankcase chamber, as these would out-last the life of the engine. Rubber seals were retained for use on the outers, as these could be easily changed without having to dismantle the crank. The crankshaft was fitted with Alpha replacement con-rods, originally intended for the Excelsior Talisman twin engine, which utilised caged roller bearings and plain small ends. The price of the completed crank, £100, was heavy by 1967 standards, but it was a work of art.

The crankcases were cast in LM4 by Ball Brothers of Stratford on Avon, at a cost of £18, and machined by Bob Tait. Made in two halves, the upper case carried the three cylinders, the central one pointing forward in the best DKW fashion, with a bolt-on Albion/Greeves gearbox to the rear. The design configuration of the cylinders ensured that the crankshaft was as short, and therefore as stiff as possible. The duplex primary drive chain, enclosed in an alloy case, drove a BSA A65 clutch unit from which one row of teeth had been removed. There was no provision for chain adjustment, but enough room was left in the chaincase if a tensioner was deemed necessary at a later date. A new splined adaptor was made by Bob, to accommodate the BSA clutch to the Albion mainshaft. The ignition system was sited on the right hand end of the crank, enclosed in an alloy cover. It comprised a single cam that operated three contact breakers and was powered by a total loss battery, for no charging system was provided on the prototype.

Again using readily available components, the motor utilised three Marcelle cylinders and heads, originally intended as replacements for the Villiers 9E engine. Modified to suit the reduced stroke, the cylinders were shortened and fitted with ported Hepolite liners by Bob Cooper, who honed them to suit the Hepolite 59 mm pistons. The cylinders and heads were reduced in width to allow for the compact fitting, held down by Greeves alloy sleeve bolts. As the motor was initially intended for use as a roadster, only one carburettor was fitted, a 30 mm Amal Concentric, to a torturous "T" shaped manifold that placed the carburettor between the twin down tubes of the frame. With no thought of expansion chambers, three separate exhaust pipes with flat silencers were fitted, one each side of the rear wheel, with the third below the crankcase.

To try out the engine, Bob fitted it into a home-brewed trials chassis, for he was also a trials enthusiast. This resulted in the most unlikely combination ever to grace the feet up scene. On its first outing, during which its creator retired due to a twisted ankle, the machine was tested by John Gleed, a regular contributor to Classic & Motorcycle Mechanics, who reported that the triple had a good power band with lots of bottom end power, which was remarkable considering the lack of any flywheel effect. It also picked up cleanly and had enough power to tackle the steepest of climbs.

As a testimony to his engineering ability, the engine was on public show at the Earls Court Motorcycle Show of 1967 and remained in regular use up until 1971, when it was removed from the bike for frame alterations that were never carried out. Bob Tait still has the engine and in 2003 the engine was on the bench, the owner considering a few modifications prior to fitting it into a road race chassis.

British Anzani

British Anzani was a pioneer name in its own right on the British motorcycle scene, having been involved in motorcycle manufacture since the beginning of the century. More recently the name had been associated with the manufacture of water-cooled two-stroke twin cylinder outboard engines for the marine craft industry. And, it was an adapted version of one of these designs that beat Villiers to the motorcycle engine manufacturing stage by some three years. Never produced in the quantities that Villiers built their 2T, it was never the less used by some of the more famous motorcycle producers of the day, for it added a twin cylinder two-fifty to its stable.

The owner and chief designer at the British Anzani Engineering Company during the fifties, based then at Hampton Hill in Middlesex, was Charles Harrison who spent his early years at the famous JAP concern. Harrison, a hydroplane racer who once held the world water speed record at 56mph, was a true motorcyclist at heart. He took the company's proven racing marine engine (the Uni-twin) and redesigned it for the motorcycle role as early as 1953.

1950s British Anzani 322cc rotary valve motorcycle engine, originally conceived for marine use, together with a 242cc version

The Uni-twin powerhead outboard racing marine engine, designed by Howard Barnes Moss, had proved unbeatable in hydroplane racing, holding many records, but its production was costly. To offset this cost, the cheaper motorcycle version was built, using as many of the marine engine's components as possible. The marine engines were available in two sizes to cover the 15 cu in (245.85cc) and the 20 cu in (327.80cc) hydroplane classes, which resulted in the manufacture of the 242cc and the 322cc engines, these sizes being passed on to the motorcycle engines.

The new Anzani 242cc motorcycle engine design was radical in its approach, having a rotary valve induction system. The valve, which fed both cylinders from a single inlet manifold, was set in the centre of the pressed up crankshaft. The central section of the crank was a large cotton reel shaped casting, which fed gas from a port in the large split phosphor bronze central main bearing (supplied by the Glacier Bearing Co), to each cylinder in turn. To accommodate the split central main bearing, the crankcases were also split horizontally, a technique normally associated with latter day Japanese multi-cylinder engines. The rest of the engine followed normal engineering practice, with a combination of ball and roller outer main bearings and a one-piece cast iron cylinder block and alloy head. A duplex chain housed within an alloy case, took the primary drive to an Albion four-speed gearbox.

The new Anzani motor, having a bore and stroke of 52 x 57 mm gave 10 bhp at 4,800rpm, good by standards fifty years ago comparing favourably with other motors of the time. The rotary valve had two drillings that extended obliquely from the centre bearing face to the adjacent flywheels, these passages being fed in turn by a window in the split central bearing. Behind the bearing, cast in to the upper crankcase half, was a large annular passage, which operated in effect as an intermediate induction chamber. This type of induction system had a two fold benefit, in that it could take advantage of asymmetric port timing to aid cylinder filling, and eliminate carburettor blow back that produced unsightly oily deposits. The asymmetric port timing was timed at 120 degrees before top dead centre, to 60 degrees after top dead centre, giving a total induction period of 180 degrees. This meant not only cleaner but also quieter engine running. With the use of this advanced technology induction system, it could be asked why, with such an advantage, the twin was no more powerful than its contemporaries. The answer was again two fold in that Anzani built the engine to a price, to reflect their intention to market a reliable, economic and profitable product. The second reason was that Anzani never intended it to be anything more than a basic motorcycle power plant.

The motorcycle engine went into production in 1953, with Greeves being the first manufacturer to use it, followed by Cotton and Norman two seasons later. In 1954 Anzani announced a 322cc version of the unit that used the same bottom end but with 60 mm pistons. The bigger motor still used the rotary inlet system, but in addition to this used extra piston controlled inlet ports to enhance its performance, which was claimed at 15 bhp at 4,800rpm.

The rotary valve timing remained at 180 degrees, with the symmetrical auxiliary piston ports being timed at 120 degrees. For 1955 Anzani included the SIBA Dynastart and reverse gear to attract minicar manufacturers. For 1956 a water-cooled version was announced, having been installed and tested in a James Captain frame by Bill Dent the previous year, but this engine had no takers. At the same time the opportunity was used to increase the cylinder and head finning on both engines, together with an increase in compression ratio from 6.5 to 7.5-1. The engine remained in production for some years, but its use in motorcycles ceased in 1960.

The Anzani motor was not a popular choice as a performance racing engine, with few examples gracing the racing scene, due to the fact that two-stroke tuning was a relatively unknown art during the fifties and expansion chamber technology was as then unexplored. Another downfall of the revolutionary rotary valve twin was the valve itself, adequate as it was in the roadster role, the centre bearing cried enough when subjected to any sustained high rpm, wearing the phosphor bronze bearing which introduced inter crankcase air leaks. As the valve seating clearance grew so did the gas leakage, the once precise valve timing becoming rather random. The torturous route of the induction path, through the intermediate induction chamber and the rotary valve itself (a path not shared by the marine version) did not lend itself to the high performance mode, neither did the use of a Siamese exhaust system in the motorcycle role. Because the twins were intended as commuter engines, the primary compression ratio was not that important, when the full circle cranks of the original marine racing engine were dropped in favour of the bob weight type to improve balance and to cut vibration.

Despite its roadster background, and the use of racing marine engine parts, the Anzani twin was not without its successes, epitomised in the July 1962 Snetterton national meeting. Bob McGregor created something of a mini-sensation with his exploits in the hotly contested 250cc race, which featured such prominent names as Dan Shorey, Terry Grotefeld and Horace Crowder. The Motor Cycling race report commented, 'Undoubtedly a future star, Bob McGregor brought his unfaired Anzani special into a very creditable fourth place.' McGregor's machine showed just what could be achieved during the early 1960s with a combination of home-brewed engineering and spirited riding talent. Unfortunately neither McGregor nor the Anzani were to match the race reporter's predictions, and both faded into obscurity.

One interesting example of the Anzani which is still ridden today, is the BSA Bantam framed water-cooled twin, built by arch special builder David Blanchard. The professional looking hybrid was good enough to take second place in the 1962 Motor Cycle News Special of the Year competition.

2T-engined sprinter, circa early 1960

Excelsior

It was not until the end of the Second World War that Excelsior became known as a producer of two-stroke engines for civilian motorcycles. In the twenties and thirties they used the proprietary Blackburne, JAP and even Villiers engines to power their models, but the later sports racers used their own engines, with Syd Gleave winning the 1933 Lightweight TT on a 248cc Mechanical Marvel, which was later to be replaced by the Manxman, available in 250, 350 and 500cc versions. Excelsior produced single cylinder motors to cover the 100, 125 and the 150cc classes, but was best remembered for the 250cc twin cylinder Talisman engines, beating Villiers into the twin cylinder market by some nine years.

Following the Second World War the Excelsior engine manufacturing shop started to produce two-stroke motors for the army's Welbike replacement, which when hostilities ended became available as the civilian Corgi. The engine that powered the Corgi was a single speed 98cc unit that used a pair of detachable transfer port windows and overhung crankshaft, and was named the Spryt. The Spryt was replaced in 1947 by a new two speed 98cc motor called the Goblin. Basically the same as the engine it replaced, the new two-speed unit had its magneto on the right hand side, with a larger casting to accommodate the gearbox, which was operated by a handlebar lever. To offer a cheaper alternative to the two-speed Goblin engine, a Mk 2 version was produced at the same time, which reverted to a single speed transmission. In 1948 a two-speed 125cc Goblin was made, but this was phased out the following year. In 1952 another single cylinder engine was produced, this time a 150cc three-speed unit, for fitting to the Excelsior light bike and scooter range. Running along side the fitment of similarly sized Villiers engines, the 150 stayed in production for ten years.

The Talisman twin

Up until 1949, all the Excelsior two-stroke engines had been in the commuter class, to power the wide range of go-to-work machines produced by the factory. But then a step was taken to break into the emerging sports-leisure market with the Talisman twin. The new twin engine, of 50 x 62 mm bore and stroke measurements, heralded the move to sporting and performance motorcycling. The Talisman engine used a three-piece, vertically split crankcase, with two pressed up cranks bolted together in the centre, supported on five ball and a single plain bearing, to form a very rigid bottom end. The rest of the engine followed conventional practice, with separate cast iron cylinders and alloy heads. A bolt on Albion four-speed gearbox, single Amal carburettor and a Wipac flywheel magneto completed the specification. The Talisman twin was not fast by today's standards, having a top speed of 62 mph, but its performance was brisk, and with a fuel consumption of 110 mpg at a steady 55 mph, it made the best use of the two gallons a month post-war petrol allowance.

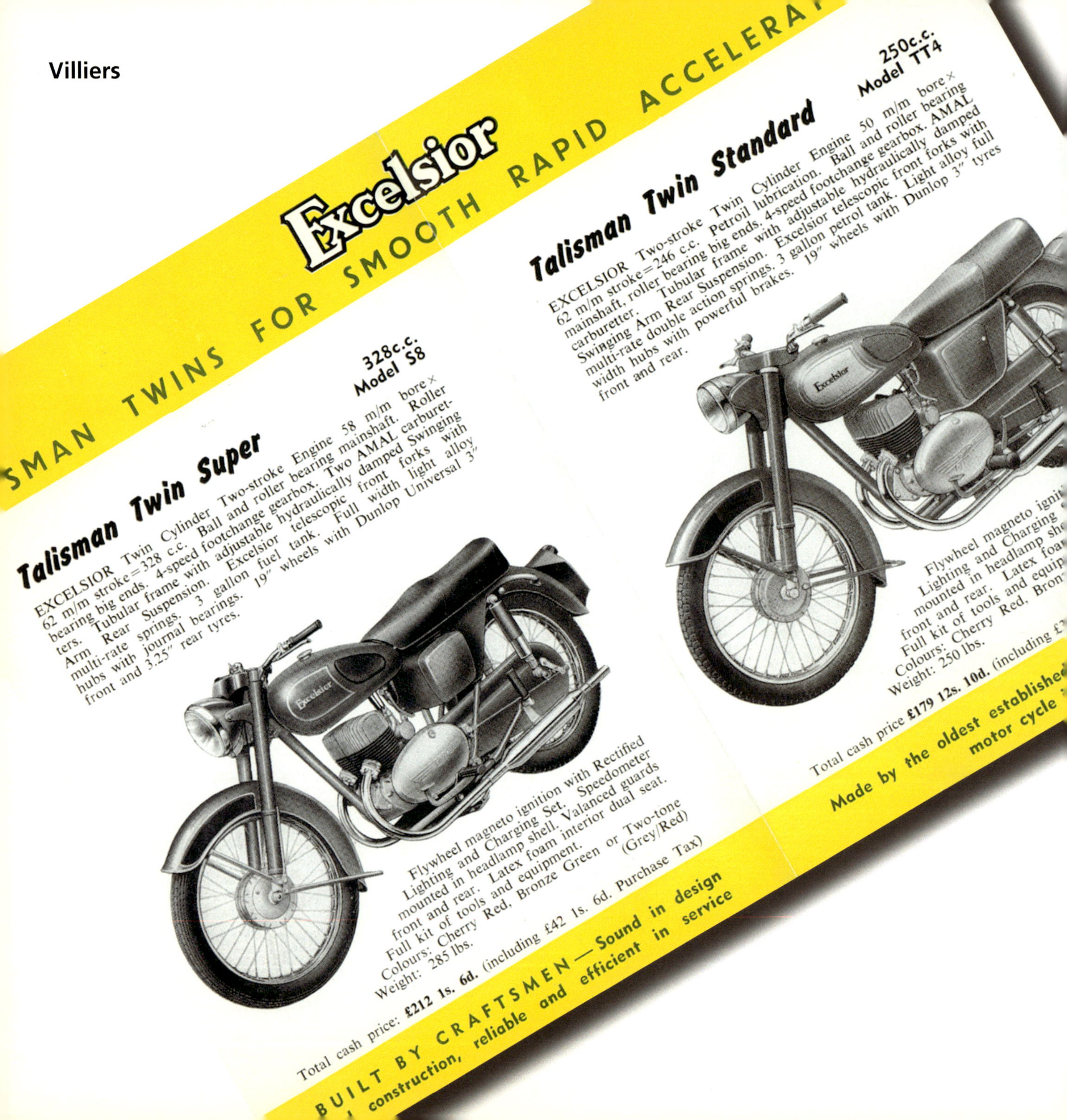
SMAN TWINS FOR SMOOTH RAPID ACCELERA
Excelsior
Talisman Twin Super
328c.c. Model S8
EXCELSIOR Twin Cylinder Two-stroke Engine 58 m/m bore× 62 m/m stroke=328 c.c. Ball and roller bearing mainshaft. Roller bearing big ends. 4-speed footchange gearbox. Two AMAL carburetters. Tubular frame with adjustable hydraulically damped Swinging Arm Rear Suspension. Excelsior telescopic front forks with multi-rate springs. 3 gallon fuel tank. Full width light alloy hubs with journal bearings. 19" wheels with Dunlop Universal 3" front and 3.25" rear tyres.
Flywheel magneto ignition with Rectified Lighting and Charging Set. Speedometer mounted in headlamp shell. Valanced guards front and rear. Latex foam interior dual seat. Full kit of tools and equipment. Colours: Cherry Red, Bronze Green or Two-tone (Grey/Red) Weight: 285 lbs.
Total cash price: £212 1s. 6d. (including £42 1s. 6d. Purchase Tax)
Talisman Twin Standard
250c.c. Model TT4
EXCELSIOR Two-stroke Twin Cylinder Engine 50 m/m bore× 62 m/m stroke=246 c.c. Petroil lubrication. Ball and roller bearing mainshaft, roller bearing big ends. 4-speed footchange gearbox. AMAL carburetter. Tubular frame with adjustable hydraulically damped Swinging Arm Rear Suspension. Excelsior telescopic front forks with multi-rate double action springs. 3 gallon petrol tank. Light alloy full width hubs with powerful brakes. 19" wheels with Dunlop 3" tyres front and rear.
Flywheel magneto igni
Lighting and Charging
mounted in headlamp she
front and rear. Latex foa
Full kit of tools and equip
Colours: Cherry Red, Bron
Weight: 250 lbs.
Total cash price £179 12s. 10d. (including £
BUILT BY CRAFTSMEN — Sound in design
construction, reliable and efficient in service
Made by the oldest established
motor cycle

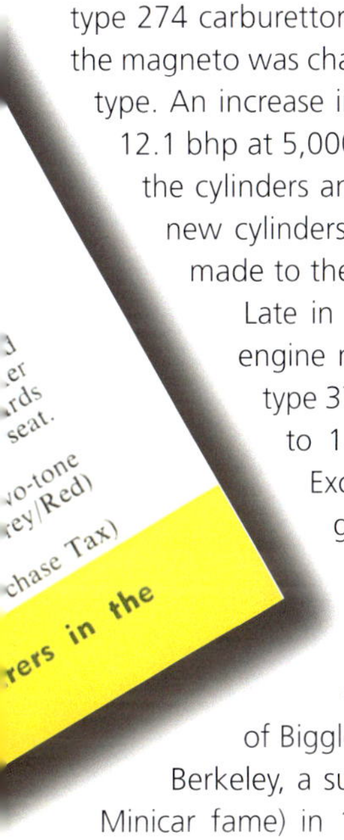

During its thirteen year production run, the 250 Talisman engine received many detailed changes to its original specification. In 1952 a sports version was made that used a pair of Amal type 274 carburettors fed by a single GP float chamber. At the same time, the bearing behind the magneto was changed to a roller, and the single row primary chain was changed to a duplex type. An increase in power during 1954 saw the output raised from 10 bhp at 4,500rpm to 12.1 bhp at 5,000rpm, but the compression ratio stayed the same at 7.7:1. Three years later the cylinders and heads were redesigned to give them increased fin depth and area. The new cylinders also received modified exhaust porting. At the same time a change was made to the carburettor specification, with the use of the type 375 Amal Monobloc.

Late in 1957 a larger version of the Talisman twin was born. The new enlarged engine now featured 58 mm pistons, which gave a capacity of 328cc. Twin Amal type 376 Monobloc carburettors were also fitted, which boosted the power output to 18 bhp at 5,000rpm. To service the light car and three-wheeler industry, Excelsior adapted the 328 twin to include a SIBA Dynastart and an Albion gearbox with a reverse ratio, the engine doing sterling service in many light three wheelers, which became popular during the late fifties and early sixties. Production of the twins ceased in 1962, when the company closed down the engine plant at Tyseley in the suburbs of Birmingham.

One of the major users of the Talisman engine was the Berkeley coachworks of Biggleswade, who used them in their range of three and four wheeler light cars. Berkeley, a successful caravan manufacturer, was approached by Lawrie Bond (of Bond Minicar fame) in 1955, with the plans for a glass fibre bodied sports car. Charles Panter, Berkeley's owner, liked the idea and launched the new car in the October of the following year. The first car was a four-wheeled two-seater, powered by an Anzani 322cc engine, but one year later Charles Panter signed up with Excelsior, for the supply of the Talisman 328cc unit to power his cars. The best remembered Berkeley was the T60 three-wheeler, which was built from August 1959, this model used the Mk 6 328cc twin, of which some 1780 examples were produced.

A 492cc triple

To counter the rumour that Berkeley were contemplating a change to BSA power for their upmarket four wheeled Sports model, Excelsior designed and built a three cylinder engine, which was basically a 328 twin with an extra cylinder, giving a total capacity of 492cc. The new triples crankcase was constructed from twin parts, and utilised two centre sections, to make the three flywheel chambers. The crankshaft again used the twin components, but this time the cranks were keyed and locked together at 120 degrees, and used a triple contact breaker magneto. All other items were from the roadster twin, except the heavy duty Albion gearbox that included a reverse ratio.

1959 Monte Carlo Rally works Berkeley entry

The 492 triple was used only in the four wheelers, as it was deemed as too dangerous in the three wheeled cars, the idea having been put to the Ministry of Transport for approval, and turned down. In its day the four wheeled three cylinder car could, due to its high power to weight ratio, match the performance of the medium engine sized traditional sports cars, with this being proved on the sporting scene. Berkeley believed that success in competition encouraged sales, and set up a competitions department, headed by Paul Garrod, to show the marque on the race track. The ultra lightweight car put up some creditable performances not only on the track, but also on the international rally scene. During the late fifties the company entered cars in the Monte Carlo rally, enlisting the help of the Royal Air Force to crew them, with the drivers and navigators coming from nearby RAF Henlow, which was then the services navigational training establishment. Other big names of the day tried their hand at rallying in the Berkeley, Pat Moss-Carlson being one, but her training session prior to one major event resulted in the total destruction of the car. Spare cars were available for the event and the damaged one returned to the factory for a rebuild.

One draw back with the use of the Albion gearbox which used the four forward and a reverse ratio was the gear shift, which employed a W shaped gate. Many drivers could not get on with this method of gear changing, and Paul Garrod adapted the motorcycle positive stop system to introduce a sequential gearshift pattern, a system favoured in today's racing cars. Other refinements he made to the engine to keep the race crews happy, was the use of a hydraulic clutch and a neutral indicator. Another modification added to the rally cars was the fitment of a manual spark retarder, fitted at the request of the Monte Carlo crews, to make the long uphill grinds easier on the engine. This was achieved by the use of a cable operated ignition back plate, controlled from the cab.

The Excelsior three cylinder engines performed well in competition, even though they had received only the minimum amount of tuning in the competitions shop, but the main failing was the rapid wear rate of the triple contact breaker system. To counter this problem the competitions shop made ready spare back plates, accurately timed (and marked); these could be quickly exchanged in record time at service halts. The short final drive chain also suffered in competition, but a change to a duplex type cured the problem.

Berkleley cars used for circuit racing were all fitted with Amal TT carburettors and large GP type float chambers, but suffered fueling problems due to the high cornering forces. To get over these faults the competitions shop came up with an ingenious modification. Swill pots were added outboard of the three float chambers, from which the floats and needles had been removed. Holes were drilled in the float chambers at the optimum fuel height level, and any excess fuel was sucked out and fed back to the tank. A second SU fuel pump kept the swill pots topped up.

The Excelsior company had been producing a three cylinder water-cooled boat engine for

Excelsior 492cc triple engine as fitted to the Berkeley four wheeler

some time, but would never allow Berkeley to use it in their cars. When Berkeley finally crashed in 1960, with Excelsior being a major creditor, Paul Garrod purchased a three cylinder motor from the winding up sale and set about building a water-cooled three cylinder three wheeler as a private venture. The motor used the marine cylinders and heads, together with a water-cooled exhaust manifold, which gave the three wheeler a frightening performance of 100 mph plus, even though it only used a single carburettor.

It is a great pity that Excelsior never did design a motorcycle to use the triple engine. It would have called for a complete new chassis and running gear to handle the power output of the engine, but this was above the capacity of the relatively small company. In 1963, Excelsior enthusiast David Blanchard actually built one that was tested for the motorcycle press by David Dixon, the neat and professional looking special beating Kawasaki to the market place with the two-stroke triple concept by eleven years.

Today many examples of the Excelsior two-stroke engine are still in regular use, in both cars and motorcycles. With good spares back up from the British Two-stroke club and the Berkeley Enthusiasts club, this ensures that the fearsome howl of a triple on full song should be heard for a long time yet.

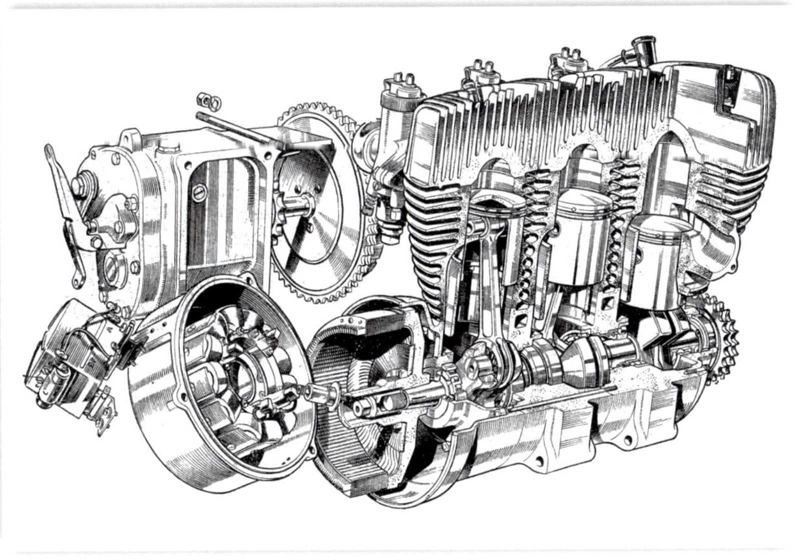

Sectional drawing of the 492cc Excelsior triple

Panther Models 35/45/50

To the Panther goes the distinction of producing the heaviest of the post-war Villiers-powered motorcycles and the last 2T-engined machines to be built. It was also one of the most durable machines to house a Villiers engine of its day and because of this a surprising number have survived - relative to production figures compared with other marques.

The first Villiers twin-engined Panther arrived in late 1956, with the 249cc (50 x 63.5 mm) 2T powerplant. This used the basic Model 10 cycle parts, previously home for the 8 and 9E 197cc singles. The 2T engined machine was known as the Model 35. As Barry M Jones recalls in his 1983 book, The Story of Panther Motorcycles, 'The Model 35 was a most potent and likable machine that outlasted the entire Villiers- engined range, reappearing as a Red Panther from Pride & Clarke in the late 1960s when Phelon & Moore had virtually disappeared from the motorcycle scene.

Next came a tuned version, the Model 35 Sports, using high compression 9.4:1 heads. Each of the Sports versions was specifically tuned and checked out prior to leaving Panther's Cleckheaton works, and gave a maximum speed of 76 mph compared with a shade over seventy for the standard model.

Important improvements to cater for the additional performance were made to the frame, with longer fork stanchions being specified, this raising the front end of the motorcycle by a small degree. There were also modified fork pivots on the Reynolds-Earls forks to provide 'safer steering and improved handling' as the P & M publicity material stated. The Sports model also sported the Model 65/75 full width 7 inch brake hubs.

A year later, in 1959 came the Model 45, using the Villiers 324cc (57 x 63.5 mm) 3T engine. And once again the factory carried out work on the frame, not only strengthening it, but also providing additional bracing to the front forks. With 18 bhp at 5,500rpm the Model 45 could top 75mph in standard tune.

For 1960 Panther introduced the new Model 50, essentially the Model 45, but with the company's own telescopic front forks, based on that which was used on Model 100 598cc ohv twin-port single.

The Model 50, of which only 372 examples were actually built, was as Barry M Jones says, 'In many ways a combination of heavyweight 100 and lightweight 35.' Essentially, the machine employed the lightweight frame suitably strengthened, and the Model 45 324cc 3T engine, initially in prototype guise with Siamese exhausts, although production versions were equipped with the conventional twin system. The remainder of the specification saw, as already stated, the 'bathtub' rear enclosure (shared with the Model 35 Sports), a unique front mudguard with deep central valances, Model 120 two-way damped front forks, a Model 100 headlamp and the huge, but attractive 8 inch deeply finned aluminium brake hubs (fitted into 18 inch rims) from the Model 120. It should be pointed out that the Model 120 front forks were reversed to reduce the trail as well as prevent the forks giving problems under braking. At 333 lb, the Model 50 was over 40 lb heavier than the standard Model 35, this additional weight providing the bike with considerable stability. A typical comment on the Model 50 was, 'Its top speed of 75 mph was not that impressive, but the sheer pulling power of the Villiers engine was typical of the long-legged top gear touring beloved of the Model 100.'

Panther's chief designer, Frank Leech, won the company a Design Council award for the Model 50; yes it was probably the most attractive twin cylinder Villiers powered motorcycle offered, together with the Norman B4 Sports and the James Superswift.

For the next two years, with falling sales, Panther struggled. Then in October 1962 the good ship P & M hit the financial rocks, with the appointment of an official receiver. The result of this was that production of all the Villiers powered models ceased in December 1962. But then, after finding that he had sufficient spares to build a considerable number of machines, combined with the fact that there appeared to be no potential buyers for the factory on the horizon, the receiver restarted production.

Actually, sales went better than expected for the 2T engined models. This resulted in Panther purchasing a job lot of Villiers 2T Dynastart engines from DMW, these having been acquired via Ambassador when the former took over the latter after Kaye Don had decided to close the Ascot works during 1962/63.

The DMW/Panther deal was done in early 1964. DMW, having moved with the times was now fitting the newly introduced 4T engine. Panther began producing the ex DMW 2T engined machines in April 1964. Distribution of this 'new' model, the Model 35 (kickstart) or 35ES (Dynastart), labelled the 'Red Panther' was handled exclusively by Pride & Clarke. In all 512 were built, 215 with the electric start the first engine number being W101A. The frames of these later bikes had a reduction in the steering head angle of some 3 degrees. The kickstart version had 6 volt electrics, the Dynastart push-button models being12 volts with two batteries in series.

Differences compared to the earlier 2T bikes included chrome-steel sports mudguards, flyscreen, a narrower dual seat, a Speedwell Italian style fuel tank (also used on the James and Francis-Barnett twins) and all vestiges of the mid-riff panelling removed. The only really black marks were the sub-standard paint finish and the fitment of the weak 5½ inch front stopper formally used on the 197cc engined Panthers. A Siamese exhaust system was also specified. One has to say that Panther was effectively using up its stock of components.

For 1966, when Panther's stock of 2T engines was running low, only the electric start versions remained. And these seem to have soldiered on until the autumn of 1968, with the final bike being sold by Whitby's of Acton (now part of the Pride & Clarke group), during mid 1969.

Also it is worth pointing out that the Dynastart equipped models with their 12 volt electrics, 90 watt output and 50 per cent overload capability not only meant efficient starting (provided the Dynastart units brushes were clean!), but remarkably good lighting for a 1960s British motorcycle.

All-in-all, the Panther series of Villiers twin cylinder motorcycles was one of the very best of the breed.

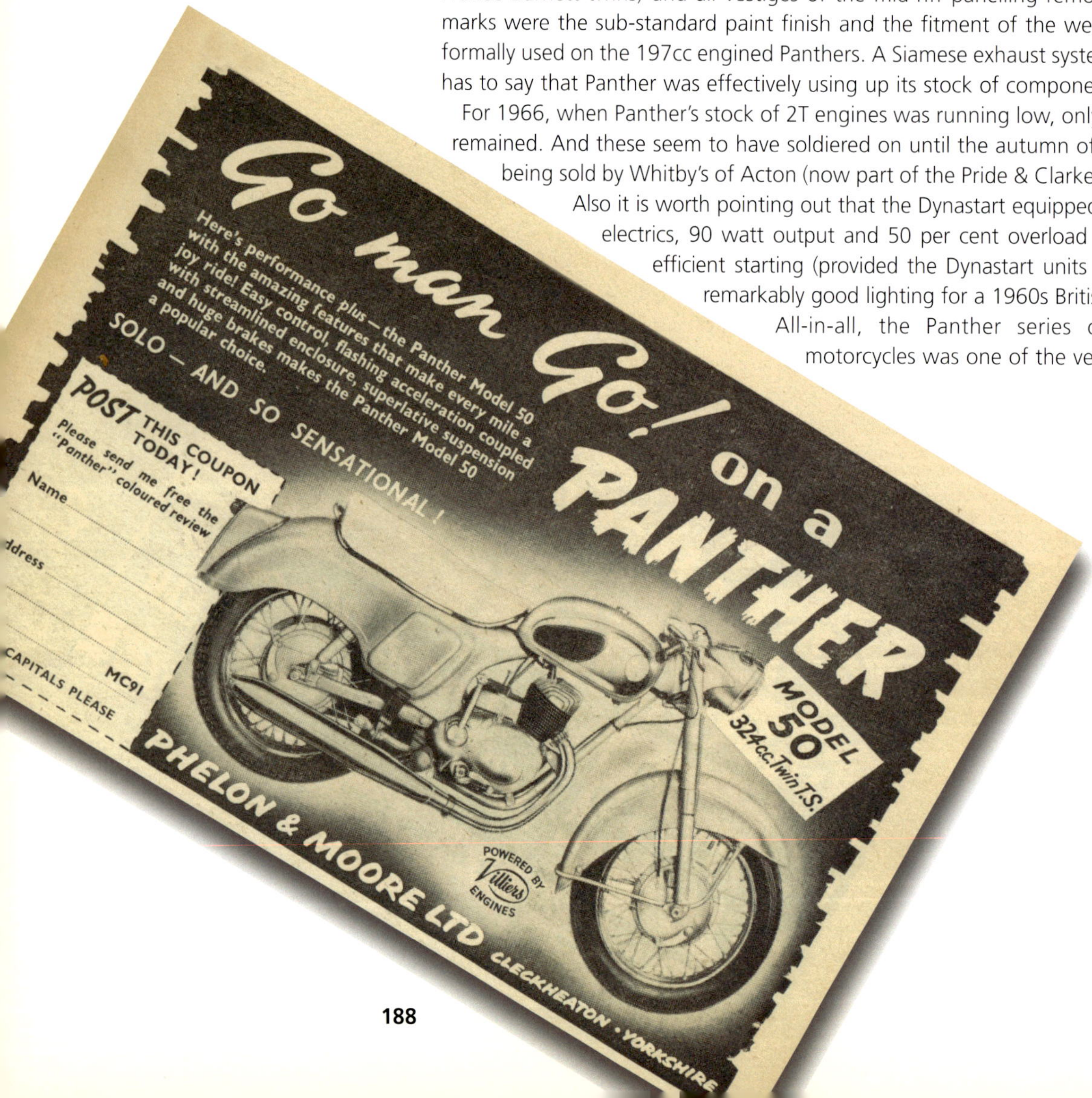

2T engine showing the ignition switch, kickstart, gearlever, points housing and carburettor cover

10 The Starmaker

For decades the Villiers company had supplied nothing more than commuter engines to the motorcycle manufacturers, who then modified them to their own requirements, by fitting items made by the peripheral manufacturers who had sprung up to fulfill this requirement. Villiers could have done the job themselves but chose not to. The expertise was on hand at the factory, and an uprated 250 could have been made, which would have had a better reliability factor than the products on offer. In 1962 this state of affairs finally came to an end with the Starmaker, when Villiers at last shook off its conservative cloak of relative respectability and produced a true competition engine for the eagerly awaiting public. Using the same trio of engine mounting bolts as the E an A range motors, the Starmaker was a direct replacement for the long-stroke motors. But not everyone was happy with the introduction of this engine, for it was rumoured that it would sound the death knell for the A series competition engines used so widely in trials and scrambles. Thankfully this was not to be the case, and the two types of engine ran happily alongside each other for a few more years.

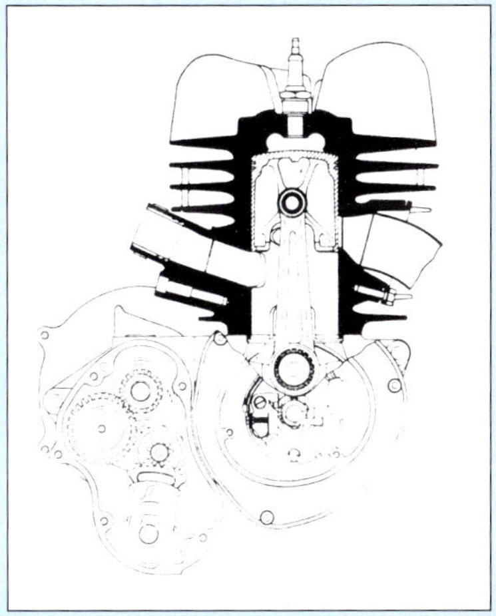

Cutaway drawing showing the unique mushroom shaped compustion chamber

A Bernard Hooper design

The new engine was designed by Bernard Hooper, who had been at the Wolverhampton factory since 1958 working on industrial engines. It was originally called the Star-Maker, but this was soon shortened to Starmaker, and was a complete breakaway from the E and A range singles of the period. Rather confusingly referred to by the factory as the Type 225H engine, the Starmaker was neither a 225 nor part of the 1H-2H range, and used very few parts from that series. In use by the general public the unit was simply known as the Starmaker. Gone was the old long stroke configuration, with the Starmaker having square 68 x 68 mm dimensions, displacing 247cc. A new wider and stiffer crankshaft, that ran in a pair of lipped roller bearings which provided both rigidity and positive crank location, was also produced for this engine. Outboard of the roller bearings was a pair of seals, and outboard of the drive side seal was a needle roller bearing lubricated from the primary drive case to support the left hand drive shaft. The crankshaft webs and drive shafts were one-piece forgings in nickel-chrome- molybdenum steel, and employed a stepped crank pin, to give the rigidity required for competition work. The crankcases were heavily webbed, and were bolted to the John Favill designed four-speed gearbox. The method of mounting the gearbox was the only feature inherited from the A range engines it replaced, the four-point mounting studs using the same dimensions, but the gearboxes were not interchangeable for the primary drive line had been changed.

John Favill was the transmission expert, and his brief was to design a gearbox that would be capable of withstanding the loadings put on it by the new motor. There was no point in rehashing the A series box, for this was only just about adequate for the 20 or so bhp that was being transmitted through it, even then it was prone to failure. The new Starmaker gearbox featured larger, wider pinions with under cut dogs, to prevent the gears jumping out under load,

DMW Hornet fitted with the wide-fin racing Starmaker and single Amal GP carb

and the wholesale use of needle roller bearings. With its solid EN36B mainshaft, which used radial needle roller trust races for positive location and involute splines for added strength, a new all-metal diaphragm clutch was used. The primary drive cases which housed a duplex chain also incorporated a clutch puller, rather than the clutch pushrod method used before on the hollow main shaft gearboxes.

The magneto used on the Starmaker was again a complete redesign, which bore no relationship to the heavy brass item used on the previous engines. Now employing an alloy flywheel of smaller dimensions and lighter weight, the unit became an energy transfer magneto, which fed low-tension power to an external HT coil that was mounted in the air stream, rather than the heat of the crankcases. The lightweight flywheel aided engine acceleration, and was tested on a special Viltool Ltd designed machine, installed in the basement of the magneto development shop. Capable of spinning components to 25,000rpm, the Starmaker magneto was tested to 17,000rpm, to ensure that it would cope with the 6,500rpm limit of the first engines. The maximum rpm of 6,500 may not sound a lot, but at this speed the engine was producing a full 25 bhp, even being equipped with a silencer to meet the newly proposed ACU noise ruling, but at the time this was not guaranteed!

Aluminium alloy cylinder and head

The most radical feature of the Starmaker was the new cylinder and head. Made of aluminium alloy the former used a spun cast austenitic iron liner, which had a coefficient of expansion only slightly less than the coarse finned cylinder casting. More radical was the head; the shape of the combustion chamber being a mushroom shaped recess with a central spark plug. The Starmaker was originally intended for use as a new generation motocross engine, and to this end needed a wide spread of power, but high performance two-stroke engines run most efficiently only at a specific rpm only. To give the engine this wide power band, an idea from the car industry was utilised. For many years high performance cars had been using the Weber progressive twin choke carburettor, which used a small choke for starting and smooth pick up, to which was added a larger choke as the instrument was opened up above half throttle. Two inlet ports were sited at the rear of the cylinder (with identical timing) to which were connected a pair of rubber mounted 1 1/8 inch (28.5 mm) Amal Monobloc carburettors. The carburettors were set so that the first instrument opened fully before the second one came into play, this being achieved by the use of a progressive cam junction box in the operating cable.

The Starmaker at this stage was hailed as a major breakthrough in high performance engine design, and was chosen by DMW, DOT, Cotton and Greeves to power their 250 motocross machines, but Greeves only used the engine as a stopgap whilst awaiting the introduction of their own Challenger engine. On show to the general public at the 1962 London Earls Court Show, the newcomer received praise from all quarters. And, the new Villiers motor performed well once

Cotton works rider Derek Minter with his Starmaker-powered racer, Snetterton, April 1965

riders learned the technique of letting the engine revolutions build up before changing up, as revs were required to overcome the lack of flywheel effect, due to the lighter but stiffer crankshaft.

Twin carburettors

The 1963 sporting season saw the introduction of the Starmaker engined Greeves 24ME motocross machine, but this liaison with the Villiers company was not a happy one and the model was axed after only 89 units. The twin carburettor engine was underdeveloped at that stage, and not up to the job of beating its rivals. The Starmaker engine, after special tuning, was at one stage destined to be fitted to the Mk 2 Silverstone, but this was not to be, as the Greeves factory had other ideas and opted to develop their own engine.

A road race engine specification 490E followed in 1964, but it still used the wide finned cylinder and the twin carburettors of the original (specification 757D) engine. Both Cotton and DMW used this engine in their new breed of 250-class club racers, which had become fashionable since the advent of the Greeves Silverstone. As the wide power spread of the twin carburettor engine was not required on the road race scene, and a misunderstanding of the system in general, Villiers produced a special road race engine with close pitch fins and a single Amal 3GP2 1$^1/_2$ inch (38 mm) carburettor. The new engine to specification 834E also used an outrigger contact breaker system which ran on its own bearings to maintain correct ignition timing at high revs, for the engine now developed 32 bhp at 8,000rpm. The Cotton Telstar, using the latest specification motor together with a Villiers built six-speed gearbox, ridden by Derek Minter and Bill Ivy scored many victories, with Minter also becoming the British champion.

A single carb

The Starmaker was also used in the trials role with a single Villiers S25/6 carburettor, but this specification still used a twin inlet port cylinder. The modification was a simple one, in that it only required a new inlet manifold to be made, which blanked off one of the inlet ports. The Starmaker was also used in a road going bike, the Cotton Conquest, but this was a racer in disguise, produced especially for the long distance production events that gained much publicity for the competing factories. DMW also entered this field and built a prototype roadster/racer called the Mosquito. At the suggestion of Peter Inchley, a Conquest was entered in the 1965 Castle Combe 500 event. Ridden by Derek Minter and Peter Inchley, the machine finished top in the 250 class. During the race they had immense fun passing 650s down the main straight. Peter Inchley, paired with Reg Everett, went on to win the Brands Hatch 500 mile race the following year.

Bill Ivy winning at Thruxton on 1st August 1965, with the Frank Higley Cotton Telstar, note Norton forks and Italian Oldani front brake

DMW 6-speed Hornet with Inchley cylinder, John Flavill designed the 6-speed box, standard Starmakers had to make do with only four ratios

The Inchley Starmaker

In 1964 Villiers decided to go racing, spurred on when earlier in the year a Cotton Telstar blew away the opposition (an Aermacchi and a Honda four excluded) at an Australian venue, and entered Starmaker development engineer Peter Inchley for that year's home events. Inchley, a brilliant engineer who learnt his trade at BSA, the Ariel Arrow development shop and later with the legendary Dr Joe Ehrlich at the De Havilland funded EMC (Ehrlich Motor Company) race shop, had been racing a works prepared Cotton Telstar. But the Villiers Company decided that it would not be very tactful for him to be seen solely on a Cotton, as they also provided engines for many of their rivals. As Villiers only made engines, in a bid calculated not upset the other Villiers engine users, an Inchley prepared Starmaker, together with the Favill designed six-speed gearbox, built in batches of 50, was mounted in a Spanish Bultaco TSS chassis. It was this model that appeared on the Villiers stand at the 1964 Earls Court Motorcycle Show together with a nicely sectioned Starmaker engine.

During that winter the Starmaker racer was thrashed round the Snetterton race circuit by both Peter Inchley and Derek Minter, the brief being to try and destroy a redesigned big-end. Between sessions the engine was stripped and the big-end bearing checked. At the end of the tests, which clocked up some 500 racing miles, the engine was again re-stripped and the bearing was found to be in perfect condition. Faith in the redesigned bearing was so high that it was put into Minter's engine, which he used at Mallory Park during March 1965. That same big-end lasted Minter all season.

Development of the Inchley engine carried on throughout the following seasons, and by 1966 it was said to be giving 35 bhp at 8,500rpm, but judging by its performance on the track it must have been more like 37 to 38 bhp, for it was 15 mph faster than its rivals. The quickness of the Inchley-Villiers special was demonstrated at the 1966 TT, when Peter took third place behind the works Hondas of Mike Hailwood and Stuart Graham. The racer was once again on display at the 1966 Earls Court Show, but the major interest that year was in its creator, for it had been confirmed that he had been offered a position as a development engineer/rider with both MZ and Suzuki.

Off Road Starmakers

The scrambles scene had not been forgotten and Norton Villiers quickly reinstated the AJS name for its new works scrambles mounts. Much speculation abounded as to who would be the new works riders, but at the beginning of 1967 it was announced that Freddie Mayes would take that position, initially riding a Rickman Brothers Villiers Metisse as a mobile test-bed. On the trials side, a bid to engage Sammy Miller as a works rider fell through when Norton Villiers decided to lower the development priorities of their trials Starmaker mounts. This decision occurred coincidently with a renewed interest in the old long-stroke 37A trials units, which were again beginning to find favour with the feet-up brigade.

Starmaker 826E Scrambles unit with single Amal Monobloc carburettor

Starmaker Engine Specifications

Specification	Description
757D	Standard scrambles specification, with twin Amal Monobloc carburettors
490E	Road racer version of above, with close ratio gearbox and rev counter drive
494E	Scrambler, as above, with 6 volt direct lighting
826E	Scrambler, with single Amal Monobloc
827E	Scrambler, with single Amal Monobloc and 6 volt direct lighting
834E	Road racer, with close finned cylinder/head, close ratio gears, rev counter drive, outrigger contact breaker, Amal GP2 carburettor
865E	Road racer, as above with 6 volt direct lighting
871E	Trials, with wide ratio gearbox, Villiers S25 carburettor
972E	Roadster, with single Amal Monobloc carburettor, 12 volt rectified lighting
091F	Special, with single Amal Monobloc carburettor, no primary drive or gearbox
131F	Trials, with 6 volt direct lighting

Minter again on the works Cotton, Snetterton, 10th April 1966

A standard production 1965 DMW Hornet with 4-speed Starmaker engine

DMW Hornet

The entry of DMW into the road racing scene came as a shock to the general public, although rumours had abounded for some time. With the announcement of the Villiers Starmaker engine, DMW saw fit to build a road racer, and with superb timing it appeared at the 1962 London Earls Court Show, arriving at 7.30 on the Saturday morning, accompanied by Harold Nock and Michael Riley, to rival the Silverstone prototype exhibited by the Greeves factory. The racer was named the Hornet, after the ill-fated French AMC dohc engined racer first shown at Earls Court in 1953. The new Hornet used the standard twin carburettor specification Starmaker motor, which was also being shown for the first time at the 1962 show. At this time there was only one Starmaker available, being basically the scrambles specification motor with coarse cylinder finning and twin Amal Monobloc carburettors. The frame followed the lines of the scramblers, manufactured in round tube, and of course employing MP forks and using Girling hubs. The new racer weighed in at only 208 lb (94.5 Kg), even with its full Jakeman fairing, and a radically softer spring arrangement was used on the front forks. To soften the springing a single centrally mounted spring damper unit was used, attached to the top yoke and a stiff fork brace fitted to the mudguard mounting lugs. This arrangement ensured that any spring or damper setting change would be a quick and easy trackside job.

It was 1963 that saw the birth of the production Hornet road racer, which now used a 1.5 inch (38 mm) Amal 3GP2 carburettor together with porting modifications to the wide fin cylinder, producing some 30 bhp. Responding to user demands, Villiers made available a close finned cylinder, which DMW soon adopted. This specification became known as the Mk 1, which had a frame number prefixed by HO. This Starmaker package, code named the 834E, was more suited to the Hornet short circuit racer than the tuned scrambles motor it replaced. The Mk 1 afforded the clubman racers of the era a fast, agile and relatively cheap machine to do combat with the Cotton and Greeves rivals that appeared at the same time.

In late 1965 DMW announced a road legal version of the Hornet called the Mosquito, to cash in on the ride-to-work racer market currently dominated by the Cotton Conquest. The Mosquito, advertised at just under £300, had just enough legal essentials to make it road worthy, for its prime aim was to enable the week-day rider to race at the weekends. To transform the sports roadster into a racer, the silencer and mudguards were quickly detachable, as was the headlamp bracket and plug-in lights. The factory aim was to have a bike eligible for the Thruxton 500, a race for production roadsters, but the project ended with only the prototype evaluation machine being constructed.

In clubman racing the Hornet showed it was on a par with its Cotton and Ducati rivals, but Harold Nock wanted a bit more power to take on the faster, but more expensive Bultaco and Aermacchi machines which were proving to be invincible. The Starmaker engine, although adequate for the lower end of the racing scene, was becoming outclassed at national level, even with the use of the Villiers produced 6-speed gearbox on the works machines. Both Greeves and Royal Enfield used the superior Alpha crankshaft assembly to good effect, but not wanting to take the long stroke route (72 mm) an approach was made to Alpha, who came up with a 68 mm crank and a set of cases to take the stronger Albion 5-speed gearbox. The 5-speed box enabled the use of a Peter Inchley tuned cylinder, which delivered more bhp at the expense of a thinner power band. The power output now was listed as 35 bhp at 8500 rpm, and to cope with this the 7 inch tls front brake, which was first used on the production Mk 1, could be uprated by using the optional extra Robinson or Oldani units. As with other Alpha crankcases, there was no provision for a flywheel magneto, the system running on points and a total loss battery. The frame geometry was unaltered except for the repositioning of the engine mounting lugs to take the new cases and gearbox, which proved that the initial design was strong enough to cope with the rigors of racing. This model became known as the Mk 2, and used the frame number prefix 2HO.

An indication of the acceptability of the Hornet racing frame can be gained from Martin Sharpe, a rider of the era who shoehorned a Yamaha TD1C and later a TD2B racing twin into his Hornet, in an effort to beat the big boys. The frame had to be modified at the front end, to allow the wider twin engine to be installed, but the extra power this unit gave did (in the end when the TD2 was fitted) adversely effect the frame and handling. The modified frame is still in existence today, now fitted with a special 197 cc Villiers engine, which is a credit to the original maker and the rider who later altered it.

In 1967 the last of the Hornet range was announced, the new 250 twin. Following on from their involvement with Alpha in the Mk 2 Hornet, the next logical step was to use the Centuri twin motor, in an effort to gain even more power, and this resulted in the twin that used an AHO frame number prefix. The Centuri engine was said to develop 44 bhp, and at a total all up weight of 224 lbs (102 Kg), the twin was equipped with the 8 inch brake as standard, together with a 4.5 gal tank to cope with the thirsty power unit. The twin was only listed for production in 1967-68 but very few if any, were actually produced. Shortly after this the single cylinder model also ceased production; engine supply being denied as the rights to the Starmaker unit had been transferred to the FB-AJS concern based at Andover, but this was not the end of DMW's involvement in two-stroke performance development.

Drag Racing

The Starmaker engine also showed its form on the drag strip, and in July 1968 shattered the world standing start kilometre record by three seconds. The Starmaker special, ridden by Des Heckle, on the Topcliffe strip put up a time of 23.87 seconds, breaking the record which had stood since 1939. Three seconds does not sound much, but over this distance it is akin to the difference between a 60 and a 100 mph lap over the TT course. Des had also set a 250cc standing-start quarter-mile record at Elvington in October 1966, when he took the Starmaker special up the strip at 13.91 seconds. This time was further reduced at the 1966 Ramsgate Sprint, when Des established another record at 13.58 seconds.

The Starmaker was seen as breakaway from the staid products normally offered by the Wolverhampton factory, and attracted the attention of many special builders. Mainly used in its original form to power home brewed roadsters, road racers and motocross machines, the components were also pressed into use as the motive power for a number of ingenious twin cylinder engines. Clive Waye built one, as did the DMW factory, but in 1965 so did Ted Davis, Chief Engineer at the old Vincent works at Stevenage. The Davis twin was again of a transverse configuration, which used a pair of high-level expansion chambers, the header pipes of which were constructed with square section tubing.

The use of the Starmaker engine was not confined to competition motorcycles, for at the January 1966 Racing Car Show, held at the London Olympia venue, a Starmaker powered car was on show. The four-wheeled racer was the Johnny Walker JW4, built to cater for the newly introduced Formula 4 series, which had started in Italy the previous season. The engine package was to the same specification as the motorcycle racing engine, complete with the large Amal GP carburettor, and when fitted to the 290 lb David Peers designed JW4, it was capable of 106 mph.

The engines approved for this new racing class included the Bultaco, Ducati Mk3, Starmaker, the rotary valve Merlin and the Montesa Impala. One motorcycle road racer who took an interest in the new formula was Starmaker development rider Derek Minter, who notched up four wins in the first five meetings of the 1966 season on his Starmaker powered JW4.

First DMW Typhoon 500 twin using two Starmaker engines

DMW Typhoon

At the DMW works the production of the 250 Hornet crept along at a sedentary pace, the factory started to look at other racing classes, and in 1965 factory boss Harold Nock came up with the idea for a 500. This was the time when British World Beater fever was at its height, and anything with the remotest chance of flying the flag, was hailed as a break through. Nock reasoned that by simply putting two Hornet engines together, a lightweight 500 cc twin of some 60 - 70 bhp could be constructed, to rival the 50 bhp Manx Norton's and other exotic foreign multi-cylinder fire engines, which dominated that class. Two Starmaker units were coupled

The second DMW Typhoon 500cc twin used Royal Enfield GP5 components

together to form the new Typhoon racer, with the primary drive being taken from between the two separate crankcases to a lay shaft that also accommodated the ignition system. A further drive transmitted the power (housed in a Starmaker chaincase) to an Albion 5-speed gearbox via a Norton/DMW clutch (RE Interceptor clutch on the second model). As the two engine units bolted to the central drive case, each unit could be released separately by the removal of the four crankcase bolts, this at least ensured maintainability of the system, for reliability was not to be its strong point.

The frame followed conventional Hornet lines, only being lengthened to take the larger unit, but it still used the single spring MP forks. A second Typhoon was constructed, this time using Royal Enfield GP5 engine components. The 500 failed to come up to expectations, being fast but exceedingly fragile, and never went into production, as the factory had wished. The two examples of the Typhoon are still in existence, with the Royal Enfield version - which was kept on permanent display at the Sedgley factory foyer alongside a stuffed bear - being exhibited, after a full and total restoration, at the National Motorcycle Museum in Birmingham until the disastrous fire of September 2003.

When the first Typhoon was track tested by Bill Smith and Jack Findlay, its shortcomings rapidly became apparent. Vibration from the engine (crank set at 180 degrees) was so bad that the rider's vision was affected, and the brakes were not up to the speed potential of the machine. These problems were enough for Harold Nock to call a halt to any further development, and the Typhoon was quietly put away, even though Bruce Main-Smith called it: 'an interesting and ambitious project' when he tested it for Motor Cycling in 1965. The Starmaker Typhoon re-surfaced and was bought, in a sad and neglected state, by Roy Martin in 1985, who decided to iron out the problems, and race it with the Classic Racing Motorcycle Club (CRMC).

As the brakes were missing, a pair of Yamaha TD2 drums were fitted, which at least solved its previously poor braking performance. To overcome the legendary vibration problems the cranks were reset at 360 degrees, instead of the original 180, which was found to be 176 when checked. This action did not stop the vibration, and took three strong men to bump start it. Compression release valves were then added which overcame some of the starting problems. As a last resort the cranks were set at 90 and then finally at 45 degrees, which restored one-man bump starting, but most importantly killed the vibration problems.

Cotton Telstar/Conquest

Winners of the 1923 Junior TT and 1926 Lightweight race, the Gloucester-based Cotton concern stormed back into the racing spotlight when short circuit star Derek Minter won the 1964 ACU 250cc Star, the equivalent of the British Championship on a 247cc (68 x 68 mm) Cotton Telstar.

In October 1962 the Telstar had become the first of Britain's new generation 'formula junior' specification racers to be publicly announced. The bike had been sparked off by the introduction of the Villiers Starmaker engine package, and like the Greeves Silverstone, by the efforts of a privateer. In Cotton's case, this was Peter Vallis, who had campaigned a racerised scrambler with some success during the 1962 season.

Although the Villiers factory had their own dynamometer, it was Cotton who privately race-developed the new Starmaker engine. This began as early as October 1962, with the Cotton staff, including Fluff Brown who is recorded elsewhere in this book and who went on to form the FB-AJS firm at Andover.

Brian Foster, Cadwell Park, CRMC meeting October 2002,Cotton Telstar production racer with 4-speed gearbox

Derek Minter was signed up in time for the 1963 season and responded by finishing an impressive runner-up, behind Mike Hailwood's twin cylinder Ducati desmodromic twin – at the Mallory Park season opener in March that year. But most of 1963 was spent squeezing out not only more power, but reliability too. These early engines were what one might truthfully describe as having borderline reliability. Minter's works machine received a variety of modifications such as remote contact breakers, a single Amal GP carburettor and a more rigid cylinder liner.

However, the most important of these changes arrived in June 1964 in the form of a six-speed gearbox, which was needed to overcome the narrowing power band of Minter's rapidly developing factory engine. The only other Cotton with this gearbox at that time was the equally rapid Frank Higley-sponsored machine campaigned by future World Champion, Bill Ivy.

Minter's and Ivy's engines progressed from the original 25 bhp at 6,500rpm to 31.2 bhp at 7,800rpm. This was more or less the power available when Derek Minter rode his Telstar to victory in the 1964 ACU 250 Star Championship. However, it wasn't the engine alone that took the title, but the combination of a competitive bike and a rare rider talent. The good handling characteristics of the 230lb lightweight also helped in this victory.

Cotton had, at that time, been manufacturing motorcycles for the previous 40 years or so and obviously knew a thing or two when it came to making them handle. Their frame consisted of a full duplex layout, manufactured from seamless 'A' grade cold drawn steel tubing. The top rail and swinging arm were constructed of 1$^1/_8$ inch x 14 swg tubing with the cradle and sub frame manufactured from $^7/_8$ inch x 14 swg tubing.

The fact of the matter was that Cotton made little else apart from the frame and swinging arm, for they employed Armstrong leading-link front forks and rear shock absorbers to control the machine's suspension. Later models used Girling dampers.

The first production Telstars were equipped with the infamous British Hub Co 6 inch SLS Motoloy brake assemblies both front and rear. However, the front stopper, famous for its lack of effect, was soon ditched and by 1964 the Telstar, along with the Greeves Silverstone, sported the newly introduced 7 inch TLS unit, which British Hub had produced to address the many complaints arising from those unfortunate individuals lumbered with the ineffective 6 inch single leading shoe component.

Unlike machines from other British factories such as DMW, Royal Enfield and Greeves, the Cotton Telstar was fitted with 19 inch wheels front and rear throughout its entire production run. This, if one considers modern trends, should have been to their disadvantage. However, it does not appear to have hampered the style of works rider Derek Minter who, along with Frank Higley's rider Bill Ivy, claimed victory after victory aboard these two-stroke 'flying machines'.

When tested by Motor Cycling in their 21st November 1964 issue, factory rider Minter and Motor Cycling staffman Bruce Main-Smith rode one of the latest four-speed production bikes.

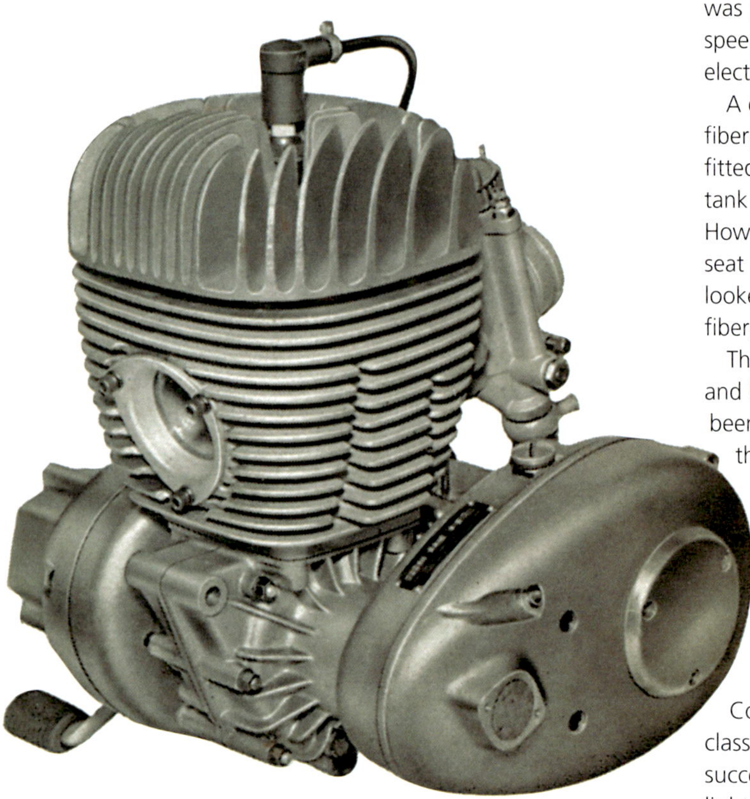

Starmaker 834E Road Racer with Amal GP2 carburettor

Held on the 1.6 mile Silverstone Club circuit, the best flying lap was put in by Minter at 1 minute 16.67 seconds, an average speed of 75.9 mph. The best speed recorded through the electronically timed trap, again by Minter, was 102.27 mph.

A distinctive feature or the Telstar was its Mitchenhall (Avon) fiberglass bodywork. Upon its introduction the Telstar was fitted out with a 2$^1/_2$ gallon jelly-mould continental style fuel tank and a rather awkward looking single-piece fairing. However with the Mk 2's appearance in 1964, the fuel tank, seat and fairing came in for a change and the Telstar now looked far more conventional with its maroon coloured fiberglass styled in the conventional British racer fashion.

The majority of Telstar production occurred during 1964-5 and by the time of its demise in 1967 over sixty examples had been produced. These found their way to various corners of the globe with Australia holding the honour of the highest numbered example, machine No 66.

Once Minter left at the end of 1966, Cotton's fortunes deteriorated rapidly, as by then the Yamaha TD1 series twin was beginning its surge to the top as the clubman's mount and in the process making all the singles, including the Cotton, obsolete virtually overnight.

The only race where the Villiers Starmaker powered Cotton could still compete after this was in the Production class. And it was here where it achieved arguably its greatest success. The Cotton Conquest was essentially a Telstar with lights. There were class victories at venues throughout Great Britain with riders such as Minter, Peter Inchley and Reg Everett. The highlights were class victories in the prestigious 500 mile race at Castle Combe in 1965 (Minter/Inchley) where they also finished a magnificent third overall, and at Brands Hatch the following year (Inchley/Everett).

The 1966 Brands Hatch 500 mile class winner boasted the full treatment: racer head and cylinder barrel; close ratio gears; external contact breaker assembly; alloy wheel rims; large capacity fibreglass fuel tank; racing seat; clip-on handlebars; tachometer; direct lighting and air scoop for the front brake.

Manx Grand Prix winner (on a Yamaha) Paddy Reid was still cleaning up with his Conquest during the 1970s, even in the open class at Cadwell Park club events. A total of 166 Conquests were produced and the price in 1966 was between £279 and £350, depending upon the exact specification.

Postscript

During the 1990s, with his son Nick as co-director, the Fluff Brown organisation built a batch of 10 Telstars, but with telescopic forks and Italian Grimeca front brakes. Nick admitted recently, 'This was very time consuming and although personally enjoyable its unlikely to be repeated.' It is also worth noting that Fluff Brown also gained the rights to use both the AJS and Cotton names, the patents having been obtained on the 9th August 1991 and the 28th April 1995 respectively.

Cotton Cobra and the Trials Machine

The summer of 1962 saw the introduction of a new prototype Cotton scrambles machine, that used the still secret – it was not unveiled until the Motorcycle Show in November - Villiers Starmaker engine unit. The new bike was an updated version of the successful Cougar that employed the Villiers 36A scrambles engine, which was fitted with the Cross and later, the Parkinson alloy cylinders. The new bike was at first still called the Cougar but when production got underway it was renamed the Cobra.

Starmaker 871E Trials with wide ratio gearbox and Villiers S25 carburettor

The prototype scrambler was an interesting machine in that it used a brand-new Villiers power plant that was shrouded in secrecy, but even at that time it was claimed to develop 25 bhp at 6,000rpm. Cotton was approached by Villiers, as were other firms, with the offer of this new motor, with a view to carrying out the testing and development under racing conditions; but there was a catch. The built up engine package was supplied by the Wolverhampton factory fitted to the Cotton bikes and ridden by Cotton riders, but looked after in the field by Villiers technicians. Although Cotton engineers could see the fruits of Villiers labours they were expressly forbidden to look inside the new motors. This ruling also had to be obeyed by the other companies who received the half a dozen experimental engines, which were not necessarily all alike.

Villiers were not happy that their A series engines were being fitted with other manufacturer's alloy top ends, and handed Cotton an offer that they could not refuse. In return for the use of Cotton works machines and Cotton works riders. Villiers offered a new prototype engine for exhaustive testing. But, there was one condition, the engine should not be stripped and inspected by the Cotton staff, this job being taken care of by the Villiers development engineer and his team of traveling mechanics. This secret operation led to the eventual introduction of the scrambles

Jack Findlay DMW Hornet prototype with twin carburettors, Lightweight Isle of Man TT, 10th June 1963

Starmaker engine unit, which was to become the number one motor to use in the early1960s.

The engine of the Cotton prototype differed from the final specification of the Starmaker, in that at this stage it was only fitted with a single carburettor; an Amal GP that was hidden behind a leatherette curtain which protected the mid-riff of the machine. When the development programme was complete the production scrambles specification motors were fitted with the twin Amal Monobloc carburettors. Changes in exhaust system design were also evident on the Cotton, for now the high-level pipe, mounted to the left, was a huge flat expansion chamber, an indication of things to come. The following year the prototype sported yet another exhaust system, this time mounted high to the right hand side of the machine.

With the new Starmaker engine producing more power and utilising a lighter flywheel, riding techniques had to be modified. Different lines could be taken through corners, which could be tighter and full power could be turned on earlier once the bike was pointed in the right direction. With the lighter flywheel power build-up was achieved a lot quicker than with the old heavy set-up of the 36A motors, but this had its draw backs and the rider had to be careful not to "lose" the engine on slow downhill sections. Exhaust system technology was beginning to show, in that the system could now be altered in length to produce peak power to suit differing tracks. Short pipes were used for fast tracks and long ones for the more twisty circuits; peak power being adjustable over a range of some 1,000rpm.

The Starmaker engine was pressed into use in all branches of the Cotton competitions department, powering the Cobra scrambler, the Trials model, the Telstar road racer and the Conquest high performance roadster, giving the Gloucester company a very high profile in motorcycle sporting activities. During the 1960s Arthur Lampkin, John Draper and Andy Robertson rode the works scramblers to a host of victories, with Draper and Alan Lampkin notching up many achievements on the works trials machines.

Cotton carried out all the early experiments - mostly in the hands of Billy Jackson - before launching the new Cobra scrambles model. Now using a widely spaced twin down-tube type frame, which positioned the engine well to the rear for better traction, full-width Motoloy 6 inch brake drums and a bright red fibre glass 1 1/2 gallon fuel tank which was especially built by Mitchenhalls, the Cobra was every inch a real eye-catcher. Over the following seasons the Cobra was modified to include the use of the single carburettor motor, with a double stage paper element air filter, a smaller 1 1/4 gallon fuel tank, a slimmer round section expansion chamber with a single tube outlet and Metal Profile forks as an optional extra. This specification remained virtually unchanged until the model was axed in 1968.

For the1965 season Villiers produced the trials specification Starmaker engine, but Cotton had been using and developing the unit for over a year. First seen at the 1964 Scottish Six Day Trial, when the Lampkin brothers and Blackie Holden, all Cotton Starmaker mounted, won special first class awards on their prototype machines. Of identical external appearance to the scrambles unit, the new trials engine featured a hammer-head type crankshaft to lower the crankcase compression ratio, a lower secondary compression ratio and a spherical combustion chamber, together with wide ratio gears and a Villiers S25 type carburettor. Said to develop 15 bhp at 5,500rpm, the maximum torque of this unit was at 3,000rpm, which gave plenty of bottom end punch.

The trials Starmaker followed the appearance of the scrambles models, the exceptions being the tyres, seat, $2^1/4$ gallon fuel tank and the exhaust system, and again carried on in production until 1968.

Cotton, by far, were the biggest customer for the Starmaker engine, using it in four differing roles, the Telstar road racer, the Conquest sports roadster (production racer), the Cobra scrambler and the Trials Starmaker. This range was seen by many enthusiasts of the era as the prettiest set of machines available.

The Cotton Telstar Mk2 - one of the few road-racing machines to successfully employ the Starmaker engine

11 Norton-Villiers

Peter Inchley's 1966 Villiers TT machine, essentially a works 6-speed Starmaker engine in a Spanish Bultaco chassis

During the period that the very successful Inchley Starmaker was being developed, the fortunes of the Villiers factory and the British motorcycle industry in general - took a turn for the worse. Like many British companies during the boom years of the fifties they became complacent, not only with sales, but also the trials and scrambles successes of the following decade. The sixties saw Villiers hit with dwindling sales, due in part to the popularity of the high performance products flooding in from the Orient. At first this did not seem to matter, but when foreign imports increased the whole of the British motorcycle industry (which shunned reinvestment) was hit very hard indeed. But, by then it was too late.

The directors of the major firms unflinchingly stood firm in the belief that their outdated large capacity products would win the day over the high revving oriental tiddlers, seeing the situation as 'a minor glitch in the sales figures.' The industry's attitude was summed up by Edward Turner, the autocratic boss of the BSA Automotive Group, 'It's a question of brand loyalty, once a Triumph owner always a Triumph owner.' Brand loyalty at that time was the last thing on the mind of the British twin owner who had been blown away by a Honda of half its size, for all he wanted was performance with a capital P, and he did not care about its origins.

Japanese imports

Japanese imports of all sizes increased during the sixties, but it was the small capacity machines that made the biggest inroads into British production, for they could offer both speed and reliability. The ride-to-work and the lightweight competition classes were the most seriously affected, putting an enormous strain on the financial resources of the Villiers empire, for this was their major market. Italian scooters, and most of all, the affordable small car, headed by the Austin/Morris Mini also played their part in the eventual decline of the industry as a whole.

The effect of foreign imports on the British motorcycle industry had been noted by Leslie Farrer, who had become chairman of the Villiers Engineering Co in 1957 on the retirement of his father, and in 1965 he decided to call it a day. Faced with mounting losses and no foreseeable solution, he resigned his position. The void created by the loss of the company chairman was soon filled when Dennis Poore of the mighty Manganese Bronze empire saved the day by putting in a bid for the Villiers shares that suddenly hit the market. It was reported that prior to this point, Manganese Bronze had been secretly buying up Villiers shares, and owned 20 per cent at the time of the take-over, to become the major shareholder, and therefore controller of the Villiers Engineering Co. Villiers was then amalgamated with fellow strugglers Norton/AMC, to become Norton Villiers. It must be said that Dennis Poore, a keen motoring and motorcycle enthusiast who wanted to re-establish the once great British motorcycle industry, had acquired Villiers because of its profitable industrial engine division.

Dennis Poore takes over

When AMC went bankrupt and the official receiver was called in during August 1966, it was Dennis Poore who put in a bid and secured the remains of that empire from the receiver, and together with a further purchase of Villiers shares these once mighty organizations were reformed into the Norton-Villiers conglomerate in 1966, taking a stand under that name at the Earls Court Show that year to prove its integrity. It is indeed ironic that these two companies joined together, for it was the AMC crash of 1966 that placed a huge financial burden on the Wolverhampton concern, in not being able to pay for engines received prior to the collapse. Owning such famous names as AJS, Francis-Barnett, James, Matchless, Norton and the Villiers Engineering Co, the new company had a good pedigree and was seen to be the answer to the problems of the ailing British motorcycle industry, but during the ensuing years this potential was never fulfilled, even though they announced the introduction of the Inchley replica racer, re-entered the off road racing scene and reached a profit-earning situation in 1971.

The new Norton Villiers company started off with good intentions; the executives now included Dennis Poore (chairman and finance director), John Neville (vice chairman and chief executive), John Pisker (managing director) and Dr Stefan Bauer (director of engineering). Initial policies included the shipment of kit-form machines to the Australian factory at Ballaarat, the acquisition of a larger financial holding in Enfield India who then used Villiers engines in their Madras-built models, and a concentration of effort in the American sporting scene. By far the most radical policy was to update the AMC racing machinery. This was aimed mainly at the United States, but with the Manx, G50 and 7R rights having been sold off to Colin Seeley, this only left the AJS two-stroke division to fly the flag.

During 1973 Norton-Villiers also took over the ailing BSA/Triumph Corporation (due to government pressure) which also included Ariel and Sunbeam, to become Norton-Villiers-Triumph (NVT). But this final move was one Norton-Villiers should never have made and the larger family did not prosper, instead the seeds of potential growth fell on stony ground and eventually the union ended in divorce after only three years of marriage. Many problems were caused and much money lost as a direct result of new policies, and the backlash resulted in the workers 'sit in' at the Meriden factory. NVT wanted to concentrate production at the Wolverhampton and Small Heath factories and close the Meriden operation, but the Triumph workforce there had other ideas. The Meriden fiasco, and meddling by politicians, caused a lot of ill-feeling throughout the group and its repercussions were felt nationwide for a very long time.

Benn causes problems

The problems centred around Poore's enforced move to acquire the remains of the BSA group (which included Triumph) was originally made under a previous Conservative government rule. When the Labour party came to power, its Trade Secretary the left-wing Tony Benn, did everything in his powers to destroy Poore and ridicule the Norton-Villiers concern.

By the 1st April 1976 the NVT Manufacturing Company was wound up, severing its links with the old Villiers Marston Road works, and NVT Engineering was set up at the refurbished Montgomery Road premises. But this new company was at pains to point out that this new concern had nothing to do with Norton Villiers Triumph manufacturing. It was just the new name of the company that made BSA and Triumph spares and carried out engineering work for Massey Ferguson and Dowty.

Some three years after taking over the BSA group, when taking part in a BBC Radio 4 phone in program during November 1976, the then Managing Director of NVT Dennis Poore advised worried listeners to hang on to their British Motorcycle industry shares, and wait for a revival. He also went on to say, 'The original government sponsored merger of Norton Villiers and BSA Triumph was a mistake. We at Norton Villiers were a profitable company and it was a mistake for us to take on the BSA Triumph businesses.'

A workers action committee

By mid 1976 the former Villiers factory at Marston Road, now run by a workers action committee on the same lines as Meriden was moving into top gear, with manufactured spares coming off the line, together with a production run of Norton Interpols. A spokesman for the facility, Mike Sampson was confident, 'At the moment we're concentrating on the spares side, but the industrial engine orders are huge and existing orders will keep us busy for the next few months.'

Unfortunately this fragmentation of NVT also saw the loss of many important Villiers records, which were destroyed in the big clear-up operation. After a brief shut-down, the industrial side of the Villiers engineering factory reopened, and for over two decades developed and manufactured even more industrial power units, many of them going overseas. So good were these foreign sales that thoughts were given to the opening of a subsidiary factory in South Africa, but political constraints prevented such a venture.

The Villiers side takes a back seat

Within the new Norton-Villiers company of 1967 the Villiers side of things had to take a back seat, for it seemed that all efforts were being put into the new Norton twins. The plan was to close the giant Plumstead factory and transfer all production to Wolverhampton, but in the now overcrowded Marston Road works there was little room left for the Villiers operation. From this point, no more motorcycle engines were built under the Villiers name, even though there was still a demand for them. It could be said that this is where the Villiers story ended.

The one saving grace was that the Manganese Bronze take-over brought with it the rights to the AJS name, and it was this marque that was resurrected to carry on with the Starmaker engine for a further two years. Engine production at the Wolverhampton facility did continue, but now this factory was turned over to the production of Norton Commando engines, to fulfill the export demand for these machines in the United States. Incidentally the Commando name was taken from the successful Villiers-engined James trials machine of the fifties, and Norton Villiers now owned the James name.

The two-stroke division of Norton Villiers continued in production, but now there was only one engine type being produced. From the vast portfolio of capacities and design configurations inherited from the Villiers empire, the only survivor was the Starmaker, which was now manufactured under the AJS banner. But even this motor was destined to finally loose its identity, be redesigned, and re-emerge as the Stormer in 1970. From the many Villiers designs that NV took over, the vast majority were scrapped, seen as outdated and outclassed; for as an extension of the NV business plan they also took over the import and marketing of the Japanese Suzuki range that included many small capacity superior two-stroke designs, this operation having been started by AMC from the back door of the James factory in Greet, during 1963.

The 197cc engine survives

Only two other Villiers designs survived the trauma of the Manganese Bronze take-over, to end up being produced by an outside company who had faith in the concept and who could see a continued demand for the product. Norton-Villiers had effectively forgotten about the ubiquitous 197cc engine and its derivatives in the big reshuffle, which led to the supply of these engines drying up. With many small firms relying heavily on this motor to power their limited range of road, trials and scrambles machines, this decision sounded the death knell for many of them, especially those firms who were unable to diversify quickly. These were turbulent times and many small companies, and some not so small, did not have the capability to survive. One company to capitalise upon the misfortunes of others was Metal Profile, who stepped in and purchased the rights to the E and A range engines, primarily to ensure an engine supply to its own subsidiary company, DMW, and to make sales of surplus engines to Cotton, Greeves and other companies for their trials models.

Metal Profile involvement

During the mid sixties the Metal Profile company was subcontracted by Villiers to rebuild and recondition the electric-start 11E invalid carriage engines for the Ministry of Pensions, but just before the Villiers facility closed down, they were again approached with a view to the purchase of all the remaining Villiers engine stock and tooling, to ensure that the reconditioning programme could continue for a further five years. There was another reason for Metal Profile taking on the rights to the 9E and 37A engines, for not only did it safeguard the invalid carriage programme but it also protected their own ongoing DMW trials machine programme. But even this market soon dried up when, as a result of a lobby by the British car industry to declare the invalid carriage unsafe. Metal Profile and DMW continued to operate their Villiers engine and spares production lines, relying on revenue received from other company's using their products.

Tony Dawson

Another person to see the potential of the DMW built engine was Tony Dawson of Astralite wheels and Scitsu frame notoriety. The Dawson philosophy of attacking engineering structure, manufacture and repair problems by employing the built-up alloy plate sandwich technique, led him to design a light-weight frame to house the DMW developed all-alloy 250 and the 125cc Upton Manx engine. Following the successes of the plate-framed Scitsu racer, fitted with a Yamaha engine, a move to the roadster market was made in 1976. The first road bikes using the bolted up alloy plate frames, the RO1 and RO2 Manxman, were fitted with all alloy DMW 250 units, and given a 1,000 mile road test to prove the concept. The road test proved satisfactory, and with backing from British Aluminium and Harmsworth Press, work started on the AR2 racer version that used the Aubrey Upton (of Fieldhouse Engineering) designed and Yamaha based Manx 125.

For a while everything looked rosy for the Manxman, with three appearances on BBC TV's Tomorrow's World, and on display at the Earls Court Show and the Westminster Road and Racing show of January 1978. With the setting up of the Manx Motorcycle Manufacturing Co to build bikes and engines on the Isle of Man, Dawson was ready to start production of the 125 and 250 variants, with designs in the pipe-line to produce 100, 175 and 200cc versions based on the 125 unit. A water-cooled version was even at the design stage.

When Hunting Industrial Plastics, who owned Fieldhouse, pulled the plug on the Manx 125 engine in favour of developing their own waterscooter engines, Dawson was left with no alternative than to abandon the Manxman and the 250 DMW projects. For with no suitable 125 engine or an alternative power source, the 250 variant, and the whole Manxman project, was doomed to failure.

Enfield India

In February 1979 Enfield India announced the introduction of a new 200cc motorcycle for its home market. This machine used a revamped version of the old 9E. Still using the original bore and stroke measurements, the new engine was said to produce 10 bhp at 5,200rpm and breathed through a Villiers S25 carburettor. But links with this country had been established some seven years before, when Dennis Poore exhibited an Indian built 175cc Royal Enfield at the 1972 Earls Court Show. Aimed at the British Police's communications and training role rather than for high-speed traffic duties, the Madras Motor Company Enfield Crusader featured a Villiers 3L engine equipped with a SIBA Dynstart and was kitted out with a British made fairing, panniers, legshields and radio set. A lavish party was organised at the show to entice potential buyers, with 40 representatives attending from 20 police forces. Motor Cycle of 18th November 1972 reported. 'An initial order of 15 machines was received.' However, the whole UK police project was eventually axed on cost grounds. But Norton Villiers still continued to supply the large capacity Commando Interpol to the British constabularies. Meanwhile the 175cc Enfield Crusader was still coming off the assembly line in Madras, and sold on the Indian market as a cheap 'two-wheeler' alternative to the 350 Bullet. The Crusader was stretched to 197cc in 1979 with the introduction of the Madras built 9E type engine.

Conclusion

During this period, the Metal Profile company carried on making suspension components and producing and wholesaling Villiers spares to kart engine builders and retailers alike, together with the sale of complete machines under the DMW brand name. But soon even this line ended, with the MP front fork being the first asset to go, with Competition Classics of Manchester gaining the rights to it in 1995. The remaining stock of Villiers spares, tooling and even the brand name passed on to Competition Classics the following year.

The Metal Profile factory was sold in 1996 to a small engineering group of companies, and is now producing commercial engineering, sub contract parts and assemblies. DMW Motorcycles Wolverhampton Ltd on the other hand was still owned by the same directors as in the preceding three decades, but they will not be actively be involved in any future motorcycle or engineering activities. By this time the Villiers logo was well and truly dead and buried. So ended the career of one of Great Britain's foremost two-stroke oriented concerns, but the fruits of its labours lived on.

Peter Inchley took charge of the Villiers/AJS racing programme

AJS

The rebirth of the AJS marque came about as a direct result of the Inchley-Villiers Special which had achieved a brilliant third place in the 1966 250 TT. Dennis Poore, who acquired the Villiers empire on behalf of the Manganese Bronze company in 1966, had a keen interest in road racing and wanted to capitalise on the Inchley result with a replica of his mount. When a replica of the 1966 special was made it could not be called a Villiers - for they never made complete motorcycles - and in any case the name had been absorbed into the title of the new company which was known as Norton-Villiers. As Poore had also snapped up the remains of the mighty AMC group which included the rights to the AJS name, this name was duly resurrected to look after the fortunes of the two-stroke side of the business.

Dennis Poore considered that the Inchley machine showed promise, insisting that it be developed further, with a view to limited production and offering a replica for general sale. The new AJS 250 racer was commissioned early in 1967 and by May a prototype was ready for testing. The engine specification for the new machine remained virtually unchanged from that off the 1966 TT mount, but was now housed in a large diameter spine frame of Reynolds manufacture, with an additional fuel tank behind the engine. The motorcycle press of the day latched on to the prototype, and blew it up out of all proportion, proclaiming yet another British World Beater. This image was soon shattered when Peter Inchley fell off at Mallory Park on the machine's racing debut. To add to this embarrassment the engine seized solid during the 1967 TT, putting paid to any further serious development.

Peter Inchley, Villiers Special at Mallory Park, 30th April 1967

The Norton-Villiers management still thought that the AJS 250 could become a winner, but they overlooked the fast developing Yamaha twins that were beginning to make a name for themselves. At this time DMW, Cotton and Greeves were all phasing out their racing 250s, due to the drastic downturn in sales caused mainly by the success of the Yamahas. With the AJS engine producing a shade more power than its Starmaker-engined rivals, due in part to the tuning genius of Peter Inchley, but down on power compared to the oriental twins, the Norton Villiers two-stroke was doomed to failure so never made it into full scale production. The demise occurred shortly after the well-meaning Dennis Poore had announced that production was imminent, with a predicted selling price of £418.00. The question has to be asked. Why did Norton-Villiers continue this outdated concept when other British manufacturers were scrapping their racing models? The answer is probably the enthusiasm of the British riders and race followers, spurred on by the Inchley successes of 1966 and 1967, the heightened motorcycle press expectations and the famous name.

When AMC crashed in 1966 the Starmaker-powered James and Francis-Barnett scramblers were hidden away in the old James factory at Greet, and once the dust of the buy out had settled it was these machines that emerged, wearing the AJS badge to become the next

AJS Stormer manufactured in 250, 370 and 410cc engine sizes

generation scramblers. With the engine development experience gained from the defunct road racer project, a new scrambler was prepared late in the 1967 season, and developed over the following year to become the Y4 250 production scrambler of 1969. By 1970 the engine unit renounced its Villiers Starmaker ancestry and became known as the AJS Stormer motocross engine, it being joined by the Y5 unit that used an 83 mm piston to bring it up to 368cc.

Mike Jackson joined AJS in 1969 as the European Sales Manager. After five and a half years with Greeves he was appalled at the lack of dirt bike understanding shown by the AJS decision makers, the only resident staff who knew anything about the sport being Fluff Brown and Bob Trigg. Together the trio set about sorting out the AJS to become a leader in its class. After a year of being a nuisance to the AJS bosses, Mike was posted to the United States to become General Manager of Norton-Villiers Corporation USA, and there he continued to ride the new Stormers in desert races, flying the British flag and increasing sales.

By the end of 1971 the Stormer had been stretched to 410cc, using the same piston as the 370, but with a slightly longer stroke at 74 mm. The new bike embodied the lessons learned in the previous season's hard testing by riders including development chief Vic Eastwood and Shell-under-21 winner Roger Harvey. Declining to enter into the horsepower race, AJS would only say that the 410 developed over 35 bhp at the rear wheel, between 5,500 and 7,000rpm, with the 250 developing 25 bhp between 6,000 and 8,000rpm. Eighteen modifications had been made to the new 410 as a result of a year's extensive testing. The clutch circlip, which had a tendency to pop out when under load, was given a deeper groove, and a steel inlet manifold replaced the alloy item which was prone to cracking. A new forged piston, a heavier forged connecting rod and an improved gear cam barrel all contributed to the extra reliability of the engine. A silencer was fitted to both models as standard equipment, but AJS offered no guarantees that it would pass the ACU decibel test.

Vic Eastwood and Graham Evans joined forces to fulfill the need to make a 500 AJS scrambler, but what started as a bored and stroked 410 vibrated so much that it had to be rubber mounted. Using Norton Commando isolastic mountings and a new frame, the 500 was ultimately tamed, but the original engine was still an animal at heart, giving out some 47 bhp. After a redesign, when a Norton gearbox was added the engine was effectively "detuned" down to 39 bhp, but it was more practical as manageable power came in from tickover, right through to its maximum of nearly 8,000rpm. To cope with the massive amount of torque, the duplex primary chain of the 410 would have to have been replaced by a triplex type, but this would have been far too wide for the cases. In the end an inverted tooth primary chain was employed, rather than a redesign of the system to use a gear drive.

Production of the 500 was initially considered, but due to the financial circumstances that AJS found themselves in, these plans never went any further than the prototype stage.

The Stormer managed to survive the troubles suffered by the Norton Villiers group and went on to win several British championships. By this time production had been relocated at Andover in Hampshire, close to other parts of what became known as Norton-Villiers-Triumph. As a result of the worker's blockade of the Meriden Triumph factory, which has already been recounted, AJS ran into trouble from which they could not recover. Production of the Stormer finished in 1974, with the remaining stock and manufacturing rights being purchased by Fluff Brown, to form FB-AJS of Andover Ltd.

Prior to the troubles of 1974, Peter Inchley, who had been closely associated with the Starmaker decided to leave, and set up shop with Frank Higley to make high performance two-stroke equipment. In 1977 Peter Inchley became involved with the Starmaker again, helping Hejira build a batch of three racers to contest the new single cylinder class. Despite the use of rider Brian Gittens, Hejira frames, six-speed gearboxes and Inchley's experience, the two-stroke just was not quick enough to catch the Vic Camp Suzukis and Ducatis that ruled the period.

DMW –The later years

In the mid sixties the company was hit hard by dwindling motorcycle sales, and even harder by the crash of the giant AMC concern. When AMC closed its doors for good, and Manganese Bronze took over the empire, in the ensuing turmoil the newly acquired Villiers factory was effectively forgotten about, which led to the supply of Villiers engines drying up. Metal Profile (the DMW parent company) again stepped in and purchased the rights to the 197 and the 37A 250cc engines, thus ensuring an engine supply to its own subsidiary company, as well as selling surplus units to the Greeves and Cotton factories.

The major reason for taking over the Villiers designs was to protect their investments. During the late sixties the company had been subcontracted by Villiers to rebuild and recondition the 11E invalid carriage engines for the Ministry of Pensions contract; a scheme that Metal Profile took on and spent a lot of money setting up. But, just before the Villiers factory closed down, they were again approached, this time to purchase all the remaining stock and tooling, to ensure that the reconditioning programme could continue for a further five years. Now Metal Profile owned both the spares making facilities and the complete engine unit manufacturing rights. But, even part of this market dried up shortly after the British car industry lobbied to brand the invalid carriage unsafe. A major protagonist was Graham Hill. The government stopped this subsidised transport and introduced a mobility allowance, used to modify a standard (out of the showroom) production car.

Metal Profile continued to produce spares and complete 9E, 11E and 37A motors under the DMW brand name, to service the needs of the fledgling kart racing scene and the well established trials bike manufacturers of the period. This state of affairs carried on for a few more years, with DMW motorcycles reverting to a 37A powered trials only range, for the Norton-Villiers policy of not supplying outside organisations meant that they had to abandon the superior Starmaker-engined racing range. During this period the 250 Highlander Trials was the mainstay, but the Spanish two-stroke trials machines were biting deeply into its sales. The Highlander was an extremely good and cheap alterative, a superb beginner's bike, but what it lacked was an up to date engine, the DMW produced 37A engine (even with its DMW alloy cylinder) being outclassed by its Iberian rivals. With this fact in mind, the factory ceased motorcycle production in 1971, to concentrate on basic component manufacture for other companies.

During these troubled times the factory had been developing the 37A motor. Now it used the Alpha crankshaft and a new wide-fin DMW cylinder, the primary chaincase carrying the DMW logo to proclaim that the engine was no longer of Villiers manufacture. This engine was chosen by Cotton to power its new trials machine. The Javelin, announced for sale in 1976, had been used to good effect by Mike Parkes the previous year to perfect the machine. During the development period the engine was in fact a DMW and the frame of Cotton manufacture, but the name did not appear on the tank in order to keep the public guessing. This was a mutual design exercise on the part of both firms to develop the 37A engine and the Cotton frame.

Alongside the Javelin, Cotton fielded an armed forces all terrain bike, in the hope of snatching the lucrative Ministry of Defence BSA B40 replacement contract. This new machine again used the DMW-built 37A motor, but was fitted with an alternator to come up to the Ministry electrical specification. The forces tested the machine, as they did many others, but dropped it in favour of the Can Am 250. A police equipment version was also planned, but that too failed to make its mark. During the same period the DOT motorcycle company announced a new trials model for general sale, which also utilised the DMW 37A engine, but was fitted with a Bosch electronic ignition system, and special gear ratios.

By the mid 1970s there were even plans for engine production to be started in the Isle of Man,

The Starmaker engine even found its way into grass track racing

to build power plants for the Tony Dawson Manxman project. But, due to unforeseen circumstances and an unwillingness of British industry to finance such a venture, this project was consigned to the dustbin, together with any further hopes of an upsurgence of interest in a British motorcycle.

The DMW trials machine reappeared in 1979, this time using a frame designed in-house which featured the fuel tank as an integral part of the chassis. A one-piece fibreglass seat and dummy tank unit was made to disguise this fact. The repositioning of the tank lowered the centre of gravity and the dummy tank cover was slim enough to allow the front wheel to be viewed at all times. The new frame was manufactured and tested by DMW works riders Colin Tipping, Steve .. and Mike Parkes. The trials machine was definitely the last of the line, and the factory built no more bikes, instead concentrating on components.

With DMW having put into production a 197cc kart racing engine in 1975, it was of no surprise to learn that Upton Karts, who were front runners in the National 210 kart class, took over the building and marketing of this engine. With the Metal Profile company still selling Villiers spares under the DMW brand name, for they had retained all the jigs and tools, supplying Upton with bare unmachined castings for his engine units. Production carried on at Sedgely, making engine spares and suspension components, but the MP front fork was the next asset to go, with Competition Classics of Manchester gaining the rights to it in 1995. The remaining stock of Villiers spares and tooling passed on to Competition Classics the following year.

The DMW story may not have ended here, for in late 1996 Clive Tomkinson of Competition Classics announced that they were considering a reborn DMW, with the blessing of its directors. The new machine was to be aimed at the commuter trail rider, and would have been powered by a Rotax 125 or 250cc engine. The project was eventually shelved, but it is not beyond the realms of possibility that one day a brand new DMW could emerge.

As a postscript, in 1972 Les "Smokey" Dawson (the founder of DMW) who then lived in Ellsmere Port, Cheshire working as a borough engineer, announced the launch of a revolutionary frame kit. For the previous ten years, Les had been working on the design of an under-slung spring suspension system. The rear suspension relied on four heavy duty springs in tension, pulling the wheel down on to the road, instead of pushing it. No damper was fitted, or needed as it was said that a spring in tension had a built-in damping effect. The front fork featured telescopic legs, which controlled a pair of long leading links, a patent he took out before the Second World War. The advantage of this system was that braking stresses were absorbed by the links and not the legs, and that the steering geometry remained unaltered under braking. A prototype frame had been built, which housed a Starmaker engine, but Les had plans to fit a Yamaha TR2 engine for short circuit racing. He planned to go into production with the frame kit, and wanted someone to invest £30,000 in the venture, but no backer was forthcoming and the project simply faded away, as did many other good British ideas.

Nevada 1971, Mike Jackson, General Sales Manager Norton Villiers Corporation, races his personal 370cc AJS Storrmer in the Mint 400, an 8-lap 400-mile desert race for by 60 motorcycles and 120 cars

1970 AJS Stormer production model, 250 and 410 engine sizes

12 Kart Racing

The thrill of driving a fast and expensive racing car on a small capacity motorcycle budget at first seems impossible, but this was exactly how and why kart racing first started. By the mid sixties the sport was well organised and controlled by the RAC (Royal Automobile Club) who formulated the rules and issued the regulations, much in the same way that the ACU (Auto Cycle Union) and the Motor Cycle Racing Control Board control all aspects of motorcycle sport. At that time kart racing was split into various classes, with class I being for beginners who were restricted to the use of direct drive industrial engines up to 100cc, class II for direct drive industrial engines up to 200cc which catered for a double-engined version of the beginner's model. Class III was for motorcycle engines up to 100cc, but the most popular was class IV. This class was split into two, with class IV Super being the most exciting, catering for karts fitted with Bultaco 196cc or bored out Montesa 175cc units. Class IV Standard was cheaper to participate in, for it was based on the use of the popular Villiers 197cc three or four-speed engine unit, with all Mks from the 6E to the 11E being used at one time or another.

Class IV Standard used the Villiers 197cc engine

Greeves made a 197cc alloy cylinder for the Class IV Super Karts, in this case used in a motorcycle

Villiers become involved

At first Villiers was oblivious to the fact that their engines were being used on the kart scene, but by 1959 had started to build engines to cater for it. The first engine was the 99cc 9F unit to service the needs of the junior classes, but by the turn of the decade they had introduced no less that four differing specification 9E motors for the larger class IV karts.

Specification 976D was a relatively standard engine unit equipped with a three-speed gearbox and an S25 carburettor mounted on a longer induction pipe. Little else in the way of tuning was carried out apart from the cylinder bore which was given an extra 0.002 inch clearance and a special fuel needle was used in the carburettor.

Specification 152D was similar, but this engine was fitted with a four-speed gearbox.

Specification 110D was a competition sports engine that used the caged roller big-end assembly, high compression head, competition magneto and competition cylinder barrel with extra piston clearance.

Specification 246D was the competition super sports engine which utilised the 110D competition components, together with a specially tuned cylinder barrel and an Amal 389/63 carburettor. In this form the engine developed 15 bhp at 5,750rpm.

During the period Villiers produced motorcycle engines, many different units were supplied to the various firms that built fun and racing karts; from the 99cc motors, the 150 types, the 175, the various 200cc versions and the 250 A range singles. In later years the Starmaker was even pressed into use.

Modified components

Many of the earlier kart racers prepared their own engines using modified components culled from the scrambles specification motorcycle engines. But ingenuity did not stop there, and experiments were carried out on short-stroke motors. The 2L motor, looking externally similar to the 9E, was pressed into use. Having a stroke of 63.5 mm and a set of full-circle flywheels as a standard fit, the 174cc motor was an ideal candidate for conversion. By substituting the standard crowded roller big-end bearing with the caged 9E sport type, the bottom end became as strong as the genuine competition engine. The cylinder barrel was then hand ported and rebored to 63 mm to accept a piston from the 225cc 1H. These modifications ended up with a 198cc motor of nearly square dimensions. The only drawback to this configuration was that the flywheels were of the standard Villiers cast type, which were not really up to the high revs expected of the racing engine. By now Alpha was producing its own machined steel full circle flywheels, and many tuners opted to use them, even though they were only available with the standard 72 mm stroke. If Alpha had put into production a smaller stroke full circle crankshaft assembly, who knows what could have happened.

A National 210cc engine

Brand new National 210cc Invader engine

Villiers

National 210cc Invader engine

With the upsurgence of interest in the use of the Villiers engine in class IV Standard racing, many manufacturers naturally produced performance equipment to cater for the increase in power that these machines needed. Alloy cylinders became the vogue and these were available from the established manufacturers of the day, which included both Greeves and Marcelle, but the fitment of such conversions put the machines into the Super class. The Greeves cylinder was specially cast with 59 mm bore and stamped GK for the 200cc kart class, and was not a sleeved down 246cc unit. It was also 1/4 inch shorter than the 66 mm bore version, for use with the short 9E con-rod. It featured superior porting and a round inlet port rather than the oval version of the motorcycle cylinder. Rule changes in the early seventies effectively banned the use of these big-fin alloy barrels, when the diameter of the cylinder finning was restricted to 160 mm. Alloy cylinders of this diameter were then produced by Aubrey Upton of Upton Karts to keep the Villiers-engined karts up among the front runners.

The increases in power that these cylinders gave had the same effects on the kart racing world as they did with motorcycle racing, namely the advanced failure rate of many of the internal engine components. To counter this problem specialist engine builders again employed the same remedies that motorcycle racers used during the period.

Modern Spanish Motoplat ignition systems ensure more reliable sparks

Another Villiers-based engine which saw service on the class IV scene kart scene was the Merlin. The roots of the Merlin design are attributed to the world of 200cc kart racing of the mid sixties. To go one better than the Villiers based engine producers of the day, Chris Merlin of Motor Karts Ltd of Kingston-on-Thames, used a rotary disc valve to control the induction phase. Having looked at piston port induction engines, Chris saw a need for asymmetric port timing to develop the power he needed, and he opted for the disc valve, which gave him the degree of control he wished for.

The Merlin disc-valve motor

To produce the 9E based 200cc Merlin disc valve kart motor, a complete Villiers engine/gearbox package was used as a starting point, but the cylinder and right hand crankcase were substituted by Merlin in-house produced items. Production was very limited and it was reported that only twenty-seven units were ever built.

The National 210cc engine also found its way into Classic motorcycle races

The class IV Standard division blossomed and eventually became the 210 National class in the late seventies, and embraced the Villiers 197cc 9E in its many guises. The name, 210 National, came about as a direct result of the maximum rebore size permissible under its rules, which allowed rebores 70 thou (1.8 mm) above the standard 59 mm bore, which gave a capacity of 209.04cc.

With the decline of the Villiers Empire, DMW took over the rights to the Villiers A and E range singles, and production continued to supply the invalid carriage market. To augment sales, DMW put into production a complete197cc kart racing engine in 1975 based on the 11E. It was no surprise to learn that shortly afterwards, front runners in the class IV racing scene, Upton Karts,

Another Motoplat ignition system, this time internal rotor type

took over the marketing of this kart engine. Aubrey Upton carried on making tuning parts for the Villiers 9 & 11E, to service the needs of this class. These parts included reprofiled cylinder heads, tuned iron cylinders with single ring high-domed pistons, full-circle cranks, strengthened rods, machined steel clutch baskets and lightweight steel flywheels. Complete engines were also built that used a total loss battery, coil and contact breaker set up; electronic ignition systems not being available in those early days. When Aubrey retired, the kart engine work was taken over by Invader UK, who developed the unit even further, and manufactured the engine until 1997.

Invader UK

Having no rights to the name Villiers or any other manufacturer who followed it, the new company marketed the engine components under the Invader banner. The engine castings were devoid of any brand name. The oval on the primary chain cover which once proudly carried the DMW and before that the Villiers logo's was still there, but now it was empty. The only evidence of the origins of the engine could be seen on the inside of the crankcase halves, away from prying eyes, for when opened up could be seen the legend DMW. Metal Profile had kept the moulds and jigs for the major engine castings, and still produced these unmachined components for Invader UK before passing the jigs and tooling on to Competition Classics in 1996.

Having inherited an uprated and successful design, Tom Thacker of Invader took the engine to greater heights, with the introduction of a steel lined alloy cylinder that employed four transfer ports, a bridged exhaust port and an inlet tract of huge proportions that used a 35 mm Amal Mk2 carburettor. The generously finned cylinder head was attached by four long crankcase studs with external nuts, for in the kart role there was unrestricted access to the top of the engine unlike the motorcycle frame, the top tube of which usually hampered cylinder removal. The sparks department was now fully electronic, using an internal or external flywheel Motoplat system, with a straight line or a retarder ignition curve. The Invader crankshaft again came from Alpha, which now sported a Yamaha big-end assembly and a needle roller small end. The crank was supported on fibre caged high-speed main bearings, of which the normal roller timing side bearing was replaced by a double row ball bearing.

With the petrol tank usually being sited on the floor of the kart, fuel had to be raised to the carburettor by means of a crankcase compression operated pump, this component being of Amal manufacture.

Rising power outputs

Power outputs had by now risen to over 30 bhp at 10,000rpm, which put a huge strain on the primary driveline. Problems in this area were overcome by the introduction of a duplex engine sprocket and chain, but the clutch sprocket remained simplex, the second row of the chain being supported by the accurately machined steel clutch drum. It may seem strange that the clutch chainwheel still retained its single row of teeth when the engine sprocket was doubled up.

Invader engine showing the bridged exhaust port to good effect

Picture showing forward-mounted carb for kart use

The reasoning behind this move was primarily one of space inside the chaincases, but this did not really matter, for the major wear points were the front sprocket and the single row chain. The standard engine sprocket used 20 teeth, of which only 9 were in contact with the chain rollers at any one time, on the other hand the clutch sprocket had 43 teeth and contact was made on 22 of them. By doubling up the front sprocket, 18 teeth came into use, which evened out the wear rate. Another good point was that the chain could be reversed after a stipulated number of races, to ensure that the wear on the rollers was equalised. This system extended the time period between the tedious task of primary chain adjustment, where the engine had to be stripped and gaskets added between the engine and gearbox to achieve correct adjustment.

As power outputs began to rise the clutch tended to suffer; and in an attempt to stop clutch slip, Upton used the heavy duty large diameter double clutch spring, which first saw service on the 1H engine and later became a standard fitment to the 35A Minicar engines. Invader strengthened this up even further by producing a 1.4 gauge single spring. This heavyweight spring, which was ideal for the foot operated clutch pedals on karts, cured any further clutch problems, but when used in the motorcycle role became a very heavy handful indeed.

Same engine showing Igor Ashwell belt drive conversion

Belt drive conversions

When the belt drive conversions for these engines became available, they had a two-fold advantage over the chain drive systems. The chain cases were dispensed with, which enabled the system to be easily adjusted and serviced without extensive stripping. But the biggest advantage was that the clutch now ran cold and dry instead of hot and wet, which enabled drivers to reduce the poundage of the clutch spring, and in some cases even reducing the number of friction plates without incurring any slippage.

Invader ceased production in 1997, but kart engine spares are still available from the 210 Drivers Club, and other members who raced with the club. The late Igor Ashwell of Newark (the 1996 210 National champion) produced high performance parts for the class, which included the belt drive primary transmission system, reed valve cylinders and a large selection of gear box ratios to suit every driver's needs. His personal engines produced over 35 bhp at 11,000 rpm, a far cry from the 8.3 bhp of their forbears.

The 210 National karting scene has its own formula, and within this rigidly adhered to set of rules, various small concerns made components to service it. Many 9E and 11E based engines, built by the numerous experts of the day, utilised components of their own manufacture, which included cast alloy primary drive cases and magneto covers. One such company to make these components was GBRD (Green Belt Racing Developments) and today much of their work is still in evidence, not only in the kart role but also the competition motorcycle scene.

GBRD (Green Belt Racing Development) one of the several companies manufacturing components for the 210cc National class

The Kartpro gear-driven primary transmission system

Kartpro

Another company who realised the shortcomings of the low powered motorcycle engine being used in kart racing was Kartpro, who designed and marketed a gear driven primary drive system suitable for the 9E and its variants. The drive system consisted of a new straight-cut engine pinion, an idler pinion and a new large pinion riveted to the back of the all-steel machined clutch basket. The idler rotated on a movable shaft, which when set up to the correct tooth backlash, could be locked in position. The kit required the use of a new set of primary drive castings that carried the idler shaft boss, which could be bolted straight onto the 9E engine. Being angular in shape, the outer cover was held on by four screws, which at least ensured that the joint remained oil tight, unlike the single nut fixing of the standard cases.

Today, much of this advanced kart technology is used in Classic and Vintage motorcycle events. Thinly disguised as a 9E or one of its variants, these engines produce a competitive machine that is capable of pushing out some 30 bhp at about 10,000rpm. These engines are slightly detuned to produce a little more tractability, for the truly wild porting of the kart engine gives a narrow power band and the extended inlet port duration hampers bump-starting.

In service, the kart engines are very reliable, but the gearbox does tend to suffer from the extra power and high revolutions put through it, for little could be done internally to beef up the box, other than the use of needle roller main and layshaft bearings. But even these have to be small for there is not enough metal in the casings to fit larger types. Solid mainshafts and externally operated Japanese clutches have been tried, but most drivers/riders tend to use the standard gearbox components, and learn to live with the repeated and regular rebuilds.

Karting kept pace with motorcycle engine developments through the following decades, and now the senior karts use both single and twin cylinder 250cc engines, which generate truly awesome speeds. But the humble Villiers 197cc engine is not forgotten, and the 210 Challenge is thriving again, bringing in new members and new technology annually.

Bottom end and gearbox of the Invader power unit

The machined one-piece clutch basket for added strength

Three kart engines ready for use

13 Industrial Engines

Mk VI-C engines saw use in both motorcycle and industrial applications

The start of the Villiers industrial engine division can be traced back to 1919, when a motorcycle engine was adapted to power a lawn mower. One of the earliest domestic applications as a result of this exercise was when Charles H Pugh, a Birmingham engineer who later founded the Atco factory that made Villiers powered lawnmowers for many years ,purchased 900 engine units and built them into domestic sized lawn mowers. Pugh's marketing technique was to send out a salesman on a motorcycle sidecar outfit, carrying one of his mowers, with instructions to stop at any house that had a large lawn. This method paid off, and started a trend towards engine power instead of muscle power, taking the effort out of domestic and industrial chores. As the industrial market progressed over the following years, the engines supplied by Villiers were all, of course, the motorcycle type, but by the late 1920s specialised stationary engines were available.

After a lot of development work, a new range of specialist fan and water-cooled two-stroke engines were introduced, with power outputs that ranged from 1/2 to 3 hp. During this early period the method of stating power ratings was to use the old RAC rating system (100cc is approximately equal to 1 horse power) and had nothing to do with the actual brake horsepower figures that were used in later years. The jobs that these engines were put to were many and varied, and included brush cutters, cultivators, sprayers, milking machines, pumps of all types and electricity generators. If the equipment requirement was for a rotary, reciprocating or linear motion, then the Villiers industrial engine was adapted to power it. This move to the world of domestic and industrial motive power created a further demand for engine units, and Villiers was only too happy to oblige.

The first production industrial engine

The first production industrial engines were based on the motorcycle A, B and C range engines, still using the original bore and stroke measurements but modified to suit the needs of the buyer. Depending on the application they could be air-cooled, fan-cooled or even water-cooled. The carburettors of these modified engines were smaller than the motorcycle variants, which gave a lower power output at an equally low speed, but this power was delivered for a longer and sustained period of time.

This range of pre-war engines included versions of the 147cc motor which were designated the Mk VIII-C; four versions of the 247cc unit, derived from the Mk XII and the 19A and a 343cc engine which was referred to as the Mk IX-B.

The outbreak of the Second World War saw the increased need for motive power in places where electricity was unavailable, due either to the remote location or as the result of enemy bombing raids. Initially the proprietary two-stroke motors met this requirement, with units of British manufacture or motors shipped in from the USA, but soon even this supply was exhausted and the government approached Villiers to see if they would design a four-stroke

A MkVI-C mounted on a 1920s Atco mower found lanquishing in a barn, hence its condition

engine to meet the demand. This new requirement ushered in the second generation of stationary engines that could run on petrol, paraffin or TVO. These were designed and ready for production in record time. The pre-war engines had used the motorcycle numbering system which identified the Mk and the size, but now the new four-strokes adopted a totally new numbering system which roughly equated to the capacity of the motor in ccs. In 1941 the first side-valve industrial engines were introduced. These were the Mk 10 (98cc), the Mk 20 (206.5cc) and the Mk 25 (256.5cc), followed in 1942 by the first Mk 12 (120cc) engine; these units being referred to as the "V" engines. Two-stroke stationary engines were still being produced during the war, giving the end user an immense choice when ordering a motor for a specific task.

War-time production

War-time stationary engine production was huge, with many thousands being built to carry out many hundreds of diverse jobs. Fire-fighting was a major task, and the National Fire Service used thousands of these units to pump water, not only for fires, but they were also used to fill static water tanks and to pump purified drinking water to areas that had lost their mains supply. Hospitals used the V engines to supply emergency lighting power, as did many other establishments that required some form of lighting when the mains power went off, which it did quite regularly. The armed services also used the Villiers product to perform a bewildering number of jobs; the RAF using them to pump fuel into aircraft, pump up aircraft tyres and in some cases they were even adapted to start the engines. Electricity generation was a major use by all the branches of the services, to charge batteries and to supply power for lights and equipment in remote locations. Users had nothing but praise for the Villiers power units, for they were reliable in operation and robust enough to deliver the goods throughout the many war theatres in which they operated.

The interest in four-stroke engines was further expanded during the war years, when Mr F Austey (the technical development chief) took out a patent on behalf of the Villiers Engineering Co, relating to the operation of overhead valves. Although the system was never used, it highlighted the diversity of the factory's forward thinking. The new system of valve operation was primarily aimed at multi cylinder engines, and used a single camshaft to operate all the valves. The exhaust pushrods were operated by direct acting cam followers, but the inlets were activated by short horizontal tappets which in turn operated a rocker that moved the pushrod vertically.

Four-stroke side-valve engines

Development of the four-stroke side-valve engines continued after the war, to produce many different engines for use in the stationary and industrial role. The next engine to emerge from the Wolverhampton premises was the Mk 7 in 1946, a 75cc unit that was available with a crankshaft speed output shaft. The following year reduction gears of 2.94:1 or 6:1 also became available to suit the nature of the equipment it powered.

The war-time four-stroke production engines were all side-valve units, but in 1948 the Mk 15 (147cc) overhead valve engine was introduced to cater for customers who required a 1.5 hp motor. This unit was available with a crankshaft speed output shaft or 3:1 and 6:1 reduction gearboxes; the reduction gear units being identifiable by the bulbous housing on the drive side and an RG suffix to the full Mk number.

Fiftieth Anniversary

The same year also saw the fiftieth anniversary celebrations of the Villiers Engineering Co, and to mark this milestone an advertisement was produced by the factory and published in the many motorcycle and engineering journals of the day. It neatly summed up the Villiers engineering company, for it depicted the industrial engine, the motorcycle engine and the bicycle freewheel, giving each separate commodity equal star billing, thus indicating the diversity of the Wolverhampton concern.

For 1949 the Mk 2 Midget engine became the main stay of the two-stroke 100cc industrial class, and was used in applications where the throttle opening could be varied by the operator to suit the load. Derived from the pre-war Midget motorcycle engine, the new industrial version differed in that the fixed head iron cylinder had a centrally mounted exhaust port and a detachable side mounted inlet manifold, and could be fitted with either an aluminium or cast iron piston, the latter being used to combat abnormally dusty conditions. The engine unit was equipped with a rope starter pulley attached to the magneto flywheel, a Villiers Junior carburettor and a small self-contained silencer. Stated as delivering a sustained 0.625 bhp at 2,500rpm, the engine could give 1 bhp, but in short bursts only.

A Mk 3 version of the Midget engine was also produced, the only difference being the provision of fan cooling and a fuel tank carried on brackets above the fan cowling. Production of this engine carried on with Mk 4 and 5 units also being produced.

A new numbering system

Two-stroke engine production continued during this period with the introduction of the Mk 25 series, but this new numbering system bore no relationship to the actual capacity, the size being again denoted by the suffix letter. The smallest of this series was the Mk 25C, a 147cc unit which used the same bore and stroke measurements (55 x 62 mm) as the post war 30C motorcycle unit. In line with motorcycle engine development, the 25C used ball races to support the crankshaft, together with spring assisted gland bushes to keep in the crankcase compression, a far better system than the bronze main bearing/seals of the wartime units. Again using fan cooling and a starter pulley on the flywheel, the 25C followed closely the lines of the Midget, except that on this model the cylinder head was detachable, and was fitted with either a Junior or Lightweight carburettor, dependent upon the power output required.

The MkI Midget was used in both motorcycle and industrial applications, here fitted to a Ransome grass-cutter

The Mk 26C followed on from the 25C, but on this motor it appeared that technology took a step backwards, for a return to the phosphor bronze main bearing sleeves was made. As this engine was mainly used in the propulsion of invalid carriages, where the motor was sited close to the ground between the rear wheels, it collected a certain amount of road dirt and dust. To counter this problem an air filter was added to the carburettor, but even with the filter, small amounts of dirt could still enter the engine, drastically reducing the life of the main bearing ball races. To eliminate this problem, Villiers specified a return to plain main bearing, but it was only for engines used in this dirty environment. Being used as a motive power unit for a road vehicle, the flywheel magneto of the 26C was equipped with lighting coils to supply power to the vehicle's obligatory lamps.

Villiers MkI Midget engine

When the need arose for more power, the Mk 25 series engines were enlarged to 249cc to become the 25A, another fan cooled two-stroke unit but this time with a bore and stroke measurement of 63 x 80 mm. Power output was in the region of 3 bhp at 3,000rpm in the continuous running mode, with short bursts up to 6 bhp. To guard against over revving the unit, a governor was fitted, operated by air pressure in the fan housing which controlled a butterfly valve in the inlet manifold and closed the engine down if the operator was a bit slow on the hand throttle. The twin exhaust engine was equipped with a flat top piston and a strong bottom end with a pair of double row main ball bearing races. Even this engine was enlarged, to become the 346cc Mk 27B, which had a bore and stroke of 70 x 90 mm, and produced 4 bhp in the continuous running role or 8 bhp in short bursts. Again 3,000rpm was the optimum working speed, with a governor coming into operation at 3,500rpm.

Triple V-belt primary transmission

From the 1953 season the 346cc 27B engine was produced, with triple V belt primary transmission that had a special application to the AC Petite three wheeler microcar. The belt driven primary drive was chosen for its ability to withstand the adverse effects of petrol and water and was said neither to slip nor stretch. The belts ran between the triple engine pulley and the clutch drum, but a chain was used for the final drive to the differential. The 27B was further enlarged to 353cc and refined in 1955, with a revised bore and stroke of 75 x 80 mm. Component parts from the 28B were also used by dedicated specials builder and trials sidecar pilot John Catchpole, in the building of an ingenious 564cc twin cylinder special. Using a pair of 80 mm stroke 28B cranks, mounted in 27B crankcases which were spaced apart by long bolts and spacers, the engine was fitted with 67 mm bore alloy cylinders and a single Amal Monobloc carburettor. Joining together the two separate but narrow engine units on the same crankshaft centre line caused little in the way of problems, and was achieved by the use of two sprockets and a length of duplex chain to hold the sprockets together. Sparks for the twin were generated by a twin cylinder motorcycle magneto mounted on the right hand side behind the cylinders. The twin performed well, producing smoothness with lots of low rpm torque, ideal for the Catchpole chair outfit.

During the 1960s John Catchpole built this trials sidecar outfit, the engine being based on Villiers industrial components

Avid specials builder John Catchpole's 564cc twin cylinder engine

The MkII Midget engine was used from 1949 for industrial purposes

Four-stroke engines continued in production after the war, seeing service in all types of environments, in the Villiers tradition of supplying a unit to meet every industrial need, together with equally as many domestic applications. To service these needs, the four-stroke Mk 10, 12, 20 and 25 side valve units were produced. The 98cc Mk 10 unit was of a square configuration (50 x 50 mm) and capable of delivering a constant 0.75 bhp at 1,500rpm to 1.3 bhp at 3,000rpm over 12 hour running periods. As with the other side valve units, this engine used a ball race supported one-piece crankshaft with plain big-end bearing shells, which were splash lubricated by a projection on the bearing cap simply scooping up oil from the sump. Ignition was provided by the Villiers flywheel magneto onto which were fitted the cooling fan blades. Again a governor was a standard fit to prevent over revving.

An increased cylinder bore

The Mk 10 was complimented by the Mk 12, an engine of similar construction, but now the cylinder bore had been increased to 55 mm. This larger unit gave increased power, 0.95 to 1.5 bhp between 1,500 to 3,000rpm over the 12 hour continuous running period. Both the Mk 10 and the Mk 12 units were available with a 3:1 reduction gear, and could be supplied with either rope starting or kick starting systems. The foot starter mechanism was a simple pedal-driven quadrant that operated a spring-loaded starter ratchet on the non-standard crank, inboard of the final drive pulley.

The Mk 20 (206cc) had a bore and stroke of 63 x 66.7 mm and was stated as delivering 1.5 to 2.5 bhp at between 1,500 to 2,500rpm. The larger Mk 25 256cc engine was equipped with a 70 mm piston, and delivered 1.9 to 3 bhp over the same rev range. Both engines could also be supplied with a 3:1 reduction gear.

TVO

In areas where petrol was in short supply, all the previously listed side valve engines could be supplied to run on Tractor Vaporising Oil (TVO). The only modifications were a lowering of the compression ratio on the Mks 20 and 25 and the addition of a two compartment fuel tank, three-way fuel tap and a special carburettor mounted on a special manifold. The engine was started normally on petrol, and once warmed up, the three-way tap was moved to the TVO position. The TVO flowed to the carburettor via the special manifold, where it was heated up to assist vaporisation. To stop the engine, the tap had to be returned to the petrol position a few minutes before killing the ignition, to ensure that the float bowl contained the correct fuel for the next cold start. If the engine was inadvertently stopped with TVO still in the float chamber, this could be easily drained away by the use of a fuel tap on the bottom of the float bowl. When using TVO, the operating instructions recommended the use of thicker lubricating oil, which had to be changed more regularly than the petrol engines. The reason for this was that the engine's lubricating oil was diluted by the fuel, and if TVO was used this would not evaporate out at normal working temperatures.

Production of industrial power units carried on alongside the motorcycle engine, and by 1957 the Wolverhampton factory, which by then controlled JAP, went on to produce a vast range of industrial units, that again were destined to carry out a wide variety of jobs. They operated in the frozen wastes of Greenland and Scandinavia, and in the steaming heat of the tropics. They were also put to work driving rock drills, air compressors and lighting sets, building the world's highest road across the Andes Mountains and drilling the foundations for electricity pylons in the Canadian Rockies. Emergency generating sets again became increasingly popular, with units being pressed into service to run stand-by power supplies for lighthouses along the Scandinavian coastline. Self-contained air raid sirens were another Villiers powered product, fully waterproofed and designed to operate in all climatic conditions. These units were supplied with either a Mk 10 or Mk 25 engine, and again sold world wide.

When Twentieth Century Fox filmed the epic motion picture "Untamed" on location in the Valley of a Thousand Hills, a few miles from Durban in the Republic of South Africa in 1955, it was faced with a severe logistics problem. Water was needed to feed the needs of 3,000 actors, technicians and extras together with some 500 head of cattle also needed for the film. The problem was that there was no water on site, the nearest supply was at the Nagle Dam, two miles away, which supplied the population of Durban. The requirement was for 30,000 gallons of water per day, and this was achieved by the use of Villiers industrial engines positioned every half-mile in the pipeline to maintain a constant flow during the ten-week shooting period. In all, these pumps delivered some 2,000,000 gallons of water, and were supplied by the local Villiers agent - McBean's Implement Co of near-by Petermaritzburg, who also supplied the many Villiers-powered electricity generators and spraying compressors used on the set.

Same engine different view, also showing the exhaust system

Australian and Spanish production

With the prestigious industrial engine manufacturers JAP and Villiers now pulling together, the merger started another empire that produced units for worldwide distribution. As well as in Great Britain, engine units were now being produced in Australia and Spain. At its peak of production the combined might of JAP and Villiers produced two-stroke industrial units from 34cc to 395cc, and four-stroke units from 75cc to 824cc. Whilst the JAP factory at Tottenham remained in production, it still produced the JAP speedway and grass track engines in 350 and 500cc form, but when the facility went into liquidation it was only the industrial engine side that was finally transferred to Wolverhampton.

Production again soared when the Wolverhampton factory took on the manufacture of BSA industrial engines in the summer of 1965, following a licensing agreement between the two concerns. This agreement, which included the supply of spares and service, freed up manufacturing space at the Redditch works which was badly needed by BSA to meet its increased motorcycle production.

Villiers

Below and opposite, the 34cc JAP industrial engine, later marketed by Villiers as the 303

With the Manganese Bronze take-over of the Villiers Empire in 1966, the industrial engine division was the only asset to survive, with production carrying on during the subsequent Norton Villiers and the Norton Villiers Triumph eras. Incidentally this operation included the rights to the BSA industrial engines, which had been acquired from Small Heath by the Manganese Bronze Group when they bailed out the ailing BSA Group in 1973. This period saw a prolific growth in the wide variety of industrial engines offered by what can only be described as Great Britain's major producer, with eight new designs being introduced in 1964 alone.

The late 1970s saw the Villiers Wolverhampton factory become another victim in the ongoing NVT saga, with the entire operation in jeopardy and up for sale. The motorcycle side of things did not survive, even after several interested parties placed bids. The industrial engine division however had been bid for during November 1976 by the Wolverhampton Industrial Engines consortium, headed by Peter Sankey. The subsequent purchase was achieved with the help of government aid, a path fraught with danger if earlier Nor Vil and NVT episodes with government cash were to be remembered. This time the buy-out was less traumatic.

After a short closing down period, production recommenced in 1977 under the Wolverhampton workers cooperative, and sales flourished once again. Sales figures climbed to such a degree that further overseas expansion was once again looked into. South Africa was considered to be the site of the next factory to take advantage of the industrialisation of the African continent, but due to the political climate of the time, this idea was shelved.

Villiers marched with the times, and in 1986 introduced the 146cc A15 four-stroke petrol engine, which used up-to-date technology in the form of an electronic ignition system. This was the first time that any Villiers engine had used such a system, for all previous engines, both motorcycle and industrial, were produced in the contact-breaker era.

In 2001 the British Villiers industrial engine factory finally closed its doors, having sold off the rights to its products to the SAEPL Co of Madras, India, who are continuing to produce industrial engines and spare parts, none of which, it must be added, can be pressed into use in motorcycle engines. In latter years all that remains of the once vast Villiers Engineering complex, is a small office on the Blakenhall Industrial Estate, off Sunbeam Street, Wolverhampton; this facility selling industrial engine spares, the factory site having been bulldozed for redevelopment.

JAP

Born in Kensington in 1874, John Albert Prestwich was a natural engineer who built a steam engine at the tender age of fourteen and a fully working internal combustion engine two years later. In 1895 he opened the small JA Prestwich Industries works in Tottenham, North London, making scientific instruments and cinematographic apparatus, including the JAP camera which accompanied Captain Scott on his Antarctic Expedition.

When JA Prestwich turned his attention to motorcycle propulsion units, the first engine to come out of the Tottenham works was the 293cc model of 1903, a four-stroke unit of 70 x 76mm which was said to deliver 2 hp at 1600rpm. This engine used an automatic inlet valve and drip feed lubrication, and to prevent the "ejectment" of oil, was fitted with a patented vacuum valve crankcase breather. The engine was sold to other manufacturers, but it was also fitted to a machine built by JAP themselves.

In 1908 JAP gave up motorcycle manufacture and concentrated solely on engines, making a variety designs both two and four-stroke up to 1400cc, to cover the various capacity classes in common use. In the run up to the First World War, JAP stayed ahead of the motorcycle engine opposition and diversified into the world of pencil making, setting up the Pencils Ltd company, who could produce the end product at ten times the rate of any other pencil maker. By the time of the Villiers merger, output had grown to a colossal figure of forty million pencils per annum.

The 1920s found JAP at full stretch building side-valve and overhead valve four-stroke units, together with small two-stroke engines, to feed the eagerly awaiting motorcycle manufacturers of the day. These engines were designs from the pen of Stanley Greening and latterly Val Page. The masterpiece of Page's design genius was the 350cc double overhead cam EXP1 engine, which Bert Le Vack used in the 1922 Junior TT, setting a new lap record. This engine was later fitted with a smaller cylinder and brought Le Vack many 250 class victories. Sporting successes were abundant during the 1930s, with JAP producing many single cylinder and V-twin sports and racing engines, for road racing and record-breaking purposes. At this time the JAP engine reigned supreme, its sporting pedigree helping the sales of the standard tune motors that were fitted to many road going machines of the period.

During the Second World War the Tottenham company helped with the war effort, building 240,000 lightweight portable stationary engines, together with 10 million time fuses and 23 million contact fuses for explosive munitions. Industrial engine production continued after the conflict had ended, with the company supplying units from the 34cc lawn mower engine up to the mighty 850cc V twin that was put to use in a variety of industrial applications.

JAP is best remembered for its speedway engines, engines that helped many riders to world titles. As far back as 1930, when Stan Greening and Wal Phillips built the first speedway unit from a road racing engine, the name JAP had become synonymous with successes in this sector of motorcycle sport, and in the post-war era it became the engine to have, an engine used by all the stars of the day. The 1950s saw JAP win every title in the speedway world, but some years later these successes tailed off with the advent of the Czechoslovakian ESO motor which then took over as the number one speedway motor. ESO later absorbed by Jawa, soon found that they were eclipsed by another British power unit. Bearing a resemblance to the JAP engine, the new four-valve Weslake was destined to dominate the sport from the mid 1970s. However, from the mid-1980s Jawa resumed its number one position, which continues to the present day.

Below and opposite, the 412H engine, used by the fire service for water pumping

The 1950s saw roadster and industrial engine sales dwindling, even though the speedway engine, hand built in small numbers, was still a good seller. Due to this situation JAP found itself in financial difficulties and with the death of its founder on 28th November 1952, drastic action had to be taken. With a brief announcement relating to 'a merger of interests' appearing in the 20th June 1957 edition of Motor Cycling, Villiers bailed out the ailing JAP empire of Tottenham, North London. The assets, which included industrial engines, the speedway engine and the pencil company, all now came under the control of the Villiers group.

The only serious attack on the Villiers utility motorcycle engine production was the introduction of the JAP 125 two-stroke of 1947. This engine unit, fitted to a number of smaller motorcycle manufacturers' machines, continued in production until 1952, when it was finally axed. But running alongside the Villiers 9 and 10D motors of the period, the JAP product did not pose much of a threat to the Wolverhampton factory, which continued to make volume sales to its traditional customers.

The Tottenham factory carried on as normal for a few more years, but in the end this too was closed down and the remains of a once great and reputable company were moved to the Villiers premises at Wolverhampton. Villiers saw fit to keep only the industrial engine and pencil making side of the JAP business portfolio, scrapping the remaining roadster engine side and selling off the speedway engine rights to George Greenwood.

The Lotus connection

When Villiers Engineering merged with JA Prestwich after the latter got into financial difficulties during 1957, JAP carried on at its Tottenham factory for a further few years, before finally going into liquidation and closing down. It was during this time that the fledgling Lotus factory, based at Cheshunt, approached JAP to machine and assemble their new Ford based twin-cam production engine, as there was no expertise and even less of a production facility at the Cheshunt factory. The task was accepted by JAP, and the third production engine, a three bearing 109E-based 1477cc unit, was shipped to them for inspection on 13th March 1962. The engine was stripped and inspected with a view to the acceptance of the Lotus contract. On reassembly, the engine was returned to Cheshunt, but unfortunately broke is crankshaft, at no fault of the JAP factory, during later testing. On 11th October 1962 the contract was issued for the project, Lotus having uprated their engine, which was now based on the Ford 116E 1500cc unit. The first production engine was completed on 21st October and tested at the Cosworth engine facility, recording a power output of 85 bhp, a vast increase over the Ford donor engine. The following month the specification was again altered, and the capacity of the engine was increased to 1558cc, which was to remain unchanged until the engine ceased production in the mid seventies.

Production of the Lotus twin-cam carried on, and in February 1963 the JAP factory installed its own dynamometer on which to test the completed engines, that were by now producing 97 bhp.

The development of the twin-cam motor was not without its problems, for the original cylinder heads were sand cast by Birmid, but they were prone to warping and leaked like sieves. A die cast head from William Mills of Wednesbury was tried, but this was no better and also leaked, until Mills reverted to the sand casting process. With the problems solved production increased, with JAP machining the bare heads, assembling the valve gear and then fitting them to the cylinder blocks that had been assembled and supplied by Ford.

When JAP finally went into liquidation, mainly due to the restrictive Union practices that prevailed at the Tottenham factory, Villiers took over the tooling and moved the machining and assembly line to their Wolverhampton site. This move placed a heavy logistics burden on the small Lotus concern, for assembled blocks were transported from Dagenham to Wolverhampton, bare heads came from Wednesbury and the completed engines then shipped down to Cheshunt for fitment into cars. When the Lotus factory moved during November 1966, to the new green-field site at Hethel in Norfolk, they decided to utilise the space available and carry out their own machining of the bare cylinder heads; also fitting the valve guides, valve seats and studs. Being more cost effective to machine in-house, the move nevertheless increased the formidable logistics problem. Now bare heads were shipped from Wednesbury to Hethel for machining, machined heads were then transported to Wolverhampton for valve gear assembly, completed cylinder blocks came from Dagenham to have the heads fitted at Wolverhampton, and the completed engines then shipped back to Hethel for fitment into Elans or Dagenham to be fitted to the Lotus-Cortina; all in all a time consuming and costly business.

When Villiers became Norton-Villiers there was a very strong union influence at the Wolverhampton site, which was alien to the Lotus staff at Hethel, who enjoyed a happier working environment. The exchange of ideas between factories became strained, with Ray Budcock, the service manager at Lotus, unable to talk directly to the Villiers fitters, having to go through the foreman. If the foreman was having a bad day, he got nowhere. Industrial trouble increased at Wolverhampton to such a degree that production of the twin-cam engine suffered, which put a huge financial burden on Lotus. Something had to be done and in mid 1967 the decision was made to move all assembly work to the Hethel site.

Fear of the Norton-Villiers unions led to a cloak and dagger operation being mounted after working hours to retrieve the Lotus engines and equipment, for it was felt that Lotus employees would be attacked by the militant Villiers union staff. But the move passed without incident and the assembly work commenced at Lotus, the line being staffed by 16 to 20 ex-RAF fitters, who were picked for their high standard of workmanship. Production increased in leaps and bounds, and in the following eight years 25,500 units were assembled, outstripping the production figures from the Villiers factory had assembled only 7,100 engines in their four-year production period.

The Wheeler Mobile Company (Canada), Beaver Amphibious vehicle powered by a Villiers 9E engine unit

This interesting aside shows yet another aspect of why the once great engineering heart of the UK industry suffered so much in the period between the late 1960s and the early 1980s.

Canadian Amphibious vehicles

The first Villiers powered Penguin was built in Toronto, Ontario some time in 1962. In 1963 a small manufacturing plant was leased in Ottawa, Ontario by Pengor Ltd. and production began. During April 1964 the Ottawa plant was forced to close and production moved to Carleton Place, Ontario. In November of 1964 the Company filed for bankruptcy, and in May, 1965 an auction was held to sell off complete machines, parts etc. The total production was approximately 800 units, with the fibreglass hulls moulded by Polyfibre Ltd of Renfrew, Ontario.

What was a Penguin? The Penguin was an amphibious 4 wheeled, two-seater all-terrain vehicle. On land a top speed of up to 40 mph was claimed from the Dynastart equipped, reversible, four-speed 9E engine unit that drove the rear wheels; this velocity being reduced to 4mph on water, when the vehicle was propelled along by the generously treaded rear tyres. If had no suspension, and the steering yoke swung right and left, instead of rotating as a steering wheel would. The throttle was located in the centre of the steering yoke and could be operated by either thumb. There was a brake pedal on the floor, and a gearshift between the seats. The dash housed the ignition switch, head/tail light switch, horn button, neutral indicator light, generator light and the passenger grab handle. The choke control and clutch lever were mounted on the gear lever.

The engine was located behind the seats, almost directly over the rear axle. There was no differential on the rear axle, and on hard ground the Penguin had a large turning radius. In the water however, the Penguin would "turn on a sixpence". The 420 lbs (empty) Penguin had a carrying capacity on land of 600 lbs, but in the water this figure was reduced to 300 lbs max. The transition from land to water travel was achieved instantly, with nothing more than a slowing down to reduce the bow wave when entering the water.

The concept of this type of vehicle particularly suited the Canadian backwoodsman, the wilderness being home to a large number of lakes after the winter snows. Penguins were even tested by the Canadian Military in 1964, but no sales were recorded.

A blue and white Penguin complete with trailer was presented to the Queen and Prince Phillip during the Royal Visit to Canada in October 1964.

Sometime after the Bankruptcy Auction at Pengor's, a somewhat similar vehicle called the "Beaver" was produced by Wheeler Mobile Ltd, of Keswick, Ontario. This one also used the Dynastart 9E unit but a similar specification 3L could be fitted if required. The steering and front axle layout of the Beaver differed from the Penguin in that the wheels were set very much closer together. Other differences were in the body dimensions, which were slightly longer and wider. The Beaver remained in production through to the early 1970s, but the number built is unknown.

14 The Classic Scene

Tug Wilson's 246cc DOT scrambler

A restored 1961 Greeves MCS scrambler with 34A 246cc 4-speed engine

Many years after its initial conception, the Villiers engine is still in general use within the many facets of the classic scene; powering many older machines that see service in the numerous road runs organised by the Vintage Motor Cycle Club (VMCC). These pre-war, and post-war, machines are lovingly prepared and ridden by members of this club, who are dedicated to the preservation of this part of our British engineering heritage. Villiers power is also a major consideration to members of the British Two-Stroke Club, for alongside products from the likes of BSA and Excelsior, the Villiers engine unit is very widely used. Throughout the year, the classic events calendar is awash with venues at which the Villiers powered road rider can air his machine, gain valuable information and spares, or just natter about bikes in general.

Pre-65 Scrambles

On the competition scene, the pre-65 and twin-shock scrambler classes have attracted many riders who now put their faith in the Villiers product. Preferring to use the relatively cheap and readily available Villiers engine units, together with the many period tuning accessories and modern day technology, these riders have injected a new level of enthusiasm into the sport which was initially dominated by the BSA Gold Star and the many Triumph powered specials. The Lightweight class now features many Villiers powered dirt bike racing machines, DOT, Cotton and Greeves to name but three, who do battle with their traditional enemies - namely the BSA and CZ variants. So popular has the Lightweight class become, that at some meetings a Greeves-only race is now run, in which the Villiers powered models are pitched against their cousins, the Challenger and short-stroke Griffon racers.

Road Racing

The road racing programmes run by the VMCC and the Classic Racing Motorcycle Club also attract a fair number of Villiers powered machines, epitomising the clubman's lightweight scene of the 1960s. In the 250 classes, Starmaker powered machines the Cotton Telstar and the DMW Hornet do battle against the 36A powered Mk 1 Greeves Silverstones, the Greeves engined Mk 2 Silverstones and the Royal Enfield engined GP5s. The CRMC 200cc class in recent years has seen the emergence of a number of 9E powered machines. Using kart engine technology, these machines are now outclassed by the screaming Japanese twin cylinder racers, that are eligible under the pre 1967 rules, but nevertheless allow riders a relatively cheap entry to the delights of circuit racing. One other Villiers powered racer which made an appearance on the classic racing scene some years ago was the 500cc double Starmaker engined DMW Typhoon.

1964 Cotton Telstar production racer seen at a recent classic meeting

The Twin-Shock Trials Scene

The twin-shock trials scene has also seen an upsurgence in the use of the Villiers engine, which has been transformed into a very competitive unit by the use of modern technology such as electronic ignition. The 197cc unit was always popular, ever since its initial successes in the 1950s when the 6E was in use, and it is still in use today. When the 9E became available, the

A DOT Works Replica trials mount restored by Cambridge enthusiast Maurice Nicholas

trend started by the competition variant of this unit was continued through to the 32 and 37A trials specification motors, which proved to be a very successful formula throughout the classic period. Today the basic engine format is still in use by experts and novices alike, and the use of such accessories as alloy cylinders and a modern carburettor ensures that the latest versions of this basic engine are still a match for their traditional four-stroke rivals. It is gratifying to note that some of the very successful modern "trick" trials machines use port timing figures not that far removed from the original Villiers dimensions formulated some five decades ago!

The Classic Scottish

The twin-shock trials scene has become so popular that the Classic Scottish, a classic two-day event run in conjunction with the annual Scottish Six Day Trial, is vastly oversubscribed, which is a lot more than can be said about the major event which nowadays is always short of competitors.

Trials riding at club level has always been popular, with riders using over-the-counter trials machines built by virtually every motorcycle manufacturer of the classic period, large and small, but now these machines have become very specialised. Altered steering head angles and close ratio gearboxes with very low overall gearing are now used in the short distance or arena type events, but for the more traditional longer distance venue, the original wide ratio gearbox is again used, albeit with a lower second gear.

The industrial engines are not forgotten, and again many examples are on show and demonstrated at the numerous vintage agricultural shows and country fairs which abound in the rural areas of Britain.

The Wolverhampton produced two-stroke power unit, initially designed purely as a commuting motive power device, saw service in many sporting activities without shaming itself. It powered TT racers (the DOT works riders gaining the Team Prize in the 1951 Ultra Lightweight 125cc TT), scramblers (Dave Bickers winning the European motocross championships in 1960 and 1961) and trials machines (Don Smith winning the European Championship in 1964 and 1967, and Billy Wilkinson winning the Scottish Six Days Trial in 1969. Many other riders achieved successes in all types of motorcycle sport, but these are too numerous to mention.

A restored 1958 Greeves 20TA Scottish Trials, with a 9E 4-speed 197cc engine

Once considered to be dirty, smelly, oily and unreliable, and the butt of many clubroom jokes, the Villiers engine initially only found favour with the ride to work brigade, until the successes of the 1960s scrambling scene opened the eyes of the general public. The 'anti-social' power unit was still shunned when the classic revival took off during the 1980s, with enthusiasts aiming to own a 'British Beef' motorcycle, which traditionally was the 650 parallel twin. As prices gradually crept upwards and supplies dwindled, enthusiasts began to look elsewhere. Finding a ready supply of machinery in the two-stroke tiddler classes, eager enthusiasts snapped up these hitherto unwanted models. So began a second lease of life for the Villiers powered motorcycle. What was earlier seen as worthless scrap now commanded sensible prices, and Villiers parts once again became sought after. Demand for spares increased, and supply initially kept up with this demand, until various items started to become rare commodities. This shortage of components heralded the birth of the specialist Villiers spares supplier.

Keeping the Villiers engine healthy

Regardless of the task to which the Villiers engine is put, its health is of paramount importance, and to keep these engines healthy an army of enthusiasts are at hand to supply standard spares, competition components, modified parts and conversion kits to uprate the standard units. Because the basic Villiers unit was originally and still is used in so many diverse roles, many of the numerous spares outlets have become specialists in their own field. Be it trials riding, scrambling, kart racing or even road riding, all these pastimes are equally catered for by enthusiasts who participate in these disciplines. Being active participants, they know what they are talking about and are willing to pass on this knowledge and expertise.

Other enthusiasts specialise in certain aspects of Villiers engine usage, with some specialising in reconditioning crankshafts, whilst others may just look after gearboxes or ignition systems. Other establishments and garden shed engineers specialise in the rebuilding of complete engine units to suit the needs of the trials rider, the pre-65 scrambler and road rider/racer, rebuilding engines to owners specifications which when completed have a reliability factor far exceeding that of the original Wolverhampton product.

World-wide supply

Today, components for Villiers engines can come from all corners of the world, sourced by eager suppliers to enhance the reputation of this masterpiece of British engineering. Pistons from Great Britain, Italy and India, needle roller big-end bearings conversions coming from Japan and ignition systems emanating from both Japan and Taiwan, all play their part in giving the venerable Villiers engine a new lease of life. Modern high-speed bearings, manufactured to closer tolerances, also play their part in producing superior and stronger bottom ends, which stand the tests of time and punishment. The crankshaft oil seal is another component that can be benefited by the substitution of a modern type. Made to a superior specification, the modern seal will afford better sealing and last longer in service. After a little machining, modern seals may be used in some of the older engines that used nothing more than phosphor bronze sleeves to keep the crankcase compression within the cases.

To build a standard Villiers engine is a bit of a misnomer, for is there such a beast? The factory built these engines to many differing specifications; road, trials, scrambles and even racing, changing these specifications at the whim of the factory they supplied to, or simply changed things because it was a good idea at the time. External appearances and optional equipment has been well documented throughout the life span of these units in their various guises, but the internal specifications cause the most problems.

Dave Bradley's 1957 James Commando trials 197cc 8E 4-speed

Depending on the use to which the engine is to be put, a bewildering array of parts are available to the builder, and it is he who must make the final choice. The many cylinders, pistons, gearbox ratios and big-ends available were all devised for specific jobs, all interchangeable with each other, and were all probably standard specification fitments at one time or another. These items were all produced by the factory and can be classified as standard parts. The dilemma comes with the fitment of non-standard parts from other sources that uprate the various systems. Should an electronic ignition system, a strengthened clutch basket and duplex primary chain, an Alpha crank or a needle roller big-end be fitted? If the fitment of such parts makes the machine more tractable, more reliable and easier to ride and maintain, then it must be yes. These items are internal and cannot be seen, but when it comes to external components such as alloy cylinders and modern carburettors the owner must decide for himself, this decision being based on his own personal needs.

Some owners want 100% authenticity on components, but this comes at the cost of effectiveness and again reliability, for it must be borne in mind that some of these systems were designed some five decades ago. Modern technology does have its place in older machines, and even the Classic Racing Motorcycle Club admits this, allowing the use of modern equipment, provided that it is hidden from view.

Post-war Engine Specification Codes

At this point it is worthwhile mentioning the Villiers post-war engine specification codes, which identify the origins and specification of the engine. Prior to the war, each type of engine was given a specific engine prefix letter or letters to denote its Mk and size, these letters varying little, other than to denote the addition of water cooling or an autolube system. After the war, motorcycle manufacturers became fussier, wanting Villiers engines to be built to their own individual specifications. To accommodate this, Villiers opted for a new specification numbering system from 001 to 999, but when this block ran out it continued with 1A to 999A, through B,C,D and E, finally finishing production half way through F. The number and letter were used as a prefix to the engine serial number, stamped on the front engine mounting lug of the earlier engines. Later engines (mid 1950s onwards) used an identification plate riveted to the inner primary chaincase.

The specification code had nor rhyme or reason, in some cases it referred to two different engine types with the same number, for there appears to be no identifiable code to the numbering system. The only information that can be gathered from it is the very rough commencement of manufacture as indicated by the letter, but in some cases even this does not work! As much Villiers information was destroyed when NVT folded, the most comprehensive specification list available appeared in the Villiers Singles & Twins book by Roy Bacon, but even this was a small percentage of the actual list. Birmingham Vintage racer John Wood has carried out a lot of research into the Villiers numbering system, and after much investigation now possesses a database in excess of some 750 specifications, which make reference to the original build specification and the original recipient. The list is now featured as an appendix in this book.

The thousands of specification numbers that Villiers used may seem an awful lot when compared with the twenty or so designs that appeared in the post-war era, but each specification detailed a specific build standard and also identified the original customer. Specification number changes in some cases meant nothing more than a single component change, a different compression ratio, a substituted carburettor, a gearbox ratio change or a magneto specification change for instance. This was a simple exercise at the Wolverhampton factory, for a great many of the components from one engine will fit other models. Interchangeability of components is one of the good points when it comes to the post-war Villiers engine range.

Simple to work on

A definite plus point is that the Villiers engine is simple to work on, but there are a few pitfalls that the enthusiastic amateur can find himself in, namely those of shaft shimming and gearbox timing. Simple as it may be, there is no substitute for the relevant information laying readily to hand regarding the engine being worked on. The Villiers Engineering Co produced maintenance manuals and exploded parts diagrams for its entire engine range, and these publications should be used when attempting an engine rebuild, for they detail the method of build together with the part number of each individual component. Specification changes are also listed, which include the part numbers of any extra components that may be used, which in some cases is quite extensive.

Information gained from these booklets is a very important tool when it comes to ownership, and the maintenance of these units, for if the correct part number is quoted when ordering spares, it will ensure that the correct part is received. Take for example the ordering of a simple gearbox output sprocket, for during the 1950s there were three different spline types:

1) the type used on the four-speed Albion type gearbox fitted to the 11D, 29C and the 6,7 and 8E units.
2) the type used on the 1H, 2H and the twin cylinder engines.
3) the type used on the three-speed gearboxes of the 122, 147, 148 and 197cc units and the four-speed gearbox used on the remaining A, C, E and L range engines.

This range was expanded to include two different chain widths, 3/16 and 5/16 inch, and further extended to cover the number of teeth required for the job in hand. From the above information it can be seen that ordering a sprocket is not the simple task it first seems, and a part number gleaned from the replacement parts manual can save the storeman and customer alike a lot of time and trouble. The number of alternative gearbox sprockets does not stop here, for the F range engines used their own type, and the Starmaker introduced yet another type of fitting spline. Today, smaller than normal sprockets are available for the 9E type gearbox, but being of special manufacture they do not have a Villiers part number.

Tim Griffin's 1967 Greeves 24CS Ranger with 37A 246cc 4-speed engine and Villiers S25 carb

Other publications

Villiers were not alone when it came to publishing product information, for such was the popularity of these engines that other publishers printed books to cover the maintenance aspects of the engine range. Examples of these publications are;

a) The Book of the Villiers Engine, by the Pitman Motorcyclists Library, first published in 1929 with the thirteenth edition being available in 1970.

b) The Villiers Engine, by BE Browning, first published in 1949 with the sixth edition being available in 1960.

c) The Villiers Engine for Industrial and Agricultural Use, again by BE Browning and first published in 1954.

d) The History of the Villiers Engineering Company, by Jack Sizer, the fourth edition being available in 2003.

e) Villiers Singles & Twins, by Roy Bacon, first printed in 1983 but later reprinted by popular demand.

f) Two-Stroke Motorcycles, by The Motor Cycle staff writers, first published early 1930s with sixth edition being available in 1938.

g) Practical Guides to Motorcycle Maintenance, produced by the service departments of the companies that employed the Villiers engine, Francis-Barnett, James, Cotton, Greeves and Bond Minicars to name but a few. These booklets contain much interesting information, reference the specification changes to the Villiers units that they used.

When the potential of the Villiers engine was realised by the karting fraternity much in the way of tuning began to be published, with one dated example being Improving Two-Stroke Performance by JW Vierdag. Years later, in 1995, the co-author Rob Carrick, in conjunction with John Wood, published a Villiers Single Improvements Handbook which brought Villiers tuning technology up to the Twentieth Century.

Marque histories again contain much in the way of valuable information, examples being: Classic British Two-stroke Trials Bikes and Classic British Scramblers by Don Morley; Greeves by Rob Carrick and Mick Walker, and Devoid of Trouble, The history of DOT Motorcycles 1903-1978, which is available through the DOT Motorcycle Club.

The Villiers engine has come a long way since its initial concept, having been conceived as a power plant to get the masses mobile, the product now ranks as the most widely used British engine type of all time, with sales of both motorcycle and industrial engines being in excess of 3,000,000 units. Thanks must be extended to the individuals and companies who now supply parts and expertise which will ensure that the Villiers product will remain in general and sporting service for many more years, as a lasting reminder of what the British engineer can do.

Villiers Services

Villiers Services started like many other establishments, as a hobby to service the needs of its owner. Paul Gollings began by collecting Villiers spare parts for his own needs, and by 1992 realised that he had amassed enough in the way of stock to offer a parts service to other Villiers engine users. Over the years more spare parts were sourced from other establishments who were clearing out old and redundant stock, to build up a spares holding that was the envy of many other specialist stockists. In later years Villiers Services acquired the ex DMW roadster spares stock from Competition Classics, and in early 2003 purchased the whole of the remaining Greeves and Villiers stock from respected Yorkshire dealer Terry Silvester, transporting it back, 10 tons in all, to the Brierley Hill premises.

When the newly formed Greeves motorcycle company started production of its Anglian replica, it was to Villiers Services that it turned, in order to get the first machines off the line, with Paul Gollings building and supplying the first five special gearboxes from his wide range of stock. Today, helped by his son Steven, Paul supplies Villiers spares worldwide, which includes parts for pre-war and industrial units.

In recent years Villiers S ervices also offered an engine reconditioning and rebuild service, the twin cylinder motors being a speciality. The motors are fully sorted, both mechanically and cosmetically, and are bench run before dispatch, but this service has proved to be too popular, resulting in a serious backlog of orders,aA problem that is currently being addressed by the proprietor.

Villiers Services, 3 Merry Hill, Quarry Bank, Brierley Hill, West Midlands DY5 1SA
Tel 01384 265797

Competition Classics

Clive Tomkinson is a building developer with an interest in pre-65 trials, and it was this interest that started the Competition Classics company. Having gained a finishers award in the 1993 Scottish Six Day Trial on his TES Greeves, through which he raised funds for the Pendlebury Children's Trust, he realised that a specialist firm was needed to look after the interests of his fellow trials riders.

When Metal Profile wanted to sell off the front fork producing side of its business, Clive stepped in and purchased it in 1995, to ensure a steady supply to the classic trials scene. The following year, Metal Profile made a further approach, this time wanting to dispose of the Villiers side of their business, which included jigs, tools, drawings and the entire stock of spares. Clive again obliged. Later the MP fork rights were sold on to the new Greeves company, and the roadster spares shipped down to Paul Gollings at Villiers Services, leaving Competition Classics with the competition spares, engine tooling and the rights to manufacture all the major engine parts. Today Competition Classics can supply in addition to the standard spares, special low ratio gearbox internals, small engine and gearbox sprockets, high compression crankcases and alloy cylinders, as well as a range of SUPA fork seals and electronic ignition systems.

At one stage Clive Tomkinson did think about resurrecting the DMW name, building a Rotax engined (125 and 250) Trail machine, but this came to nothing. Today he concentrates on the manufacture of competition components for the Villiers range of engines, Starmaker included. He still produces castings and gearbox components for the E and A range engines, and even supplies them to Greeves for use on their brand new Anglian and Pathfinder models.

Competition Classics is now known as Norton Villiers, and comprises DMW Motorcycles Ltd and Villiers Engines Ltd.

Norton Villiers, Tynesbank Works, Walkden, Manchester M28 0SF
Tel 0161 790 5277

Nametab Engineering

Nametab Engineering is another specialist company which concentrates on the sporting side of the Villiers engine unit. Run by Simon Bateman, an accomplished 210 National kart racer who started racing in 1983, he looks after the many needs of the competition driver/rider, but also caters for the needs of the road and sporting rider who requires a greater degree of power and or reliability from his motor. When Invader Engines ceased trading, Simon took over much of their work on a part time basis, looking after his kart racing acquaintances, but as the workload increased and redundancy loomed, he became full time in 2002. Specialities of this company extend to the re-sleeving of cylinder barrels back to standard, or any specification required by the owner. Crankshaft reconditioning and gearbox modifications are another area in which racing experience gives added reliability, with the use of standard or needle roller bearing big-end conversions for both the single and twin cylinder Villiers engines. Simon is a time-served engineer and a qualified machinist, who can produce special components from a drawing or pattern, or simply modify any standard part to gain that extra degree of power or reliability.

Carrying many thousands of new or used, standard or uprated components, an engine reconditioning service is also available to the owner who wants his engine rebuilt to a particular standard or competition formula, this work being carried out by a qualified and experienced engineer who learnt his trade by hard work on the kart racing scene.

Nametab Engineering, Unit 18 Bartleet road, Washford, Redditch, B98 0DG
Tel 01527 522266

Greeves Motorcycles Ltd

This Essex company started as an offshoot of Chelmer Classics based in Chelmsford, who marketed, amongst other competition commodities, spare parts for Villiers engine units. With the acquisition and registration of the Greeves name and logo in March 1999, Richard Deal entered the field of motorcycle production, but on a very limited basis. The first machine was the Greeves 24 TJSB Anglian, a faithful replica of the 1968 model marketed by the original Greeves factory at Thundersley. This was followed by another general-purpose trail machine, the Pathfinder. Not the original Greeves bike powered by a 170cc Puch engine, but a brand new Villiers powered version based on the Anglian, it used some up to date technology to bring it up to modern day standards. The Pathfinder was kitted out with disc brakes and Paoli forks.

As with other companies who have recognised the shortcomings of the original ignition system, Greeves Motorcycles now markets modern electronic systems. Available are two individual conversions; the Tolmin trials system, with or without lighting output coils, and the PVY system.

Greeves Motorcycles Ltd can also supply many specific parts for the Thundersley manufactured Greeves machines, which are true replicas of the original items and are produced from the original drawings. One recent addition to upgrade the original Villiers engine is a four-petal reed valve cylinder with extra boost ports.

The ultimate aim of Richard Deal is to produce a modern Greeves trials machine to take on today's established stars.

Greeves Motorcycles Ltd The Briars, Mayes Lane, Sandon, Chelmsford, Essex CM2 7RP
Tel 01245 227667.

Moto-Ward Ltd

This company can be traced back to the golden years of the Villiers engine unit, when it was known as Meetens Motor Mecca, situated on the New Malden roundabout at Shannons Corner on the Kingston By-Pass. In 1965 the owner Tommy Meeten retired and the business closed, but a young salesman, Dick Ward bought the motorcycle stock and transferred it to down the road to Ewell, where he set up Meeten and Ward. Dick retired in 1993 and the company passed to his son Martin, who had worked within the business since 1980 and had a firm grounding in the art of Villiers two-strokes. Martin later relocated to a new shop on Brighton Road, Surbiton, with a name change to Moto-Ward Ltd. A further move in September 2003 saw Martin Ward operating from Rudgwick in West Sussex.

Today the company still retains its strong tradition of Villiers spares supply, both to this country and worldwide, and can supply a wide range of post-war items from its extensive in-house stock of genuine and pattern replacement parts. Parts that are in short supply are sourced from all corners of the globe. One example of this is the pressed aluminium 8E type magneto covers that in Australia. In addition to the Villiers spares, Moto-Ward can also supply consumable parts to service the pre 65 competition scene, including seats, chains, control levers, brake shoes and cables.

Moto-Ward Ltd, Victoria House, Church Street, Rudgwick, West Sussex RH12 3HJ
Tel 01403 823222

Dave Whitehouse (owner) talking to Andy Ward of Motorcycle Enthusiast magazine (white tee-shirt) about Dave's 1966 six-speed DMW Hornet, Donington Park, 1st July 1984

FB-AJS

Fluff (David) Brown started his motorcycle engineering career in 1954 with Cotton, working his way through the various departments, learning the trade as he went. When Villiers stopped supplying the Starmaker to the independent motorcycle manufacturers in the mid 1960s, he foresaw the collapse of these small businesses and decided to take employment with the new Norton-Villiers competitions department. This department was AJS, and there he helped to shape the Starmaker based AJS Stormer. When this facility fell on hard times, it was Fluff who stepped in and saved the day, by taking over the Stormer tooling and manufacturing rights in 1974.

After acquiring the Stormer rights and stock from NVT, Fluff Brown carried on the good name of AJS, operating from his premises near Andover, Hampshire, producing both 250 and 370cc machines for enduro and motocross use. The deal permitted him to use the AJS initials only if they were accompanied by the prefix FB. Later a check was made on the register of company titles, only to discover that the AJS name was no longer registered, and consequently any claims to this title were questionable. In later years the FB part was conveniently dropped. The FB-AJS team, of Fluff and his partner Roger Jeffery, being small and unburdened by outside interference from head office, carried on at a leisurely pace, producing only a handful of completed bikes per week. Being competitions orientated, Fluff Brown reformed the AJS team, with David Wells, Adrian Yallop and test rider John Foot flying the flag for the Andover concern at the January 1975 Tweseldown event.

The product FB-AJS produced was less complicated than the front-runners of the day, easier to ride and less costly to maintain. This appealed to the average clubman who wanted a manageable and affordable mount to enjoy himself on at weekends. Initially the FB Stormer was a faithful replica of the NVT product, but as stocks of NVT chassis parts dwindled, new tooling was introduced. A new frame, simpler in design and manufacture, was introduced, being built on the FB jig. The forks used on the FB Stormer were of an NVT competition design, built by Metal Profile, and available in short or long travel versions.

During production, the FB Stormer was continually updated to feature electronic ignition systems and long travel suspension systems. Most of the time at the factory was spent on the manufacture of spare parts to service the many Starmaker based machines that were still in use. In recent years, this wealth of experience and spares has been put to the good of the company, for now Fluff and his son Nick offer frame kits for the Cotton Cobra scrambler and the Telstar racer. The Cobra came first at the request of pre-75 racer Dave Heaton, who wanted to have a go at pre-65 events. Using a borrowed Cobra frame, a jig was made up and the replica frame was born. Now using Betor or Marzocchi forks, AJS hubs and glassfibre components from the original Cotton suppliers, the Cobra was willingly accepted by the pre-65 authorities. As the Cobra frame is basically the same as the Telstar, this became the next project: 'for no other reason than I fancied building one' said Fluff. The Telstar replica made its successful debut in October 1991 and was exhibited at the following year's International Stafford Classic Bike Show. The Cotton range was extended in 1992, to include a frame kit that accepted the Triumph 3TA or 5TA unit constructions engine.

The Starmaker has not been forgotten, and FB-AJS still produce Starmaker/Stormer engine spares, and a complete engine unit in any state of tune can be supplied if required. Still having the rights to the Starmaker and Stormer engines, he is able to supply spares 'off the shelf' together with components for the six-speed Starmaker road racing gearbox.

During the early years of FB-AJS, Fluf Brown announced his intention of marketing an all British trail bike. The new machine, destined to go into production during 1976, used the Talon-Mickmar 250cc engine in a frame that was derived from the Stormer. Developed from the Mickmar one-day trials unit that led the Welsh trials championship of 1975, the AJS versions specification was arrived at by West Country trials rider Nigel Hallett, who covered many miles on the prototype machine. Another venture into the road bike market was announced in 1978, when AJS launched the Apollo project, an all-British machine (except for the ignition system) based on the Stormer engine. The following year the Apollo was shelved, due in part to the six strong staff being fully occupied making the enduro and motocross machines. The Apollo and Talon never made it into full scale production and the concepts faded away, as did many other good ideas from the drawing boards of British designers. Fluff Brown now imports motorcycles under the AJS name.

AJS Motorcycles, Flint Farm, Goodworth Clatford, Andover, Hants SP11 7RP. Tel 01264 711160

The 1952 98cc 4F Villiers-engined James, customised by Englishman James Moore to break the 100cc Modified Vintage land-speed record at Bonneville Salts Flats, Utah in 2009

John Wood (149) on his 197cc Greeves Hawkstone at a VMCC meeting Pembrey, Summer 1993

The Greeves on which Brian Stonebridge won a Gold Medal, 1958 ISDT, Bavaria

Peter Thorne 197cc DMW, IOM 1997

Rob Carrick, 197cc Invader-engined Greeves, Sculthorpe, 1996

Peter Thorne, Invader-engined Greeves, Snetterton early 1990s

DMW Hornet CRMC, Snetterton, 2nd May 1988

Cotton 247cc Telstar, Snetterton, CRMC, mid-1980s

Appendix 1

Villiers Motorcycle Engine Classifications

CC	Dims	Mks/Model	Production yrs	Pre-war prefix
49	40 x 39.7	3K	1959-1960	
98	50 x 50	Midget	1931-1940	CY/CYA
		Junior	1934-1939	SH
		Junior de Luxe	1941-1948	XX/XXA
99	47 x 57	1F	1949-1953	
		2F	1949-1958	
		4F	1952-1958	
		6F	1956-1964	
		9F	1959-1965	
122	50 x 62	VI-D(1.25 hp)	1926-1927	
		8D	1936-1938	AA
		9D	1938-1940	AAA
			1941-1948	AAA-A
		10D	1948-1953	
		11D	1953-1954	
		12D	1953-1954	
		13D	1953-1954	
147	55 x 62	VI-C	1922-1923	H
		VII-C	1923-1924	L
		VIII-C	1924-1947	
		29C	1954-1956	
		30C	1954-1959	
148	53 x 67	XII-C	1931-1940	GY/GYF
		XV-C	1934-1940	CUX/CUXF
	57 x 58	31C	1956-1964	
172	57.15 x 67	Sports	1924-1932	T
			1924-1932	TL Autolube
		Super Sports	1925	Y Autolube
			1926	XY Autolube
		Super Sports TT	1926-1932	BZ Autolube
		Brooklands	1925-1934	Y Autolube

174	59 x 63.5	2L	1957-1962	
		3L	1960-1966	
196	61 x 67	1E	1928-1938	1E
		Super Sport	1929-1940	KZ/KZB
		2E	1930-1940	XZ
197	59 x 72	3E	1939-1940	VV
		5E	1946-1948	
		6E	1948-1953	
		7E	1953-1956	
		8E	1953-1958	
		9E	1955-DMW	
		10E	1957-1959	
		11E	1958-DMW	
224	63 x 72	1H	1953-1957	
246	66 x 72	2H	1957-1964	
		31A	1958-1960	
		32A	1960-1966	
		33A	1958-1959	
		34A	1960-1962	
		35A	1962- DMW	
		36A	1962-1964	
		37A	1965- DMW	
247	67 x 70	VI-A	1922-1923	J
		VII-A	1924-1925	S
		VIII-A	1925-1926	X Autolube
		IX-A	1926-1929	DZ Autolube
		X-A	1930-1932	JZ
		XVI-A	1934-1940	AXF
	68 x 68	Starmaker	1962- AJS	
249	63 x 80	XIV-A	1932-1940	
			Aircooled	BYP
			Autolube & Aircooled	BY
			Autolube & Watercooled	RY
		XVII-A	1935-1938	BYX
		XVIII-A	1939-1940	UU
	50 x 63.5	2T twin	1956-1968	
		4T twin	1963-1967	

269	70 x 70	I	1913-1916	O
		II	1916-1920	A
		III	1920-1921	B
		IV	1921	C
		V	1922	D
324	57 x 63.5	3T twin	1957-1964	
343	79 x 70	VI-B	1922-1923	K
		VII-B	1924-1925	M
		VIII-B	1925-1926	AZ Autolube
		IX-B	1926-1929	CZ Autolube
			1929-1932	CZA
		X-B	1928-1932	HZ Autolube
344	57.15 x 67	Twin	1927-1928	TW
346	70 x 90	XIV-B	1931-1940	YZ YZP
			1931-1940	YZ Autolube
		XVII-B	1931-1940	WY Watercooled
349	75.5 x 80	1st four-stroke	1911-1912	

Appendix 2

Villiers Industrial Engine Classifications

CC	Dims	Mks/Model	Start date	2/4 stroke
34	35 x 35	303H	1964	2
		303V	1964	2 Vertical shaft
50	43 x 34	505H	1966	4
70	43 x 48	2G,3G	1950	2
		4G,5G,6G,7G,8G	1954	2
75	50 x 38	7	1946	4
		7/1RG	1947	4 Reduction gear
75	53 x 34	507H	1966	4
80	46 x 48	308H	1964	2
		308V	1964	2 Vertical shaft
90	55 x 38	409H	1964	4
98	50 x 50	Midget	1931	2 Prefix CYZ/CYF
		10	1941	4
		Midget Mk2,3,4,5	1949	2
		10/1HS	1955	4 High speed
		10/1RG	1955	4 Reduction gear
		10/1	1959	4
		410H	1964	4
99	47 x 57	7F	1956	2
		7F/1	1964	2 Vertical shaft
		8F	1964	2
119	55 x 50	12	1942	4
		12/1	1959	4
		12/1HS	1959	4 High speed
		12/1RG	1959	4 Reduction gear
		412H	1964	4
		C12	1974	4
120	59 x 44	F12	1973	4

122	50 x 62	VI-D (1.25hp)	1926	2
125	58 x 47	512H	1966	4
		512V	1966	4 Vertical shaft
146	65 x 44	F15	1967	4
		A15	1986	4 CDI ignition
147	55 x 62	VI-C	1922	2 Prefix H
		VII-C	1923	2 Prefix L
		VIII-C	1924	2
		Water cooled	1926	2 Prefix LZ/LZH
		XI-C	1927	2Prefix WZCP WZFC
		Water cooled	1933	2 Prefix WAT/WAH
		24C	1951	2
		25C	1951	2
		26C	1951	2
147	63 x 47	15	1948	4
		15RG	1948	4 Reduction gear
		15/2	1964	4
		15RG	1964	4 Reduction gear
		415H	1964	4
		515H	1966	4
		515V	1966	4 Vertical shaft
169	70 x 44	F17	1967	4
206.5	63 x 66.7	20	1941	4
		20RG	1952	4 Reduction gear
		20PP	1952	4 Paraffin/Petrol
		420H	1964	4
		420HS	1964	4 High speed
247	67 x 70	VI-A	1922	2
		VII-A	1924	2
		VIII-A	1925	2
		IX-A	1926	2
		XII-A	1927	2
		Water cooled	1930	2 Prefix WXII/LZH
		Water cooled	1933	2 Prefix WBT/WBH
		19A	1927	2 Prefix WW or BYX

249	63 x 80	25A	1947	2
		26A	1955	2
256	70 x 66.7	25	1941	4
		25RG	1952	4 Reduction gear
		25PP	1952	4 Paraffin/Petrol
		425HS	1964	4 High speed
		425H	1964	4
		C28	1974	4
		C30	1969	4
269	70 x 70	II to V	1919	2
		D270	1964	4 Diesel
		D270RG	1964	4 Reduction gear
342	79 x 70	VI-B	1922	2
		VII-B	1924	2
		VIII-B	1925	2
		IXB	1926	2
346	70 x 90	27B	1954	2
353	75 x 80	28B	1955	2
395	77.8 x 82.5	40	1952	4
		40HS	1960	4 High speed
		440H	1964	4
415	80 x 82.5	D415	1964	4 Diesel
		D415RG	1964	4 Reduction gear
433	82 x 82	444H	1964	4
		C45	1973	4
		C46	1973	4

Appendix 3

Villiers Motorcycle Power Unit Users

This list reflects the Villiers worldwide sphere of influence and is the most comprehensive yet published. The dates given indicate the period the company was in production; but not necessarily the period when Villiers engines were utilised.

ABC (Birmingham)	1920-1924
Abendsonne (Germany)	1933-1934
Aberdale	1947-1959
ABJ	1950-1954
AC Cars	
AEL	1919-1924
AER	1931-1950
Ajax	1923-1924
AJS	1910-197
AJW	1926-1977
Albatross	1954
Alfa (Germany)	1925-1928
Alge (Germany)	1923-1931
Alldays	1903-1915
Allegro (Switzerland)	1925-1960
Allright (Germany)	1901-192
Ambassador	1946-196
AMS (Spain)	1954-196
Ancora (Italy)	1923-194
Anglo-Dane (Denmark)	1912-1914
Appollo (Sweden)	1951
Arab	1923-1926
ARC (Spain)	1954-1956
Arden	1912-1920
Armstrong	1913-1914
Attolini (Italy)	1920-1923
Austria (Austria)	1930-1933
Autoglider	1919-1922
Automoto (France)	1901-1962
Avis-Celer (Germany)	1925-1931
Avon	1919-1920
Avro	1905-1926
AWD (Germany)	1921-1950s
BAC (Bond Aircraft)	1951-1953
Baker	1927-1930
Banshee	1921-1924
Baron	1920-1921
Batavus (Holland)	1911-1976
Beccaria (Italy)	1924-1928
Bema (Holland)	1950s
Berwick	1929-1930
Bodo (Germany)	1924-1925
Bond	1949-1962
Bown	1922-1924
Bown	1950-1958
British Standard	1919-1923
Brough Superior	1919-1940
Buckler Cars	
Bulldog	1920
Burford	1914-1915
Butler	1963-1966
Caesar	1922-1923
Cain	1950
Calthorpe	1909-1939
Campion	1901-1926
Carfield	1919-1924
Carlton	1937-194
Carlton (Scotland)	1922
Casoli (Italy)	1928-193
CC	1921-192
Cedos	1919-192
Chater-Lea	1900-193
Cheetah	1967-196
Chell	1939
Clua (Spain)	1954-196
Cofersa (Spain)	1953-196
Comery	1919-192
Commander	1952-1953
Condor (Switzerland)	1901->>>
Consul	1916-192
Cotton	1919-200
Coventry Eagle	1901-1940
Coventry Star	1919-1921
CR (Germany)	1926-1930
Crest	1923
Cyc-Auto	1934-1956
Cyrus (Holland)	1931-1971
Dayton	1913-1920
Dayton	1954-1960
Defy-All	1921-1922
De-Luxe	1920-1924
Despatch Rider	1915-1917
Diamond	1910-1938

Dilecta (France)	1920-1939
Disa (Denmark)	1954
DKR	1956-1966
DMF (Holland)	1950-1957
DMW	1950-1976
Dorman (Hungary)	1920-1937
DOT	1903-1978
Douglas	1907-1957
Dreadnought	1915-1925
DSH (Austria)	1924-1932
Dunelt	1919-1957
Dunkley	1913-1920
EBS (Germany)	1924-1930
Edeta (Spain)	1951-1960
Edmund	1907-1924
Elig (Spain)	1956-1959
Elmdon	1915-1921
Elstar	1968-1971
Endurance	1909-1924
Escol (Belgium)	1925-1938
Europa (Germany)	1931-1933
Excelsior	1896-1964
Eysink (Holland)	1899-1970s
Fagan (Irish Rep)	1935-1937
Faggi (Italy)	1950-1953
Fama (Holland)	1938
Federation	1919-1937
Firefly	1960s
FLM	1951-1953
Fmschauf (Germany)	1928-1933
Francis-Barnett	1919-1966
Frisoni (Italy)	1952-1957
Fuji (Japan)	1946-1964
Gadabout	1948-195
Gamage	1905-1924
Garanzini (Italy)	1921-1931
Gasuden (Japan)	1946-196
Gazda (Austria)	1924-1927
Gazelle (Holland)	1903-195
Ge-Ma-Hi (Germany)	1924-195
Gerard	1913-1915
Germaan (Holland)	1935-1966
GH (Czech)	1924-192
Givaudan	1908-1914
Gladden (USA)	1946-1950s
Glendale	1920-192
Gloria	1931-1933
Goetz (Germany)	1925-1935
Gordon Cars	
Goricke (Germany)	1903- 1980
Governer-Villiers	1914
Greeves	1954-197
Grigg	1920-1925
Grindlay-Peerless	1923-193
Grose-Spur	1934-1939
Hailstone & Ravenhall	1923
Harewood	1920
Harper	1954-1955
Hascho (Germany)	1923-1926
Haschut (Germany)	1929-1931
HEC	1922-1923
Hecker (Germany)	1922-1956
Henley	1920-1929
Hercules (Germany)	1904-1939
HJ	1920-1921
HJH	1954-1956
Hobart	1901-1923
Hoffman (Germany)	1949-1954
Hoock (Germany)	1926-1928
Hoskinson	1919-1922
H&R	1922-1925
Hulsman (Holland)	1939-1955
Huracan (Spain)	1957-1959
Invicta	1913-1923
Iresa (Spain)	1956-1959
Ixion	1906-1923
James	1902-1966
Jawa (Czech)	1929->>>>
JH	1913-1915
Johnson (USA)	1946-1950s
Jones	1934-1936
Juno	1911-1923
Kapiscooter (Spain)	1950s
Kenilworth	1919-1924
Kieft Cars	1955-1957
Koehler-Escoffier (France)	1912-1957
Krammer (Austria)	1926-1929
Kumfurt	1914-1916
Lady (Belgium)	1925-1938
Lafour & Nougier (France)	1927-1936

La Mondiale (Belgium)	1924-1933
Lethbridge	1922-1923
LGC	1926-1932
Lily	1906-1914
Lion-Rapide (Belgium)	1936-1953
Lutetia (Spain)	1920s
Mammut (Germany)	1925-1933
M&M	1914
Marlow	1920-1922
Mars	1923-1926
Mars (Germany)	1903-1958
Martin (Japan)	1956-196
Massey-Arran	1920-1931
McEvoy	1926-1929
Mead	1922-1924
Meray (Hungary)	1921-1944
Mercier (France)	1950-1962
Mercury	1956-1958
Metro	1912-1919
Mezo (Austria)	1923-1926
Miller High Boy	1968-1969
Mohawk	1920-1925
Monarch	1919-1921
Monark (Sweden)	1920
Monet-Goyon (France)	1917-1959
Monfort (Spain)	1957-1959
Monopole	1911-1924
Montgomery	1905-1940
Moonbeam	1920-1921
Motobic (Spain)	1949-1965
Moto Bloc (France)	1948-1950
Moto Muller (Italy)	1950-1979
Motopiana (Italy)	1923-1931
Motor Karts	
Mountaineer	1902-1926
MT (Austria)	1925-1937
Mustang (USA)	1945-1965
Neander (Germany)	1924-1929
Necchi (Italy)	1951-1953
Nestor	1913-1914
New Comet	1905-1932
New Henley	1920-1929
New Hudson	1903-1958
New Imperial	1903-1939
New Knight	1923-1931
New Rapid (Holland)	1933-1936
New Ryder	1913-1922
New Scale	1906-1925
Newton	1921-1922
Nickson	1920-1924
Norbreck	1921-1924
Norman	1939-1962
NSH (Germany)	1923-1928
NUT	1912-1933
Oberle (Germany)	1927-1929
OEC	1901-1954
OK Supreme	1899-1939
OMC	1930
Omega	1919-1927
OMN (Italy)	1924-1925
Omnia (Germany)	1931-193
Oscar	1953-1955
Overdale	1921-1922
Panther (P&M)	1904-1968
Pallion	1905-1914
Pashley Truck	
Pengor Ltd (Canada)	1962-1964
Phillips	1954-1964
Phoenix	1955-1964
Piana (Italy)	1923-1931
Planet	1919-1920
Pierton (France)	1922-1925
Pony (Spain)	1952-1954
Pouncey	1930-1938
Poustka (Czech)	1924-1934
Powell	1921-1926
Pride & Clarke	1938-1940
Premier	1908-1915
Priory	1919-1926
Progress (Germany)	1901-1914
Progress	1956-1958
Pullin	1955
PV	1910-1925
Radco	1913-1932
Radco	1954
Radco-muter	1966
Radmill	1912-1914
Rambler	1937-1961
Ray	1922-192
Raynal	1914-195
Ready	1919-192
Ready (Belgium)	1924-1939
Rebro	1922-1928
Reddis (Spain)	1957-1960
Revere	1915-1922

Make	Years
Rex (Sweden)	1908-1957
Rex Acme	1900-1933
Reynolds	1931-1934
Rickman	1959-1970
R & K (Czech)	1924-1926
RMW (Germany)	1925-1955
ROA (Spain)	1952-1960s
Rockson	1920-1923
Roulette	1918-1919
Rovena (Spain)	(see Sanglas)
Royal Enfield	1901-1970
Royal Enfield (India)	1950s->>>
Royal Nord (Belgium)	1950-1960s
Royal Ruby	1909-1933
Rudge Whitworth	1911-1939
Rulliers (Czech)	1924-1929
Ruter (Spain)	1957-1960
RW Scout	1920-1921
Sadrian (Spain)	1956-1963
Sagitta (Czech)	1928-1930
Salira (Belgium)	1955-1960s
Saltley	1919-1924
Sanglas (Spain)	1942-1982
Sapphire	1966
Sarco	1920-1923
Scorpion	1961-1966
Scootercars	
Scott	1908-1950
Scott Cyc Auto	1934-1950
Seal	1912-1923
SGS	1926-1933
Sharratt	1920-1930
SHL (Poland)	1935-1939
Sieg (Germany)	1922-1930
Sirrah	1921-1925
Silver Prince	1919-1924
Simplex (Holland)	1902-1968
Sirocco (Czech)	1925-1928
Smart (Austria)	1925-1930
SMW (Germany)	1923-1933
Socovel (Belgium)	1947-1955
Soriano (Spain)	1934-1950s
SOS	1927-1939
Souplex (Belgium)	1947-1953
Southey	1905-1925
Spark	1921-1923
Sparkbrook	1912-1925
Sparta (Holland)	1931-1972
Sprite	1964-1974

Make	Years
Stabil (Belgium)	1931-1933
Stanley	1932
Star	1919-1921
Sudbrook	1919-1920
Sun	1911-1961
Supermoco	1921-1923
Swallow	
Tandon	1948-1959
Tempo (Norway)	1949
The Fly (Belgium)	1949-1950
Three Spires	1931-1932
Tilbrook (Australia)	1947-1953
Trafford	1919-1922
Triplette	1923-1925
Tripol (Czech)	1925-192
Triumph	1902->>>
Tyler	1913-1923
Unibus	1920-1922
Victoria	1902-1926
Vincent HRD	1928-1956
Villiers- Strand	1914
Villof (Spain)	1951-1961
Wabo (Holland)	1957
Walker Cars	
Harry Walker (Spain)	
Walter (Germany)	1903-1942
Warrior	1921-1923
Warath (Australia)	1924
Warwick	1924
Watney	1922-1923
Weaver	1922-1925
Wecoob (Germany)	1925-1930
Westovian	1914-1916
Wheeler (Canada)	1967-1970s
Whitwood	1935-1936
Willow	1920
Witall	1919-1923
Wolf	1901-1939
Wurring (Germany)	1921-1950s
X-Tra	1920-1922
Zenith	1905-1950
Zwi (Israel)	1952-1955

Appendix 4

Post-war Engine Identification List

The following list has been compiled by John Wood and is the result of his detailed investigation, with information being gathe from many sources. It is by no means complete, but is now considered to be the most comprehensive list available to Villiers motorcycle engine users. Some industrial engine codes have been added.

Note 1
The pre-war engine numbering system usually saw the letter/letters as a prefix to indicate the mark, being stamped into the crankcase mouth at the rear and just below the cylinder joint.

Note 2
The post-war Villiers engine numbering system was vast and haphazard, covering some 5000 plus Motorcycle and Industrial engine specifications. The full engine number included a number, or a number and letter, as the prefix to the actual engine number. This was the specification code, which referred to the type, standard of build and the customer to whom the engine was supplied.

Note 3
Post-war, up to the mid 1950s this number was stamped on the front mounting lug of the crankcases. Fifty years later, after much swapping around, these numbers now mean little, and must be viewed with scepticism, for interchangeability of components is a strong suit with all the Villiers designs. Today the number appearing on the crankcases of a 6E guarantees the authenticity of the crankcases only, with little or no regard to the cylinder, magneto and gearbox specification.
These earlier numbers stamped on crankcase lug never gave the engine Mk /Model, and to find this the Villiers engine number sheets must be checked. For example:

389A 12345, refers to a three-speed 10D supplied to the OEC factory for fitment to the 1953 Atlanta D55 and D55RS models.

Note 4
After the mid 1950s the number was to be found on an identification plate riveted to the inner primary chaincase, and gave not only the engine number but also the engine unit type. This identification plate again only guarantees the authenticity of the inner primary chaincase, that is if the plate is still attached. For example:
950A 12345 Type 2T, refers to the 2T twin supplied to Ambassador for their 1958 Supreme Twin roadster. But, to add to the confusion, specification 950A can also identify other twin cylinder engines which were fitted to certain Cotton, Dayton, Greeves, Panther and Sun models. In certain cases the same specification number could identify two different Mks of engine.

Note 5
Experimental engines used their own numbering system, which in the 1960s used the prefix P or PRO.

Ident	Type	Production Period	Customer	Model	Carb
278	Mk11C	Ind	John Allen	Motor Scythe	LW
301	2F	45-58	Bown	Auto Roadster	Junior
364	10D	48-53	Kieft Cars		V3/4
411	9D	38-48	Tempo		LW
431	Mk11C	Ind	Lee Howl		LW
434	JDL	38-40	Francis-Barnett	Powerbike 50	Junior
451	JDL	38-40	Sun	Autocycle	Junior
459	19A	Ind	Unknown		MW
539	9D	38-48	James	ML	LW
597	9D	38-48	Francis-Barnett	Merlin 51	LW
623	9D	38-48	Tempo		LW
624	10D	48-53	DOT	125	V3/4
641	9D	38-48	James	ML	LW
649	Mk20	Ind	Unknown	V type Engine	Type V
662	5E	46-48	Ambassador	S1, S2	MW
716	1F	48-53	Bown	Standard L/weight	VJ6
			Bown	Auto Roadster	Junior
			Sun	Motor Cycle 98	VJ6
756	Mk20	Ind	Unknown	V type Engine	Type V
761	9D	38-48	Tempo		LW
763	10D	48-53	Tempo		V3/4
			OEC	Atlanta, C1,S1	V3/4
797	4F	52-58	Bown	98	VJ6
			James	J3, J4, J10	VJ6
801	2F	48-53	New Hudson	Autocycle	VJ6
			Bown	Auto Roadster	Junior
			James	Superlux Autocycle	Junior
			Norman	Model C Autocycle	Junior
			Francis-Barnett	Powerbike 56	Junior
			Sun	Motor Cycle 98	Junior
805	10D	48-53	Swallow	Gadabout	V3/4
809	6E	48-53	Ambassador	S3	V4/5
812	10D	48-53	OEC	S2	V3/4
823	10D	48-53	Francis-Barnett	Merlin 53	V3/4
824	6E	48-53	Francis-Barnett	Falcon 54, 55	V4/5
838	10D	48-53	Francis-Barnett	Merlin 52	V3/4
843	10D	48-53	Norman	B1	V3/4
844	6E	48-53	Norman	B2	V4/5
848	10D	48-53	James	Cadet	V3/4
849	6E	48-53	James	Captain	V4/5
872	Midget	Ind	Ransomes	Lawnmower	Junior
876	Midget	Ind	Ransomes	Lawnmower	Junior
932	10D	48-53	Francis-Barnett	Merlin	V3/4
			OEC	Atlanta, D1	V3/4
933	10D	48-53	Unknown		V3/4

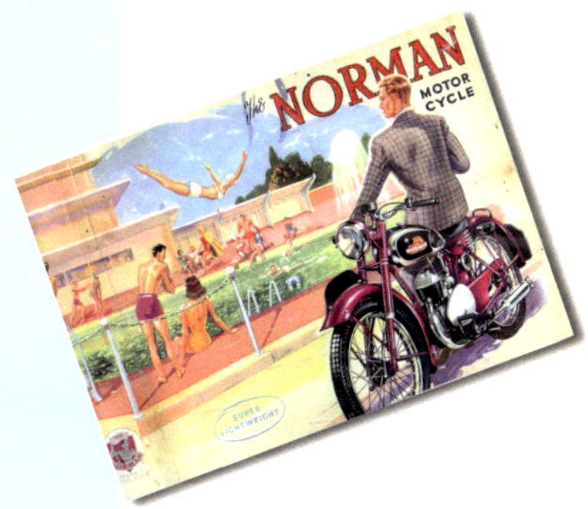

934	10D	48-53	Unknown		V3/4
935	10D	48-53	Francis-Barnett	Merlin	V3/4
936	10D	48-53	Unknown		V3/4
937	10D	48-53	Unknown		V3/4
938	10D	48-53	Norman	B1 Standard, deluxe	V3/4
			Tempo		V3/4
939	10D	48-53	Unknown		V3/4
940	10D	48-53	Unknown		V3/4
941	10D	48-53	DMW	Standard	V3/4
			Sun	122 Deluxe	V3/4
942	10D	48-53	Unknown		V3/4
943	10D	48-53	Unknown		V3/4
944	6E	48-53	Ambassador	S3	V4/5
945	10D	48-53	DMW	125DL	V3/4
			OEC	Atlanta C2, SD2	V3/4
946	6E	48-53	Francis-Barnett	Falcon	V4/5
947	6E	48-53	Norman	B2	V4/5
948	6E	48-53	James		V4/5
949	6E	48-53	Ambassador	Courier, Embassy, S5	V4/5
950	6E	48-53	Unknown		V4/5
951	6E	48-53	Francis-Barnett	Falcon	V4/5
954	6E	48-53	DOT		V4/5
955	6E	48-53	Unknown		V4/5
956	6E	48-53	Unknown		V4/5
957	6E	48-53	Unknown		V4/5
960	6E	48-53	Unknown		V4/5
983	1F	48-53	Norman	Model D L/W deluxe	VJ6
036A	10D	48-53	DMW	125C	V3/4
066A	10D	48-53	Tempo		V3/4
083A	31C	56-64	DMW	150P Mk9	S19
129A	31C	56-64	Bond	P1 Scooter	S19
			DKR	Pegasus	S19
133A	Midget	Ind	Unknown	Lawnmower	Junior
134A	Mk20	Ind	Unknown		Type V
139A	6E	48-53	Ambassador	Supreme	V4/5
145A	Mk40	Ind	Auto Culto	Garden Tractor	B10
158A	6E	48-53	Francis-Barnett	Falcon 60	V4/5
	7E	53-56	Francis-Barnett	Falcon 60	S24/25
161A	1F	49-53	Bown	Standard L/weight	VJ6
166A	11D	53-54	Francis-Barnett	Merlin 59 Trials	V3/4
171A	2F	48-58	New Hudson	Autocycle	Junior
189A	2F	48-58	Francis-Barnett	Powerbike 56	Junior
206A	10D	48-53	Francis-Barnett	Merlin 52, 53	V3/4
207A	6E	48-53	Francis-Barnett	Falcon 54, 55	V4/5
208A	10D	48-53	Francis-Barnett	Merlin 57	V3/4
209A	6E	48-53	DMW	200	V4/5
			Francis-Barnett	Falcon 58	V4/5

213A	Mk25C	Ind	Unknown		V3/4
216A	10D	48-53	OEC	Atlanta S1,SS1,D1,SD1,C1	V3/4
			Tempo		V3/4
218A	10D	48-53	DMW	125 Comp,Standard,deluxe	V3/4
221A	13D	53-54	Norman	B1, B1S, E	S19
227A	6E	48-53	Ambassador	Popular	V4/5
228A	6E	48-53	OEC	Atlanta S2,SS2,D2,SD2,ST2,ST3	V4/5
			Sun	Challenger	V4/5
229A	6E	48-53	Norman	B2, B2S	V4/5
231A	6E	48-53	Ambassador	Embassy	V4/5
236A	6E	48-53	DOT		V4/5
237A	6E	48-53	Unknown		V4/5
238A	6E	48-53	Sparta	200	S24/25
247A	6E	48-53	Greeves	Prototype	S24/25
262A	10D	48-53	Sun	122 Deluxe	V3/4
299A	4F	52-58	Excelsior	F4S Consort	VJ6
300A	6F	56-64	Excelsior	F6S Consort	S12
302A	7E	53-56	DMW	Competition	S24/25
			Norman	B2C	S24/25
319A	6E	48-53	James	J9 Commando	V4/5
333A	9E	55-66	Excelsior		S25
339A	6E	48-53	Norman	B2C	V4/5
			Sun	Challenger Deluxe	V4/5
348A	12D	53-54	Tempo		S19
350A	4F	52-58	Excelsior	F4S Consort	VJ6
361A	8E	53-58	Greeves	20R	S24/25
			OEC	Atlanta ST2	V4/5
363A	6E	48-53	Ambassador	Popular, Embassy	V4/5
	8E	53-58	USA Market		S24
364A	8E	53-58	Norman	B2 Standard, deluxe	S24
365A	6E	48-53	Sun	Challenger	V4/5
			James	Captain	V4/5
366A	8E	53-58	USA Market		S24
367A	8E	53-58	Greeves	20R3	LW
368A	8E	53-58	DOT		S24
369A	8E	53-58	Excelsior	R Type	S24
374A	7E	53-56	Francis-Barnett	Falcon 62,64,72,76	S24/25
375A	7E	53-56	Francis-Barnett	Falcon 62,64,77	S24/25
376A	8E	53-58	Francis-Barnett	Falcon	S24
379A	8E	53-58	Pashley WR	3-wheel truck	S24
380A	7E	53-56	James	K7C Cotswold	S24/25
			OEC	Atlanta ST3	S24/25
381A	7E	53-56	Norman	B2C Competition	S24/25
	8E	53-58	DMW		S24/25
			James	K7 Captain	S24/25
382A	8E	53-58	DMW		S24

383A	8E	53-58	Bond		S24
385A	8E	53-58	Tandon		S24
387A	7E	53-56	Francis-Barnett	Falcon 62, 64	S24/25
	8E	53-58	Francis-Barnett	Falcon 54, 55, 58, 67	S24
389A	10D	48-53	OEC	Atlanta D55, D55RS	V3/4
391A	12D	53-54	Aberdale Cycle Co		S19
392A	10D	48-53	DMW	Coronation	V3/4
	12D	53-54	DMW	Coronation	S19
			Sun	De Luxe	S19
394A	12D	53-54	Norman		S19
396A	12D	53-54	James	Cadet	S19
399A	12D	53-54	Tandon	Imp	S19
402A	12/4D	53-54	Francis-Barnett	Merlin 61	S19
	11D	53-54	Francis-Barnett	Merlin 61	S24
403A	12/4D	53-54	Francis-Barnett	Merlin 63	S19
	11D	53-54	Francis-Barnett	Merlin 63	S24
404A	12D	53-54	Francis-Barnett	Merlin	S19
405A	10D	48-53	Francis-Barnett	Merlin 57	V3/4
	12D	53-54	Francis-Barnett	Merlin 57	S19
411A	1H	53-57	Dayton	Albatross	S25
			Sun	Cyclone Mk II	S25
			Tandon	Monarch	S25
415A	11D	53-54	Francis-Barnett	Merlin Competition	S24
416A	7E	53-56	James		S24/25
417A	11D	53-54	James		S24
418A	7E	53-56	James		S24/25
419A	6E	48-53	Sun	Challenger	V4/5
420A	10D	48-53	Francis-Barnett	Merlin 61	V3/4
440A	Mk40	Ind	Landmaster	Rotary Hoe	Type V
470A	6F	56-64	Excelsior	Scutabyk SB1	S12
489A	6E	48-53	Sun	Challenger deluxe	V4/5
491A	8E	53-58	Greeves	20T, 20S, 20D	S24/25
			Tandon		S24/25
501A	8E	53-58	USA Market		S24
517A	8E	53-58	Sun		S24
521A	4F	52-58	James		V6/0
534A	4F	52-58	Norman	Model D deluxe	V6/0
548A	8E	53-58	Pashley WR	3-wheel truck	S24/25
549A	7E	53-56	Greeves		S24/25
569A	13D	53-54	James	J5, J6 Cadet	S19
573A	8E	53-58	Vernon Industries	Gordon Cars	S24
574A	11D	53-54	James		S24
575A	7E	53-56	James		S24/25
586A	30C	54-59	Sun	Challenger MkIA	S19
588A	8E	53-58	Tandon		S24
617A	8E	53-58	Francis-Barnett	Falcon	S24

618A	13D	53-54	Francis-Barnett	Kestrel 66	S19
			James	J5 Cadet	S19
			Norman	B1,B1S	S19
620A	7E	53-56	Norman		S24/25
630A	8E	53-58	DOT		S24
631A	8E	53-58	DOT		S24
637A	8E	53-58	General Steel		S24
639A	7E	53-56	Edgar Bros		S24
643A	8E	53-58	Bond		S24
646A	7E	53-56	DOT	TDH	S24/25
	8E	53-58	DOT		S24
652A	4F	52-58	Excelsior	F4, F4S Consort	V6/0
654A	8E	53-58	Ambassador	Supreme	S24/25
			USA Market		S24
659A	7E	53-56	DMW	MX Mk5	S24/25
660A	7E	53-56	DMW	Competition	S24/25
663A	8E	53-58	Francis-Barnett	Falcon	S24/25
666A	8E	53-58	DOT	TDHX4	S24
668A	7E	53-56	Francis-Barnett	Falcon 65 Scrambler	S24/25
	8E	53-58	Francis-Barnett	Falcon 65 Overseas	S24/25
671A	8E	53-58	Tandon		S24
673A	8E	53-58	Pashley WR	3-wheel truck	V4/5
676A	8E	53-58	DMW		S24
677A	8E	53-58	DMW		S24/25
691A	8E	53-58	Sun		S24
693A	8E	53-58	Pashley WR	3-wheel truck	S24/25
710A	8E	53-58	Norman	B2, B2S	S24
713A	8E	53-58	Pashley WR	3-wheel truck	V4/5
716A	1F	48-53	Sun	98 Deluxe	VJ6
	4F	52-58	Sun	98 Deluxe	VJ6
722A	8E	53-58	J Smith		V4/5
739A	4F	52-58	Sun	98 Deluxe, Hornet	VJ6
743A	Mk28B	Ind	AC Cars	Petite Mk II	S24/25/B
750A	7E	53-56	Francis-Barnett	Falcon	S24/25
775A	7E	53-56	DMW	Competition	S24/25
776A	7E	53-56	DMW	Competition	S24/25
777A	7E	53-56	James		S24/25
788A	7E	53-56	James		S24/25
797A	4F	52-58	James		VJ6
799A	1H	53-57	Greeves		S25
			James	K12 Colonel	S25
801A	8E	53-58	Ambassador	Supreme, Popular	S24/25
808A	8E	53-58	Projects & Developments - Oscar Scooter		S24
809A	12D	53-54	Projects & Developments - Oscar Scooter		S19
811A	11D	53-54	DMW		S24
835A	12D	53-54	Excelsior		S19

842A	1H	53-57	Francis-Barnett	Cruiser 68,71,75	S25
844A	30C	54-59	Rex		S19
846A	Mk12	Ind	Unknown		V10
865A	30C	54-59	James	Cadet	S19
894A	8E	53-58	Stanley	Harper Scootamobile	S24
896A	12D	53-54	Stanley	Harper Scootamobile	S19
897A	7E	53-56	Norman		S24/25
899A	8E	53-58	Greeves	20R	S24
900A	8E	53-58	Greeves	20S, 20D, 20R	S24
916A	12D	53-54	Stanley	Harper Scootamobile	S19
917A	8E	53-58	Stanley	Harper Scootamobile	S24
935A	1H	53-57	Ambassador	Supreme	S25
936A	8E	53-58	Sheepbridge Engineering		S24
937A	13D	53-54	Norman		S19
946A	8E	53-58	WE Barnett		S24/25
947A	8E	53-58	Motor Meyer		S24
949A	8E	53-58	Sheepbridge Engineering		S24
950A	2T	56-68	Ambassador	Supreme twin	S22
			Cotton		S22
			Dayton	Albatross twin	S22
			Greeves	25SA, DB, DC	S22
			Panther	35, 35 Sports	S22
			Sun	Overlander	S22
953A	8E	53-58	Vernon Industries	Gordon Cars	S24
958A	30C	54-59	Francis-Barnett	Kestrel 69	S19
			James	Cadet	S19
959A	30C	54-59	Francis-Barnett		S19
960A	11D	53-54	Norman		S24
965A	8E	53-58	Cotton		S24
970A	30C	54-59	Norman		S19
971A	7E	53-56	Francis-Barnett	Falcon	S24/25
975A	7E	53-56	Francis-Barnett	Falcon	S24/25
981A	8E	53-58	Smiths Service Station		S24
993A	1H	55-57	DMW	Cortina	S25
009B	8E	53-58	Pashley WR	3-wheel truck	V4/5
011B	7E	53-56	DOT		S24/25
013B	9E	55-67	Ambassador	Envoy	S25/1
014B	31C	56-64	Ambassador	Popular	S19
015B	31C	56-64	Ambassador	Popular	S19
018B	9E	55-67	Ambassador	Envoy	S25/1
019B	9E	55-67	Ambassador	Envoy	S25/1
021B	2T	56-68	Ambassador	Supreme twin	S22
027B	11D	53-54	Excelsior		S24
030B	30C	54-59	Ambassador	Popular	S19
			Tempo		S19

043B	7E	53-56	Norman	B2C Competition	S24/25
044B	8E	53-58	DMW	200P Mk1	S25
045B	8E	53-58	Ambassador	Envoy, Embassy	S24/25
			USA Market		S25
046B	8E	53-58	Sun	Challenger, Mk IV, V	S25
			Tandon	Imp Supreme	S24/25
047B	8E	53-58	Greeves	20R3	S25
049B	6E	48-53	Excelsior		V4/5
	8E	53-58	Excelsior	R4, R5, R6	S25
052B	8E	53-58	DOT		S25
053B	8E	53-58	DMW	200P, 200 Deluxe	S25
			James	K7 Captain	S25
054B	8E	53-58	Greeves		S25
055B	8E	53-58	Sun	Trials	S25
056B	8E	53-58	Tandon	Imp Supreme	S24/25
057B	7E	53-56	DMW	Competition	S24/25
058B	7E	53-56	DMW	Competition	S24/25
060B	8E	53-58	Vernon Industries	Gordon Cars	S25
061B	8E	53-58	Unknown		S24/25
062B	8E	53-58	Bond		S25
063B	8E	53-58	Tandon	Imp Supreme	S25
064B	8E	53-58	Ambassador	Embassy	S24/25
			USA Market		S25
065B	8E	53-58	James	K7 Captain	S24/25
			Norman		S25
066B	8E	53-58	Norman	B2S, deluxe	S25
067B	8E	53-58	DOT		S25
068B	8E	53-58	DOT		S25
069B	8E	53-58	DOT		S25
070B	8E	53-58	Francis-Barnett	Falcon 70, 74	S24/25
071B	8E	53-58	Francis-Barnett	Falcon	S25
072B	7E	53-56	James		S24/25
073B	8E	53-58	James	K7 Captain	S25
074B	7E	53-56	James		S25
	8E	53-58	Greeves	20R3	S24/25
075B	8E	53-58	James	K7 Captain	S25
087B	8E	53-58	Greeves		S24
088B	8E	53-58	Mercury Industries		S24
089B	8E	53-58	Mercury Industries		S24
095B	Mk20	Ind	Unknown		V10
102B	Mk12	Ind	Unknown		V10
127B	8E	53-56	Norman	B2S Standard, deluxe	S24/25
	30C	54-59	Norman	B1S Standard,deluxe	S19
133B	29C	54-56	DMW	150P Leda 55	S25
138B	2F	48-58	Norman		Junior
145B	8E	53-58	James	K7 Captain	S24/25
			Stanley	Harper Scootamobile	S25

146B	8E	53-58	Cotton	Vulcan	S25
			James	K7 Captain	S24/25
147B	1H	53-57	Dayton	Albatross	S25
155B	7E	53-56	Greeves	20R4	S24/25
164B	8E	53-58	Greeves	20D	S25
168B	8E	53-58	Phoenix	S200	S25
169B	8E	53-58	Stanley	Harper Scootamobile	S25
170B	8E	53-58	Stanley	Harper Scootamobile	S25
173B	6F	56-64	Excelsior	Consort	S12
176B	2F	48-58	New Hudson	Autocycle (BSA built)	Junior
	4F	52-58	James	Comet	VJ6
177B	2F	48-58	Francis-Barnett	Powerbike 56	Junior
178B	2F	48-58	Norman	Model C Autocycle	Junior
184B	Mk26C	Ind	John Allen	Motor Scythe	Junior
211B	30C	54-59	Tempo		S19
214B	8E	53-58	WL Manuel		S24/25
223B	30C	54-59	Powerdrive		S19
224B	8E	53-58	Soden & Sons		S25
228B	9E	55-67	Cotton	Vulcan	S25/1
230B	7E	53-56	Bond		S24/25
243B	8E	53-58	Southampton Ice Rink		S25
249B	7E	53-56	Sun		S24/25
251B	8E	53-58	Soden & Sons		S25
257B	8E	53-58	Powerdrive		S24/25
268B	8E	53-58	DOT		S24/25
269B	8E	53-58	DOT		S24/25
270B	9E	55-67	Excelsior	A9 Autocrat	S25/1
			Greeves	20D	S25/1
281B	10E	57-59	Francis-Barnett	Falcon 81	S25/3
286B	8E	53-59	Harry Walker		S24/25
287B	29C	54-56	Harry Walker		S25
295B	30C	54-59	Francis-Barnett	Plover 73, 78	S25
			James	L15 Cadet	S19
296B	8E	53-58	James	K7 Captain	S24/25
297B	7E	53-56	James		S25
298B	7E	53-56	James	K7T Commando	S24/25
	8E	53-58	Francis-Barnett	Falcon	S24/25
310B	4F	52-58	James	L1 Comet	VJ6
311B	8E	53-58	James	K7 Captain	S24/25
313B	9E	55-67	Ambassador	Envoy	S25/1
			Cotton	Vulcan	S25/1
			Excelsior	A9 Autocrat	S25/1
			Greeves	20D	S25/1
			Panther	10/4	S25/1
317B	8E	53-58	Greeves	20SA	S24/25
318B	9E	55-67	Bond		S25/1

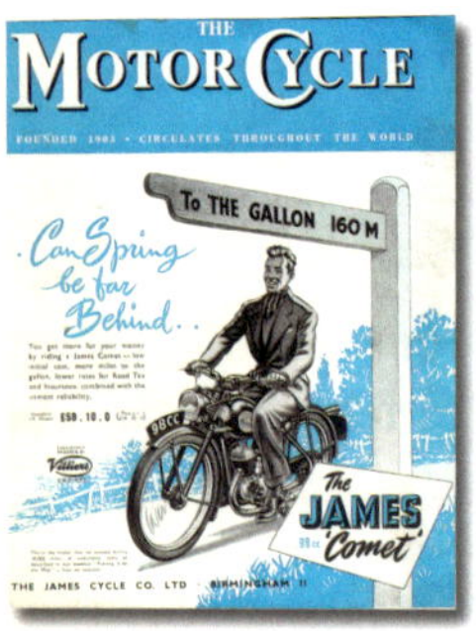

323B	8E	53-58	Greeves		S24/25
324B	9E	55-67	Greeves	20D	S25/1
326B	9E	55-67	DMW	200P Mk9	S24/25
			DOT		S25/1
329B	9E	55-67	Bond		S25/1
331B	9E	55-67	Greeves	20T	S25/1
332B	9E	55-67	Greeves	20TA	S25/1
340B	31A	58-50	Greeves	24TAS	S25/5
342B	9E	55-67	Unknown		
355B	8E	53-58	James	K7 Captain	S25
356B	30C	54-59	Excelsior	U9, U9R	S19
357B	8E	53-58	Stanley		S25
359B	6F	56-64	Excelsior		VJ6
365B	4F	52-58	DMW	Bambi Scooter	VJ6
369B	9E	55-67	Norman	B2CS Competition	S25/2
370B	9E	55-67	Norman		S25/1
372B	9E	55-67	Bond		S25/1
373B	9E	55-67	Bond		S25/1
375B	9E	55-67	Norman	B2S deluxe Sports	S25/1
377B	9E	55-67	Sun	Wasp	S25/2
384B	9E	55-67	Excelsior		S25/1
390B	1H	53-57	James	K12 Colonel	S25
391B	8E	53-58	DMW		S25
393B	6F	56-64	James	L1 Comet	VJ6
410B	6F	56-64	Sun	Geni Scooter Mk I,II	S12
411B	9E	55-67	DOT		S25/2
412B	7E	53-56	Francis-Barnett	Falcon 77	S25
413B	7E	53-56	Francis-Barnett	Falcon 76	S24/25
414B	9E	55-67	DMW	MX Mk6, Mk7	S25/2
415B	9E	55-67	DMW	Trials Mk 7	S25/2
433B	30C	54-59	DKR	Dove	S19
434B	9E	55-67	H Meadows Vehicles		S25/3
437B	9E	55-67	Sun	Wasp, Wasp Comp	S25/1
455B	9E	55-67	DOT		S25/1
459B	9E	55-67	RP Frogatt		S25/1
475B	9E	55-67	DMW		S25/1
478B	9E	55-67	Cotton		S25/1
480B	9E	55-67	Greeves		S25/1
485B	Atco	Ind	Built under licence for Atco Lawnmowers		
490B	9E	55-67	DMW		S25/1
493B	9E	55-67	Sun		S25/1
497B	9E	55-67	Greeves		S25/2
498B	9E	55-67	DOT		S25/1
500B	4F	52-58	Mercury Industries		VJ6
501B	9E	55-67	Greeves		S25/1
504B	33A	58-59	Cotton	Scrambler	A389

506B	30C	54-59	HB Engineering Co		S19
507B	8E	53-58	Vernon Industries	Gordon Cars	S24/25
508B	8E	53-58	Greeves		LW
509B	8E	53-58	Stanley		S25
511B	31C	56-64	DOT		S19
512B	2L	57-62	Ambassador	Statesman, Popular	S22
513B	31C	56-64	DOT		S19
514B	8E	53-58	Smiths Service Station		S24/25
515B	2L	57-62	DOT		S22
517B	2L	57-62	DOT		S22
518B	9E	55-67	Tourette	Supreme	S25/1
519B	8E	53-58	Phoenix	S200	S24/25
525B	31C	56-64	Ambassador	Popular	S19
532B	9E	55-67	Greeves		S25/1
537B	9E	55-67	Bond		S25/1
538B	31C	56-64	Norman	B1S deluxe	S19
539B	9E	55-67	Stanley	Harper Scootamobile	S25/1
540B	8E	53-58	DMW		S24/25
541B	9E	55-67	Sun		S25/1
543B	2H	57-64	Ambassador	Supreme	S25/5
544B	9E	55-67	Cotton	Vulcan	S25/1
			Panther	10/3A	S25/1
545B	6F	56-64	Excelsior		S12
550B	9E	55-67	Ambassador		S25/1
563B	2T	56-68	DMW	Dolomite II	S22
564B	31C	56-64	DMW	150P	S19
567B	6F	56-64	Mercury Industries		S12
568B	6F	56-64	DMW		S12
571B	9E	55-67	DOT		S24/25
573B	Mk25HS	Ind	Unknown		Z 24T
580B	8E	53-58	DOT	SH	S24/25
	9E	55-67	Ambassador	3 Star, Envoy	S25/1
583B	9E	55-67	Stanley	Harper Scootamobile	S25/1
585B	30C	54-59	Wooddisse		S19
598B	31C	56-64	Rowe SE		S19
599B	2L	57-62	Rowe SE		S22
600B	4F	52-58	DMW	Bambi Scooter	VJ6
601B	4F	52-58	Excelsior		VJ6
602B	4F	52-58	James	L1 Comet 100	VJ6
603B	4F	52-58	Mercury Industries	Pippin Scooter	VJ6
604B	4F	52-58	Sun	Hornet	VJ6
605B	6F	56-64	Excelsior	F4,F6S,SB1,CA8,CA9,C10,F10	S12
606B	6F	56-64	Excelsior	CA9,CB1,F4F,F6S,F10	S12
607B	6F	56-64	James	L1 Comet 100	S12
609B	6F	56-64	DMW		S12
612B	9E	55-67	DOT		S25/1

617B	9E	55-67	AC Cars		S25/1
618B	9E	55-67	DOT		S25/1
620B	2T	56-68	DMW		S22
625B	9E	55-67	Greeves	20TC,TD,TE,DB,SCS	S25/1
626B	9E	55-67	Greeves	20SAS,SCS,DC,DB,SA	S25/1
628B	2F	45-58	BSA		Junior
632B	9E	55-67	Tourette	Supreme	S25/1
633B	9E	55-67	Tourette	Supreme	S25/1
			DKR	Defiant Scooter	S25/1
634B	2L	57-62	DMW	175P Mk9	S22
638B	2T	56-68	Dayton	Albatross twin	S22
642B	30C	54-59	Tourette	Supreme	S19
643B	8E	53-58	Tourette	Supreme	S24/25
648B	2T	56-68	H Meadows Vehicles		S22
649B	2T	56-68	DMW		S22
652B	10E	55-59	James	K7, K7T	S25/1
653B	2T	56-68	DOT	SCH Works Rep	S22
659B	9E	55-67	Phoenix	S200	S25/1
662B	10E	57-59	Francis-Barnett	Falcon 81	S25/1
664B	9E	55-67	Vernon Industries	Gordon Cars	S25/1
672B	2H	57-64	Dayton	Albatross	S25/5
675B	6F	56-64	Mercury Industries		S12
676B	9E	55-67	Harry Walker		S25/1
694B	9E	55-67	Panther	Princess	S25/1
696B	9E	55-67	Harry Walker		S25/1
			Panther	Princess	S25/1
697B	2T	56-68	Harry Walker		S22
699B	2T	56-68	Cotton	Continental	S22
702B	30C	54-59	HB Engineering		S19
			Phoenix	S150 Scooter	S19
703B	9E	55-67	Bond	P2 Scooter	S25/1
705B	9E	55-67	Bond	P4 Scooter	S25/1
707B	34A	60-62	Norman	B4C Scrambler	A389
714B	9E	55-67	Scootacar		S25/1
716B	9E	55-67	Bond		S25/1
722B	9E	55-67	Bond		S25/1
723B	9E	55-67	Greeves	20TCS	S25
726B	9E	55-67	Sun	Wasp	S25/1
729B	2T	56-68	H Meadows Vehicles		S22
731B	4F	52-58	Excelsior		VJ6
	6F	56-64	Norman		S12
732B	9E	55-67	DOT		S25/1
			Norman	B2S Roadster,deluxe	S25/1
733B	9E	55-67	Norman	B2SC Competition	S25/1
734B	2T	56-68	James	Superswift	S22
			Norman	B3&B4 Roadster,Sports	S22

737B	9E	55-67	DKR	Defiant	S25/1
739B	9E	55-67	Excelsior		S25/1
741B	31C	56-64	Panther		S19
742B	10E	57-59	James	K7, K7T	S25/1
750B	2T	56-68	HB Engineering		S22
761B	6F	56-64	Sun		S19
762B	9E	55-67	Ministry of Health		S25/1
763B	9E	55-67	Ministry of Health		S25/1
764B	9E	55-67	Ministry of Health		S25/1
765B	9E	55-67	Ministry of Health		S25/1
766B	9E	55-67	Ministry of Health		S25/1
770B	9E	55-67	Ambassador	3 Star Envoy	S25/1
771B	9E	55-67	Scootacars		S25/1
772B	31C	56-64	DKR	Pegasus Scooter	S19
781B	4F	52-58	James	Comet	VJ6
	6F	56-64	Mercury Industries		S12
782B	2T	56-68	DMW		S22
786B	31C	56-64	HB Engineering		S19
788B	9E	55-67	HB Engineering		S25/1
790B	6F	56-64	Excelsior		S12
793B	9E	55-67	F Tippen		S25/1
804B	31C	56-64	DKR	Dove II Scooter	S19
806B	2L	57-62	Ambassador		S22
807B	2L	57-62	Ambassador		S22
808B	2T	56-682	Ambassador	Super S	S22
810B	2T	56-68	Panther	35	S22
			DOT	Scrambler	S22
812B	9E	55-67	H Meadows Vehicles		S25/1
814B	30C	54-59	HB Engineering		S19
823B	9E	55-67	Greeves		S25/1
826B	9E	55-67	Panther		S25/1
832B	9E	55-67	DKR	Defiant	S25/1
835B	2T	56-68	Ambassador		S22
847B	3T	57-64	Cotton	Messenger	S25
			Panther	45 Sports, 50 Grand Sports	S25
848B	2T	56-68	DKR	Manx Scooter	S22
854B	31C	56-64	Bond	Scooter	S19
859B	31A	58-60	Bond	Minicar Mark F	S25/5
860B	31A	58-60	Bond	Minicar Mark F	S25/5
862B	2T	56-68	Greeves		S22
863B	9E	55-67	Cotton	Trials	S25/1
	32A	60-65	Greeves	24TCS, TDS, TD, TE	S25
864B	32A	60-65	Greeves	24DB, DC	S25
879B	32A	60-65	DOT	Trials	S25
880B	32A	60-65	DOT	Trials	S25
883B	2L	57-62	Panther	Princess	S22

884B	2L	57-62	Panther	Princess	S22
885B	2L	57-62	Dayton	Albatross	S22
887B	2L	57-62	Sun	Wasp Scooter	S22
888B	31A	58-60	Greeves	24SAS	S25/1
893B	3T	57-64	Greeves	32DB	S25
			Panther	45 Sports, 50 Grand Sports	S25
897B	9E	55-67	Stanley	Harper Scootamobile	S25/1
904B	3K	59-60	Phillips	P45 Gadabout	SM10
906B	3K	59-60	Norman	Nippy Mk 4	SM10
907B	3K	59-60	Norman	Lido, Nippy Mk 4 S	M10
909B	3K	59-60	Norman	Nippy Mk 4	SM10
916B	3L	60-66	Ambassador	Scooter	S25
952B	10E	57-59	Francis-Barnett	Falcon 81	S25/1

176C	Mk10	Ind	Unknown		B10
498C	Mk12/1	Ind	Unknown		B10
546C	Mk12/2	Ind	Unknown		Type V

004D	2T	56-68	Cotton	Herald, Gloucester	S22
			Panther	35, 35 Sports	S22
005D	9E	55-67	Phoenix	S200	S25/1
007D	32A	60-65	Greeves		S25
008D	32A	60-65	Greeves		S25
009D	32A	60-65	DOT	Trials	S25
010D	32A	60-65	DOT	Trials	S25
014D	9E	55-67	Greeves		S25/1
015D	9E	55-67	F Tippen		S25/1
016D	33A	58-59	Cotton	Scrambler	A389
017D	30C	54-59	Ministry of Health		S19
023D	2T	56-68	DMW	Deemster Sport	S22
027D	32A	60-65	DMW	Trials	S25
028D	33A	58-59	DMW	Mk 12 MX	A389
030D	9E	55-67	AC Cars		S25/1
035D	3T	57-64	DMW	Dolomite	S22/3
039D	2T	56-68	Cotton	Herald, Gloucester	S22
040D	3T	57-64	Cotton	Vulcan	S22/2
049D	9E	55-67	H Meadows Vehicles		S25/3
051D	31C	56-64	Excelsior	U10, U14	S19
053D	3T	57-64	Panther	50 Grand Sports	S22/2
054D	3T	57-64	Cotton	Messenger	S22/2
059D	9E	55-67	Excelsior	R10, R11, ER11	S25/1
066D	2L	57-62	Panther	Princess	S22
067D	2L	57-62	Panther	Princess	S22
070D	34A	60-62	Cotton	Scrambler	A389
			Greeves	24SCS, MCS, MDS	A389
076D	9E	55-67	Aero Controls		S25/1

077D	6F	56-64	Aero Controls		S12
079D	31C	56-64	Excelsior		S19
084D	9E	55-67	DMW		S25/1
085D	2T	56-68	DMW		S22
086D	31C	56-64	RA Harding		S19
089D	3T	57-64	DMW	Dolomite 11A	S22/3
090D	31C	56-64	RA Harding		S19
103D	2L	57-62	Phoenix	S175	S22
104D	2L	57-62	Phoenix	S175	S22
105D	9E	55-67	Phoenix	S200	S25/1
106D	31C	56-64	Phoenix	S150	S19
108D	32A	60-65	DOT	Trials	S25/5
110D	9E	55-67	Keele Engineering	Sports Kart	S25/1
114D	32A	60-65	DOT	Trials	S25/5
115D	32A	60-65	DOT	Trials	S25/5
117D	9E	55-67	Phoenix	S200	S25/1
118D	3T	57-64	DMW	Dolomite	S22/3
123D	9E	55-67	H Williams		S25/1
125D	2L	57-62	DKR	Pegasus II	S22
128D	9E	55-67	Buckler Cars		S25/1
130D	9E	55-67	Stanley	Harper Scootamobile	S25/3
131D	9E	55-67	Greeves		S25/1
135D	2L	57-62	Phoenix	S175	S22
136D	9E	55-67	WF Bartlett		S25/1
138D	31C	56-64	Phoenix	S150	S19
139D	6F	56-64	Excelsior		S12
143D	34A	60-62	DOT	Demon	A389
149D	32A	60-65	Cotton	Trials	S25
150D	9E	55-67	Cotton	Trials	S25/1
151D	9E	55-67	DOT		S25/1
152D	9E	55-67	Motor Karts	Standard Kart	S25/1
160D	9E	55-67	Progress Chassis Co		S25/1
161D	32A	60-65	DMW	Mk 15 Trials	S25
162D	3T	57-64	Phoenix	S250	S25
169D	31A	58-60	Bond	Minicar Mark F	S25/1
171D	31A	58-60	Bond	Minicar Mark F	S25/1
179D	31A	58-60	Bond	Minicar Mark F	S25/8
180D	31A	58-60	Bond	Minicar Mark F	S25/5
181D	2L	57-62	Motor Karts		S222
182D	32A	60-65	Motor Karts		S25/6
184D	2L	57-62	Adler		S22
187D	31C	56-64	DKR	Pegasus	S19
188D	31C	56-64	DKR	Pegasus	S19
189D	2L	57-62	DKR	Capella	S22
190D	2L	57-62	DKR	Capella	S22
191D	9E	55-67	Scootacars		S25/10

192D	9E	55-67	Scootacars		S25/10
207D	3L	60-66	Ambassador	Scooter	S22/3
208D	2T	56-68	Ambassador	Electra 75	S25/3
			Ambassador		S22
			Panther	35	S22
211D	9E	55-67	Phoenix	S200	S25/3
214D	2T	56-68	Ambassador		S22
221D	2T	56-68	Greeves	25DC	S25/2
222D	3T	57-64	Greeves	32DC, DCX, DD	S25
226D	32A	60-65	Norman	B4C Trials	S25/6
227D	34A	60-62	Norman	Scrambler	A389
228D	2T	56-68	Dayton	Albatross	S22
			Norman	B4 Roadster	S22/2
229D	2T	56-68	Cotton	Continental Sports	S22
			Norman	B4 Sports	S22
231D	2L	57-62	Sun	Sunwasp Scooter	S22/3
237D	2T	56-68	Greeves	25DC	S25/2
239D	35A	62	Bond	Minicar Mark G	S25/8
240D	35A	62	Bond	Minicar Mark G	S25
241D	2T	56-68	Ambassador		S22
246D	9E	55-67	Unknown	Super Sports Kart	A389
248D	34A	60-62	Norman	Scrambler	A389
251D	9E	55-67	Cotton	Vulcan	S25/1
			Greeves	20DC, TE	S25/1
269D	2T	56-68	Ambassador	Super S	S25/3
270D	2T	56-68	Cotton		S22
284D	34A	60-62	DMW	Mk 14 Scrambler	A389
			Greeves	24SC, SCS, MDS	A389
285D	9E	55-67	Pashley WR	3-wheel truck	S25/1
287D	3L	60-66	Sun	Sunwasp Scooter	S25
292D	9E	55-67	AC Cars		S25/3
305D	34A	60-62	Greeves	24MCS	A389
309D	35A	62	Bond	Minicar Mark G	S25/8
332D	31A	58-60	Bond	Minicar Mark F	S25/8
337D	2T	56-68	DMW		S22
338D	2T	56-68	DMW	Deemster Sport	S22
339D	2T	56-68	Norman		S22
340D	2T	56-68	Norman		S22
341D	2T	56-68	Greeves		S25/2
342D	3T	57-64	Greeves	32DC	S25
343D	2T	56-68	Ambassador		S22
344D	2T	56-68	Ambassador		S25/3
345D	2T	56-68	Ambassador		S22
346D	34A	60-62	DOT	Scrambles	A389
356D	2L	57-62	DKR	Capella	S22
357D	2L	57-62	DKR	Capella	S22/8

358D	2L	57-62	DKR	Capella	S22/8
360D	3L	60-66	Ambassador	Scooter	S22/4
378D	2T	56-68	DMW		S22
379D	2T	56-68	DMW		S22
380D	31A	58-60	Bond	Minicar Mark F	S25/1
381D	9E	55-67	Pashley WR	3-wheel truck	S25/1
384D	2L	57-62	DKR	Capella	S22/8
393D	2T	56-68	Cotton	Continental	S22
398D	34A	60-62	Greeves	Scrambler	A389
400D	31A	58-60	Cotton	Corsair	S25/5
409D	31C	56-64	Pashley WR	3-wheel truck	S19
423D	9E	55-67	Davidson WK		S25/3
427D	31C	56-64	Davidson WK		S19
428D	2T	56-68	James	M25 Superswift	S22
429D	2T	56-68	Francis-Barnett	Cruiser 89	S22
430D	3T	57-64	Pashley WR	3-wheel truck	S25
432D	2L	57-62	Davidson WK		S22/2
433D	9E	55-67	Excelsior		S25/8
452D	32A	60-66	Greeves	24DC	S25
453D	32A	60-66	Greeves	24TE, TES, TFS	S25/6
500D	9E	55-67	Greeves	20SC, DC, TE	S25/2
501D	32A	60-66	DOT	Trials	S25/5
507D	9E	55-67	Ambassador	Popular	S25/1
514D	11E	58-67	AC Cars		S25/3
522D	32A	60-66	DMW	Trials	S25/6
528D	34A	60-62	DMW	Mk 14 MX	A389
533D	11E	58-67	Unknown	Dynastart	S25/3
559D	9E	55-67	Ministry of Health		S25/3
560D	9E	55-67	Ministry of Health		S25/3
561D	9E	55-67	Ministry of Health		S25/3
606D	2T	56-68	Cotton	Continental	S22
607D	32A	60-62	Cotton	Trials	S25
617D	11E	58-67	Unknown	Dynastart	S25/3
718D	2T	56-68	Greeves	25DC, DCX, DD	S22
725D	2T	56-68	Cotton	Herald	S22
747D	32A	60-62	Greeves		S25
757D	STM	63-69	Cotton	Cobra	A389
			Greeves	24ME	A389
976D	9E	55-67	Unknown	Standard Kart	S25/1
004E	9E	55-67	Cotton	Vulcan	S25/1
016E	C12	Ind	Alcon	Pump	B10
072E	Mk15/2	Ind	Unknown		Type V
085E	36A	62-64	Greeves	24MD, MDS	A389
				24RAS	A-GP
086E	36A	62-64	Greeves	24MD, MDS	A389

			Cotton	Cougar	A389
146E	9E	55-67	Cotton	Vulcan	S25/1
296E	36A	62-64	Greeves	24RAS	A-GP
300E	2T	56-68	Francis-Barnett	Cruiser	S22
			James	Superswift	S22
326E	32A	60-62	Francis-Barnett	Trials 92	S25
			James	M25T Commando	S25
338E	11E	58-67	Unknown	Dynastart	S25/1
352E	36A	62-64	Francis-Barnett	Scrambler 93	A389
			James	M25R Cotswold	A389
353E	4T	63-67	Cotton	Continental	S25
			Greeves	25DC II	S25
490E	STM	63-69	Cotton	Telstar	A-GP
494E	STM	63-69	Unknown	Scrambles 6v lights	A389
531E	9E	55-67	Pengor Ltd	Penguin Amphibian	S25/1
687E	4T	63-67	Cotton	Continental Sports	S25
688E	4T	63-67	Francis-Barnett	Cruiser 91	S25
701E	4T	63-67	Royal Enfield	Turbo twin	S25
760E	Anzani	Ind	Built under licence	for Anzani Easimow	B10
826E	STM	63-69	Cotton	Cobra	A389
			James	M25RS Cotswold	A389
827E	STM	63-69	Unknown	Scrambles 6v lights	A389
834E	STM	63-69	Cotton	Telstar	A-GP
863E	31A	58-60	Cotton	Corsair	S25/5
865E	STM	63-69	Unknown	Road race 6v lights	A-GP
869E	4T	63-67	Greeves	25DD II	S22
871E	STM	63-69	Cotton	Trials	S25/6
972E	STM	63-69	Cotton	Conquest	A389
086F	4T	63-67	Greeves	25DC II	S22
091F	STM	63-69	Unknown	Special no gearbox	A389
131F	STM	63-69	Cotton	Conquest	A389
161F	37A	65-68	Cotton	Trials	S25/6
			Greeves	24TGS,THS, TJ, TJS	S25/6
203F	34A	Exhibit only	Greeves Museum	Replica of 24SCS	A389
310F	11E	58-67	Unknown	Dynastart	S25/1
313F	11E	58-67	Unknown	Dynastart	S25/1

Appendix 5

Villiers Industrial Power Unit Users, Great Britain

Company	Location	Product
Abrey & Gerratt Ltd	Slough	Sweepers
Abtus Ltd	London SW 1	Track layers
AC Cars Ltd	Thames Ditton	Invalid cars
A.C.E Machinery Ltd	London SW 2	Road rollers
Aeraspray Associated Ltd	Birmingham	Paint sprayers
Aerex Ltd	Stockton-on-Tees	Air fans
Aerograph Co Ltd	London SE 26	Paint sprayers
Aerostyle Ltd	London NW 10	Road liners
Air Industrial Developments Ltd	Lichfield	Air compressors
Air Units Co	Wigan	Air compressors
Alfa Laval Co Ltd	Newport Mon	Milking machines
E P Allam & Co Ltd	London SW 1	Concrete vibrators
John Allen & Sons (Oxford) Ltd	Oxford	Motor scythes
Allen & Simmonds (Auto-Culto) Ltd	Reading	Cultivators
E Allman & Co Ltd	Chichester	Fire pumps
Argyll Motor & Engineering Co Ltd	London N 8	Rail trolleys
Associated Pumps Ltd	London SW 6	Pumps
Atlanta Motors Ltd	Stains	Pumps
Austin Burrell Motors Ltd	Leicester	Marine engines
Auto Diesels Ltd	Uxbridge	Generating sets
F W Baggett Ltd	Wolverhampton	Lawn mowers
Bamfords Ltd	Uttoxeter	Harvesters
Barber-Green Olding & Co Ltd	Hatfield	Ditchers
Barford (Agricultural) Ltd	Grantham	Cultivators
W & F Barrett	Bristol	Invalid cars
Barronia Metals (GB) Ltd	Hereford	Grain dryers
William, Bateman Ltd	Preston	Air compressors
Benford Ltd	Warwick	Dumper trucks
James Beresford & Sons Ltd	Birmingham	Pumps
Keith Blackman	London N 17	Air fans
Blackstone & Co Ltd	Stamford Lincs	Elevators
John Blake Ltd	Accrington Lancs	Pumps
A B Blanch & Co Ltd	Malmesbury Wilts	Elevators/balers
Frank Bonser Ltd	Nottingham	Auto trucks
Boscome Precision Ltd	Boscome	Marine engines
F W Brackett & Co Ltd	Colchester	Pumps
Braham, Peterson & Benham Ltd	Enfield	Bitumen mixers
British Anzani Engineering Co Ltd	Hampton Hill	Tractors
Bristol Pneumatic Tools Ltd	Bristol	Air compressors
British Hoist & Crane Co Ltd	Compton Berks	Hoists & winches
British Vacuum Cleaner & Eng Co Ltd	Leatherhead	Suction cleaners

J Brockhouse & Co Ltd	West Bromwich	Sweepers
Broome & Wade Ltd	High Wycombe	Air compressors
Alfred Bullows & Sons	Walsall	Air compressors
Burtonwood Engineering Co Ltd	Wigan	Air compressors
Byron Farm Machinery Ltd	London E 17	Grain elevators
Calor Gas (Distrib) Co Ltd	Weybridge	Grain dryers
Cartem Engineering Ltd	London SW 1	Bitumen mixers
Carter & Co (Nelson) Ltd	Nelson	Sirens
Catchpole Engineering Ltd	Bury St Edmunds	Grass cutters
J W Chafer Ltd	Doncaster	Crop sprayers
Chinook Heaters Ltd	London N 19	Grain dryers
Clifford Cultivators Ltd	West Horndon	Cultivators
Climax-Fraser Tuson Ltd	Orpington	Sweepers
J Clubley Armstrong Danarm Ltd	London SW 1	Chain saws
Colcrete Ltd	Rochester	Concrete mixers
Colour Sprays Ltd	London NW 3	Paint sprayers
Columbus-Dixon Ltd	Wembley	Suction cleaners
Compactors Ltd	London SW 2	Soil compactors
Cooch & Sons Ltd	Northampton	Potato sorters
William Cook & Co Ltd	Peterborough	Elevators
Cooper Pegler & Co Ltd	Burgess Hill	Crop sprayers
Cooper-Stewart Engineering Co Ltd	Letchworth	Sheep shearers
R H Corbett & Co Ltd	Burgess Hill	Loading equipment
W J Craven & Co Ltd	Evesham	Crop sprayers
Crawley Metal Productions Ltd	Littlehampton	Tractors
Crown Pump Manufacturing Co Ltd	Feltham	Pumps
Cylinder Components Ltd	Birmingham	Motor scythes
Dale Electric (Yorkshire) Ltd	Filey	Generating sets
A F Danbridge & Sons	London SE 10	Pumps
Dawson MacDonald & Dawson Ltd	Ashbourne	Paint sprayers
Diesel Equipment Ltd	Uxbridge	Generating sets
Dorman Sprayer Ltd	Cambridge	Crop sprayers
Drake & Fletcher Ltd	Maidstone	Crop sprayers
J B Edlington & Co ltd	Gainsborough	Potato sorters
Electrical Equipment Co (Leicester) Ltd	Leicester	Generating sets
Electro Dynamic Construction Co Ltd	St Mary Cray Kent	Generating sets
Douglas Ellison Ltd	London W 5	Pumps
En-Tout-Cas Co Ltd	Leicester	Grass rollers
Joseph Evans & Sons (W'ton) Ltd	Wolverhampton	Pumps
J W Evans & Co	Burslem	Flexible drives
Excelsior Motor Co Ltd	Birmingham 11	Auto trucks
Gordon Felber & Co Ltd	London W 1	Grain elevators
Flexible Drive & Tool Co Ltd	Edenbridge Kent	Concrete vibrators
Flexible Drives (Gilmans) Ltd	Smethwick	Concrete vibrators
Flextol Engineering Co Ltd	London W 5	Flexible drives
Folland Aircraft Ltd	Southampton	Jet starter packs

Forest City Electric Co Ltd	Manchester	Traffic signals
Four Oaks Spraying Machine Co Ltd	Sutton Coldfield	Crop sprayers
Franki Compressed Pile Co Ltd	London SW 1	Pile drivers
Frisky Cars Ltd	Wolverhampton	3-wheel/light cars
R J Fullwood & Bland Ltd	Ellesmere	Milking machines
Gascoignes (Reading) Ltd	Reading	Milking machines
Geest Industries Ltd	Spalding	Auto trucks
Gilbert Gilkes & Gordon Ltd	Kendal	Washing machines
Girdlestone Pumps Ltd	London W 1	Pumps
Sir George Godfrey & Partners Ltd	Hanworth	Air compressors
H J Godwin Ltd	Quenington Glos	Pumps
Goodbourne & Byrne Ltd	Lymington Hants	Power screens
Goodenough Pumps Ltd	London SW 1	Pumps
Goodyear Tyre & Rubber Co Ltd	Wolverhampton	Tyre ballasters
Thomas Green & Sons Ltd	Leeds 2	Motor mowers
John Gregory (Nelson) Ltd	Nelson	Floor planers
Hampson Industries Ltd	West Bromwich	Generating sets
Hamworthy Engineering	Poole	Compressors
R A Harding (Bath) Ltd	Bath	Invalid cars
W Hargreaves & Co Ltd	Cheadle	Turf aerators
Hart Agric Engineering Co Ltd	Brierley Hill	Elevators
L Hathaway Ltd	Oswestry	Fire pumps
Hayters Ltd	Bishop's Stortford	Grass cutters
C E Heinke & Co Ltd	London SE 1	Air compressors
Heli-Strand Tools Ltd	Rye Sussex	Chain saws
Hill-Barnes (Pumps) Ltd	Leicester	Pumps
Hogg & Pudsey	Leeds 11	Saw benches
G E Holt Ltd	Kingston-on-Thames	Grass cutters
E C Hopkins Ltd	Birmingham 16	Polishers
Hymatic Engineering Co Ltd	Redditch	Air compressors
Hydran Products Ltd	Wenlock Staffs	Oil burners
Industrial Machinery Equipment (Bimpex)	London SW 19	Loading equipment
Ingersoll-Rand Ltd	Manchester 17	Air compressors
Invacar Ltd	Thundersley	Invalid cars
Alec Jackson Ltd	London N W 10	Speedway bikes
C H Johnson (Machinery) Ltd	Stockport	Concrete vibrators
E Johnstone	Brighton	Midget coaches
JP Engineering Co Ltd	Leicester	Motor mowers
Kine Engineering Co Ltd	Redhill	Saw benches
Adam Knox Ltd	Glasgow	Palm nut crushers
Landmaster Ltd	Nottingham	Cultivators
Laycock Engineering Co Ltd	Sheffield	Washing machines
Le Grand Rochester Ltd	Rochester	Oil well gauges

Lead Wool Ltd	Snodland Kent	Air compressors
Lee Howl & Co Ltd	Tipton Staffs	Pumps
Lightfoot Refrigeration Co	Wembley	Refrigeration
Liner Concrete Machinery Ltd	Gateshead 8	Concrete mixers
R A Lister & Co Ltd	Dursley Glos	Auto trucks
Lister-Todd Engineering Corp Ltd	Dursley Glos	Crop sprayers
Lloyds & Co (Letchworth) Ltd	Letchworth	Motor mowers
James F Low & Co Ltd	Dundee	Concrete mixers
Arthur Lyon & Co Ltd	Stamford Lincs	Generating sets
Manus (GB) Ltd	Morton-in-Marsh	Milking machines
Markham Traction Ltd	Stamford	Concrete mixers
Victor Martin & Co Ltd	London N 17	Speedway bikes
Massey-Ferguson (GB) Ltd	Coventry	Harvesters
Matisa Equipment Ltd	Chertsey	Track layers
Matling Ltd	Wolverhampton	Sweepers/trucks
Max Arc & Electrics Ltd	Walton-on-Thames	Generating sets
Mayfield Engineering Co Ltd	Dorking	Motor scythes
Mellotte Separator Sales Ltd	Grantham	Milking machines
MHH Engineering Ltd	Guildford	Marine engines
Micron Sprayers Ltd	London S W 11	Crop sprayers
Mitchell Colman & Co Ltd	Manchester	Grain elevators
Mitchell Ropeways Ltd	Peterborough	Elevators
ML Aviation Co Ltd	Maidenhead	Air fans
Mono Pumps Ltd	London EC 3	Pumps
George Monro Ltd	Waltham Cross	Cultivators
B C Morris Ltd	Coventry	Flexible drives
Morrison Pumps Ltd	Loughborough	Pumps
A G Morrison (Engineers) Ltd	Southampton	Generating sets
Robert Moreton & Co Ltd	Burton-on-Trent	Pumps
H R Nash Ltd	Ashtead	Grass cutters
New Holland Machine Co Ltd	Aylesbury	Harvesters
Nixon & Co	Littlehampton	Auto trucks
Normand Ltd	London NW 10	Refrigeration
Northern Aluminium Co Ltd	Smethwick	Hydraulic presses
F O'Brian & Co Ltd	Swadlincote	Concrete mixers
G C Ogle & Sons Ltd	Derby	Elevators
Oil Equipment & Engineering Co Ltd	Kew Gardens	Oil burners
Onneley Implements Ltd	Crewe	Pumps
S E Opperman Ltd	Boreham Wood	Auto trucks
Oswalds & Ridgeway Ltd	Kew Gardens	Pumps
Frederick Parker Ltd	Leicester	Concrete mixers
E Pass & Co Ltd	Denton	Hydraulic pumps
H Pattisson & Co Ltd	Stanmore	Compost mixers
Pegson Ltd	Coalville	Concrete mixers

Petbow Ltd	Sandwich	Generating sets
Phoenix Engineering Co Ltd	Chard	Bitumen mixers
George Pike Ltd	Birmingham 6	Traffic signals
Pioneer Mixers Ltd	Monkseaton	Concrete mixers
Pneulec Ltd	Smethwick	Compost mixers
Powerco Ltd	London SW 18	Generating sets
The Precision Engineering Works	Wigston	Concrete mixers
Pressure Jet Markers Ltd	London W 4	Grass cutters
Charles H Pugh Ltd	Birmingham 9	Grass cutters
Grahame Puttick Ltd	Canterbury	Generating sets
Qualcast Ltd	Derby	Grass cutters
E F Ranger (Ferring) Ltd	Littlehampton	Motor mowers
Ransomes & Rapier Ltd	Ipswich	Pumps
Ransomes Sims & Jefferies Ltd	Ipswich	Garden tractors
Raven Engineering Co Ltd	Kingston-on-Thames	Cultivators
Reliancce Trucks Ltd	Heckmondwike	Auto trucks
Road Machines (Drayton) Ltd	West Drayton	Cement silos
Robinsons Developments Ltd	Winchester	Cultivators
Rollason Aerocessories Ltd	Croydon	Aircraft de-icers
Rollo Industries Ltd	Bonnybridge	Tractors
Romac Ltd	London NW 9	Air compressors
Rose Bros (Gainsborough) Ltd	Gainsborough	Turf aerators
Rotary Hoes Ltd	West Horndon	Cultivators
Russells (Kirbymoorside) Ltd	Kirbymoorside	Elevators
Ruston's Engineering Co Ltd	Huntingdon	Grain elevators
Salmon Engineering Co Ltd	Dunmow	Elevators
Saunders Valve Co	Wolverhampton	Pumps
Scootacars Ltd	Leeds	3-wheel cars
Scottish Mechanical Light Industries Ltd	Ayr	Grain dryers
Sealed Motor Construction Co Ltd	Bridgewater	Pumps
William G Search Ltd	Leeds 12	Concrete mixers
William R Selwood Ltd	Southampton	Pumps
Service Engineers (Newcastle) Ltd	Newcastle-on-Tyne	Hoists & winches
Sharpe Commercials Ltd	Preston	3-wheel cars
J E Shay Ltd	Basingstoke	Cultivators
Siebe Gorman & Co Ltd	Tolworth Surrey	Air compressors
Sigmund Pumps Ltd	Gateshead	Pumps
Simplex Dairy Equipment Co Ltd	Cambridge	Milking machines
K Skinner	Lincoln	Marine engines
Standard Insulator Co Ltd	Camberley	Motor scythes
Stanley Engineering Co Ltd	Egham	Invalid cars
Star Engineering Co Ltd	Leicester	Hydraulic presses
E G Steele & Co Ltd	Glasgow C 2	Shunters
Siskol Machines Ltd	Sheffield	Quarry drills
Stothert & Pitt Ltd	Bath	Road rollers
Stovis Engineering & Co Ltd	London SE 15	Air compressors

Sturtevant Engineering Co Ltd	London EC 4	Suction cleaners
Supercar Co (Coventry) Ltd	Leamington Spa	Amusement cars
H Sykes Ltd	London SE 1	Pumps
Sylvan Engineering Ltd	London S E 19	Saw benches
N Tamplin& Co Ltd	Chichester	Grain transporters
W T Teagle (Machinery) Ltd	Truro	Elevators
Teles Smith Ltd	London W 2	Chain saws
Thomas & Sons Ltd	Worcester	Pumps
Thompson Bros (Engineers) Ltd	London SE 9	Hoists & winches
Tidemaster Ltd	Deal	Marine engines
F Tippen & Sons Ltd	Coventry	Invalid cars
E J Tong & Sons	Spilsby Lincs	Potato sorters
Toogood & Jones Ltd	Tankerton Kent	Marine engines
Tractors (London) Ltd	Barnet	Cultivators
Trupal Engineering Ltd	Sheffield	Concrete vibrators
William Turner (Kismet) Ltd	Sheffield	Air compressors
S Tyzack & Son Ltd	London E C 1	Saw benches
Volspray Ltd	Gravesend	Paint sprayers
Voucher Ltd	Walsall	Power drives
Warsop Power Tools Ltd	London S W 1	Rock drills
Warwick Pumps Ltd	Feltham	Pumps
Wayne Tank & Pump Co Ltd	London SE 26	Pumps
The Weaver Manufacturing & Eng Co Ltd	Bedford	Steam cleaners
H C Webb & Co Ltd	Birmingham 6	Motor mowers
Welding Industries Ltd	Bristol	Brick making
Welland Engineering Ltd	Spalding	Generating sets
Wessex Industries (Poole) Ltd	Poole	Auto trucks
Wickham Engineering Co Ltd	Stevenage	Hoists & winches
D Wickham & Co Ltd	Ware	Pumps
M B Wild & Co Ltd	Birmingham 7	Hoists & winches
Winget Ltd	Rochester	Concrete mixers
Williams & James Ltd	Gloucester	Air compressors
C I Wilson	Liverpool 3	Hedge trimmers
Wolseley Engineering Co Ltd	Birmingham 6	Pumps
W A Wood & Co Ltd	Horsham	Saw benches
Worthington Simpson Ltd	Newark-on-Trent	Pumps
Wroxham Engineering Co	London SW 18	Generating sets
York Forge Welding Co Ltd	Birmingham 14	Concrete mixers
Yorkshire Patent Steam Wagon Co	Leeds 10	Sweepers

Index